Huarochirí

Karen Spalding

HUAROCHIRÍ
An Andean Society Under Inca and Spanish Rule

Stanford University Press, Stanford, California

Stanford University Press, Stanford, California
© 1984 by the Board of Trustees of the
Leland Stanford Junior University
Printed in the United States of America
Cloth ISBN 0-8047-1123-2
Paper ISBN 0-8047-1516-5
Original Printing 1984

Last figure below indicates year of this printing:
97 96 95 94 93 92 91 90 89 88

Who built the seven gates of Thebes?
The books are filled with names of kings.
Was it kings who hauled the craggy blocks of stone?
And Babylon, so many times destroyed,
Who built the city up each time? In which of Lima's houses,
That city glittering with gold, lived those who built it?
In the evening when the Chinese wall was finished
Where did the masons go? Imperial Rome
Is full of arcs of triumph. Who reared them up? Over whom
Did the Caesars triumph? Byzantium lives in song,
Were all her dwellings palaces? And even in Atlantis of
    the legend
The night the sea rushed in,
The drowning men still bellowed for their slaves.

Young Alexander conquered India.
He alone?
Caesar beat the Gauls.
Was there not even a cook in his army?
Philip of Spain wept as his fleet
Was sunk and destroyed. Were there no other tears?
Frederick the Great triumphed in the Seven Years War. Who
Triumphed with him?

Each page a victory,
At whose expense the victory ball?
Every ten years a great man,
Who paid the piper?

So many facts.
So many questions.

To the creativity,
the endurance,
and the courage
of the people who
built Lima's houses,
mined its gold, and
paid the piper.

Acknowledgments

THIS study is the product of twelve years, much of which were spent not in research but in mulling over, dissecting, and reconstructing, time and again, the material that I present in the following pages. It is impossible to thank all of the friends and colleagues who have helped me clarify my ideas through their comments and their criticism over the years, although in any expression of appreciation the students with whom I worked over the years at Columbia University and, for one short term, at Yale University belong at the top of the list. Many of these people are now colleagues and friends whose continuing friendship and comments I depend upon heavily. In particular, I want to thank Brooke Larson, Steve Stern, and Florencia Mallon, friends to whom this book is in part a response to their questions, their stimulating comments, and their support.

I also owe debts of gratitude, first, to the staff of the Archivo Nacional del Peru, where I spent many months with the aid and help of the staff and director, Dr. José Duran; second, to the Biblioteca Nacional del Peru, and in particular to Srta. Graciela Sanchez Cerro, one of the most able and helpful bibliographers I have met on either continent; and third, to the Archivo Nacional de la Nacion Argentina, repository of much valuable material-on southern Peru and Bolivia for the period from 1776 to 1810. The staff of the Museo Mitre in Buenos Aires also made working in that lovely center a pleasure to remember. The able notaries of Peru, in towns and cities throughout the country, have always responded with graciousness and interest to my appeals for help, opening their archives—invaluable collections of important materials—to me. The people of Huarochirí shared with me and Tom Patterson their knowledge together with their beer in many hours that I remember fondly during the field season that I spent in the province in the summer of 1968. And many other friendships in Peru, built over the years, have made me always eager to return to a country I have grown to love.

I have received a great deal of support for this project, which began as a doctoral dissertation supported by the Woodrow Wilson Foundation. I want to thank the Social Science Research Council for making it possible for me to spend a year studying anthropology on a Research Training Fellowship in 1970–71, and for supporting my return to Peru on a related project in 1973. My summer work has also been supported by Rutgers University in Newark, where I worked from 1966 to 1970, and by the University of Delaware, which also supported the typing of the final manuscript. I also owe a debt of thanks to Marie Murray, who not only typed the final manuscript but corrected my grammar and caught my errors as we entered the final stretch together. And to Peter Kahn, whose editorial skills and discreet and patient prodding are responsible for getting this book into print, I owe very special thanks.

And finally, I want to thank the friends, now of more than a decade's standing, who have been the source of ideas, comments, and criticism, who have stretched my mind, shared their knowledge and their insights, and put up with the long years I spent in building up and tearing down theories and concepts. My thanks to Saul Newton for the challenge and the support that finally got this book written. To John Rowe, John Murra, Herb Klein, Craig Morris, Tom Patterson, Anibal Quijano, and Manuel Valladares, in the United States and in Peru, thank you for your generosity and your friendship. And to the friends whose presence and interest laid the foundation for thinking and working over the years, thank you all.

K.S.

Contents

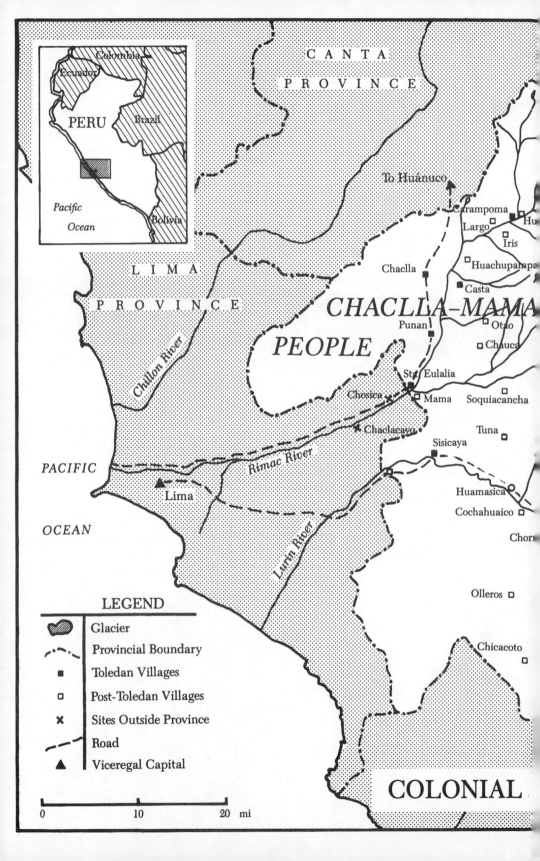

CANTA
PROVINCE

To Huánuco

Carampoma
Largo   Hu
              Iris
              Huachupalpa

Chaclla
          Casta

CHACLLA–MAMA
PEOPLE

Punan   Otao
                Chauca

Sta Eulalia
Chosica   Mama
                Soquiacancha

Chaclacayo   Tuna

Sisicaya

Huamasica

Cochahuaico

Chon

Olleros

Chicacoto

LIMA

PROVINCE

Chillon River

Rimac River

PACIFIC

Lima

Lurin River

OCEAN

LEGEND

🪨	Glacier
·—··—·	Provincial Boundary
■	Toledan Villages
□	Post-Toledan Villages
✗	Sites Outside Province
——	Road
▲	Viceregal Capital

0   10   20 mi

COLONIAL

Inset map

Colombia
Ecuador

PERU

Brazil

Pacific
Ocean

Bolivia

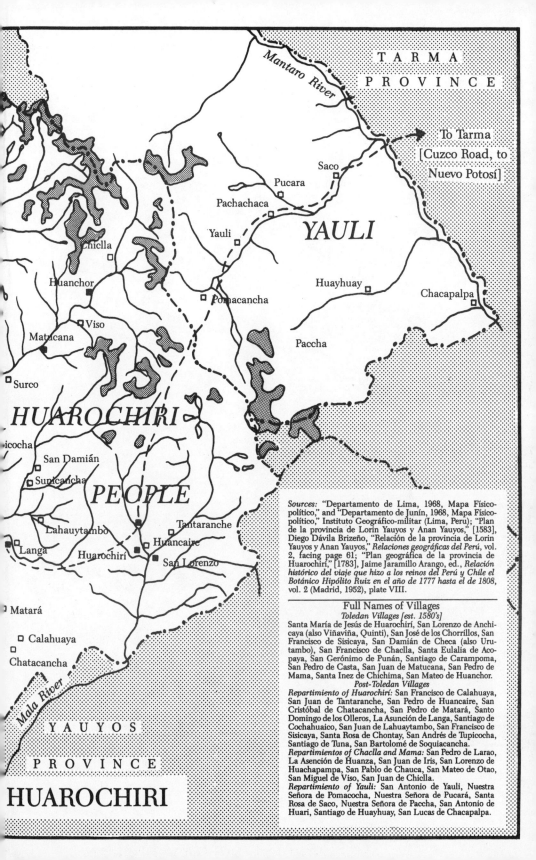

TARMA
PROVINCE

Mantaro River

To Tarma
[Cuzco Road, to
Nuevo Potosí]

Saco

Pucara

Pachachaca

YAULI

Yauli

Chiclla

Huanchor

Huayhuay

Chacapalpa

Pomacancha

Viso

Matucana

Paccha

Surco

HUAROCHIRI

icocha

San Damián

Sunicancha

PEOPLE

Tantaranche

Lahauytambo

Huancaire

Langa

Huarochirí

San Lorenzo

Matará

Calahuaya

Chatacancha

Mala River

YAUYOS

PROVINCE

HUAROCHIRI

Sources: "Departamento de Lima, 1968, Mapa Físico-político," and "Departamento de Junín, 1968, Mapa Físico-político," Instituto Geográfico-militar (Lima, Perú); "Plan de la provincia de Lorin Yauyos y Anan Yauyos," [1583], Diego Dávila Brizeño, "Relación de la provincia de Lorin Yauyos y Anan Yauyos," *Relaciones geográficas del Perú*, vol. 2, facing page 61; "Plan geográfica de la provincia de Huarochirí," [1783], Jaime Jaramillo Arango, ed., *Relación histórico del viaje que hizo a los reinos del Perú y Chile el Botánico Hipólito Ruiz en el año de 1777 hasta el de 1808*, vol. 2 (Madrid, 1952), plate VIII.

Full Names of Villages
Toledan Villages [est. 1580's]
Santa María de Jesús de Huarochirí, San Lorenzo de Anchicaya (also Viñaviña, Quinti), San José de los Chorrillos, San Francisco de Sisicaya, San Damián de Checa (also Urutambo), San Francisco de Chaclla, Santa Eulalia de Acopaya, San Gerónimo de Punán, Santiago de Carampoma, San Pedro de Casta, San Juan de Matucana, San Pedro de Mama, Santa Inez de Chichima, San Mateo de Huanchor.
Post-Toledan Villages
Repartimiento of Huarochirí: San Francisco de Calahuaya, San Juan de Tantaranche, San Pedro de Huancaire, San Cristóbal de Chatacancha, San Pedro de Matará, Santo Domingo de los Olleros, La Asunción de Langa, Santiago de Cochahuaico, San Juan de Lahuaytambo, San Francisco de Sisicaya, Santa Rosa de Chontay, San Andrés de Tupicocha, Santiago de Tuna, San Bartolomé de Soquiacancha.
Repartimientos of Chaclla and Mama: San Pedro de Larao, La Asención de Huanza, San Juan de Iris, San Lorenzo de Huachapampa, San Pablo de Chauca, San Mateo de Otao, San Miguel de Viso, San Juan de Chiclla.
Repartimiento of Yauli: San Antonio de Yauli, Nuestra Señora de Pomacocha, Nuestra Señora de Pucará, Santa Rosa de Saco, Nuestra Señora de Paccha, San Antonio de Huari, Santiago de Huayhuay, San Lucas de Chacapalpa.

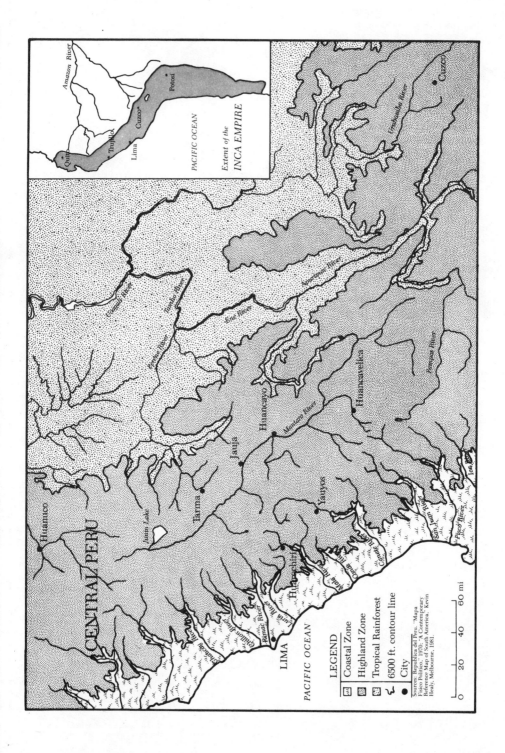

CENTRAL PERU

Huánuco

Tarma

Janja

Huancayo

Huancavelica

Tauyyas

LIMA

PACIFIC OCEAN

LEGEND

Coastal Zone

Highland Zone

Tropical Rainforest

6500 ft. contour line

City

Sources: Republica del Peru. "Mapa
Fisico Politico, 1970: "A Contemporary
Reference Map of South America. Kevin
Healy, Melbourne, 1981.

0   20   40   60 mi

PACIFIC OCEAN

Extent of the
INCA EMPIRE

Amazon River

Quito

Trujillo

Lima

Cuzco

Potosí

Cuzco

Introduction

THIS BOOK tells the story of the construction of a social relationship—a relationship of inequality and oppression—in a portion of the Andean highlands of Central Peru from before the European invasion of the sixteenth century to the end of the eighteenth century. The area is the former colonial—and republican—province of Huarochirí, located on the western slopes of the Cordillera Occidental, the westernmost range of the Andes. The province, which included three river valley systems, was bounded on the north by the Chillón River, on the south by the province of Yauyos, on the west by the foothills of the mountains along the coast of Peru, and on the east by the high *puna* of the mining region today occupied by the mines of Centromín, modern successors to the colonial mines of Nuevo Potosí.

Huarochirí is no more representative of the Andean area as a whole than any other part of this highly complex alpine region. Although it lay across the main route to the rich southern area of Peru during the Spanish colonial period, Huarochirí was not part of the heartland of the Spanish colonial world in the Andes, whose real center was the silver mines of Potosí in contemporary Bolivia, source of the silver that was the lifeblood of the European society in the Andes for over three hundred years. The colonial economy can be described in terms of a line running from Lima, capital of the viceroyalty of Peru, through the mercury mines of Huancavelica, source of the mineral used to reduce the silver ore, through Cuzco to the mines of Potosí in the Bolivian highlands.

Along that line, Spanish settlement was denser and the integration of the native population into the colonial system more thorough than in areas that were more peripheral to the colonial economy. That integration did not mean that the people living along the Lima-Huancavelica-Potosí artery conformed completely to the Spanish colonial model as expressed in legal regulations and theory. On the contrary, it might simply mean—

as recent studies suggest it did in many ways—that the preconquest forms of social relations characteristic of Andean society were modified and altered to a greater degree along that line than elsewhere.[1] Particularly in the south, from Huancavelica to Potosí, the condition of the bulk of the native Andean population reflected to a large degree modern definitions of colonialism as a social system in which a subject, exploited peasantry supports with its labor and goods an elite that may or may not define itself as native to the same area as the subject population.

Huarochirí lies along the first part of the Lima-Huancavelica-Potosí artery, immediately outside Lima. But for a variety of reasons, which I hope will emerge in the course of this study, the area cannot be defined, even in terms of the Spanish colonial system, as a region of "classic colonialism." I did not choose to focus upon this area because of any *a priori* definition of colonialism that I wanted to test against the historical record. The region has become the focus of my interest over the years not because of its "fit" in terms of any preexisting model, but rather because of the vividness and vitality that emerged from the large body of surviving materials and documents produced in and about the area. There are other regions perhaps better suited to test a particular hypothesis or assumption; there are important lacunae in the materials on Huarochirí; and to a considerable extent the material I had available to me has set the range of questions I have felt competent to try to answer—though not to ask.

The documents dealing with Huarochirí that remain in Peruvian archives, both national and local, touch upon virtually every aspect of life in the area. They include a collection of local myths and rituals gathered under the direction of a Spanish parish priest at the end of the sixteenth century, records of idolatry trials from 1660 to 1750, court records of land trials and other disputes, house-to-house censuses, and the records of protest and rebellion, including a diary of a revolt in the province in 1750. Much of the picture I present depends heavily upon the study of other disciplines, particularly anthropology, and of the often cryptic but honest record of daily living in the detritus of garbage dumps, abandoned structures, and cemeteries—the laboratory of the archaeologist.

This variety of material has made it possible for me to get close not only to events but also to the people who took part in them. There are even cases in which it is possible to follow the actions of particular individuals through a variety of sources prepared for different purposes, returning to these people their personalities, their actions, their motivations, and their voices.

In attempting a reconstruction of the process of change within Andean society under Spanish rule in a particular area, I am not making a case for additional similar studies in order eventually to piece together the story of the colonial system of the Andes as a whole. I do not object to such a procedure, but I am primarily concerned with illuminating the process of structural change in a society and the peculiar character of that society's integration into the expanding European world. If I emphasize the kind of detail that can be obtained by the limited focus I have chosen, it is because I have found such significant detail extremely valuable in delineating the relationships, the alliances, and the conflicts among groups of people that are, in my opinion, the sources as well as the products of the structural transformation of their societies.

The story that follows is in many ways an abstraction—a picture reconstructed from a wide variety of sources that refer to particular sites and places within the region known as Huarochirí. Though Huarochirí was one province, and a relatively limited part of the Andean region as a whole, it is by no means susceptible to the practice of "microhistory," the narrative of a single town or village. This is not a community study in time. The province of Huarochirí was roughly equivalent in size to Massachusetts and contained diverse environments and communities, each with its own particular history and conditions. In order to reconstruct the general process of change in the region as a whole, I have had to select and generalize, to abstract from the sources the structures that clearly refer to traditional Andean patterns of social organization and to set those against the overlay of institutions and relations introduced by the Spaniards. In the course of the three centuries following the European invasion, Spanish overlays merged with the older structures to form a "salad" of elements from different times and different social systems, a pattern of contradictory and conflicting relationships that made up the essence of what can be defined as the colonial system.

That system was built upon the Andean social systems that preceded it, and indeed depended for its survival upon the maintenance of the traditional social relations of Andean society and the economic surplus it could generate. For that reason, a considerable part of this study is devoted to delineating Andean society before the European invasion. The Spanish conquest of the Andes precipitated a change of cataclysmal proportions for the people who lived there before the arrival of the Europeans. The destruction of the native American state that existed in the Andes when the Europeans arrived—the Inca state—and the subsequent history of the former subjects of that state form a chronicle of destruction and brutality that has divided later observers into two distinct camps: those who have condemned the brutality of the Spaniards and tended to look upon the world that was destroyed as automatically better for all; and those who have celebrated the expansion of the superior European civilization and progress, despite its inevitable destruction of the customs and practices of "primitive savages." Neither side in this quarrel has been particularly honest in its use of terms that carry a load of emotional overtones, so it might be well here to define just what I mean by one term that is commonly applied to the native American societies conquered and used by the Europeans. That term is "primitive." The societies that developed in the Andes before the entry of the Europeans have been classified among what are often called the "primitive peoples," and in one sense, and one only, that definition can be accepted as valid. The basis of any society is the fulfillment of need, which begins on the material level with such basic requisites for survival as food, essential goods, and future members of society. The political and ideological structures of any society, primitive or modern, are conditioned by the social relationships into which people enter in the process of producing the goods and tools to meet those needs, and those structures in turn condition and reinforce the existing social relations. That general definition applies to Andean society at the beginning of the sixteenth century, as it applies to the Europeans themselves. The level of material development of both societies was limited and set real constraints upon the direction and the quality of the social relations erected upon that base.

In societies such as that of Huarochirí under the Inca state or prior to its conquest by the Incas, as well as in societies such as that of Castile in the sixteenth century, the development of the forces of production, the material elements available to people to supplement their own labor and the natural environment, are limited—i.e. primitive. The Spaniards may have had a somewhat greater range of technology available to them, but even if that is so, the Spaniards in Peru came to live on the productive system of Andean society. The relatively limited development of the forces and techniques of production in Andean society meant, quite simply, that people had to devote a very large proportion of their time just to reproducing the conditions of life as they lived it, so that little time was left over for experimentation, change, or the introduction of new practices. A primitive society is in this sense relatively static; there is little room for innovation if its members are to survive. People depend heavily upon tradition, upon the authority of rules and norms attributed to agents defined as outside and above the society: ancestors, deities, or similar ideological figures created by the society and in turn regarded as its authorities. And this, in turn, slows down the likelihood of major change within the system.

In order to lay a foundation for the analysis of change in such a social system over time, I chose first to delineate some of the basic relationships upon which local Andean society was based. The picture that I present, drawn in the first three chapters, is not organized in terms of traditional divisions of social science research. It is virtually impossible to unravel the closely knit fabric of social relations in order to reconstruct the outlines of an economic system, a political system, or an ideological system in provincial Andean society prior to the arrival of the Spaniards. It is also impossible to apply the other traditional division of a society into base and superstructure. Relationships that might be assigned in the abstract to the sphere of the economy, the polity or political system, or the patterns of values and beliefs all functioned, when seen from another perspective, as part of the set of mechanisms that maintained and facilitated the production and distribution of material goods. I have chosen to set my discussion of those relationships in that latter perspective, in order to provide a basis for analyzing how the incorporation of Andean societies into the political structure of a European state affected the internal structure of those societies, undermining, over the long term, the social relationships that facilitated their prosperity and even their material survival.

I have begun with a discussion of Andean definitions of the environment and the Andean organization of production, both of which were old—considerably antedating the Inca state as far as we are now able to tell—and constituted the bedrock ensuring the survival of the local population under the difficult conditions of an alpine environment. Local prosperity was founded upon cooperation. Given a limited development of the techniques and means of production, only by organizing relatively large numbers of people could a society produce sufficient surplus to permit the growth of social differentiation and the rise of state systems.

State systems emerged as a particular group expanded from its home territory and conquered other communities and local societies, incorporating them into a political structure that functioned to siphon off the surplus produced by the conquered population for the benefit of the conquerors. According to the archaeologists, such state systems existed in the Andes by the time of the birth of Christ, the first clear example being the Huari Empire, which expanded from the Ayacucho Basin during the first millennium A.D. in a rapid series of conquests that brought all of Central Peru under its authority. The Huari state fell in approximately A.D. 500 and was followed, a millennium later, by the Inca Empire, which expanded from the Cuzco Valley sometime in the early part of the fifteenth century, rapidly building a political system that reached from present-day Ecuador in the north to northwest Chile and Argentina in the south. The state structures built in the Andes—in particular the Inca state—redirected the surplus production of local societies to mobilize massive amounts of labor for the benefit of the state. The great Inca road system and the huge monuments that today provide the Peruvian government with another source of income from tourists are the material evidence of the enormous volume of labor that could be extracted from local societies.

Investigations of the social organization of Andean society to date have tended to approach the subject from two distinct directions. On the one hand, historians and those anthropologists interested in the Inca Empire have followed the material left by members of Spanish society. That material was in turn obtained by the Spaniards principally from informants from Cuzco, members of the ruling Inca elite with their own model of society and picture of the ways local societies were integrated into the Andean state—a state that they had participated in building and maintaining. On the other hand, anthropologists and ethnographers interested in the contemporary village peasantry of the Andes have recorded local interactions, kinship relations, and trade and exchange patterns on the village level.[2] The few who have attempted to comprehend the impact of the Spanish conquest upon Andean society and trace the process of change from the time of the Inca state could do little beyond forcibly imposing one of those pictures upon the other. They came up with the by now well-worn vision of an all-powerful native state whose destruction by the Spaniards left a multitude of atomized local communities without links to one another, stagnating in anonymity until their rediscovery in the twentieth century by scholars seeking to record and preserve these "fossils" of social history.

In the course of the last two or three decades, new approaches to traditional sources used since the nineteenth century have developed, and new materials have become available that deal with local societies under the Inca state.[3] This in turn has begun to make it possible to offer a picture of the Inca state that takes it out of the realm of scholarly myth and makes of it a human construct, a structure of political organization and control that loses none of its scope and grandeur through being firmly rooted in the pre-Inca societies upon which it was built.

In Chapters Four and Five, I alter my focus to the relationship between Andean and European societies in more general terms. In these chapters, the society of Huarochirí moves back to permit me to look more closely at the crisis of the conquest period. The arrival of the Europeans in the Andes in 1533 brought an end to the Inca state and initiated the development of a colonial system in which traditional social relationships and patterns of internal organization were distorted to meet European demands for precious metals and material support. The conquerors initially sought to appropriate the mechanisms of surplus extraction developed by the Inca state for their own benefit, but the sheer size of their demands combined with the decimation of the Andean population by European diseases to which the people of the Americas had no immunity brought on a major crisis by the 1560's.

Though the process of change in social systems characterized as "primitive" on the basis of the definition outlined above is relatively slow, a rapid and major intervention from outside the system can result in changes that can only be described as cataclysmal. Indeed, scholars interested in the transformation of socioeconomic systems have recently begun to look at the role of violence in the transformation of societies.[4] It does appear that in the study of change, there are some periods when the basic social relationships of a society can be described as relatively static, or as changing only slowly, and others when the rate as well as the nature of change are transformed as new elements set up contradictions that can only be resolved by introducing new relationships and constraints. In a precapitalist system this occurs almost inevitably on the level of the political structure, and the long-term impact is the transformation of society.

The Spanish conquest of the Inca Empire and the subsequent erection of a colonial system in the Andes, characterized by massive violence and destruction, was a process of this kind. From 1533 to the 1580's, the contact of European and Andean cultures stimulated a process of rapid transformation. During this half century, the rate of change in the Andes was bewildering and confusing, as the members of each culture—the conquerors and the conquered—were forced to adapt to and seek to comprehend the other in order to survive, and if possible to take advantage of the new situation. In this relationship, the odds were weighted in favor of the Europeans. The members of Andean society were forced to adapt to their conquerors, although the latter rapidly learned that they could profit from their ostensible control of a population that outnumbered them by a factor of some 50,000 to one only by using the existing social relations of the society they ruled.

In order to understand this process of rapid change and crisis, I found it necessary both to narrow my temporal focus and to broaden my geographical frame to take into account the relations of the Andean area with Europe through its conquerors, and the problems on both sides of the Atlantic involved in the development of a political system that would permit the members of European society in the Andes as well as the Crown in Castile to benefit from their new possession. During this half century, changes in the social organization of local society originated not in the local area but outside, in the political centers of the European conquerors both in the Andes and in Spain. So to use an idiom from film, I have cut, for the half century following the European invasion of the Andes, to the centers of power in Peru and in Spain—to sources originating largely from Lima and from Madrid—and focused on the conflicts and alliances through which the sociopolitical form of the new Spanish colony was developed.

Once that form took on its basic shape, I could again move back to the regional scale, to trace the impact of the colonial system as it was framed in Lima and Madrid upon the internal structures of Andean society in Huarochirí. With the help of primarily local sources that permit me more immediate access to the members of Andean society, I examine in the remainder of the book how the local people responded to or resisted the political structures imposed upon them, and how they dealt with, were exploited by, or benefited from the Europeans who occupied their land and made it their own. I hope that the resulting study will illuminate and clarify the origins of the social relationships in provincial Andean society that took form during the long centuries of Spanish colonial rule.

ONE

The Human Landscape

IN THE sixteenth century, the people of Huarochirí told a myth to explain to themselves the origins of human life, or perhaps better, the origins of life in their homeland, which was what was important to them.

The story is told that from the heights of the universe there fell blood onto a place called Huichicancha; it fell onto the fields where the *quinua* grew, and there, in those places, the peoples were formed, from Allauca to Cunisancha, from Satpasca to Yuriñaya, from Sullpachca to Chuparacu, from Uacataca to Pomasa, from Musica to Chaucachimpita, from Cacasica to the already named Huarcancha and Llilicancha, of the Yañcas.[1]

The link between *quinua*, the high-altitude grain that grows on the upper reaches of the slopes of the Andes, and the people of the highlands who cultivate and live from it is explicit in this myth. The peoples of Huarochirí, by their own testimony, were part of the mountain slopes they inhabited, born of the same lands that gave them the food they ate.

The relationship between human groups and their environment in the Andes is basic to any understanding of the patterns of Andean society. In many ways, the Andes seem to present a formidable obstacle to human occupation. This alpine land, whose people live at an altitude regarded by many in other parts of the world as fit only for mountain goats and viewing from afar, often seems too huge and overwhelming for men and women to comprehend. The Andes reduce human beings to insignificance, tiny spots on a picture scaled for far more imposing centers of interest. And yet this land, one of the handful of places in the world where people have developed great civilizations, is also of particular interest because of how men and women have turned its characteristics to their advantage. In the Andes, people developed patterns of access to and control of the land that permitted them to produce a surplus sufficient to maintain an elite and to elaborate complex, stratified societies based upon differential access to goods and resources.

Photos 1–4. Four views of land under cultivation in the highlands of Huarochirí. Photo 1 (above) shows relatively level land with mountains rising in the distance. Photo 2 (below) shows the effects of erosion along the edges of one of the many highland streams. Photos 3 and 4 (right) show terracing on the steep hillsides.

Photo 5. The unpromising nature of the highland soil is shown in this photo of a dry wash and a scrub growth near a highland settlement.

The steep slopes of this mountain land were the raw material from and in which the Andean peoples built their cultures. That raw material was not everywhere the same, and the societies that developed in the Andean region appear from recent studies to have been quite different from one another. Setting aside the fertile irrigated valleys of the coast, however, we can describe in general the structure of the central Andes.

To a person from Europe or the United States, or indeed any of the relatively flat lowland areas of the world, the Andean landscape appears harsh and forbidding. On the western slopes of the central Andes, the actions of men have slightly altered the look of the land through terracing and irrigation, and have undoubtedly accelerated the process of erosion, but the basic characteristics of the landscape have remained essentially the same from the sixteenth century to the present. European travelers since the sixteenth century have described the rainless coastal desert covered with thick fogs through much of the year; the steep, jagged mountain slopes on which farmers must grow their crops on inclines of 30° or more; the flat plain, or *puna*, lying farther above sea level than the peaks of mountain ranges in other parts of the world and so cold that the ground is frequently frozen. Peru has the distinction of being classified by European scholars as one of the "problem climates" of the world, which simply reflects the fact that this jagged land of extremes presents great difficulties to the technology developed by Europeans for the cultivation of their temperate, relatively flat agricultural lands.

Peru has also been described as a "vertical land." It is an alpine environment, similar to that of the Alps and the Himalayas. In this part of the continent, so near the equator, climate and vegetation are far more a function of altitude than of latitude, and seasonal variation is less than the changes of temperature from night to day. The vegetation of the coast and the lower parts of the river valleys above the coastal fog line is dry and sere except along the river banks, where the presence of water facilitates the growth of river grasses, trees, and cultivated plants. As one moves higher along the mountain slopes, whether along the rivers or perpendicular to them, the vegetation alters to the columnar cactus and cultivated fields of the sierra slopes, then to scrub brush, and finally to *ichu*, the bunch grass of the high puna above the zone of cultivation.[2]

To a member of Andean society, and in particular someone from the central Andes, the core of his world is the high mountain valleys located between 9,800 and 11,200 feet above sea level. These valleys are relatively broad scoops of rich land scoured out by glaciers during the last ice age, the sites of the headwaters of the coastal rivers. They stand in sharp contrast to the heavily eroded, precipitous slopes downriver. These scattered oases of relatively level land, good water, and easy access to other environmental zones became the core territories of most of the highland population on the western slopes of the Andes, defended and disputed by rival tribes. Their proximity to the equator makes them more temperate than their high altitude might lead one to expect. Though the temperature drops sharply as soon as the sun is gone, it rises with the return of the sun, warming the ground wherever it is not in shadow. Rainfall is most regular at this altitude, the upper portions of the region getting dependable annual rains. The region is the zone of overlap between the basic food staples of Andean society—maize and potatoes. In the upper slopes of these valleys, where the air is thin, frosts are sharp, and the sun is hot for only a very short part of the day, potatoes can be cultivated up to about 11,800 feet. In the lower slopes and warm bottomlands, maize—which needs more warmth, tolerates less frost, and requires regular irrigation—can be grown.[3]

These high valleys are not tiny Edens. If the rains are insufficient or come at the wrong time, before the ground cover is sufficient to retain the earth, the waters can cut steep gullies down the slope, washing out even stone retaining walls facing hillside terraces. Sudden frosts or insufficient sun may ruin or stunt the harvest. Land is scarce and prized, and water is often scarcer. Myths and folk traditions often center around the search for water, the construction of irrigation canals, or the magical appearance of springs. Nonetheless, when worked with care and attention, these pockets of land provided a large proportion of the requirements for feeding and clothing a population that, according to estimates made shortly after the Spanish conquest, was larger in 1535 than it was in 1940.[4]

The land of the people of Huarochirí did not always look exactly as it does today. Wooded areas were more extensive in the fifteenth century, before the Europeans denuded the sierra slopes of wood to build houses and make charcoal for the stoves of Lima. Hardwoods, including the tough *molle* trees that grow today only in the lowlands near the mouths of the coastal rivers, though scarce even then, were much more plentiful than today. (Eucalyptus, imported from Australia at the end of the nineteenth century, is now the principal wood of the highlands.) The brush forest of the mountain slopes hid mountain lions or pumas, as well as white-tailed and *hueymel* deer, the latter being small, dun-colored animals whose forked horns, somewhat like those of an antelope, were used as musical instruments in feasts and ceremonies. The puma and both forms of deer were hunted for ceremonial purposes and for meat. On the higher-altitude puna, people hunted the wild vicuña, relative to the llama, with its fine, soft wool, and the *guanuco*, another small camelid that ranged throughout the highlands.

From the high valleys members of Andean society reached out to other places both above and below for additional resources important to them. Above the agricultural zone, the high puna provided pasture for llamas and alpacas, which served both as sources of wool and meat and as pack animals; the high puna also contained the lakes from which sprang the rivers whose waters supplemented rainfall through irrigation. These high plains were also the zone of great mineral deposits: first the gold and silver valued by members of Andean society for ornaments, and the copper used for implements; then the silver that became the major colonial export to the Spanish metropolis; and still later the nickel, copper, and other metals valued by the industrial powers. The puna was not extensive in the central Andes, nor was it a zone of concentrated settlement, but it was an integral part of the social and economic—as well as the political—relationships of the people who inhabited the region. It was a source of specialized resources and the home of the ancestors, the gathering place for ceremonial observances, and the passageway to core settlement areas claimed by the distinct social groups of the region. The high-altitude grain quinua, which appears in the origin tale of Huarochirí, grows near the crests of the high valley slopes, and these crests and the puna above were the sites of the tombs of the dead. Neither the puna nor the steep mountain peaks were regarded as barriers; people moved from one river valley to another along mountain crest and high plain.

Below the core zones, down along the banks of the rivers or toward the coast, lay lowland areas, warmer regions that could produce coca and *ají* (chili peppers), avocados, *guayaba, pacay,* and other native fruits. These areas, like the puna, were not regions of dense settlement, but their resources were highly valued by members of both Andean and European societies. Still farther down, along the coastal desert, was another valued resource that the peoples of Huarochirí gained access to only after they were incorporated into the Inca Empire: the *lomas.* These desert oases occur only at altitudes of 1,300–2,600 feet because of the peculiar climatic conditions of the coast, where a combination of water-laden air blocked by the Andes and the cold Antarctic current offshore produces a continual fog over a dry earth. It almost never rains below about 5,300 feet along the western slopes of the Andes in Central Peru, but humid clouds and heavy dew during the winter months of July to October give rise to a dense ground cover of plants that draw their moisture from the air rather than the soil. These lomas provide pastureland during the winter months when the high puna pastures are sere and dry.

From the sierra pockets of relatively rich land, the highland peoples reached out to more distant resource areas for crops or other goods they sought. The network of access to more distant areas was not confined to a single river valley system, or even closely linked or proximate valleys. A resident of the village of Huarochirí today is more familiar with the headwaters of the Lurín and Rímac rivers, reached by crossing the puna to the north, than he is with the area downriver from his village to the mouth of the Mala River. This focus reflects the characteristics of the land on the western slopes of the Andes. The landscape there is a multitude of small resource areas, pockets of specific ecologies, each with its own particular conditions, that can be reached not only by following the river valley toward the crest but also, and frequently more easily and efficiently, by moving down the valley slope from puna to river's edge.

There is little level land in Huarochirí, and the green patches of cultivated land are scattered in tiny pockets that hug the sides of slopes and the narrow valley floors. The land is almost literally vertical. The rivers that flow from the peaks of the western cordillera to the sea are relatively flat and shallow, and their channels are steep. The Rímac, the most northerly of the rivers of Huarochirí, drops sharply from the mountain peaks through a valley gorge whose sides slope at an angle of 40° or more, leveling off to a more gentle incline only about 1,500 to 2,000 feet above sea level. The Lurín, with its mouth at the temple of Pachacamac, the famed god of earthquakes and one of the most powerful deities of ancient Peru, has a more gentle slope in its lower reaches, not climbing fast until well above the fog line.

The coastal range makes for a bewildering variety of conditions within a limited geographical area. The upper Mala Valley, for example, is crossed by a river that since the last glacial period has cut a gorge some 6,500 feet deep from the broad upper slopes of the valley basin. Further, there are not only continuous changes in climate and accompanying flora and fauna as one moves down the valley slope from the puna to the river, but also significant differences between one parcel of land and another at the same altitude. The angle of the slope, the degree of erosion, and consequently the depth of the soil cover vary considerably from one small piece of land to another. Where the gorge narrows sharply, the surrounding rock masses cast some lands into shadow for large portions of the day, affecting the growing season. Similar variations occur in the amount of rain that falls on a given parcel of land, the direction and intensity of winds, and the intensity and frequency of frosts.

The same conditions can be found throughout the Andes. In the longitudinal valleys of the highlands between the western and eastern cordillera, there is rich, relatively level valley land, but other specialized resource areas can be found on the puna or across the eastern cordillera along the upper reaches of the Amazonian tributaries. In the south, the high puna is an ancient granite plain uplifted in past millennia and then rumpled by the folding and faulting that built mountain ranges rising from foothills up to two miles above sea level. It stretches for scores of miles, the homeland of Andean domesticated camelids and the cradle of the most powerful states to arise in the Andes. But even there, people accustomed to travel can reach down to the savannah grasslands of eastern Bolivia or to the Pacific Ocean, where goods and resources can be obtained that are unknown up on the roof of the world above.

The variety of the landscape was a basic factor in the organization of social and productive life in the Andes. People there turned what flatlanders have often seen as formidable barriers to advantage, developing a productive system that incorporated and used the maximum number possible of different resource areas. There has been much written about the Andean ideal of self-sufficiency, or, as it has often been called, "verticality."[5] The idea behind this concept is essentially simple. All societies rely upon a considerable variety of goods to survive, reproduce their members, and maintain the culture patterns and the organization of their lives. European societies, living in relatively uniform climate areas, developed extensive trade networks through which they obtained the goods they wanted to meet their needs. But human groups in the Andes developed another pattern. They tried to gain access to goods by laying claim to resource areas in which they could be produced. A community attempted to control as great a variety of different kinds of resource areas as possible, thus assuring the access of its members to the goods upon which it depended and protecting against crop failure and famine by avoiding undue reliance upon one bit of land that might fail to produce in a given year while another nearby piece, with slightly different conditions, would bear a crop. The goods obtained or produced in the lands claimed by the group were exchanged among its members not according to any abstract standard of value but according to a complex system of equivalencies that specified the proper exchange between people in terms of their personal relationships. At the frontiers of the territories claimed by a group, its members faced people from other groups also seeking to obtain access to desired goods by occupying and cultivating lands in propitious areas.

This pattern of access to relatively far-flung resource areas can be found operating today, but it is extremely difficult to prove for the more distant past, giving us very little evidence upon which to build our assumption that the ideal of group self-sufficiency is an old one in Andean society. The archaeological record—virtually our only source of information about the period prior to the rise of the Inca state—gives us little help except in the case of a complex of sites in the Lurín River valley in Huarochirí.[6] About midway up the Lurín Valley, at an altitude of about 1,500–2,100 feet, a survey team in 1967 located five small villages or hamlets that have been dated to about A.D. 500. This area is in a shifting frontier between the coastal societies and those of the highlands, and it is at the upper limit of the latitudes at which avocados and other warm-climate crops thrive. A warm, sunny region roughly equivalent to the present-day resort area of Chaclacayo—also in the Lurín, just above and free of the fog belt along the coast—it is a fine area for growing the maize sought by different groups not only as a foodstuff but also as a basis of ceremonial feasts and celebrations.

The five hamlets in the Lurín Valley are all within a half-mile of one another. Each was close enough to its neighbors for us to assume that the residents could hardly avoid some kind of contact. Enough elements of pottery styles of the five hamlets are shared for archaeologists to be confident that all are contemporary with one another, but there are significant variations. Three very different pottery styles can be distinguished among the five hamlets. The hamlet at the lowest elevation, closest to the coast, was evidently part of the coastal culture pattern, for its pottery had the same style of decoration and shapes for cooking and storage ware as contemporary lowland sites. The decorated wares of the three middle hamlets were characteristic of coastal styles, but their cooking pots were like those of the highland peoples up the river. The fifth and highest hamlet was a highland settlement, whose people made their cooking pots and their few decorated pieces in the image of the highland culture.

Photos 6, 7, and 8. Three views of a typical highland village. Photo 6 (above) is taken from across a valley (note the nearby terraced fields). Photo 7 (below) shows an approach to the village. Photo 8 (right) shows a typical street.

Pottery styles and shapes are useful indicators of culture patterns. There are few inherent limitations to the shapes into which a pot, bowl, dish, or beaker can be molded, and virtually any kind of decoration can be applied to these vessels. Yet the boundaries within which imagination and creativity are given full play are defined rather narrowly by each culture. Tradition and continuity play an important part in determining style, which in turn becomes an index to the self-definition of a given social group. The distinct styles in groups so close to one another suggest strongly that the ties of these five hamlets were not with one another, but with other social groups a considerable distance away. One of them was clearly linked to the coastal peoples, whereas another was part of the highland culture. The three middle hamlets may have looked either upriver or downriver, or may have been part of a distinct mid-valley culture with traditions of its own despite influence from both directions.

Though the evidence is not conclusive, the pattern described above reflects what we would expect to find on the ground in the physical remains of related but separate cultures with considerable contact with one another. Since these five sites were located in a particularly good area for the cultivation of one of the highly valued goods of Andean society—maize—we may have here the remains of a multiethnic frontier, an area in which distinct ethnic groups, each seeking access to a particularly valued resource, faced one another in a kind of uneasy standoff in which coexistence could easily turn into conflict as the balance of force shifted among them. That pattern was in any event part of the social ecology of the Andean area a half millennium later, a period for which we have written records that provide a glimpse into the efforts of distinct ethnic groups to obtain and hold resource areas for the production of particularly valued crops.

In the Rímac River valley, one valley to the north of the Lurín, sometime before the Inca conquest of the central highlands in the fifteenth century, three distinct culture groups cultivated crops in the warm valley lands of Quives, at an altitude of approximately 1,500 feet above sea level. The lands were originally held by a coastal group that had sent some of its members upriver to cultivate cotton, coca, maize, and other crops for their fellows on the coast. Some time shortly before the Inca conquest of the area, the Chaclla people in Huarochirí raided down the valley in search of lowland fields. They threatened the coastal people occupying Quives, sending emissaries down from the hills to meet with their rivals. After some negotiation, the two groups reached an agreement in which they established new boundaries and the Chaclla people took over a part of the lands, settling some of their members there to send coca and other lowland fruits up to their home communities in the highlands. The Canta people, another highland group to the north, also moved into the Quives lands, settling their people on other plots of land taken from the lowland group.[7] The members of each group kept themselves apart from the others, cultivating their crops for exchange within their home communities rather than dealing with their nearby rivals in the area. The geographical reconstruction of the Quives settlement is strikingly similar to the picture of the five hamlets in the good maize lands of the Lurín Valley about A.D. 500. As the archaeologists continue to add to our understanding of the physical patterns of settlement and their relation to one another on the western slopes of the Andes, we will get closer and closer to being able to reconstruct the geography of past societies—and ultimately the character of social relations.

The creative use of their environment made it possible for human groups in the Andes to build societies that were seen as comfortable and prosperous by Europeans. In 1611, a member of European society in Huarochirí—the resident priest—described the people of the region as prosperous farmers. They were, according to him, "Indians of good character, who go about well dressed in wool and not poor; rather there are among them many who have good plots or fields, herds of goats and other forms of income and affairs."[8] The prosperity of earlier Huarochirí societies was based upon a complex pattern of household production and access to distant goods and resources. The basic goods cultivated locally included maize, quinua, potatoes, ají, and other grains and native fruits common to the mountain slopes. Llamas, more common in the high puna steppes of the south and the basis of wealth there, were not as important a part of life in the central highlands, although they were important to the peoples of the Mantaro River valley to the east of the Cordillera Occidental. Still, camelid bone became common in sites in the northern part of Huarochirí, in the area of Chaclla on the boundaries of the Chillón River valley, by the time of the birth of Christ.[9]

We know that the people of Huarochirí prior to the European invasion enjoyed not only wool, grains, and the standard agricultural crops of the highlands and the puna but also goods that were more difficult to obtain or that came from a greater distance. They used *mullu*, the shell of a mollusk obtained only along the coast of Ecuador, in ceremonial activity. Ceremony also provides a glimpse at luxury goods. The Jesuit missionary to the province in 1571 reported that in celebration of festivals honoring local deities, "some came dressed in silver shirts, and others in shirts of gold, and all had caps of silver, with a great quantity of feathers on them."[10] Yet all sources on Andean society, whether from Cuzco or more recent local research, insist on the absence of trade and markets in most areas of the Andes. In the highlands there existed only a petty local exchange of foodstuffs between households, through which people obtained the little extras that flavored meals and met temporary shortages.[11]

Access to resources beyond the limits to which group members can move, or access to more specialized goods such as worked gold and silver, is virtually impossible without considerable organization and specialization. It took the organized labor of many people to free specialists to mine silver or gold, to turn mercury ores into pigments, or to perform any of the other tasks that meant the difference between living poorly on what the immediate surroundings provided and living comfortably with access (at least for some members of the society) to all of the goods defined as desirable. The small, fragmented villages of the Andes today are poor— both in European terms and in terms of their own values and needs. Their poverty is at least in part a problem of scale: they no longer have access to the agencies and sources of power as they are defined today.

Life was in many ways simpler prior to the arrival of the Europeans, but it was never easy. We have seen that crops could easily fail and that survival was a matter of a precarious balance between too much and too little water. Access to land and to water were both crucial, and at least in the period just prior to the expansion of the Inca state there is evidence, both archaeological and cultural, that competition was endemic among the societies of the central Andes over the resources that meant the

difference between the survival and the disappearance of groups. Archaeologists are familiar with the fortified sites that can be found on top of
steep slopes, particularly in the coveted region between coast and highlands where water was relatively plentiful and maize, ají, and prized lowland fruits grew easily. The Andean chronicler Huaman Poma de Ayala
spoke of the period before the Inca expansion as an age of war, or "auca
runa," when people

> lived in the heights and the mountains and the cliffs, and to defend themselves
> began to build fortresses that are called *pucara*; they built walls and enclosures
> and inside them houses and fortresses and hidden wells for water, where they
> lived, and they began to quarrel and there was fighting and much war and killing,
> with their captains and lord and with other lords. They were brave and valiant
> captains and eager men and . . . there was much death and bloodletting and they
> took many captives and took their wives and children and appropriated their fields
> and chacaras and irrigation ditches and pastures and they were very cruel, taking
> clothing, silver, gold, and copper—even to the grinding stones. [12]

Competition for land and goods was clearly an aspect of life on the
western slopes of the Cordillera Occidental. The traditions of the people
of Huarochirí, corroborated by testimony taken in the decades following
the entry of the Europeans, emphasize both the highland origin of the
peoples who held the region in the sixteenth century and their bellicose
nature. These people were warriors, proud of their ability in battle,
whose origin stories described their advance down the mountain slopes
toward the coast, driving out the coastal or *yunga* peoples previously settled along the valley slopes. "At that time . . . all the peoples of whom we
have spoken, those that form the group of peoples of the province of
Huarochirí and also of the province of Chaclla-Mamaq, had yungas. Pariacaca pushed them down to the lowlands, saying 'My sons will live here.'
These victors were each one sons of Pariacaca." [13]

Both conquest and the organization of the spoils of conquest demanded
the combined labor of many people working together. Cooperation was
needed to build the irrigation canals that run for miles along the highland
valley slopes, bringing water from the high springs or glacial lakes of the
puna above. Cooperation was needed to maintain those canals, to clean
and repair them so that they could continue to serve the needs of the people through whose lands they ran. People had to work together to build
the dikes and dams that harnessed the highland lakes to provide water;
they had to join forces in order to expand agricultural land by terracing
the valley slopes. Today those same terraces stand abandoned, many of
the stone facings destroyed or scattered by sudden mud slides or the
slower but inexorable processes of time. It is no longer possible to mobilize the large-scale labor needed to maintain—let alone expand—produc-

tive resources. The integration of large numbers of people was the key to the prosperity found and described by the Europeans, and the remainder of this chapter will be devoted to a discussion of the social mechanisms through which labor was mobilized and goods produced and distributed before the arrival of the Europeans.

Andean society has been commonly described as a communal one in which group membership determined access to the resources that made production possible. But communal does not mean equal, as recent work by anthropologists has made amply clear.[14] Andean society was not egalitarian, nor did cooperation mean that people freely shared their labor and the products of that labor. This was not a society of plenty. People worked hard to reproduce the conditions of life as they knew them, to produce or obtain the goods defined by their culture as necessary or desirable. Productive activity was organized according to recognized rules of behavior and interaction.

Societies of the Andean type commonly organize social relations around rules of behavior that are assigned to particular roles fixed from birth and defined in terms of kinship. A person is regarded as stepping at birth into a particular set of relationships—responsibilities toward others and claims upon them—that provides the framework he or she manipulates to gain certain objectives. Kinship ties, in the view of the members of the society, provide both the basis of the organization of production and distribution, and the foundation of the political order. The rights and claims that people have upon one another by virtue of kinship define who a person may call upon for labor or other assistance and what will constitute the productive unit for different tasks. Kinship terms provide a vocabulary—a set of rules of behavior—that is socially defined as prior to and above any mundane activity such as the maintenance and reproduction of physical and social life. Kin ties link small groups of people with larger groups, thus providing the rationale for political organization. They can link past and present, providing an ideology to explain and justify the distribution of access to productive resources, the organization of ritual, and the participation of the people in maintaining and preserving the social order.

It is virtually impossible to unravel the closely bound web of social relations in order to reconstruct the outlines of an economic system, a political system, or a religious or ideological system. Production was organized through these relations, providing systems of internal organization and authority that ensured that the cultivation of crops and the maintenance of the llama herds were efficiently done. Patterns of authority or the organization of worship and ritual were integral parts of the social relationships through which the production of goods was organized. Ritual was socially defined as one of the factors that—properly carried out—maintained and augmented the means of production, i.e. the natural resources upon which the group depended, including the cooperative labor of its members. If, in this, there was also considerable room for the accumulation of goods and power, this is hardly surprising and also played a part in the maintenance and expansion of the society.

The rules of behavior that can be reconstructed for any society may appear fixed and rigid, as indeed they do in the Andean case if we limit ourselves to reproducing the often complicated diagrams and models of kinship systems dear to certain schools of anthropology. But it is clear from even the fragmentary data now available that the members of Andean society, though accepting and reproducing the basic relationships that structured their behavior, used those relationships creatively in their struggle for status and wealth, some losing in the process and some gaining. The rules may seem immutable, but the varied fortunes of the social groups depicted in the myths and tales of Huarochirí show a process of change that is revealed graphically, on a larger and longer scale, by the archaeological record.

The basic productive unit in local Andean society that emerges from myths and historical records, as well as archaeological materials, is the household. Archaeological surveys in the central Andes point strongly to a residence pattern of relatively small household units. In Huánuco, an extensive field survey of sites dated to the period of the European conquest found a few components that consisted of several house foundations enclosed by a low wall. But these units stood out in the general picture of single-house foundations, and have been classified by the investigators as high-ranking households, probably those of chiefs.[15] In the region of Huarochirí, virtually all the sites that have been dated to the period just before and during the Inca expansion and that contain remains not totally destroyed and scattered reveal a pattern of relatively small, one-room house foundations, usually of stone.[16] There are exceptions, of course, but those are generally sites with some purpose other than or in addition to the basic day-to-day labors of an agricultural society. The evidence, then, suggests strongly that the basic working unit of the society was the household. And we can further posit—on the basis of contemporary ethnographic data, the age-grades of Inca census categories, and the testimony of a member of Andean society at the end of the sixteenth century[17]—that the household was composed of a limited number of people differentiated by age and sex.

Huaman Poma de Ayala, the third of our sources just mentioned, described a system of age-grades for both men and women. Both sexes passed through a series of stages from infancy to young adulthood: boys gradually assumed light tasks such as herding and hunting, and girls began gathering and drying herbs for dyes, learning household chores, weaving, and herding. As the young people neared full adulthood, the boys served as runners or messengers between local groups, spent time in the puna shepherding the animals belonging to the chiefs or elders as well as to their own household, and began to join their elders in war parties; the girls cared for the llamas and learned to spin and weave fine cloth. By about twenty, according to Huaman Poma's rough and fluctuating age calculations by year, young people became eligible for marriage and adult status. With marriage, both men and women became full members of the society, bringing to the organization of a new household the property they had accumulated both from parents and relatives and from their own labor as they moved through the stages from birth to marriage. As adults, they could take possession of the fields and other resources passed on to them as they grew, and assume responsibilities that carried with them obligations to aid, support, and maintain the people who had helped bring them to adulthood. [18]

The household was composed of parents and children at various stages of growth, together with older adults who had passed on to the status of honored elder. Though limited in size, it could perform alone most of the tasks involved in the cultivation of crops and the care of herd animals over the course of the year, though it might well need extra help at planting and harvest time. But these units could not invest the labor necessary for the maintenance of basic resources or their expansion: a couple needed help to build a house or to obtain effective access to goods not produced by the local unit. Thus the prosperity of Andean society depended heavily upon the integration of household units into more extensive groups, relations among which were regulated according to the same ideology that structured behavior in the household unit. At the end of this process of progressive integration we are dealing with units that have become in fact political entities, tribes, or whatever we choose to call them.

At this level, cooperation in productive or other activities becomes a far more complicated affair, and it is here that we can perceive the presence of another group that cuts across the structure of household units integrated on a steadily expanding scale. That new group is an elite, or class, whose function is that of command, administration, or organization—in short, of government—and who enjoy privileged access to the resources and the products of production without themselves personally participating in the work process. That elite also perpetuates itself through kin ties, forming lineages of descendants whose birth is the basis of their privileged access to the goods and resources of their societies. Relations between the elite and the people among whom they live and to whom they are bound by the same structure of mutual claims and responsibilities are not symmetrical and bilateral, but asymmetrical. These two sets of relationships—those regulating interaction between people with the same kind of claim to the resources and products of their society, and those regulating interaction between those who produce the goods and those who rule or administer—together constitute the organizing principles of the societies of the central Andes in the period just prior to the invasion of the Europeans.

In order to obtain a clearer idea of how kin ties were used to mobilize labor in the productive process, let us move back to the household level for a short while and follow the net of reciprocal claims and responsibilities accepted by the households of two people who established a new social unit with each other. The joining of two people to form a new household linked the kin of each partner, who were henceforth expected to behave toward one another as brothers and sisters.[19] The people who regarded one another as brothers and sisters prior to the expansion of the kin group by marriage included not only the brothers and sisters born of the same parents, but also first, second, and third cousins (i.e., those who traced their ancestry back to the same great-grandfather), which made for a large group of people.[20] All of the members of this larger group were expected to aid one another in tasks that demanded more hands than could be mobilized within the household alone. Within the group, the ideology of proper behavior between kinsmen insisted that support and assistance should be ungrudging and open, a norm spelled out by Huaman Poma de Ayala as the "law of marriage and good order." "These *compadres* helped one another in their work and in other necessities and when they were ill and in eating and drinking and in the celebrations and in the sowing and in the mourning at death and at all times as long as they lived, and afterwards their sons and descendants, grandchildren and great-grandchildren aided one another and kept the ancient law of God."[21]

The language fuses the vocabulary of kinship and of labor obligation and assistance. Take, for example, the word *mit'a*, used to designate a labor turn or exchange owed by people to one another, to chiefs, or to the Inca state, and later applied by the Spaniards to the labor draft for work in the mines and other colonial enterprises. In the construction *cananmittan* it means "the entire clan, lineage, or generation of a person, or their descendants, sons, or grandsons."[22] One's brothers and their offspring make up the group from whom a person can claim *mit'a*, a "turn" of labor, and to whose similar claims one should respond. The "brothers" were the contributors of labor to one another and to the new "brothers" created by a marriage, a responsibility and a role so taken for granted that the language did not distinguish between kin terms and the terms of labor exchange and the sharing of goods.

Kinship, as recognized by the society, was not the source but the expression of the reciprocal rights of people to the aid and support of specific other people among whom they lived. As in most societies prior to our contemporary industrial system (in which a person's claim to the labor of someone else is openly based on his monopoly of the tools and materials needed by the other to work), the basis of the claims people had to the labor of others was rooted in the arena of social relations. Custom and tradition specified acceptable behavior of one person toward another. Such "acceptable behavior," defined as responsibilities toward and claims upon kin, governed the presentation of labor in the production process as well as the exchange of the products of that labor. In Andean society, there was so little difference between access to kin and wealth that material prosperity was counted in terms of available kin. "The woman who was held in most esteem as a marriage partner was she with most kin, and not the wealthiest, because she who had more relatives brought with her friends and people, which was what had most value as the greater thing, and in this they placed high honor and authority and power."[23] Again, language is telling: The word *wak'cha*, for example, means "potato-eater," "poor," and "orphan"; the word *capak*, which alone means "king," "lord," or "rich," is also the root of the word *capakhaheque*, meaning "to have many people, to be many in one house, family, or group."[24]

Within the household, it is clear that women as well as men gained access to land through the kin group of their birth. In the myths and tales of Huarochirí, women appear frequently as the cultivators and holders of lands and water sources, although those who marry in the tales commonly leave their family homes to follow their husbands.[25] A suggestive hint here is offered by a contemporary scholar working in an Andean Aymara community, whose traditions and practices are strikingly similar to those recorded in the tales of Huarochirí. Aymara women tend to move to their husbands' lands, but they retain their claims to the lands and properties of their own parents and can pass such claims on to their own children or grandchildren. Until recent years, the women continued to hold lands at a distance, going to work them themselves or retaining brothers or close kinsmen to work them instead.[26]

The union of a man and a woman therefore became the basis of a new productive unit with access to resources contributed by the kin of each partner, and with claims to the support and aid of those same people. Though evidence both from the myths and tales and from contemporary ethnography strongly suggests that men in Andean society placed considerable emphasis upon sons as the foundation of a lineage that could become the basis of prestige and rank, it is at the same time clear that the men alone did not control the resources of the society. Kinship for a member of Andean society seems to have been relatively flexible and malleable. It might be useful to think of Andean kinship and its rights and responsibilities as a model of the way in which a member of that society visualized his social world. These groupings did not make up a formally organized class lasting through many generations, the skeleton and reference points of that society. There is no evidence that the formalized, relatively permanent class perceived by anthropologists in Africa ever existed in the Andes. The kinship structure of Andean society describes the alternatives available to a given member, who chooses among them to his own best advantage, seeking to construct a position of authority and wealth through the labor of his own household and the relationships he can establish with the members of the two groups linked to him by marriage. If he is successful, his new status can permit him to establish an enduring lineage, and ensure service by his descendants not only in this world, but in the next as well.

The structure of kinship, which made it possible for people to claim aid and support from one another, also laid the basis for more enduring social units linked through time as well as space. Domingo de Santo Tomás, a Dominican friar with real sympathy for the Andean people, described the organization of these more enduring groups succinctly in the 1560's: "Among them, if a gentleman is particularly known in some way, his children take on his name; and not only the children, but all his descendants, and in that way are formed among them the lineages that they call *ayllu* and *pachaca*. And so it goes in all of the rest of the provinces of Peru, [where] particular lineages, which they call *ayllus*, take the name of their ancestors."[27] The ayllu, formed of a number of lineages regulated internally by an ethic of sharing and cooperation, can be viewed as the basic political as well as productive unit of Andean society. Twentieth-century scholars have commonly defined it as a localized kin group living in a single village and holding lands in common.[28] More recent attempts at definition not only point to the territorial aspect of the group but also add that membership can be defined in terms of accepting the ritual responsibilities connected with the cycle of production and reproduction of goods and of people.[29] Sixteenth-century dictionaries, however, defined the ayllu as a family: the descendants of a common ancestor. The term was commonly defined as any group—family, lineage, or generation—whose members were related to one another through their descent from a common ancestor. In the myths of Huarochirí the term is applied to groups of very different extent, but at one point the narrator defines an ayllu broadly as a group of people "who are like a single son."[30]

Dictionaries clearly indicate just how functional the basis of ayllu membership was. The act to which the root (*aylluy*) refers is that of grouping elements or persons together on the basis of similarity or species, or dividing up a larger group on the basis of the same criteria. *Ayllupura*, meaning "to join together those of a lineage, or things of a single genus or kind," is opposed to *aylluchani*, "to divide people according to their segments (*parcialidades*) or put them into their separate places."[31] Essentially, any group whose members could be regarded as "of the same kind" was an ayllu. The basis of membership might be birth; more broadly, it might be simply the acceptance of the responsibilities, ritual as well as productive, inhering in membership.

The origin story of an actual ayllu of Huarochirí in the sixteenth century, remembered as one of the most recently formed ayllus of the province, provides good evidence of the internal structure of these groups and the basis of membership.[32] The ayllu Concha, like the majority of the other groups of Huarochirí, was formed by conquest, its lands and resources the spoils of war with the lowland peoples who, according to local tradition, occupied the lands later claimed by the people of Huarochirí. The ayllu was composed of five lineages, the descendants of five brothers who expelled the coastal people and took their lands and shrines. However, the lands were held by only three of the lineages, and the lack of access to land of the others was explained with the tale that the remaining two brothers had gotten lost and had to retrace their steps, arriving at the site that had been occupied by the coastal people too late to claim any of the spoils. Even within the ayllu, therefore, access to resources was not shared with the non-landholding lineages as long as there were direct heirs in the other three to receive the lands and goods of their parents, as also attested to by information from another area of the Andes, where a witness testified that "All the lands are divided among the Indians, and each one has marked out what is his."[33] But if a man with control over resouces and a position within the ayllu found himself without heirs to claim his property, he could adopt heirs, thus preserving his line. In the case of Concha, the leading elder and founder of the ayllu, Llacsamisa, lacked direct descendants and so adopted two men as his sons. The first of these was a direct descendant of one of Llacsamisa's brothers who lacked access to resources, and on being adopted this man gave up his own lineage name and took that of Llacsamisa, thus preserving the line of the founder and taking on his authority.[34] The other man was an outsider, a coastal survivor of the Concha conquest of his lands whom Llacsamisa saved as a boy and brought up in his home, defending him from his brothers and eventually marrying him to his sister.[35]

The relation between ayllu membership and willingness to assume the traditions and customs of the group is even more clearly stated in another case. The narrator of the tales of Huarochirí, in speaking of the ceremonies performed for Pariacaca, chief deity of the province, adds: "When someone [from Huaylas] has married a woman of [the community of] Surco, and subsequently performs these duties [accepting the 'cargo' associated with the worship], it is said that the members of that community do not take away his fields or anything else, in spite of his being an outsider. On the contrary, they account him worthy, they help him."[36] Despite the lack of immediate familial ties, the members of an ayllu were ideally expected to aid and support one another and to act toward one another as "brothers" in terms of the ideology of kinship. A description of access to land within the ayllu from outside Huarochirí but probably expressing the principles prevailing in that province as well, clarifies both the pattern of access to land and resources described earlier and the statement found in most sources since the sixteenth century that the members of an ayllu held lands in common. Ultimately, the larger group did hold claim to the resources and the property of its members, exercising that claim if the individual lineage died out. "When an Indian dies without leaving children but leaving his wife, part of the lands are assigned to his wife and the rest divided among the Indians of his ayllu who are in need, and if the deceased leaves no heir all the lands are divided up among those of his ayllu."[37]

That broader relationship between people defined as kin made it possible for households to throw the net of their holdings wider, cultivating land at different altitudes, in as many of the microecologies to which the larger group held access as possible. In a real sense, access to kin, defined as people who could—and would—act to protect a person's interest, could be equated with wealth. A "brother" not only helped his kinsman in productive tasks; he could also be called upon to protect his brother's interests.[38] This structure of support explains how it was possible for ayllu members to lay effective claim to lands scattered over a broad area. Despite the fact that the lands claimed by ayllus were frequently widely separated—even to the point of being in different river valley systems—there is considerable evidence that ayllu members continued to claim, and cultivate, lands spread over a wide area throughout the Spanish colonial period. The remnants of that pattern can be found today. In 1968, the comunidad or ayllu of Yambilla in Huarochirí still held lands at various altitudes. According to the treasurer of the comunidad, Sr. Hector Chuquimuni, each ayllu ideally held lands in three zones: the high or cold zone, from 9,600 to about 10,800 feet; the middle or temperate zone, from 8,400 to about 10,200 feet; and the hot or low zone, from 5,400 to

8,400 feet. The last of these areas produces squash and pumpkins, yuca, apples, oranges, tomatoes, maize, ají, avocados, lemons, plums and Andean fruits. The temperate middle area is the zone of wheat, corn, and other grains, plus beans, melons, and the high-altitude *rocotta*, a fiery hot chili. Up high, near the puna, people harvest *oca* and *ulluco* and other tubers, as well as a variety of potatoes, beans, a little wheat, and barley. Above, on the puna, each ayllu held pasture for llamas and sheep, as well as lakes whose waters are diverted to irrigate the fields, particularly in the temperate zone.[39]

As we move back in time, we find evidence that the reach of the people of Huarochirí formerly extended to even greater distances from their home communities. The testament of a resident of Huarochirí in 1631, for example, reveals that he held parcels of land ranging from the warm areas down along the banks of the Mala River up to the cold territory of the puna. The parcels were not contiguous and were scattered over an area that would take several days to cover on foot.[40] Those who sought to hold more land aimed not to concentrate their holdings but to fling them wider. The lands passed on to the heirs of a member of the village of Quinti in 1684 extended from the present village of San Juan de Tantaranche, located at about 11,400 feet in the province of Yauyos to the south, to the high puna pastures of the community of Tanta, fourteen hours' journey from Quinti.[41]

This pattern is clearly not a European one, and in fact the Andean people's efforts to maintain access to a variety of parcels scattered over a broad area brought them into direct conflict with the European authorities, particularly those not familiar with the Andean traditions described by the more perceptive among the Spaniards in Peru in the sixteenth century. Indians living in the village of San Damián, located at about 10,500 feet in the Lurín River valley, held access throughout the colonial period to lowland fields in Soquiacancha, in the Rímac River drainage to the north, at an altitude of about 4,800 feet. At the end of the sixteenth century, the local Spanish administrator discovered these people living in Soquiacancha for much of the year. Since they were so far from San Damián, their ostensible home settlement, he founded a new village and parish on the site. But though the people continued to work their lands in Soquiacancha and to live there much of the year, they refused almost a century later to sever their link with San Damián, insisting that they belonged to the latter settlement despite their extended residence in lands more than 20 miles away in another river drainage.[42]

The idea of a system of overlapping access to land held and cultivated by household groups organized into larger entities on the basis of common descent—whether that descent is fictional or not—adequately explains the available data, but those data are sketchy, and the picture painted above is strikingly monochromatic. "Brothers" who owe one another aid and support and yet have claims upon one another's property may in fact act as the norms and rules of behavior say they should. But they may not, and quarrels between brothers over property are among the most common sources of lasting discord in contemporary Andean society.[43] Either we assume that Andean people prior to the arrival of the Europeans were never tempted to seize their brother's property or to cheat one another (which smacks of the early friars' occasional arguments that the people of the Americas were the original children of Eden, unaffected by the greed and jealousy characteristic of the descendants of Cain and Abel), or we assume that they were as human in the fifteenth century as they are today, in which case we must return to the data and search for the mechanisms that limited this kind of conflict and ensured at least a general congruence between the norms and values of the society and the behavior of its members.

A suggestive clue is provided by material from sixteenth-century inspections of both the province of Chucuito, in the area of Lake Titicaca to the south, and the province of Huánuco, to the east of Huarochirí on the upper slopes of the eastern cordillera of the Andes, in the area called the *ceja*, or "eyebrow," of the jungle. In speaking of land access among the people of Chucuito, our informant, after noting that "all the lands are divided among the Indians," added that "the *kurakas* are in charge of inspecting them each year to guard against some entering into the land of others."[44] Our informant here clearly assigned the task of assuring that each person's claim to the lands and other resources inherited from his household or acquired in the course of his life was respected by his fellows to a community authority: the kuraka. Material from Huánuco is even more explicit. There, a kuraka in 1562, in speaking of land access, specifically assigned to his office the responsibility of ensuring that the "brothers" of a lineage or ayllu respect another's claims to land and other resources. "The sons succeed their parents in the lands and they divide the goods and the *chacaras* among themselves, and sometimes the brothers quarrel with one another over the division of the goods and the *cacique* [kuraka] puts them at peace."[45] The authority to mediate such quarrels at the minimal or household level was in all likelihood held by one of the elder and more respected and successful members of the local group. Huaman Poma de Ayala, in his descriptions of the age-grades of Andean society, specifically assigns to the elder members the responsibility for instructing and counseling the young and punishing transgressions, in return for which their fields or chacaras were cultivated and their animals cared for by the rest of the community.[46] At the ayllu level, these people were called *principales*, defined by a Spaniard in 1586 as "[chiefs] of lesser degree . . . who serve as chiefs in each division . . . called ayllus."[47]

Beyond the level of the household or small group, the kuraka was part of a privileged elite, hierarchically organized, whose members enjoyed special access to the goods and resources of their society by virtue of their position. There was considerable debate among the members of European society about the origin and "legitimacy" of the kurakas as a separate privileged estate in the sixteenth century, but despite strenuous efforts to prove that the kurakas were not "natural lords" (a medieval term referring to the members of a hereditary nobility in Europe), the general consensus was that these people did form part of a hereditary elite that the Europeans had no difficulty in defining in terms of their own culture as a native nobility.[48] Both the responsibilities and the privileges of the kuraka were inherited. In Huánuco, the kurakas reported that "the caciques [kurakas] succeeded their fathers as long as they were capable and able to do it."[49] Succession varied, the position sometimes passing from brother to brother rather than from father to son, but certainly at the time of the entry of the Europeans into the Andes (and according to the testimony of the chiefs in Huánuco and Chucuito, at least, by the time of the Inca expansion) the kurakas at all social levels formed a separate, hereditary elite, linked by kin ties to the society to which they belonged, but set apart by their special claims to the labor and support of their kin.

Even when the direct line died out or the heir could not succeed, the position remained within the group formed by kurakas of the various units of the society, who in turn were linked to one another by ties of kinship and intermarriage. Two examples of the failure of direct succession, from Huarochirí and from Huánuco, give some indication of how at least the fiction of kinship remained the basis for succession to authority. In the case of Huánuco, a census of the native population in 1562 found the principal kuraka of a group dead, and his heir a young boy who could not undertake the job. According to another kuraka, the principales (minor chiefs) of the group, together with their Spanish encomendero, chose one of their number, Don Francisco, as principal chief.[50] In Huarochirí, the history of the ayllu Concha, when it came to be recorded at the end of the sixteenth century, noted that the then lineage chief of the ayllu, Lazaro Puypurocsi, traced his descent not to Llacsamisa, the founder and head of the group, but to a younger brother, Hualla, one of the two brothers who had gotten lost on the way to conquer new lands and had failed to receive any share of the goods and resources taken from the coastal people. As we have seen, Llacsamisa adopted Hualla's descendant into his line at the time of his death, passing his control over the water source of his group, together with the responsibility for maintaining the rituals connected with its use, to a related but at that time unprivileged lineage.[51]

The kuraka's privileged position within his community was insisted upon both by members of native society and by European observers. Juan de Matienzo, no great admirer of the native elite, described the kurakas caustically in the 1560's, noting that "their function is to be idle and drink."[52] The kurakas themselves noted that they were the only members of the society who did not join in the physical labor of their communities but rather received the labor services of others. A kuraka of Huánuco in 1562 described the relationship of the members of Huánuco communities to their kurakas. "They serve the chiefs in turn by preparing their fields and houses and providing them with straw and wood and firewood . . . and they give [each chief] an Indian to guard his herd and he gives them food when they work and some wages and meat when he has it and some coca."[53] Again, Matienzo's judgment, though admittedly prejudiced, clearly conveys the kurakas' privileged status: "They do not work inherited properties nor hire themselves to labor for others, but maintain themselves from the tribute given them by the Indians of their ayllu."[54] From the perspective of an energetic member of the Spanish bureacracy, himself of nonnoble origin, the kurakas belonged to an idle class, providing no services to state or society but living on the labor of others.

The chiefs clearly did live from the work of the other members of their society, and were according to their own testimony the only group to do so. But they did not compel the services of the people among whom they lived. The kuraka had to request the services of the members of his community; the mechanisms of compulsion lay in the social norms and values of the society. As Don Francisco, a kuraka of Huánuco noted, "they serve the chiefs at their request."[55] The kuraka's function can be broadly described as governing or administering. Let us complete here Juan de Matienzo's description of the function of the kurakas begun in the phrase quoted above: "Their function is to be idle and drink, and to count and divide up; they are very capable at this—more so than any Spaniard—and they keep accounts with multicolored stones, so ably that it is a pleasure to watch them."[56] The importance of counting and measuring, of "keeping accounts," is well known in Andean society. Terms specifying measurement and the process of allocation and division are common in the language; the Quechua dictionaries of both Diego González Holguín and Domingo de Santo Tomás abound with them. Most people who have read about or traveled in the Andes have heard of the *quipu*, the mnemonic counting device of knotted cords that has been found in archaeological sites dated to centuries before the rise of the Inca state; and *quipucama-yoq*, or specialists in keeping records with the quipu, can still be found in isolated areas of the Andes today. The age-grades listed by Huaman Poma de Ayala assigned the function of quipucamayoq to the aged members of Andean society, whose experience and skills were placed at the service of their communities once their physical ability had gone.[57]

Now in some societies the justification for the privileged position of an elite class is ability in war. The Andean chiefs were indeed war leaders, and at least some of the sources argue that leadership in battle was the origin of their authority. War parties, both before the rise of the Inca state and under its authority, were organized and led by the kurakas.[58] But there was another function, more closely related to the relations of production and distribution in Andean society, that was performed by the kuraka: he ensured that all members of society gained the access to the goods and labor they were entitled to by the formal relationships of kinship.

All witnesses from Andean native society in the sixteenth century testify to the absence of markets and trade on any scale beyond that of the household—at least in the highlands. Don Francisco of Huánuco, for example, told the Spaniards that "in the time of the Inca there were no large-scale merchants as there are among the Spaniards, save for a few Indians who only traded a little food among themselves; and cloth was not bought because everyone made what he needed."[59] Despite convincing evidence of both merchants and long-distance trade in the coastal areas— and indications that trade may well have extended into the highlands prior to the expansion of the Inca state—it is increasingly clear that there were large differences in the social organization of coast and highlands.[60] The Incas may well have restricted trade that had previously taken place in the highlands, but it is probable that unless a substantial part of the exchange that took place was organized outside of a market context prior to the Inca expansion, some evidence for markets would have emerged from the testimony of members of Andean society in the sixteenth century or from archaeological investigation.[61] We have evidence of exchange, but to date no archaeologist has uncovered evidence of a market center. All of this suggests strongly that exchange took place along other than market lines. And other evidence further suggests that distribution was also a function of established relationships within Andean society that provided access to both labor and the products of that labor for the members of the community.[62] Here is the principal function of the kuraka in the community. He supervised and counted, and according to Don Francisco of Huánuco in 1562, he divided up tasks and assigned labor.[63] The kuraka ensured that the lands of the widowed and the aged were cultivated by their kinsmen, and that the products of labor were shared according to the same rules.

One of the best descriptions of the role of a local kuraka in the productive system I have found in Huarochirí is contained in the history of the ayllu Concha.[64] This ayllu was known in the traditions of Huarochirí as among the youngest "sons" of the deities of the province—so young that it was "scarcely taken into account."[65] This suggests that the group, already declining sharply by the end of the sixteenth century, was not particularly large. According to tradition, the founder of the ayllu, Llacsamisa, transmitted to his heirs the instructions for the care of the dikes and reservoirs, and the rules for the distribution of irrigation waters. These were in turn said to have been vouchsafed to him by the ayllu's guardian deity. Llacsamisa instructed his heirs in how to determine when the reservoir should be opened and the fields flooded, telling them that they "must give the order for the performance of these duties."[66] And after he taught them how to read the stones placed to measure the height of the lake, "the descendants of these men, generation after generation, to this day, obey the instructions that he gave for the distribution [of the water]."[67]

In this particular case, water is the resource distributed according to the rules and customs attributed to the ancestor and maintained by the kuraka. In other cases the kuraka takes the responsibility for administering and maintaining other rules of proper behavior structuring access to labor and distribution of production. At the household or minimal group level, distribution was a product of established relationships and responsibilities backed by the social pressures that could be brought to bear upon a lax or reluctant kinsman by those people defined as his brothers. The kuraka intervened here only when normal practice broke down and the "law of good behavior" failed to function. At higher levels, however, the kuraka intervened more directly, especially in supervising the group's access to productive resources at a distance. For the administrative role of the kuraka was an essential aspect of the process by which a group claimed and maintained access to resource areas far from its core territories.[68]

The term *mitmaq* or *mitimaes*, describing colonists sent from their home territory to settle in distant areas, is a familiar one to anyone who has read a little about the Incas. Until recently it was thought that the mitimaes derived from an Inca practice of resettlement used as a tactic of pacification and control by the expanding state. But the general term *mit'a* refers only to periodic service. A *mitayoq* is defined in González Holguín's great dictionary as "someone working his time, or turn." "Those who serve in turn" are *mit'aruna*.[69] The root can be combined with other terms to refer to a person's descendants, who take their own "turn" at using the resources of their society in the course of their lives, and who retire at the end of their active lives in favor of their offspring. González Holguín even noted a construction where the composite of which mit'a formed a part defined a conversation in which the right to speak was passed along from one person to another.[70] Recent scholarship has altered the earlier view of mitmaq and made it increasingly clear that in the absence of markets and commercial exchange, the people doing a "turn" of service far from their home communities were an integral part of the productive system of Andean society.[71]

An extensive system of pre-Inca mitmaq settlements far from the home territories of the groups involved has been reconstructed by John Murra for the region of Chucuito, in the puna steppes of southern Peru. Murra has also described what he terms an "archipelago" system of access to resources in central Peru, in Huánuco as well as in the area of the Rímac and Chillón river valleys at the northern edge of the province of Huarochirí.[72] In Huarochirí itself, the limited numbers of the population relative to Huánuco would have constrained the geographical reach of such a system, but fortunately ecological factors made such a wide reach unnecessary. The two major social groups of the province, the people of Huarochirí and the people of Chaclla-Mamaq, sent mitmaq up to the headwaters of the Santa Eulalia River, near the later colonial village of Carampoma, to mine silver and mineral powders for pottery, body paints, and ornaments.[73] Huarochirí people also received products from their mitmaq settlers to the east in Jauja, on the other side of the Cordillera Occidental, and from other mitmaq on the coast near what later became Lima, a particularly fine area for maize.[74] Several decades after the Spanish conquest of Peru, there were still some 170 household heads in the Lima area who were defined as part of the society of Huarochirí.[75] South of Yauyos in the colonial province of Chocorvos, the people of Huarochirí held pastures assigned them by the Incas to supplement the scanty pasturage available in Huarochirí itself.[76] In the 1570's, forty years after the Spanish conquest, there was a settlement of almost 500 Huarochirí people, one of over 600 Chaclla people, and yet another of some 80 Mamaq people (22 households) in Chocorvos.[77]

Within Huarochirí province itself, colonists from all the component social groups settled in prized resource oases, charged with cultivating goods sought by their home communities. Huarochirí people sent mitmaq to cultivate coca and other lowland crops in Quives, in the Chillón Valley three rivers to the north. They and the people of Checa also sent mitmaq to the maize lands of Chaclacayo near Lima on the coast. The

Chaclla people, another group centered in the Santa Eulalia Valley, sent mitmaq upriver to the mines of Carampoma, as well as downriver to . Chaclacayo.[78] Good pottery clay was found near the colonial village of Olleros, on the boundary between the core territories of highland and coastal groups, and people from Huarochirí and Yauyos to the south both sent mitmaq to exploit it. The Olleros region was still a major producer of pottery cookware in the 1960's.

Who were these colonists? There is some suggestion that at least some of them were specialists who sent the products of their crafts back to their home communities. In the case of Huánuco, John Murra has demonstrated that there were colonies of woodworkers (or *q'erocamayoq*) and potters living in settlements close to the source of their raw materials.[79] In Huarochirí, the narrator of the myths and tales of the province provided a suggestive note when, speaking of a particular ayllu called Yasapa, he added, "when we say 'Yasapa' we mean 'silverworker,' because Yasapa has that meaning and the Yasapas had that occupation."[80] Craftsmen with particular skills probably had most of their needs met by their kinsmen through the network of reciprocal claims and obligations. That is particularly likely in the case of miners, for the mining region of Huarochirí lies at an altitude where crops are stunted and often fail. Where the activities of the mitmaq were agricultural, a portion of the lands they cultivated may well have been set aside for their own use, permitting them to satisfy most of their needs without depending on other members of their society.

In one case we have a fairly detailed account of a resource area controlled by the people of Huarochirí and Chaclla: the warm lowland fields of Quives, which produced fruits and particularly coca for the highland societies.[81] In 1559, the Spanish courts intervened in a dispute between the people of Chaclla and those of Canta to the north over the land of Quives. In the course of the trial, all witnesses agreed that the lands of Quives had originally belonged to a lowland community subject to a coastal group. Seeking new lands, the Chaclla people sent out a war party that was stopped by the coastal group but managed to lay siege to Quives and finally gain access to a portion of the lands. The Canta people also moved into the region shortly before the Inca conquest, and both groups established mitmaq in the lands. The Inca claimed land in Quives after the conquest of the area, and granted the Chaclla people additional land at the expense of the people from Canta. It is clear from the account that the respective mitmaq sent the produce of the lands, particularly coca, back to their own communities.

What was done with these goods? Here the kuraka again enters into the picture. The overlapping character of claims to land by both the community and the kuraka is clear from colonial court records. I suspect that the confusion of claims to ownership during the colonial period derived from the nature of the kuraka's relationship to his own community. He was part of the society he administered, with the same claim to its resources as any other member of the community, and yet at the same time he was set apart, with a special claim to labor and goods by virtue of his social position. And in the case of the distant resource areas, worked for the benefit of the larger group, the kuraka as the representative and leader of the group became the channel through which the products of those areas were distributed. In the case of Quives, the kuraka of the Chaclla people used the prized goods harvested there—chiefly maize and coca, both high-prestige goods—to reinforce his ties with other kurakas. According to a local witness in 1559, the kuraka of Chaclla "went sometimes to Huarochirí . . . to see the chief of the settlement of Huarochirí, called Ninavilca, . . . bringing ears of maize and coca and ají and other foodstuffs for the chief Ninavilca, saying 'I bring you this from my chacara, Quives.' "[82] Prized goods distributed by a kuraka might go to other kurakas, or to the Inca, or even to community members. Particularly valued luxury goods, such as precious metals, were marks of rank and status within the group, as indicated by the description of a local celebration in Huarochirí left by a Jesuit priest in 1570. He described the silver ornaments woven into the cloth of the ceremonial shirts worn by the important members of society. Some people had bits of silver woven into their shirts, others had shirts with yet more silver, and the most important people wore shirts decorated with gold.[83]

An important part of the kuraka's function was ceremonial. A good kuraka was, in Huaman Poma de Ayala's terms, "generous and hospitable"—which explains much of Juan de Matienzo's complaint that they had no other function than to drink and be idle. As noted above, the kuraka was expected to reciprocate with gifts and food for the labor he asked from the members of the society. He should always be free with drink for those who came to see or consult him; he fed those who worked for him, and he carried out periodic distributions of llamas, coca, and other goods in his community.[84] His privileged access to the products of his society permitted him to maintain the role expected of him within his community as well as to forge, with gifts, bonds of reciprocity with the other members of his class and with the state to which he and his people were subject.

The goods that derived from his special position were also used for ceremonial purposes, for the kuraka's role as administrator and guardian of his community extended to the dead and the mythical as well as the living. Again, the origin story of the ayllu Concha of Huarochirí underlines this function. As we have seen, the founder, Llacsamisa, controlled the lake from which the group drew its water and was said to have established the rules for distributing that water and maintaining the system of reservoirs and dikes by which it was channeled. But his role went beyond merely practical concerns to include that of "venerating the lake Yansa, of serving it."[85] He was expected to feed the *wak'as* of the lake, the husband-and-wife guardian deities of the group's essential resource, and llamas and *ticti* (a gruel used only in ritual) were specially prepared as periodic offerings.[86]

The existence of a redistributive system of this kind, in which particularly valued goods were remitted to the community and distributed by the kuraka, demanded another element that, like markets in a different kind of society, can be detected and examined in the material remains of a society. For when goods must be held for later consumption, some kind of storage facilities are necessary. The existence of such facilities on the state level has been amply proved: the Incas maintained huge storehouse complexes, both in Cuzco and at the provincial level, whose broken remains have yielded clear evidence of their function.[87] At the local level, however, though the testimony of Huaman Poma de Ayala and the language itself contain evidence of storage, it is difficult to locate the remains of storage facilities, or to distinguish between storage for the group and storage for the kuraka. I suspect that community and kuraka stores were not distinguished from one another. The Andean term for the good of the community as a whole is *sapsi*, translated by González Holguín as "something belonging to everyone."[88] The sapsi can be defined as the goods or the productive resources claimed by a group, as in the term *sapsichacara*, "that belonging to the community," a composite term linking community stores and cultivated fields together. Huaman Poma de Ayala, in describing the agricultural cycle, noted that at harvesttime in May, "the communities and the community store [sapsi] of maize and potatoes and all the foodstuffs and the community herds were inspected . . . and all of the storehouses were swollen, and the houses of the poor; and the *yuyos* [an Andean root crop] were dried and the goods prepared for storage so that there would be enough to eat for the entire year and there would not be hunger among the poor."[89] Local stores may well have been located in the residence compound of the kuraka, which on the basis of both written and archaeological evidence seems to have been considerably larger than the residence areas of the other members of his local community.[90]

Material remains from Huarochirí also offer suggestions about the character and location of storage. In a living complex in the area of Mamaq at the fork of the Rímac River dated to the Inca period, there are rectangular storage areas approximately three by two yards in size in the corners and along the sides of the rooms, some of them roofed with slabs of stone.

Some of these possible storage areas may have been tombs or places where household idols were kept; others may well have served as local storage. Foodstuffs could be easily stored in these in pots and baskets for use as needed.[91]

On the local level, it seems clear that the members of highland Andean society had developed, at least by the time of the Inca expansion and probably well before, a culture pattern that utilized the particular characteristics of the alpine landscape to advantage. The "ecological mosaic," as Olivier Dollfus describes it,[92] offered the men and women who lived in that environment a wide variety of climates and ecological zones in a relatively limited area. The social relationships governing access to both resources and goods in Andean society were integrated with this mosaic, and aimed at ensuring the members of the group the greatest variety of access and the least chance that climatic reverses and natural disasters would bring crop failure, famine, and death. Access to a variety of micro-ecologies at different altitudes is perhaps the primary characteristic of this structure. By reaching out from its major area or "nucleus" to other specialized resource areas or "islands" cultivated by colonies of mitmaq sent out from the home community, a group could acquire a far greater range of goods and products than would be possible under a nucleated, concentrated agricultural system.

But a reconstruction of the social structure of Andean society on the most reduced social level, that of the household or the minimal productive unit, cannot complete our picture of the organization of relatively large-scale societies or political entities. The remnants of traditional social organization on the minimal level can be perceived today in the more isolated areas of the Andes, in villages and communities that have kept at least some of the social organization that was so well adapted to the Andean landscape through a half millennium of foreign rule, first by Europeans and later by the Europeanized ruling class of the state formed of the one-time Spanish colony in the nineteenth century. But more extensive social units, from the scale of the Inca state to that of smaller but still substantial entities of twenty or thirty thousand people, no longer exist. And it is precisely this kind of scale that is the key to the wealth of local society described by the Spaniards in the sixteenth century. At this more extensive level, though social relationships were still phrased in the terms outlined above, the scale of the operation itself meant a change from the level of personal relationships among specific people to that of political structures. The subject of the next chapter is the nature of this larger-scale organization—in other words, the organization and structures of the local political system.

TWO

The Sons of Pariacaca

O NE OF the major problems faced by anyone who attempts to understand and portray a social system quite different from those of Western Europe is that of definition. The terms that we commonly use to describe or refer to social groups must be broken down and reconstructed to build up a context of associations and meanings that link the term used to the reality described. In the case of local Andean society prior to the arrival of the Europeans, this procedure becomes essential. In the following pages I want to build up a context for defining the more extensive social groups of the western slopes of the Andes, based as far as possible upon a broader comprehension of how the members of those groups acted toward one another, of what forces drew them together and what pushed them apart. In short, I want to build up a picture of what I broadly call the political structure of the region of Huarochirí.

Most of the preceding chapter was an effort to begin to lay down some of the context necessary for defining local Andean society on the basis of how the members of that society interacted with one another in the production and reproduction of their material lives. But in dealing with the mechanisms of social relations on what might be termed the minimal scale of households or small groups, we limit ourselves at best to a fragmentary understanding of the organization of the larger social system. For these small groups were part of larger systems that in turn were part of a state structure at the time of the Spanish conquest of the Andes. And it is just that integration of small groups into larger units that underlay the strength and the productive capacity of Andean society. In order to get a general sense of the change of scale implied by our move from the level of the household to that of societies reaching over a relatively large area, it would be well to begin this discussion with an effort to estimate just how many people we are talking about when we speak of the society of Huarochirí.

Population estimates for the region of Huarochirí before the Spanish invasion, as well as for the Andean area in general, are extremely difficult to make, even by the often imaginative extrapolation from information filtered to the Europeans through Inca informants. One of our earliest sources of specific information on the population of the region dates from 1583. It was prepared by a Spaniard, the first civil administrator of the province, Diego Dávila Brizeño.[1] Dávila Brizeño said that the first census of the native population of the area by Francisco Pizarro in the 1540's counted 10,000 Indian tributaries, or adult men who were heads of households, in the entire Inca province of Yauyos, the upper part of which became colonial Huarochirí. By 1571, the date of the first general count of the Indian population of Peru, the number of tributaries had declined to 7,000.[2] The tributary population of Huarochirí alone in 1571 was 4,224; by applying the same ratio of decline for the upper region as for the entire province, I came up with an estimate of approximately 6,000 household heads for Huarochirí in the 1540's.

Six thousand households means a population of between 24,000 and 30,000 people, a respectable political unit. But though we need as background an approximate sense of the numerical size of the society of Huarochirí—always an efficient reminder of the scale we are dealing with—numbers alone cannot explain the structure or the productive capacity of the society. We cannot think of Huarochirí as a society of some 30,000 people divided into autarkic, self-contained fragments on the model of the isolated village communities of the Andes today. In order to comprehend the social relations of this society, we must refer to larger groups of which the minimal units—households or ayllus—were a part, for a member of any minimal unit was at the same time a functioning member of other groups that made claims upon him and owed him rights and support in turn. For that reason, I found myself in Chapter One using terms such as "community" that carry a load of accumulated meanings and references that can seriously distort their application to the world of the Andes. My first task in the following pages, then, will be to repair that omission and set the context for understanding what I mean when I refer to the Andean community or communities.

As should be clear from the earlier discussion of the social geography of land use and residence in central Peru, the European picture of a community as a nucleated group, generally a village, occupying a defined territory or geographical area, cannot be applied to the Andes. An Andean "community" did not look like that at all. The ideal described as "verticality"—that is, of access to multiple ecological zones, each exploited or cultivated for particular goods or crops—did not produce a nucleated village pattern. According to Spanish testimony in the sixteenth century, the people of Huarochirí lived in scattered hamlets in the puna pastures and on the boundaries of the patches. of cultivable lands wrested from the mountain slopes by the labor of the group. The first Spanish administrator of the region reported that before the Spanish conquest the inhabitants of the province had lived scattered in more than 200 small settlements throughout the area.[3] Archaeological work in the upper Mala River valley has resulted in the location of a number of sites that have been dated to the period just before the Inca expansion. All of the sites with habitation refuse are quite small—as for example three located within a few miles of one another in the contemporary villages of Yambilla, Lupo, and Santiago—and the small collections of the debris of living there indicate that the groups occupying these sites were also quite small. Bits of pottery and refuse have been found in isolated fields and terraces nearby, suggesting even more dispersed living arrangements. High on the puna, where llamas are pastured, there still stand today the stone foundations of individual shepherds' huts with attached stone corrals built of fieldstone.

The oral histories and origin stories of the province also bear witness to a dispersed settlement pattern. The story of the ayllu Concha, after describing the conquest of new lands and resources by the founders of the group, notes that after the spoils of conquest were distributed among the victors "each began to live on his own, alone."[4] The geographical model proposed for the Andean community by John Murra, which fits the pattern of evidence from Huarochirí, posits a series of groups that held not only core territories cultivated by group members but also other resource areas, or "oases" (often quite far from the core territories), that could produce particularly valued crops or goods, at both higher and lower altitudes. As noted in Chapter One, the ideal of a social group was to obtain access to a variety of such "oases" in each of the altitudinal and climatic zones: in the high puna; in the upper levels of the *quishwa*, or mountain valley slopes; in the midvalley areas; and in the warmer, lowland regions with access to water for maize and coca. The more distant oases were cultivated by resident colonists or mitmaq, who sent the produce of their zone back to their own people. This pattern has been described as an archipelago structure, with a central or core zone surrounded by more or less distant "islands" or "resource oases."[5]

But a community is more than a geographical entity, no matter how nucleated or dispersed. What were the relationships between people that defined who was a member of a given group—a community—and who was not? If we cannot define the community in geographical terms, are there other bases for determining the membership of the group? The previous chapter has provided a basic definition of the relations between people that structured their access to the productive resources of their society. We can use approximately the same approach here, for by reconstructing the structure of claims to land—a resource valued highly by both Andean and European societies, and therefore one about which controversy generated useful information—we can gain some idea of the social units defined by rights to land in Andean society. From there, we can look for the social relationships through which those units were organized. Since most of the information relating to claims to land that can be extracted from colonial records was generated from court papers and administrative documents, we can take these materials and first compile a list of the various claims to land presented by members of Andean society and recognized by the colonial authorities, and then extract those claims that clearly reflect European forms of property and access to land in order to arrive at the group of claims that seem to reflect Andean traditions.

Spanish colonial law recognized native tradition and custom as binding in cases involving members of Andean society, unless that custom specifically conflicted with the laws of Spain or the dictates of the Catholic religion.[6] In practice, local authorities often maintained native custom even when it conflicted with decrees emanating from Spain or from Lima. As a result, the court records include a great deal of material describing the character and variety of Andean forms of land access. Further detailed information can be found in contracts, testaments, and similar records, though here Andean relationships and colonial innovations are all present and must be disentangled from one another.

There are some claims to land in the colonial records that were clearly postconquest and European. During the colonial period, individuals who purchased land not recognized as the property of the Andean groups held it as private property. Full private tenure as a result of the purchase of land as a commodity was clearly European and recognized as such by the courts. Land was also assigned to the local Catholic parish for the support of the priests and the Church. The local *cofradías*, or religious brotherhoods, held lands that they acquired through purchase or donation as corporate entities. The income from the produce of these lands was supposed to be used in the celebration of the festival of the saint to whom the cofradía was dedicated. These two kinds of claims to land—made by individuals operating within a European system of private ownership or by institutions that were part of the colonial system—can be set aside as clearly non-Andean.[7]

There were a multitude of other kinds of claims to land, however, that were recognized in Spanish colonial courts as derived from preconquest forms of land tenure. These claims, pressed in the courts on the grounds that they dated "from time immemorial" and were therefore part of the local tradition to be respected by the authorities, involved both individual and group tenures. Claims to land were pressed by the kurakas, the Andean chieftains, on the basis of their privileged position in preconquest society. As noted in Chapter One, the kurakas held special access to the goods and resources of their society. The lands they claimed were cultivated first. They could make special calls upon the aid and labor of the people they led, in return for which they were expected to be generous, lavish with their feasts and gifts, and free with their goods in case of need.

Lands were also claimed by corporate groups of different extent. The Spanish authorities adapted for their purposes the administrative divisions of the Inca state. The Andean population was divided into a hierarchy of nested units, on the basis of which the authorities assigned tribute payments, labor levies, and other assessments. The largest unit in the system of colonial Indian administration until the establishment of the intendancy system in 1783 was the province. Each province was divided into a varying number of smaller units, called *repartimientos*. Each repartimiento, in turn, was divided into several *waranqas*, and each waranqa consisted of a number of ayllus. Though in the course of time these units came to approximate geographic areas more and more closely, they were never defined in terms of territorial boundaries. A repartimiento or a waranqa was a group of people. In the sixteenth century, there was a great deal of difference between geographic proximity and group membership. Some of the members of a given repartimiento or waranqa lived far from the core territories of the group to which they belonged. Even as late as the eighteenth century, two and a half centuries after the Spanish conquest, group membership could not be entirely equated with geographic location. The Indians belonging to the ayllu Concha and living in the colonial village of San Damián belonged to an entirely different waranqa from the rest of the residents of the village, a waranqa whose other members lived in villages located at a considerable distance from San Damián.[8]

Another unit that appears in colonial administrative records, the village, was not completely a part of this administrative structure. The village, a colonial creation, was a fixed territorial unit on the European model whose population might include members of a number of different groups, as in the example of the village of San Damián above. Furthermore, the residents of a village did not usually constitute a landholding unit. Whenever a village included a number of ayllus, lands were claimed by the ayllus and not by the village as a whole. During the colonial period villages claimed land as corporate units in only two circumstances. First, when a village consisted of a single ayllu, thereby making ayllu and village coterminous, the village appears in the sources as the landholding unit on some occasions, and the ayllu on others. The apparent confusion, however, is purely verbal; ayllu and village being the same, there was little reason to distinguish clearly between them. Second, the village appears as the corporate group claiming land when it contained no component ayllus, something that occurs more frequently in the latter years of the colonial period. (In the course of three centuries, many villages became ghost towns that were later reoccupied by migrants from other places.) In these cases, the colonial authorities assigned land to the new settlers as a single, newly formed corporate unit: the village. [9]

The colonial province was an administrative unit that never bore any relation to landholding; it appears to have been adopted from the Inca administrative system by the Spanish conquerors with little modification. The colonial province of Huarochirí was the more populous and important northern half of the old Inca province of Yauyos; it was the upper moiety of the old province and the residence of the principal kuraka. The repartimiento, the largest of the smaller units into which the province was divided, appears initially to be an entirely postconquest creation totally unrelated to the organization of local society. At the time of the Spanish conquest, the native population was divided up among the conquerors. A given kuraka and all those subject to him were assigned *in encomienda* to a Spaniard. The term derives from the Spanish verb *encomendar*, meaning to give in charge or entrust. The person who received an encomienda, as the kuraka and his people were called, was charged with the responsibility for their conversion to Catholicism in return for the privilege of using their labor essentially as he saw fit. The repartimiento, derived from the verb *repartir*, to divide up or hand out, was used early in the Spanish occupation of the Americas and became an administrative term later, designating the administrative unit equivalent to an encomienda. [10] In the colonial administrative system, a repartimiento consisted of all the people who had been originally awarded as a single encomienda.

The people of Huarochirí were divided into three encomienda-repartimientos: Chaclla, Mamaq, and Huarochirí. The core territories of the first two were located in the Rímac River drainage, whereas those of the third centered in the upper Lurín and Mala river valleys. After Francisco de Toledo reorganized the Viceroyalty in the latter part of the sixteenth century, the encomiendas were redefined for administrative purposes as repartimientos. Each of the three encomiendas of Huarochirí—Mamaq, Chaclla, and Huarochirí—appears in colonial administrative records as a repartimiento of the same name.

The Quechua term *waranqa* is translated as the number one thousand; it is a numerical designation with no particular social referent. A deity in Huarochirí was described as receiving, before the Spanish conquest, the services of "a waranqa of men." [11] The Inca state used the term to designate census categories of people, and the Spaniards adopted the same categories. In the Spanish colonial system, the repartimiento of Mamaq contained two waranqas, that of Chaclla three, and that of Huarochirí five.[12] Though this information does not permit us to assume that the population of the three repartimientos at the time of the Spanish conquest was, respectively, 2,000, 3,000, and 5,000 households, the number of waranqas did bear a rough relation to the relative population size of the repartimientos. Mamaq was the smallest, and in fact was designated in local traditions as part of Chaclla—Chaclla-Mamaq. Chaclla was somewhat larger, and the repartimiento of Huarochirí had considerably more people at the time of the first available colonial census in 1572, and most likely at the time of the Spanish conquest as well. Whatever the changes introduced by the Spaniards in the realm of colonial administration, it seems that on the local or provincial level they essentially took over and maintained the decimal categories of the Inca state with little or no modification.

The ayllu, the smallest of the administrative units recorded in tribute records and other administrative documents, has been discussed in Chapter One. Here let me offer a summary definition of the ayllu as a group of people claiming access to productive resources, including the support and labor of one another, on the basis of the relationship established between them and defined by themselves and their culture as kinship. At this minimal administrative level the identity between kinship and claim to land is clear. The ayllu was a group of kin that held land as a corporate unit. The priest of Huarochirí in 1611, Francisco de Avila, defined the ayllu succinctly for his European superiors as "a group of people with a single origin, as we would say, 'Mendozas,' or 'Toledos.'"[13] The traditions of the ayllus themselves described an ayllu as a group of lineages holding land conquered or occupied by their ancestors, heroes who were credited with originating all of the rules by which the group lived.

This structure of nested units ranging from the ayllu to the waranqa and beyond to the level of the repartimiento was more than a system imposed from outside, either by the Spaniards or by the Inca state that preceded them. Throughout the Spanish colonial period, each of these units in Huarochirí claimed land and fought, often successfully, for those claims in the colonial courts. They argued their claims on the basis of preconquest tenure from "time immemorial." The lands farthest from the core territories of any given group were held by the largest units, the repartimientos. The repartimientos of Huarochirí and Chaclla both claimed maize lands in the warm, sunny region of Chaclacayo near the coast, and pastures in the province of Chocorvos to the south.[14] The coca fields of Quives, in the Chillón River valley on the northern boundary of Huarochirí, were claimed by the repartimiento of Chaclla, and a dispute over possession of the fields that erupted in the 1550's between Chaclla and Canta to the north was phrased in terms of claims to the lands presented by the two rival repartimiento-encomiendas. In some cases the lands claimed by repartimientos were granted them by the Incas, but in others, such as Quives, the members of the group stated specifically that they had entered the lands, expelling the original holders, prior to their incorporation into the Inca state.[15]

The waranqas, divisions of the repartimientos, appear as landholding units throughout the Spanish colonial period. As late as the eighteenth century, one of the waranqas of Chaclla still held lands in Carapongo and Huampaní, in the warm lower reaches of the Rímac Valley just above the fog line, and the other two held lands nearby in Pariachi. The waranqas of the repartimiento of Huarochirí still held their maize lands in Chaclacayo.[16] In the various sales of land carried out by the Spanish Crown to obtain cash during the seventeenth and eighteenth centuries, the waranqa frequently appears as purchaser. In the general land sale, or *composición de tierras*, carried out in the early years of the eighteenth century, one of the waranqas of Chaclla offered money to retain its coastal lands in Carapongo and Huampaní; a few years later this waranqa paid 30 pesos to retain highland pastures that it claimed as part of its traditional territories. In 1717, the waranqa Chaucarima (of Huarochirí) offered 120 pesos to the Crown in order to retain its traditional grazing lands in the puna region between the Lurín and Mala drainages. In each of these cases, the petitioners stated that they were purchasing the lands in order to maintain their access to lands that they had held before the entry of the Europeans.[17]

The Inca census categories are fairly well known. Informants from Cuzco presented a picture of a highly organized state, in which the population was divided for the purpose of assigning state labor service into a hierarchy of nested units, ranging from groups of ten households (a *chunca*) to a group of 100 households (a *pachaca*) to one of 1,000—a *waranqa*. The largest group was the *huñu*, a unit of 10,000.[18] Now the importance of counting and records in a socioeconomic system founded upon redistribution rather than market exchange need hardly be stressed, and the real administrative value of the Inca decimal categories is underlined by their adoption virtually intact by the Spaniards who succeeded the Incas. But the Inca state was relatively short-lived. The time span that is increasingly agreed upon by scholars for that Andean state, from the beginning of its expansion to its defeat by the Spaniards, is slightly more than a century and in many areas of the Andes, including Huarochirí, only about 75 years.[19]

It is simply impossible to believe that an administrative category imposed upon conquered people within the memory of some still alive at the time of the Spanish conquest could erase all preceding forms of access to productive resources and become the basis of the social relations of production for the following three hundred years. It is far more reasonable to assume, as others who have seriously considered the same problem have done, that the high degree of administrative organization achieved by the Inca state was founded upon the adaptation of decimal categories to existing social units that continued to exist after the Spanish conquest. The minimal units of the Inca census (the chuncas) do not appear in colonial administrative records, and both the pachaca and the huñu also disappear shortly after the Spanish invasion, at least in Huarochirí, so it is impossible to speculate about the nature of these units on the basis of colonial records. There are, however, considerable colonial data on ayllus, waranqas, and repartimientos as landholding units that support the contention that these units were social entities with deep roots in local Andean society rather than merely administrative categories imposed by the Inca state.

It is not easy to provide detailed evidence to support this assumption, but there are numerous situations (unfortunately some of them rather late in the colonial period) that can best be interpreted in terms of the framework set out above. A dispute over pasturelands in Huarochirí that landed in the Spanish colonial courts in 1798 is a particularly interesting example.[20] In that year, people from the ayllus Concha and Sunicancha (waranqa Chaucarima) complained to the Spanish authorities that people from the ayllu Lupo (waranqa Colcaruna) and from ayllus of the waranqa Checa were edging over into their pastureland, destroying the boundary markers that divided the pastures and sending their animals into their neighbors' lands. The colonial courts supported their claims, warning off the delinquents from the other ayllus. The ayllu Lupo did not protest the decision, and the members of that ayllu who had moved into their neighbors' pastures withdrew their animals to the lands belonging to their own group. The people belonging to the ayllus of the waranqa Checa, however, whose core territories were slightly closer to the lands in dispute, did not accept the decision. In their appeal to the court, they raised the stakes, presenting their case not in the name of the specific ayllus to which the offenders belonged, but in the name of the entire waranqa Checa. In return, the ayllu Concha turned to the kuraka of its waranqa, and the answer to Checa was accordingly presented by the kuraka of the waranqa Chaucarima "in his name and in the name of the section of the settlement of Concha."[21] The case went on, with new complaints, until 1799, when the authorities finally ordered a new delineation of boundaries.

Here we have, quite clearly, a set of larger units—the waranqas—entering as the ultimate, or maximal, claimants into a dispute over land access, notwithstanding the fact that the actual use of the land was based upon ayllu membership. Puna pastureland is scarce in Huarochirí, where much of the land is steep and jagged, and the relatively flat high plain between the headwaters of the Lurín and Mala rivers, crisscrossed today by animal trails and dotted with stone corrals and shepherds' huts, was a prized resource used by groups throughout the two river valley systems. Control of pastureland and protection from encroachments upon it were vested in the larger social unit, the waranqa, to which the shepherds appealed in cases of trouble. In a conflict like the one described above, the disputants sought the support of the larger units to which they belonged; since all of the people involved belonged to the repartimiento of Huarochirí, the dispute had no particular meaning beyond the waranqa level. The issue was one not for the common maximal unit—here the repartimiento—to decide, but for the smaller groups, each represented by its own leaders and authorities, to argue before a superior authority, in this case the colonial courts. Prior to the Spanish conquest, that superior authority was probably the kuraka of the next higher level or the Inca governor.

If we accept this picture of a structure of nested units that incorporates people in larger and larger groups, we have one remaining problem. What was the basis of membership in these groups? We know the basis of membership in the ayllu, the minimal unit. In the eighteenth century, a Spaniard offered an explanation of the character of the larger groups that fits so well with other information on the structure of the ayllu and on how the larger groups functioned that it is worth quoting.

All the gentile Indians lived according to their families, separated one from another, forming on that basis an ayllu, [a term] that in Spanish means the genealogy of one family in contrast to another; and this name of ayllu or tribe was applied up to the level of one hundred families, at which level the name "ayllu" became "pachaca"; and when their numbers rose to one thousand, it was given the name of "waranqa," and thus there is no waranqa that does not contain within itself pachacas and ayllus. As a result they live one and another so interrelated among themselves, that even though they change names or surnames in baptism, by knowing to what waranqa they belong, or to what pachaca or ayllu belonging to a given waranqa, they recognize themselves as kinsmen in these extended families. [22]

Though this description may be suspect owing to its relatively late date, its basic content is corroborated by one of the most observant and sensitive members of Spanish society in the decades immediately following the conquest, Fray Domingo de Santo Tomás, who also described the larger social units as built upon the same principle as the ayllu: "Among them, if a lord is very distinguished in something, his children take his name; and not only the children, but all the descendants. And from this are formed the lineages that they call ayllu, and pachaca. . . . ."[23]

From this material, we can finally define the term "community" in a way that can be applied to the Andean context. The Andean community was a social group of varying size whose members were linked by their common claim to access to the resources of production held by the group and the goods and foodstuffs produced by it. The community was a land-holding unit at all levels, and it claimed access to resource areas or "islands" more or less distant from its core territories that were exploited by some of its members sent to those areas for that purpose. Membership in the community was defined in terms of kin ties, although at the maximal level the ideology of proper behavior among kinsmen must have become so attenuated as to be little more than a political fiction, an ideology that carried with it a set of norms structuring political behavior within the group. The flexibility of the notion of community in terms of both geographical reach and population size may seem to present a problem, but the problem in itself provides some insight into the social world of the Andes. A person or a household was a member of an entire hierarchy of communities, in each of which he had particular responsibilities to his fellows, and particular claims upon their labor and support. At the minimal level, day-to-day interaction was likely to be most intense and most constant. As Huaman Poma de Ayala noted, people at the lowest level were linked by ties of marriage, by rituals that made them responsible for guarding the rights of one another's children, and by other associations. Even at the ayllu level, as noted earlier, membership could be as much a function of observing the customs of the group as of formal lineal descent or affinal ties. And at the level of the larger group, the fiction of common ancestry was not only a fiction but one recognized as such by the people themselves. The oral histories of the people of Huarochirí include groups such as the ayllu Sutca, part of the waranqa Checa in the sixteenth century. According to local traditions, Sutca was originally a lowland group living in the lands conquered by the Checas, but its people agreed to adopt the deities of the highlanders and were permitted to retain their lands. " 'In my lands, in my fields, among my people I will fear and adore Pariacaca and Tutayquiri' [highland wak'as]; so saying they returned."[24]

Another aspect of community structure in the central Andes is the essentially historical character of the groups composing the larger society. The series of nested units to which people belonged cannot be defined as segmentary lineages, groups regarded as permanent and unchanging. Andean society was intensely hierarchical and concerned with power and status. In one of the myths of Huarochirí, a female deity impregnated without her knowledge by a male wak'a threw herself into the ocean when she discovered that the father of the child she bore was a "potato-eater," or *wak'cha*, who went about in rags and tatters.[25] Yet changes in the relative status and position of groups composing the larger society were not reflected in oral history, which rather continued to present pictures that in some cases were hardly flattering. For instance, the Checas and the Quintis were two waranqa communities of Huarochirí who in the sixteenth century were separate and rival units of essentially equivalent status. The Checa traditions, however, spoke of a far different relationship in the past. The narrator of the myths of Huarochirí, when speaking of his own group, the Checas, noted that his people were "younger brothers of the Quintis, and for that reason the Quintis despised them, because they were formed later."[26] Since there is no Quinti version of the same story in the collection, it is impossible to tell whether the other side of the story would be significantly different.

The stories make it clear that the groups forming the Andean communities at all levels were neither permanent nor regarded as such. Even on the minimal level there is evidence of fission and the formation of new ayllus. Again returning to the myths, we find a story describing the ayllu Chahuincho, which split from an ayllu named Cupara. The parent ayllu still existed in the eighteenth century, but Chahuincho disappeared in the course of the Spanish colonial period.[27] The Andean community was temporal. Communities arose, gained power and status, and declined—yet their traditions were not adjusted to fit their altered condition.

At the level of the larger community, where personal relations and interactions became more attenuated and the fiction of being one large family was less easily maintained, the importance of leadership became greater. At the waranqa or the repartimiento level—the highest at which the fiction of brotherhood was the charter of membership in the colonial period, although perhaps not prior to the arrival of the Spaniards—the role of the kuraka as administrator, mediator, and guardian of community norms and behavior loomed large. As noted earlier, the kuraka elite formed a governing class that cut across the norm of brotherhood and reciprocity among kinsmen and was privileged with special access to the labor and the products of its society. Each community had its own ethnic chief, and the group of chiefs formed a hierarchy that reflected the nested scale of communities, from the level of the ayllu to whatever the repartimiento was termed before the Spanish conquest. The hierarchy of authority within this elite as it was described by one of the kurakas of Huánuco to a Spanish inspector in 1562 reflects the structure of political authority in Huarochirí and Chaclla-Mamaq as well. "The major chief of the four waranqas was in charge of the other chiefs of each waranqa, and those of the waranqas commanded the [units] of one hundred called

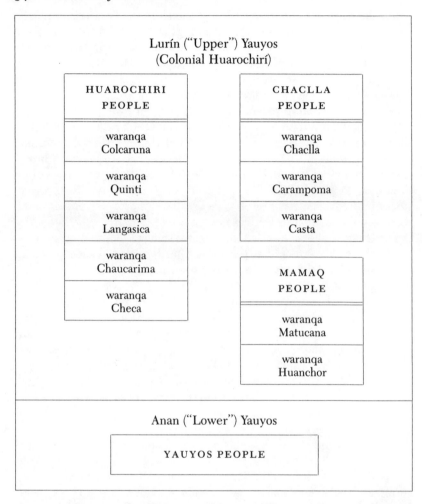

Figure 1. The Inca province of Anan and Lurín Yauyos. Lurín Yauyos became the colonial province of Huarochirí, administratively separate from Anan Yauyos. The three "peoples" of Lurín Yauyos were assigned to Spanish encomenderos to whom they paid tribute. The waranqas, the internal structure of the encomiendas, remained the same.

pachacas, and those of the pachacas oversaw the [chiefs of] chuncas who are the leaders of ten Indians."[28]

Beyond the level of the repartimiento or tribe there was under the Incas a still larger political entity: the province. (For a graphic summary of the political structure of the province, see Figure 1.) Huarochirí was the

upper, "right," or superior half of the Inca province of Yauyos, and contained three of the province's five tribal units (Huarochirí, Chaclla, and
Mamaq). There is some indication that the people of these two halves had
some established relation to one another, for the tales of Huarochirí describe the people of Yauyos, a poorer area in the present, and probably
the past as well, as their "brothers," whom they hated and despised as
savage and "wild."[29] But the relationship, whatever it was, was limited
and vague.

Even within the moiety of Huarochirí, the kurakas of the three tribal
groups comprising the upper half of the province did not apparently have
any authority to intervene in the internal affairs of any group other than
their own. According to Juan de Matienzo, the kuraka of the upper moiety of the province was "the first of all and rules over those of *hurinsaya*
[the "left," or lower moiety]. He calls and holds meetings and governs in
general, although he does not command in particular."[30] A kuraka governed by persuasion and mediation rather than by imposing his authority.
In the Inca province of Yauyos, one kuraka exercised moral authority over
all the tribal groups, but he could not reverse or alter decisions made by
their kurakas. The kurakas of Chaclla and Mamaq sent gifts of coca and
foodstuffs from the fields of Quives to the kuraka of Huarochirí in recognition of his status, but when one of these kurakas was apparently tricked
by his encomendero and the encomendero of the neighboring province of
Canta into agreeing to give up the lands in exchange for llamas, the kuraka of Huarochirí could not reverse the decision, and had to resign himself to scolding the wayward kuraka for selling the patrimony of his people.[31]

At the political level of the tribe or repartimiento, however, the kuraka
was responsible for the observance of the norms of proper behavior within his group, which included the distribution of services and the settlement of disputes. Juan de Matienzo's description of the function of the
kuraka as "counting and dividing up," taken in the Andean context, essentially refers to the function of government—that of determining, on the
basis of a detailed knowledge of the particular situations of the households under their authority, the contribution that each member should
make to the larger group.

One of the most detailed and dynamic descriptions of the process of local government in action that we have was prepared by Juan Polo de Ondegardo in 1571. Polo's description of how the kurakas went about their
task of "counting and dividing up" refers specifically to how they allocated
the tribute requirements assigned them by the Spaniards, but the process
was probably the same as that used in the distribution of community tasks
or the settlement of disputes within the community. Polo presented a

picture of the gathering of the kurakas of the component units of the community, together with the quipucamayoq, or keepers of the knotted-cord records or quipu. They "laid out the stones and beans with which they make up their accounts on the floor in the accustomed order," and in a few hours they completed a complicated task in which they took into account "the peculiarities of the lands and the mines and the productivity of the regions, . . . after which they break [their assessments] down by ayllus and *parcialidades* [lineages], each one taking into consideration his particular situation."[32]

These meetings looked to Polo like total chaos, in which "they talk all together without listening to each other and come to a conclusion in less than two hours; and the people charged with the division, without asking anyone, take into consideration things that would be impossible for any outsider to see even if he were there for two years."[33] The representation of the interests of the smaller component groups of the community was guaranteed by their own kurakas, who participated in these sessions; as Polo insisted, "once their discussions and accounts are understood, it is obvious that no one would agree to any injury or affront to his own group."[34] Finally, the kuraka was probably the supervisor of his community's participation in projects undertaken either within the group or in conjunction with other members of the larger community to which they belonged. Although Polo here speaks of group organization and operation as a whole, the presence of the kuraka hovers behind his description of community participation in common tasks, in which "although many lineages go to do a community task, they never begin without figuring out and measuring what each should do, and among the members of the same lineage they also divide up the labor into shares that they call *suyos*, and no one helps another for any reason even though he completes his task first."[35]

Polo's comment points to another aspect of social relations in Huarochirí that was an important part of social and political life. This society, on all levels, was a highly competitive one in which rank and prestige were important counters in the struggle for position. In a system in which property accumulation was limited, both because of real limits on the productive capacity of the society and because most of the valued goods were relatively impermanent and easily spoiled or destroyed even with storage, wealth was measured more in what we think of as intangibles. The rank and status of a lineage or ayllu within the larger community was something to be jealously guarded. It was ultimately a measure of security, the basis of a network of people who would respond to calls for assistance and support in the expectation of future return. In the larger communities,

the component groups or ayllus were ranked in a hierarchy that determined the order of their participation in feasts, worship, or the division of
the spoils of war. Each time the narrator of the tales of Huarochirí speaks
of the ceremonies performed in honor of a wak'a (deity) of the group, for
example, he carefully lists the ranked order of the participants: "They entered to serve him, ayllu after ayllu. . . . Allauca began, as the principal
[ayllu]. 'Let us enter,' said the others, and they began the celebration, in
an orderly way, by mutual agreement."³⁶ Within this ranked order, the ayllus competed with one another in the performance of ritual or other joint
activity, testing the established order. Even today a myth explaining the
origin of ayllu divisions recorded in a village in the province of Ayacucho
in the south-central Andes links the existence of ayllus to competition
within the larger group. Though presented in contemporary terms, it
bears witness to the competition that emerges clearly from descriptions of
ritual and ceremony centuries earlier. "Before, when there were no ayllus
and everyone was equal, the people had gone to Jajamarca to carry the
church bell 'Maria Angola' and some rosewood beams for the construction
of the church. Since everyone was equal, no one had any energy to work,
so then they thought, 'Let us compete with each other. Well, you are
going to be Qullana and we, Sawqa. . . . ' "³⁷

Competition is presented here as a stimulus to group effort. But in a society of even relative scarcity, competition has a sharper edge, for it can
be—and was—a mechanism for the exhibition and reaffirmation of relative status within the group, which was ultimately a basis of security and
power. The intensity of jealousy over relative rank and the seriousness of
competition is vividly depicted in a myth of Huarochirí about a poor man
from the highlands, a "potato-eater" (as such ragged people were derog-
atorily called), who won a daughter of a wealthy chief by curing him of an
illness brought on by his wife's infidelity—an illness that had defeated all
the efforts of the local diviners and curers.³⁸ The husband of the chief's
other daughter was outraged when he discovered that the chief would accept the poor man as his son-in-law, saying "How can he join her with that
poor, miserable beggar, when she is the sister-in-law of someone as powerful as I am!"³⁹ As a result, he determined to challenge his new brother-
in-law, Huatyacuri, and "leave him in the deepest shame" through a series of competitions. The two participated in a series of trials in which the
poor man's only support came from his father, Pariacaca, the major deity
of the province. Since aspects of this myth repay extended analysis, I
present it in fairly full form.

One day the challenger said to Huatyacuri, "Today we will compete in singing and
drinking." Then Huatyacuri, the poor man, went to consult his father. Pariacaca

said to him, "Go to a mountain. There, pretend to be a dead guanaco [Andean wild camelid] and throw yourself on the ground. In the morning, early, a fox and his skunk wife will come to pay homage to me. They will bring *chicha* [maize beer] in a small gourd, and also a little drum [*tinya*]. Believing that you are a dead guanaco, they will put the drum and the gourd on the ground, together with a panpipe, and begin to eat you. Then you get up, revealing yourself as the man you are, and yell loudly as if you are hurt. The animals will flee, forgetting everything. You take their things and go to the competition." Poor Huatyacuri did everything just as his father told him. And so, in the place where the competition was to be held, the rich man began. All kinds of women, about two hundred of them, sang and danced in his behalf. When they finished, the poor man entered, accompanied only by his wife. And when he sang, accompanying himself with the skunk's drum, the whole world shook. And Huatyacuri won the competition.

Then the drinking began. The rich man invited men from everywhere; he drank with them without rest. Meanwhile Huatyacuri, just like guests today who seat themselves at the head of the gathering, waited alone with his wife. And although he drank everything, he remained quietly seated. Then, after the rich man sat down, happy and untroubled, Huatyacuri began to drink with all the people, serving them from his little gourd. The people all laughed at him, saying "How can he satisfy so many people with that tiny gourd?" But Huatyacuri began at one end and, while the others laughed, he served them very rapidly, and they all fell down drunk, one after another, right where they sat.

Defeated once again, the rich man challenged Huatyacuri to another competition on the following day. The test consisted of dressing up in the finest clothing. Huatyacuri went back to his father. Pariacaca gave him a gift of a tunic made all of ice. With this tunic he dazzled everyone's eyes and won the competition. Then the rich man brought many pumas and challenged Huatyacuri to compete once more. The poor man went back to his father and told him about the new competition proposed by his rival, and this time Pariacaca made a red puma appear at dawn at the bottom of a spring. And when Huatyacuri danced with the red puma, a many-colored rainbow appeared in the sky.

After that, the rich man challenged Huatyacuri to compete in house building, and since he had so many men at his service, he raised the walls of a great house in a single day. Huatyacuri, on the other hand, could only lay the foundations, and went about all day with his wife without doing anything. But at night the birds, the serpents, every living thing in the world helped him. And when his rival saw the work concluded, he took fright and challenged him to roof the house. Huatyacuri loaded the straw and the bindings and everything necessary for the roof on vicuñas. His rival loaded everything needed for the roof on llamas, and when the string of animals passed by a precipice, mountain cats that Huatyacuri had begged to help him jumped out and scared the llamas, who fell into the abyss. The loads were destroyed and the test was won.

Since he had won in everything, Huatyacuri said to his rival, obeying his father's instructions: "So far we have competed in tests that you proposed; now I will propose a competition." "Fine," answered the rich man; and Huatyacuri said, "We will dress in blue *huaras* [loincloths that cover the waist and legs] and our tunics will be white. Dressed this way, let us sing and dance." "All right," the rich man answered; and since he had begun all the competitions, he began to dance, and once he was dancing Huatyacuri let fly a yell from outside the dancing space. All his strength was concentrated in that yell, and the rich man, terrified, turned into a deer and fled.

This myth is especially interesting in that it systematically inverts the behavior expected of kinsmen toward one another. It contradicts every element of Huaman Poma de Ayala's "Law of marriage and good order," in which kinsmen are expected to help in common labor and illness and particularly "in eating and drinking and in the celebrations."[40] The story depicts the uglier emotions that underlay brotherly reciprocity. The contests between Huatyacuri and his wealthy brother-in-law are mirror images of the vocabulary of reciprocity, repeating in reverse the entire range of the claims and support that brothers were trained to expect of one another.

The first competition—singing and dancing—was part of the regular cycle of feasts and ceremonies held to honor the deities of the community. The dances were occasions for exhibitions of skill that brought either prestige or shame to the participants. Everyone was taught the ritual dances that were a mark of group membership, and skill in dancing and knowledge of the songs of the group were a measure of social acceptance. "All of the men have to sing and dance from the time they are children; they make them compete among themselves," noted the narrator of the tales of Huarochirí.[41] For an outsider, participation in the dances stood for acceptance of the responsibilities of group membership; hence a man from a distant area who married into an ayllu of Huarochirí was helped and praised by his new kinsmen as long as he joined the dances marking the agricultural cycle in the tales of the province.[42]

The second contest was a test of generosity and proof of wealth and social position. Food and drink, particularly chicha, were important elements on any occasion when people gathered. It was a sign of wealth to offer food and drink freely to others, for it took a considerable amount of chicha to get a large group of people drunk. The host who met his obligations lavishly built up credit among his kinsmen; the one who did not was hardly likely to get a ready response to an appeal for support. According to the Spaniards, when people gathered for cooperative labor of any kind, "the common bond of such groups is to drink until they fall down."[43] Another important element of ceremonial was cloth. The importance of cloth in Andean society has been widely recognized.[44] Every young girl learned to weave, for weaving was an important skill. Cloth was given as gifts on important occasions during people's lives, and it was a part of the treasured possessions of a household. Shirts ornamented with silver or gold, or caps of silver and feathers, were valued possessions, usually gifts from the kuraka who controlled the production and distribution of precious metals within the community.[45] The dead were dressed in their finest clothing for burial. Fine *cumbi*, or tapestry cloth woven by male specialists, was wrapped around mummy bundles when they were taken out for community ceremonies and feasts. The myth points up the social importance of clothing as well as the fact that such dressing up, though undoubtedly pleasurable for at least some of the participants, was a serious affair, in which points were gained or lost according to the luxury and brilliance of one's clothing.

House-building was yet another situation in which cooperation could easily become an occasion for scoring points against one's neighbors. The construction of a new house required calling upon the labor of others, and the household that not only had many kin, but had kept its claims upon those kin strong through generous participation in the network of reciprocity that structured the flow of goods and services in the community, could get the job done quickly and easily. The close proximity between reciprocity and the competition that could mask resentment and hatred is brought out clearly by the myth of Huatyacuri, the outwardly indigent newcomer to a wealthy family.

The myth also expresses the resentment and anger bred by a social system in which prosperity depended upon the support of other people who in turn had first claim to the property of the person to whom they owed assistance. In such a system, common to any social structure defined in terms of kin ties, small slights could assume large importance.[46] The struggle for position could easily lead to splits within any group, and indeed Spanish priests in the sixteenth century seeking information about the maintenance of forbidden rituals among the Andean communities were instructed to question people about their neighbors' practices rather than their own, because "there are generally divisions and enmities between the clans and factions and they inform upon one another."[47] The language also provides evidence of the link between reciprocity and revenge, as in the term *aynicapunacuni*, "to take revenge on," built on the root *ayni*, a term for equivalence that today is used to indicate labor exchange within a community.[48] And "friendly" competition slid easily into enmity. The word for competitor, *atillchamaciy*, contains the term *atillcha*, which can combine to signify either a drinking partner or competitor (*upiyaypac atillchay*), or an enemy (*aucanacuypi atillcha maciy*).[49]

The competition and rivalry that were part of the social relations of Andean society fostered enmities and divisions, making it necessary to have mechanisms that functioned to maintain group cohesion. There is clear evidence of the fission or splitting of groups in the tales of Huarochirí, together with much information on the kinds of mechanisms brought into play to erase, or at least minimize, such tensions. Much of what the Spanish priests—and all of us who have taken our cue from them—defined as religion in Andean society was in fact mechanisms designed to overrule or repair the angers and rivalries generated in an intensely competitive society. I do not intend to offer here any definition of "religion." Rather, I want to concentrate on the social function of systems of belief that provided the members of the society with explanations for illness, defeat, or the other seemingly inexplicable events of daily life. These explanations provided the basis for rituals intended to erase divisions within the community and repair the damage to social relations that those divisions generated. Their function was social as well as particular, and the objective was the maintenance of the social group as a productive entity. We might define a ritual as a drama designed to produce a change in the condition of the subject. It is a treatment intended to produce a specific end, such as the termination or infliction of illness (curing or witchcraft), or to mark the passage to a different state of being or social existence (name-giving, baptism, marriage, or death).

Any definition of the organization of the Andean community as a social and productive unit must deal with the mechanisms that could be set in motion to maintain and preserve that community. They involved specialists who did not enjoy the particular privileges of the kurakas (the kurakas were also expected to do their part to maintain community norms and values) but who did derive some profit from the performance of their services. To understand those mechanisms, we must again broaden the definition of community elaborated earlier, for the social dimension of the community extended through time as well as space to include the dead. Every group derived its identity and its claim to lands from a recognized ancestor, real or mythical. The bodies of dead leaders were dried and then bound in a flexed position with the knees bent tightly against the breastbone and the arms folded around them. Richly dressed and then wrapped in finely woven cloth, the bodies were stored in above-ground tombs, from which they could be brought out periodically to share in the ceremonies and festivals of the group. The ancestors had to be fed, honored, and propitiated with offerings of chicha and coca, for their good will ensured good harvests and the increase of the llama herds, just as their ill will could bring illness and death. Spanish priests investigating Andean beliefs at the end of the sixteenth century found that the people believed "their illness has come because their *malquis* [ancestors] and wak'as are angry at them."[50] And the narrator of the tales of Huarochirí, describing the worship of the wak'as by his people, noted that offerings were accompanied by a request to the wak'a being served to "help me, and aid this people. You are the one who guards it; you cure all illnesses."[51]

The social origins of misfortune in the ideology of Huarochirí emerge clearly from the tales of the province. The myth of Huatyacuri, the poor man who won his wife by curing a wealthy chief, underlines this principle. The great chief became ill because, as Huatyacuri told him, "your wife is an adulteress. And because of her acts you have become sick."[52] As a result of her behavior, two snakes had settled in the roof of his fine house and were wasting his strength, and a two-headed frog sat beneath the grinding-stone of the house. The damage to the integrity of the house and of the hearth had to be removed before the illness that was the outward evidence of social discord could be cured. The opposite effect was produced when people gave proper and generous service to the ancestors or the deities who represented the integrity of the social group. The wak'a Macahuisa, son of the principal deity of the region, was guarded and served by a community of Huarochirí. The people assigned the wak'a a field that was cultivated by an entire waranqa of men. "They put all their strength into that field, so that Macahuisa would have a lot to drink. And for that reason, those people became very wealthy."[53] Even death had to be placed in the social context. At the end of the traditional five-day mourning period, when the dead person had been properly served and bidden goodbye, a diviner was asked to find out the source of the person's death. The answer might be that the person died because of the anger of an ancestor or a deity. If that was the case, then offerings and sacrifices had to be made to calm the rage of the spirit so that more members of the community would not die.[54]

The rituals that had to be performed to propitiate angry ancestors, both in myths and in reality, were intended, as we have noted, to repair strains or breaks in social relations. Illness or disaster was regarded as the product not of intent, but of action. As the Spanish priests later complained, the people did not "confess inward sins but such sins as having stolen [something] or mistreated someone or having had more than one wife."[55] Because community survival and prosperity depended so strongly upon ties of reciprocity and cooperation—ties that had to be continually reinforced to counter the jealousy and suspicion that could so easily arise in a highly competitive system—the admonition of the priests of the major deities of the province to people who came to consult them is significant.

In the old times, all the wak'as questioned the people who went to them: "Do you come in the name of your sons, to the least of them; in the name of your father and your grandfather—can you represent them all?" And to whoever said "no" they answered: "Go back. Listen first to the last son, the least [of your group]." And they left and returned; and only then did the wak'as answer them: "you have angered or offended this or that person," they said.[56]

A wak'a might take the physical form of an oddly shaped rock or other natural formation, for wak'as were regarded as hero-deities who had performed great exploits (such as constructing the irrigation canals that watered community fields, or opening springs for water) and had then turned themselves to stone to guard the resources they had created for their people. A wak'a might be the guardian of a particular community or a more general deity consulted by people of a broader area. Wak'as were regarded as the sources of prosperity or good fortune, and the invasion of the western Andean slopes by the highland people in their expansion toward the coast involved not only the capture of productive resources (particularly land) but also the appropriation of the wak'as defined as the guardians and protectors of those lands. The capture of wak'as—who continued to be honored and served by their new possessors—as well as of lands was part of the oral tradition of Huarochirí, and the distribution of the spoils among the victorious ayllus and larger communities was carefully listed in the traditions. Wak'as might also appear suddenly: an oddly shaped stone that stubbornly resisted all efforts to extricate it from a field could be recognized as a wak'a that demanded service from the community it had decided to favor.[57]

From household level to lineage to ayllu to waranqa and beyond, the solidarity that ensured the prosperity and survival of the members of this nested structure of communities was guarded by the complicated structure of wak'as and mummies viewed as the overseers of group norms and behavior. At the household level, the oldest member held the guardians of the welfare of the household—small idols, stones, or odd-shaped objects called *conopas*. The conopas were the material representation of the family's resources, passed down from father to son and wife to daughter. They oversaw family behavior and, properly fed and propitiated, ensured the welfare of the immediate members of the household.[58] Worship of these idols and prayers made to them were private. As late as 1660, a woman in the village of Santiago de Quinti described her petition to her conopa, kept in a hole in the wall at the head of her bed. After sprinkling the idol with special chicha made for the occasion, and also pouring some chicha on the floor, she prayed, "father, father, son, nephew; I am poor; give me maize and potatoes."[59] Households with higher rank in the community had more of these idols, and some families held additional conopas said to ensure the maize or potato harvest or the health of the llama herds. A Spanish priest at the beginning of the seventeenth century noted that "they are the principal inheritance of the family and sometimes they have two, three, or four of them. A cacique [kuraka] I know showed me eleven, and his wife five, each with its own name."[60] As in the case of kinsmen, the powerful family was one that claimed the support of more conopas to intercede for its members with the wak'as and the mummies of the larger group.

Maintenance and service of the wak'as was public and was the responsibility of the larger lineages or clans—the ayllus, pachacas, or waranqas. On the local level, the most important and powerful wak'a was generally that of the ayllu or kin group, who was often regarded as the founding ancestor or the donor of particularly valuable productive resources held by the group, such as a spring, a lake, or an irrigation ditch. These wak'as often carried the name of the kin group and were located at a site revered by the members of the group as their place of origin. The wak'a Huanchorvilca stood in the village of San Mateo de Huanchor; the wak'a Huancanana, belonging to the ayllu of the same name, stood in the high puna outside the colonial village of Tantaranche. Here a crack about sixteen feet high in the face of a rock opened into a cavity between two and three feet across, and this formed a shrine into which offerings and sacrifices were placed.[61] The Hualcaraya wak'a, the wak'a of one of the ayllus of the Quintis, consisted of two standing stones outside the colonial village of San Lorenzo de Quinti.[62] Other wak'as were revered throughout the region, and served by people from many ayllus. Huarochirí had three principal deities worshiped throughout the province: Pariacaca, revered throughout Central Peru; his sister-wak'a Chaupiñamca, or Mamaq, described as the wife of Pachacamac, the earth-shaker (whose shrine on the coast in the Lurín River valley was one of the richest and most powerful in the Andes); and Tutayquiri, ancestor and hero of the Checas, whose mummy, carefully preserved and honored, was located in the early seventeenth century by a Spanish priest ferreting out native religious practices.[63]

There were a great many wak'as. Some stood along frequently traveled roads, where the traveler would stop to offer small sacrifices of burned coca leaves in hopes of a journey without accident or attack. Some were wealthy and powerful, with men assigned from different ayllus as their personal servants (*yanakuna*), and with rich storehouses stocked with maize and coca, finely woven tapestry cloth, and gold and silver ornaments.[64] Petitions and sacrifices to the wak'as marked all important events: a journey, a raid for new lands, the death of a powerful member of the ayllu, an illness, or the events of the agricultural calendar—clearing, planting, and harvesting. The year was divided into a multitude of ritual occasions when petitioners were reminded of their obligations to the wak'as and the power of the wak'as and the ancestor-mummies to influence their lives for good or ill. The deities were so numerous that particular kin groups could have their favorites, whose answers to their questions or petitions were preferred. The narrator of the tales of Huarochirí noted that the Checa peoples preferred to address their petitions to a sister-wak'a of Chaupiñamca located outside the village of Huarochirí. "They particularly venerated [this wak'a] because they believed that Chaupiñamca did not tell men the truth, that at times she lied."[65] The Spanish priests noted that each lineage had its own idols and each ayllu its wak'a and attendant priest. Francisco de Avila stated in 1611 that in a population of a little over 7,000 adults, he had located more than 5,000 wak'as and mummies.[66]

This multitude of wak'as was served and interpreted by large numbers of priests, or *yañcas*, as they were called in Huarochirí. Trained specialists, guardians of the lore and the traditions of their communities, the priests were responsible for preserving and transmitting the histories of the various communities, for maintaining proper behavior among the members of the group, and for directing the ceremonies related to the agricultural cycle. They signaled the onset of the planting season, led the rituals aimed at obtaining needed rains, and organized and led community efforts to stop unwanted rains, floods, or other disasters. They were the people who determined what ancestors or deities were the sources of personal or community disasters, why they were angry, and how to restore the community or its members to good health.[67] In Huarochirí, access to the priesthood was reserved to members of particular ayllus. The Checa peoples told the following myth to explain the monopoly of ritual knowledge by specific groups.

In that period, Huallallo Carhuincho . . . made an animal appear in the mountain where Pariacaca lived. "It will bury him," he said. This animal, called *huhi*, spread out everywhere. If the huhi had managed to survive, it would have ended Pariacaca's life. And for that reason, he ordered all the men of Tahuantinsuyo to capture it. Scarcely had they received the order when the people began to search for the animal and hunt it everywhere, but they did not find it. Pariacaca hurled rays of lightning and torrents of rain, but he could not kill it.

Then, in a faraway place, a man of Checa, of the ayllu Cacasica, succeeded in trapping the animal. And another man of Quinti said to him, "Brother, you must be very happy. Go and present him the brillant tail of the animal; let me carry the carcass." "Fine," answered the man of Checa. But taking another road, the man of Quinti reached Pariacaca first and said to him, "Father, I caught it."

Pariacaca rejoiced and praised the man. This individual of Quinti was named Chucpayco. A little later, the other man arrived with the animal's tail, and then Pariacaca said to the man of Quinti: "For having lied to me you will fight with the Quintis; 'pestilence,' they will call your children," and he went on excoriating him horribly. Then, referring to the ayllus Cacasica and Huarcancha, even Llilicancha, Pariacaca himself said, "You, for having caught this animal, will be raised to the class of yañca. I will listen to all that you tell me about your peoples, and the other communities must talk to me through you as intermediary; they must tell you first anything that they want me to learn." And he himself gave a name to the man who caught that huhi: "You will be called Nancaparya," he said. From that time on, the peoples that we have named are yañcas. Those of Concha are also yañcas, designated as such by Pariacaca himself, who gave them the name of Huatusi. And thus all those who are yañcas were instituted by Pariacaca himself.[68]

The yañcas were the masters and teachers, whose function was to perpetuate the socially accepted explanations of reality and maintain group cohesion by asserting the power of the wak'as and the ancestors. The yañcas presented the offerings to the wak'as and interpreted their replies to questions. As noted above, the yañcas interrogated the people who came before them on whether or not they had settled accounts with their kinsmen and could approach the ancestors free of either the anger or the envy of their fellows. The yañca, speaking for the wak'a, was in a position to elicit the resentments and slights that were part of life in relatively small competitive communities. They prescribed penance for the neglect of obligations toward either kinsmen, ancestors, or deities, and such penance often took the form of the sacrifice of llama kids or, if the supplicant was too poor, of a quantity of maize or coca.

The competition for place and position and the fear of humiliation in the battle for status and rank are leitmotivs of the myths of Huarochirí, and it is certain that the yañca, a "wise man" trained in the rules of proper behavior, knew about the disputes and the slights, the jealousies and quarrels that were threats to stability in his community. His privileged status as the exclusive interpreter of the wak'as and the ancestors enabled him not only to find out about quarrels and enmities but also to enforce compliance with the rules of proper behavior. I suspect that the yañca played an important part in maintaining the cooperation that held the Andean communities together on all levels beyond that of the minimal household and made it possible to produce the resources upon which the community depended. He not only prescribed punishment for transgressions but apparently had some authority to adjust rank within the community: for example, if a person brought an oddly shaped stone to the yañca for his inspection, he could define it as a conopa or household guardian, thereby increasing the number of household deities protecting that person's group and providing public recognition of the group's increased status in the community.[69]

As we noted earlier, the yañcas had special calendrical knowledge and determined the time for planting and harvesting, for cleaning the irrigation ditches, and for opening the dikes that fed the canals from the high puna lakes. In the ayllu Concha, for example, the yañca supervised the system of dams and dikes, determined the number of days for irrigation, and kept a watch on the water level to prevent overflow and flooding. The yañca "was careful to watch day and night, keeping the rules that had been learned by memory. 'We live because of him; otherwise the maize would have no strength, and no one would be alive if he did not protect us,' they said, and feared him."[70] The yañca's authority and direct participation in the productive process are amply clear in this case. The yañca's technical role is also illustrated by his part in determining the agricultural cycle, marked by community rituals. The narrator of the tales of Huarochirí, describing the role of the yañca in determining the times of ceremonies, alluded to a local calendrical system that marked the seasons by the angle of the sun's shadow. "A man of the ayllu Cacasica, which from olden times knew the reason for this test and for that reason are masters, one or two of these, called yañca by all the peoples, looks at the path of the sun from a well-built wall, and when the sun reaches the wall, he calls the people and tells them that they should go [to worship the wak'a] tomorrow."[71]

The principle here is well known by archaeologists and quite old in the Andes; it was based upon the apparent movement of the sun across the horizon as the earth turned. Three pillars of stone were erected on hills at some distance from a settlement and the wall from which the yañca in the description made his observations. As the earth turned, the sun appeared to rise at a different place in relation to the pillars, moving from one end of the line of stones to the other. At the time of the winter solstice in June, the sun appeared to rise directly above the pillar at one end of the line; at the summer solstice in December, it rose directly above the pillar at the other end; and the central pillar marked the equinoxes, about March and September. The major Andean festivals marked these times, and the yañca, taught the practice and the calculation as part of the skills of his profession, could fix the time for the yearly celebrations to mark the agricultural cycle with real precision.[72]

Not only the yañca or priesthood, but the community as a whole took part in the celebrations marking the major cycles of the year. Part of the complex web of mechanisms that bound the smaller elements together against the centrifugal pull of competition and rivalry, these festivals were public and corporate reenactments of the group's history that denied the existence of internal conflicts. Here the descendants of the wak'as and the ancestors acted out the great deeds of their forebears, as in the festival of the Checa, when the people celebrated their common unity as sons of Tutayquiri, their ancestor-deity, "traveling the road followed by his strength."[73] In Huarochirí, the major festivals of the year were the ceremonies in honor of the three principal deities described earlier: Tutayquiri, Chaupiñamca, and Pariacaca. At each the people came together for days of dancing, drinking, feasting, and games in which unity was reasserted through celebrations that people were expected to join in as brothers, without the enmity and conflict that might have separated them at other times.

In these festivals the priesthood did not lead the celebrations above or separated from the other members of the society. Rather, responsibility for leading the dances and other festivities was rotated among the members of the community. Every year, after the harvest festival of Chaupiñamca, each ayllu chose one of its members to lead the singing and dancing at the next three major celebrations. These people were called *huacasa*, and no one was expected to refuse the position (the narrator of the tales of Huarochirí noted that if anyone did refuse, and then died in the course of the year, his death was said to be the result of his refusal). For that reason, children were carefully trained in the traditional songs and dances from the time they were small.[74]

The myths contain many examples of the fear of shame or humiliation associated with the glitter of the dancing costumes and the lavishness of food and drink at the great festivals. But they were also occasions for fun and contests of skill—foot races, javelin-throwing competitions, and similar merriment. Some members of the community undoubtedly paraded their status and wealth, but others probably saw the festivals as a release, a time of relaxation and enjoyment after the harvest or just before the next ground-breaking. People could clown and joke, drink and get drunk as part of a group, at least some of whose members thoroughly enjoyed the fun.

The feast of Chaupiñamca, a fertility deity particularly sacred to the people of Mamaq, in the Rímac River valley, was an occasion for great festivity, since it marked the maturation of the crops. People brought animals (often *cuyes*, or guinea pigs) for sacrifice to the wak'a, and for five successive nights everyone, men and women, spent the entire night dancing and drinking. The feast of Tutayquiri, by contrast, marked the beginning of the rainy season and was characterized by a great hunt. Men from all the settlements went out on the day of the hunt, the huacasas together with the rest. Those who succeeded in bringing down a guanaco or a deer, or any other animal, gave it to the huacasa of his ayllu after first cutting off the tail to dance with later. That night all the hunters danced together on the high plain called Mayani, above the settlement of Tupicocha, where they had gathered for the hunt. The following day, the hunters left for the place where Tutayquiri was said to have first appeared. People from everywhere gathered there, at the traditional site of origin of the Checa peoples, to wait for Tutayquiri. All but the hunters brought chicha, and there they worshiped Tutayquiri. Then the huacasas, carrying the carcasses of the animals caught in the hunt, went to Llacsatambo, the principal settlement of the Checas, where people waited for them with chicha. As the travelers arrived, people threw jars of chicha on the men, the ground, and the gateway through which they entered the settlement. Then all gathered on the plain to sing and drink. Once the ceremonies were concluded, everyone waited for the rains to begin.[75]

The major festival of the year was the summer feast of Pariacaca, probably coinciding with the solstice in December. The shrine of Pariacaca was located in the peaks of the mountains behind the colonial village of Huarochirí, overlooking the high pass through which people traveled from the coast to the Huancayo Valley. The yañca announced the festival and led the pilgrimage to Pariacaca. The huacasas of the ayllus made the climb, carrying the ritual ticti, coca, and other offerings sent by the ayllus to the wak'a. Pariacaca was worshiped throughout the central highlands after the Inca expansion, but the myths only note that before the appearance of the Spaniards, "men from everywhere went to Pariacaca himself."[76] The pilgrims brought back word of whether Pariacaca was satisfied or angry with his people. Their return marked the onset of five days of drinking and dancing in all of the communities.

The feast of Pariacaca also marked the time when those who had died during the year were finally put to rest. If the dead were not properly fed and mourned, they could not rest quietly and might return to earth to bring illness and ill fortune to their kin. After the date of the festival was announced, all households in which persons had died during the year gathered together to cry and mourn for the dead for a night. They called the dead to eat for the last time, offering them food and feasting throughout the night. If a family could manage it, they also offered a llama kid; if not, they substituted a large bag of coca. These offerings were received by the priest, who read the heart of the animal for signs of the behavior of the family members. If the priest was content with the behavior of the family, he accepted the offering in the name of the dead kin; if he was not, he named those he regarded as sinners. They had to do penance and make an offering to Pariacaca in order for the dead kin to be able to rest quietly and not return to haunt the family.

Perhaps the most vivid example of community solidarity was the feasts honoring the ancestors, the mummies of the dead. The mummy bundles were kept in above-ground crypts or caves. A possible example of one such site is a large complex of buildings near the contemporary village of Huancaire.[77] High on the flank of a mountain, in a flat area, stand a large number of low oval structures roofed in stone as well as the foundations of other buildings with many rooms. The structures are grouped around a plaza opening to the south, and there are other small plazas at the site, some of them paved, surrounded by oval crypts. Such a site could well have been used for storing mummy bundles prior to the Spanish conquest. The "house of the dead" is periodically mentioned in the myths of Huarochirí as the burial place of particular groups, and these complexes in which the dead were stored and offerings made to them may well have been the largest sites in this region of dispersed settlement. The clothing of the mummies was changed at regular intervals. Kin presented them with jewelry, necklaces, shirts overlaid with silver, and drinking gourds for the chicha that was offered to them by pouring it in front of the bundle. Instruments—drums for dancing or panpipes—were also presented to the ancestors. The associated rooms may well have stored the rich cloth or jewelry offered to the mummies.

On feast days, the mummies were brought out of the crypts and arranged in a circle around the plaza. The most important ancestors—founders or important members of the largest ayllus—were placed on the inside and the less important on the outside of the circle. The priests also brought out the wak'as worshiped in general—at least those that could be moved. In the plaza, people danced and sang, offering the mummies chicha and food. The women kept the beat on the small drums called tinyas, while musicians may well have played the panpipes or Andean wood flutes known as *quenas*, whose high, sweet sound is a part of highland tradition today. These burial sites had none of the debris of living, for the living came to them only to do honor to the dead. Such places were a material symbol of the larger groups whose members were usually dispersed and that gathered together periodically to commemorate their common membership in the same family. The sites stand vacant today, their crypts and rooms empty, plundered clean even of bones. Viewed with fear as places of evil spirits, they stand as reminders of a time when people saw themselves as members of groups larger than the local village or segment of a village.

The productivity of the Andean community rested upon the reciprocal rights and responsibilities that reached from the household level through larger and larger units up to the maximal extent of the community. Access to a variety of goods, as well as the generation of sufficient surplus to permit the development of an elite that enjoyed greater access than others to those goods, depended upon the maintenance of group cooperation and solidarity. In the central Andes, the group cohesion and cooperation was based upon the definition of group members as descendants of a common ancestor, and consequently as "brothers and sisters" who owed one another reciprocal aid and assistance when called upon. In reconstructing this organization, it is misleading or worse to attempt to isolate economic, political, and ritual elements of the society from the fabric of which they are part.

What we might designate as political relationships or structures—the function and privileges of the kuraka, for example—or as "religious" or ritual and ceremonial elements—the institution of the yañca or the worship of the wak'as—were all part of productive activity, essential to the prosperity of the society. The goods expended on sacrifices to ancestors or wak'as, or consumed in feasting, drinking, or gifts, were viewed by the members of the society as part of the structure of reciprocity, which not only included the living but also reached back through the generations to encompass the dead and the deities. The reciprocity shown the ancestors ensured a return in the form of good harvests and adequate rainfall. The relationships and practices that were basic to this system, guarded and reinforced by the elites and specialists in charge of the social norms of the community, underlay the development of sociopolitical systems of considerable size and complexity at the time of the incorporation of the central Andes into the expanding Inca state. On this foundation, the Incas were able to build a state system capable of extracting immense amounts of surplus from the people it ruled. The character of that system and its presence in the local society is the subject of the next chapter.

THREE

Tribes Become Peasants

T HE WEALTH, the organization, and the panoply of the Inca state amazed the first Europeans to encounter it, and the organizational and productive structure that underlay what was perhaps the wealthiest state in the New World has continued to amaze and baffle people since the sixteenth century. An early description by Francisco de Jérez, a member of the first body of Spaniards to enter the Andes, provides a graphic illustration of the Inca state apparatus on parade.

First came a squadron of people dressed in a red-and-white check livery, who picked up the straws from the ground and swept the road; then more bands in different liveries, all singing and dancing, and after them a number of men with breastplates, . . . medallions, and gold and silver crowns, in the midst of whom came Atahuallpa in a litter lined with multicolored parrot feathers and decorated with gold and silver plates. The ruler was borne on the shoulders of many men and behind him came two more litters and two hammocks containing persons of importance, who were followed by many more who wore gold and silver crowns. [1]

The barbaric splendor of this picture is striking. But it also carries a further message, implicit in the description itself, about the organization necessary to mobilize the people described and to outfit them: the gold and silver came from mines in the Andes, the parrot feathers from the lowlands and near-jungle regions; clothing in standardized patterns, in sufficient amounts to outfit entire squadrons of men, implied many labor-hours of weaving; and the ornaments, medallions, and crowns implied the existence of skilled metalworkers, who in turn had to have behind them a productive system sufficient to feed and maintain them while they learned and practiced their craft.

Atahuallpa's troops were only the surface of an organized bureaucratic structure at which the Spanish conquerors marveled while they dismantled it, and which many of them strongly advocated retaining. Since the sixteenth century, conquerors, Spanish administrators, and later scholars have passed on the story of a state structure of overarching power, able to draw enormous amounts of surplus from a highly organized population. Karl Marx himself noted that Inca society appeared to be something of a sport, a system in which highly developed forms of cooperation and division of labor coexisted with a very limited development of the productive forces of society.[2] After the expansion of the Incas, just as before, human labor was the basic source of productive energy, supplemented to a limited degree by the *taclla* (foot-plow) and similar tools. Metal was used primarily for ornaments, and the llama, though used to carry burdens, would bear only a limited load without stubbornly refusing to move. The only large domesticated herd animal in the New World, the llama was a source of wool and meat, but not of productive energy. The wealth and glitter of the Inca state was the product of the labor of men and women.

But despite such apparently limited tools, the organization of the Inca state and the goods commanded by its rulers were a marvel to the Spaniards. The gold and silver collected to ransom Atahuallpa from the Spaniards was the greatest sum of treasure assembled at one time in the New World, an amount that probably exceeded any ransom paid to redeem a medieval lord or king in Europe during the Middle Ages. The conquerors marveled at the state storehouses filled with foodstuffs, ornaments, weapons, and, particularly, cloth. One of them wrote back to Spain that "there was so much cloth of wool and cotton that it seemed to me that many ships could have been filled with them."[3] They could scarcely believe the road system that ran from north to south along the spine of the Andes; and among those who remained in Peru, their amazement at and admiration for the organizational capacity of the Inca state grew rather than decreased with time. They recorded the detailed state records kept on *quipu*, or knotted cords, and the state census system based on ranked age-grades, so that the Inca state has come to symbolize a degree of organization and supervision—or regimentation, depending on one's perspective—of its citizens that is difficult to conceive of in any but the most modern bureaucratic systems.

The enormous scale of the Inca state and its wealth have tended to draw the attention of modern scholars to the state bureaucracy and capital at Cuzco—as they did that of the conquerors centuries earlier. Faced with evidence of armies in the hundreds of thousands, state storehouses containing millions of bushels of goods, and a road network thousands of miles long with rest stations and administrative centers spaced all along its length, many historians have fallen back upon the time-honored, if often misleading, solution of letting the actors speak for themselves: they have translated for members of a European cultural tradition the explanations of the origins and the structure of the state given by the Inca bureaucracy to the conquerors centuries earlier. This solution has generated further problems of explanation, notably how to account for the growth in less than a century of a small group in the Cuzco basin into a conquest state extending over a geographical area divided today among five nation-states and organized on a scale difficult to conceive of even without considering the problem of time. This problem has led some scholars to deny all credence in Inca evidence on their own history, and to argue that Inca historical traditions must be regarded as myths that collapsed long periods of evolution into the string of great deeds of particular hero figures.[4] But that alternative, too, must be tested against the evidence that we have available. We cannot throw out data that might yield up information unless it is clear that the source is so muddled or abstruse that it is more misleading to use it than not. And in the case of the problem of Inca historical traditions, we do have an independent source of data that can be used to test the interpretations of Inca history offered by the historians: the evidence of the archaeologists. The Inca period, the latest in the long span of human occupation in the Andes, has not drawn the attention of archaeologists in large numbers, since most have until recently been drawn to the long process of human evolution and the rise of early state or proto-state systems many centuries before Inca armies appeared outside the Cuzco Valley. But historians, archaeologists, and anthropologists have now begun to join forces, and recent evidence both helps clarify some of the important problems of late Andean states such as that of the Incas and indicates the value of interdisciplinary approaches to these problems.

Let us take a look at the problem of Inca history, and then see what recent evidence suggests about the relative time span to be attributed to that history. When the Spaniards entered the Inca Empire, the rulers of that state held sway over an area they called Tawantinsuyu, "the land of the four quarters." Their authority reached the length of the Andean chain, from above Quito, near the twentieth-century boundary of Ecuador and Colombia, to the Maule River in central Chile—roughly equivalent to the distance from New York City to the Panama Canal. Most Inca oral traditions (from which the Spaniards drew) record a list of some twelve Inca rulers from the first Inca to the rival claimants Huascar and Atahuallpa, who were disputing control of the state at the time of the entry of the Spaniards into the Andes in 1532.[5] But the first eight Incas are shadowy figures at best, and Inca history seems to be the stuff of legend prior to the figure of Pachacuti Inca, credited with the massive expansion of Inca authority and the organization of the structures of the new state. According to the traditions, Pachacuti, otherwise known as Cusi Inca Yupanqui, was one of the sons of the Inca Viracocha, who passed him over as heir presumptive in favor of another son. Viracocha began organizing Inca conquests for the continued benefit of the conquerors instead of restricting his operations to raids that left the defeated groups able to recover their strength. The wisdom of such a policy was shown late in his life, when Cuzco itself was attacked by a rival tribe, the Chancas, from the region of Andahuaylas to the north. The Chancas almost succeeded in taking the city, forcing Viracocha and his forces to withdraw to a hilltop fortress outside it. Pachacuti, aided by war chiefs loyal to him, rallied his followers and routed the Chancas, saving Cuzco.[6] After the battle, Pachacuti brought the stones of the battlefield back to Cuzco as wak'as, claiming that in the heat of the battle the very stones became men and took up arms to help the Inca forces.[7] Following this great victory, Pachacuti deposed his father and brother and took over the throne.

Pachacuti followed his father's lead in the matter of organizing his conquests and extended Inca control both throughout the southern highlands to the north of Cuzco and into the lands of the Lupaqa, a highly organized society in the Lake Titicaca area, centered in the high puna pastures that were the homeland of the llamas. His successor, T'upa Inca Yupanqui, pushed Inca authority far to the north, incorporating both the highland and the coastal areas of central and northern Peru as far as Cajamarca. His armies marched as far north as Quito and as far south as the Maule River in contemporary Chile. His successor, Huayna Capac, who died of smallpox between Francisco Pizarro's first appearance on the Peruvian coast in 1527–28 and the arrival of Spanish forces prepared for conquest in 1532, was credited with the consolidation of Inca rule in this immense area, and the protection and defense of the frontier areas facing the Amazon, from which raiders threatened the highland farmers producing for their new rulers.[8]

John Rowe, in an article published in 1945, assigned a date of approximately 1438 to the defeat of the Chancas by Pachacuti and his accession to the throne, thus consigning the rapid expansion of Inca authority throughout the Andes to less than a century, from the late 1430's to the appearance of the Spaniards in the Andes in 1532.[9] Though he warned against assigning undue precision to these dates, noting Andean disregard for a chronological system based upon anything equivalent to the European calendar,[10] he did argue that the expansion of the Inca state took place less than a century before the Europeans arrived in the Andes. Others have been extremely reluctant to accept these dates, arguing that Inca narrative traditions were more mythic than historical, and should be assigned to the timeless realm of myth in which sequence and chronology are jumbled and rearranged to make a "deeper" point about social and structural relationships.[11] Debate about the antiquity of the Inca state began with the conquerors themselves, and those who objected to any notion of absolute chronology for the Incas can find evidence for their contentions in the impossibly long reigns attributed to Inca rulers by some of the chroniclers. Inca traditions, many of them liberally seasoned with mythical figures and events, were preserved in long narrative poems and songs composed by selected members of Inca society and sung on regular occasions to remind the people of the great deeds of their kings. Those scholars who argue against accepting dates reconstructed from Inca sources have suggested that our wish for some relation to chronological time may be cultural, a demand for something with little relation to the purpose for which such sources were composed.

Yet despite the fact that some histories recorded after the Spanish conquest extended the origins of the Inca state well back in time, most external evidence indicates that this Andean state system was a relatively young one when the Europeans entered the Andes. In proposing his chronology, Rowe drew upon the available archaeological evidence, noting that stratified refuse containing Inca material was thin and that local styles existing before the appearance of Inca remains continued, indicating that Inca influence was short-lived enough so that local styles maintained their vitality until the Spanish conquest. Later archaeological evidence has continued to support the assumption that the Inca state was a young one despite its enormously rapid conquest of a huge area. Despite the relatively large number of sites assigned to the Inca period on the basis of pottery evidence (and despite their relatively good state of preservation), the depth of habitation refuse is relatively shallow for the population density posited from other sources. And pottery recovered from Inca-period sites shows less change in form and decorative style than Detroit cars have shown over the past twenty years. Though it is true that modern society places a premium on stylistic change for its own sake, the relatively small degree of style change that can be determined by archaeologists has led them increasingly to support the assumption that the Inca state lasted for less than a century before its defeat by the Spaniards, agreeing tentatively with the chronicler Cabello Balboa, who dates the beginning of Inca state formation to the early part of the fifteenth century.[12]

With this independent evidence of the antiquity—or rather, relative youth—of the Inca state, we can return to the traditions to see if we can extract some information on the evolution of the political structure through which this enormous territory was administered and ruled. Inca tradition places the territorial expansion of the Incas and the organization of the state in or about the early decades of the fifteenth century, during the reign of Pachacuti. Some students of Inca social organization have argued that the first seven rulers were essentially mythical figures, and that all of the ten kin groups or royal ayllus supposedly descended from past Inca rulers already existed in Cuzco in the fifteenth century, and were reordered and reorganized as part of the development of the state system of the Incas.[13] Since I am concerned not with the origins of Inca society, but rather with the state structure developed to administer conquered areas, I can set aside such problems and just point out that all traditions agree that Inca society was quite different before and after the Chanca War. Before that war, the Incas were one among many bellicose ethnic groups in the Cuzco Valley who raided one another for booty and captives and then withdrew again. After that war, the outlines of a state system began to take form, with an organized elite class and an elaborate organization for extracting labor and its products from the conquered tribes and states that became part of the new political structure.

But the assignment of a chronology to both the military expansion and the political organization of the Inca state raises new problems. For it implies that in less than a century, the Incas built thousands of miles of road and dozens of large administrative centers with elaborate stone construction. They terraced mountainsides and filled in valleys, and accumulated immense volumes of goods, much of which were consumed in enormous destructive ceremonies while the rest maintained an elite in great luxury. How did they do it? It takes time to impose new patterns of behavior, to accustom people to levies and demands that they had not faced before their incorporation into a new political entity. It takes time, in other words, to build a state system. How can we explain the organization of a complicated state system in so short a time, particularly in a society with such a limited degree of development of its productive forces?

It has been pointed out that the Inca state was not the first state system in the Andes. From about A.D. 650 to 850, an Andean state whose capital was at Huari in the contemporary province of Ayacucho in south-central Peru expanded to include much of the area of central Peru. The Huari state also constructed great storehouses in the area of Casma, Huamachuco, and Cuzco, which strongly suggests that the pattern of ceremonial destruction combined with judicious hospitality that underlay the organization of the Inca state was an old one in the Andes. The Huari state lasted only a few centuries. By A.D. 850 the capital was abandoned, and by 1000 or shortly thereafter Huari pottery styles had been replaced by local designs and traditions throughout the area of what was once the Huari state.

But it is difficult to assume that state traditions could last through centuries to reemerge in the Cuzco Valley some four hundred years later. It would be well to look closer to hand for an explanation of the rapid consolidation of the Inca state system. An explanation for the apparent contradiction between the organizational complexity of the Inca state and the limited development of the productive forces upon which it was raised was advanced by John Murra some twenty years ago, and his argument that the answer to this problem must be sought in the social systems of the local communities incorporated into the Andean state has gained strength and conviction with the years.[14] It is far easier to comprehend the extremely rapid growth of the state if we assume that the Incas built upon local economic and political structures, using them as the basis for political integration and state demands, and in the process forming a new structure whose very difference of scale meant a new formation. All of the material presented in the two preceding chapters has attempted to lay a basis for this assertion. I have argued that local society was structured on a complex network of reciprocal rights and responsibilities phrased in terms of relations between people expressed through kin ties, and that this web gave people access to the productive resources of their society and the labor of their fellows. Through the cooperative labor mobilized on the basis of such socially accepted claims, productive resources could be expanded and improved by building terraces that extended cultivable land area, by dikes, dams, and canals that controlled and channeled water sources. The same network of claims and responsibilities, extended to include larger and larger groups of people, were the basis of political organization. The same relationships, phrased in terms of fictive or real descent from a common ancestor, were the idiom of membership in nested series of groups ranging from a minimal level of the household or several households to larger and larger groupings that could include as many as 20,000 or 30,000 households in ethnic or tribal polities that in degree of organization can easily be described as small states.

The rapidity with which the Inca state was built can be much more easily comprehended if we assume that the new rulers built upon long-standing economic and political structures developed on the local level, structures that were common to them as well. As the young Andean state grew from a local political system to the behemoth it became, the mechanisms of political integration and authority, the channels through which labor and goods were mobilized, and the local claims that had been appropriated and rephrased into a state ideology were stretched and changed until the sheer difference of scale transformed them into something else, and the relationships that structured local integration became the basis of the mechanisms of control of a conquest state. Exchange phrased as responsibilities toward kin was translated into labor appropriated by a central authority for the benefit of the ruler and the military and bureaucratic apparatus surrounding him. Ethnic chieftains, responsible for the organization and the group cooperation of their communities, were transformed into the local representatives of a ruling state, sharing to some degree in the material benefits of authority in exchange for their function as part of the structure of local rule, and buttressed by the potential of punitive force from outside in the form of the Inca armies. There is ample evidence that the people incorporated into this expanding state did in fact perceive the real change in their status overlaid by the Inca's practice of phrasing new demands in old forms, and expressed their resistance to the changes in revolts against Inca rule.[15] Inca responses to these rebellions and the solutions adopted toward defeated rebels introduced still further changes into the political and economic structures of this Andean state, which may well have been pushing the political system in new directions in the decades immediately before the Spaniards entered the Andes.[16]

The hypothesis outlined above is tentative and incomplete. It needs testing and elaboration against data that can reveal, through sensitive and careful interrogation, the transformation of traditional relationships into something very different over the course of the short lifetime of this Andean state.[17] Ethnic groups such as the Cañaries, rebels later transformed into permanent military units, need to be studied. The transformation of traditional Andean institutions and statuses—such as the *yana*, or retainer group, and the *mitmaq*, or resident colonists—under the pressures of the sharply changing scale of state operations needs further study, although some exciting and valuable initial work has been done.[18] The region of Huarochirí itself, far from the centers of power—even the regional centers—may not be the best focus for such a study. The data on the role of Huarochirí within the Inca state are thin, although we have some highly suggestive fragments, and there is little justification for choosing this particular area as a means of gaining insight into the changing relationships between local polities and the larger state system in the century before the Spanish conquest. But it is equally impossible to comprehend the long-term history of the communities of Huarochirí under a political structure totally alien to them—that of an overseas European state— without taking into account the place of the region as a part of an Andean state at the time of the European conquest. So the pages that follow represent less an attempt to throw new light upon the Inca state than an effort to place the region within the context of the Inca state of which it was a part when the Europeans entered the Andes.

According to Inca traditions, the province of Yauyos, which included Huarochirí, was incorporated into the state in the 1460's during the reign of Pachacuti. Under the command of his son T'upa Inca Yupanqui, the Inca armies moved north through the central highlands, taking the regions of Jauja, Chocorvos, Huarochirí, and Canta before moving on to defeat the small highland kingdom of Cajamarca and its ally, the rich coastal state of Chimor near the twentieth-century city of Trujillo on the north coast. At the same time, another expedition was sent south to take the Titicaca basin and the Collao. With these campaigns, the major quarter of the Inca state, Condesuyos, was essentially complete. Inca traditions say little about the developing organization of the Inca state as its territories grew. The balladeers charged with remembering events and composing them into narrative poems to be sung at festivals and state gatherings recorded great deeds and conquests, leaving little of the day-to-day conflicts that reflect major transformations in social organization and state formation over time.

Pachacuti was credited by the Inca traditions with the organization of the entire state structure.[19] As a result, we have little beyond the occasional suggestions of myths and tales that gives us a glimpse of the conflict that inevitably accompanied the transformation of Inca society into the ruling class of a stratified state system. But while the sources are not available that would permit us to trace the changes brought about in a local society such as Huarochirí by its incorporation into the Inca state, we do have access to a variety of sources that tell us something about the region under Inca rule. By disentangling those aspects of local society that clearly reflect the presence and the operation of the state from the fabric of local social organization and authority, I hope to comprehend something of what the presence of the Inca state meant in local society. And through this examination of a local society and the state, we may also be able to understand more of the relationship between state and local structures in the Andean world.

The rapid expansion of the Inca state in itself is not easily comprehended. There is no evidence that Inca warriors had any real advantages in either military technology or tactics over their neighbors before the rapid string of victories that built the Inca state. They seem to have been a society of raiders and warriors, but that was also true of many highland societies at the same time. Huaman Poma de Ayala described the period before the Inca state as the "fourth age," the *aucaruna*, characterized by wars, fortresses, and raiding for lands, women, and plunder.[20] Each victory, of course, increased the Incas' relative advantage over other tribes, for they incorporated the warriors of defeated groups into their own forces. In the case of Huarochirí, for example, the Spaniards were told in the 1550's that the people of the repartimiento of Chaclla, already disputing access to the prized coca fields of Quives with the people of Canta to the north, joined the Incas in the conquest of the valley of Quives.[21] Long-standing enmities and rivalries between ethnic groups, stimulated and maintained by endemic conflict over particularly prized resource areas, could easily be turned to advantage by the Incas, who offered substantial benefits in lands, gifts, and privileges to sweeten their offer. Such surrenders were rewarded with gifts that bound the recipient to the giver. Testimony provided by a kuraka of Jauja in 1570 noted that the grandfather of the witness, who surrendered with his people to the invading Inca forces, was presented by the Inca with "shirts and *mantas* [shawls] and goblets for drinking."[22]

The state appropriated lands in the newly conquered areas for the production of goods for its own purposes. Some sources have asserted that the Incas appropriated all lands in conquered territories and divided it into thirds, reserving one portion for the state, one for the sun and the Inca deities, and one for community production. But such wholesale expropriation of productive resources without major resistance by the people whose survival was threatened so directly is difficult to comprehend; and in fact, local records make it clear that the Incas were much more selective in their appropriation of the spoils of war. According to Juan Polo de Ondegardo, the Incas took lands from the newly incorporated areas for the Inca and for the sun and other Inca wak'as, but the remainder of the lands remained in the possession of the communities incorporated into the state.[23] In disputes over land after the Spanish conquest, people regularly testified that they had held their lands "from time immemorial," and in the earliest of those cases now available, between the repartimientos of Canta and of Chaclla over the coca lands of Quives, it is clear that the reference was to the period before the Inca expansion.

The story of the coca fields of Quives is itself useful for an understanding of the practice of the Incas in the regions they conquered.[24] The Chaclla people, who allied with the Incas, profited from the establishment of Inca power, for although T'upa Inca Yupanqui took a part of their lands for the state, the Chaclla were also assigned additional lands in the valley of Quives at the expense of their rivals, the Canta. Chaclla mitmaq were sent to the lands to cultivate coca, ají, and other foodstuffs for both the Inca state and their home communities. Huayna Capac, T'upa Inca's successor, expropriated more coca lands for the state, again at the expense of the Canta people, who later seized their chance during the disruption following the entry of the Spaniards into Cuzco to attack the Chaclla people and drive them from the valley.

In the case of Huarochirí, there is evidence that the Incas not only expropriated lands for the benefit of the state, but also added lands to the holdings of the local communities as well as to those of the wak'as. The people of Huarochirí were assigned lands by the Incas in the puna pastures to the south to supplement their own scanty pastures.[25] According to

Polo, the other major resource appropriated on a large scale by the Incas was llamas. These animals, the source of the wool for the fine cloth so prized by the state, were taken by the Incas and formed into state herds from which the Inca then granted animals to kurakas and others as marks of particular favor and status. Some were also assigned to communities to supply wool for clothing,[26] though I suspect that what we have here may well be community herds retained despite the presence of the state, much like the familiar fiction that assigned the Inca state total ownership of all lands cultivated by the people belonging to the new polity. But the pretense, at least, of state control over herds would be easier to maintain in the case of movable resources such as animals, and Inca largesse would also be easier to comprehend if the Incas added to the herds of particularly valued or loyal subjects as marks of favor.

And all witnesses agreed that the people of the Inca province of Yauyos, which included Huarochirí, were favored by the Incas. According to Diego Dávila Brizeño, the first Spanish administrator of the region, who probably got his information from the people he supervised, the Yauyos were warlike people, "used by the Inca in all his wars."[27] But Dávila Brizeño specifically noted that "the Yauyos" referred not to all of the communities of the province, but only to the communities of Lurín, or lower Yauyos, a much smaller ethnic group whose ability in war was said to be the reason they gave their name to the province as a whole. However, the favor of the Incas toward the people of Huarochirí was also mentioned independently in 1554. In referring to the favor shown the Chaclla by the Inca, a witness added that "the Inca was very pleased with them and loved them because they were his servants."[28] The prestige of Huarochirí was also increased by the assignment of lands to the major deities of the region for their support, and the participation of the people of the province in Inca armies was rewarded by additional gifts of lands and animals to the wak'as.[29]

Inca access to the productive resources of the territories outside the Cuzco Valley may have been the direct product of conquest and outright expropriation, but the lands were of little value without access to labor for their cultivation. In order to gain that access, the Incas phrased their demands for labor in terms of the established mechanisms of reciprocal aid and support owed by kinsmen to one another on the local level. But whereas the local kuraka, even in large polities such as that of Chucuito in the region of Lake Titicaca, "begged" for the aid of his kinsmen and specifically noted that it was not given until he requested it,[30] the Inca state's "requests" for the services of the people it ruled could not be ignored. The state's claims upon the labor time of its subjects were backed, at least implicitly, by all of the coercive power of its armies. The failure of a kuraka to respond to "requests" for labor time from the state could result in the loss of his position, and was probably the first step toward open rebellion.[31]

The political fiction was that the state asked only for the labor service of people on its own lands, responding to that service with "gifts" of food and clothing. Inca tradition assigned to the second Inca, Sinchi Roca, the responsibility for initiating the pattern of chiefly generosity and reciprocity. "This one established the style of attracting and entertaining these nations so that his court and his house never angered anyone. His way was to keep the table set and the goblets full for whoever wished to come, and natives as well as strangers were always, day and night, occupied with dancing and music in their own style."[32] Just as local Andean traditions assigned the origins of particular practices or techniques to a mythical ancestor, so the Inca state adapted the ideology of chiefly generosity to new needs, attributing its origins to the sponsorship of probably apocryphal early rulers. As the state grew, the generosity expected of the ruler—the foundation of his claim to the labor of the people under his rule—was elaborated into a yearly cycle of feasts and ceremonies.

Labor time was the only demand made by the state upon its subjects, the source of the enormous wealth that amazed the Spaniards when they arrived in the Andes less than a century later. As Polo de Ondegardo put it, "All that the Indians gave their sovereign lord was personal service, because all the rest that there was, such as lands and herds, belonged to the Indians as their own; and although the tribute given the Incas consisted of many things, everything was the product of the labor of the people."[33] The state made its "requests" for labor time at one of the monthly feasts. The kurakas who attended were feasted and honored, and once tasks were assigned, all returned to their homes laden with gifts: fine cloth, gold and silver bracelets, jewelry, and other prestige articles. The labor time given the state varied from province to province and time to time, undoubtedly depending upon the bargaining position of the kurakas present at these highly ceremonial gatherings. But however great the ceremony and however important the gifts, the scale was clearly weighted in favor of the requests of the state; open opposition to the state's requests was unlikely to receive much of a hearing. Once the tasks were distributed, the kurakas carried the news of them to their people, distributing them among the communities at each level in the kind of local meetings discussed earlier.[34]

When agricultural work was done, it was done in sequence, beginning with the cooperative labor for the state and the local hierarchy. Lands were cultivated in turn, beginning on the fields of the wak'as, passing to those of the state, passing next to the fields of the kuraka, and ending with those of individual households. The cultivation of state and wak'a lands was rotated along with those of the community, the state's share passing into cultivation along with the fields chosen by kuraka and religious specialist in any given year. According to Polo de Ondegardo, who was familiar with the difficult agricultural lands of the high puna to the south, where crops failed often and harvests were meager, "[the lands] were sown every seven years, and when they were divided up for the settlement and its members, the share of the Inca and of the sun was also designated; and in the warmer lands it was designated only in some areas and in others it was designated anew each year, and the sun also had pastures and hunting grounds."[35] In accord with cultural expectations fostered by the state, the one who claimed labor was obligated to feed and support those who worked for the duration of the job. The stored goods harvested from state lands were used to feast people while they worked those lands, and the wak'as were also expected to feed, through their priests, the people working their fields from the products harvested earlier from their property.[36]

The services provided the state by the people it ruled are almost impossible to enumerate. The Spaniards later argued that the people worked at whatever task the Incas assigned them, and local testimony bears some relation to that assertion. Some tasks, such as the cultivation of state lands and the care of state herds, were regular and recurrent; others were called for as needed or wanted by the state. Summaries of the variety of services provided the state by local communities can be reconstructed from local censuses and testimony gathered in the decades following the Spanish conquest, material that has become widely available to scholars only in the last decade.[37] By any standard, both the volume and the variety of services provided the state were extensive. In addition to agricultural tasks, the kurakas of the Chupacho of Huánuco, for example, provided people to work in Cuzco, to serve in the Inca armies, to guard fields, and to build and maintain roads.[38]

It is impossible to calculate the proportion of the total labor time of the population appropriated by the state. It has been calculated that it took 30,000 people to build the great fortress of Sacsahuaman in Cuzco.[39] If we estimate a total population of approximately twelve million for the Inca state, it means that a quarter of one percent of the total population, or perhaps one percent of the adult male population, would have been occupied on the construction of the fortress at any one time. And as massive as Sacsahuaman is, the investment of labor that it represents pales in comparison with the enormous amount of building done in the short century of Inca rule. The Incas built a massive road system, with *tambos* [hostels, rest stops] by the hundreds, as well as provincial administrative centers

along the length of the great Inca road. Populations were moved and settled in new centers; valley floors were filled in and hillsides terraced; ceremonial centers were built and furnished—of which Cuzco, the capital,
was the finest and most lavish of all. The material infrastructure left by
the Inca state is the greatest testimony possible to the immense amount of
labor appropriated and expended by this Andean state in the course of its
short lifetime, and it is also a source of much valuable information on the
organization of state control.

A graphic illustration of both the volume and the variety of labor time
and productive activity appropriated by the state is contained in the testimony of the people who provided that labor. A kuraka of the Lupaqa of
Chucuito in 1567 noted that his people gave the Inca

. . . many Indians for war and to build houses and chacras in Cuzco and men and
women to serve in his house. [The Inca] had daughters of chiefs and principales
for concubines, and they gave him men and women to kill in sacrifice to the wak'as
and men to put as *mitimaes* in many parts, and from here they took him chuno and
other foodstuffs to Cuzco and fish carried quickly by *chasquis* [runners] in order to
arrive fresh, and cloth of cumbi and abasca; and the Inca sent men to pick them
up, and besides they gave him llamas in tribute and men to mine gold in Chuquia-
bo and silver in the mines of Porco; and there were men set aside to make feathers, and they gave him sandals and charqui, that is a meat dried in the sun, and
they gave him wool from the community herds and they gave him *llautos* for his
head and slings for war and axes of copper for war and copper picks for his house
and all else that the Inca asked of them because they were very obedient. [40]

Records of labor and goods provided to the state—read to the Spaniards
from quipu, or knotted cords—have not emerged for Huarochirí, although a basic idea of at least some of the variety of labor services can be
elicited from more general sources. The wak'as in Huarochirí, and undoubtedly the Incas as well, had llama herds cared for by shepherds
drawn from specific communities. The ayllu Allauca, of Checa, provided
the shepherds, and another ayllu, Yasapaya, gave men as the personal servants (*yanas*) of one of the important wak'as of Huarochirí. [41] There is no
mention of service to the state in this source aside from the wak'as, but in
the replies of local kurakas to questions about labor services, only formal
state services and not labor for the wak'as is mentioned. The people were
probably not eager to provide their conquerors with more information
than they demanded, particularly since wak'a lands and treasure were in-
variably appropriated by the conquerors as part of the spoils of war. In
the case of the data from Huarochirí, the information requested was specifically about the wak'as. There is little or no mention of any state service
in this source, although internal evidence strongly suggests it. In view of
the similarity of the type of service given the wak'as to that provided the

state in other contexts, I think we can examine the data above for what they suggest about both the character and the form of labor recruitment for state and deities together.

The ayllu specialization indicated by the assignment of particular services for wak'as to specific ayllus suggests that continuous, repeated tasks may well have been performed by particular communities that assumed the responsibility of providing and replacing people as needed. Community reciprocity, backed in this case by the additional coercive power of the state, would ensure that the claims of someone removed for such services would be respected. As Father Bernabé Cobo later noted, in such cases, "the other Indians of the community worked the fields of the absent man without asking or receiving any compensation beyond their food."[42] People were also assigned to work fields in specific resource areas claimed by the state, such as the coca fields of Quives. Since Huarochirí had mines as well as specialized silver-workers—the members of the ayllu Yasapa were "of that profession"—it is likely that the state drew upon the same miners and skilled metalworkers who extracted the ore and turned it into ornaments to be offered to the wak'as.[43] As noted earlier, the people of Huarochirí, proud of their ability in battle, also served the state in its wars. They remembered and recounted their military services to the Inca in myths and tales that glorified the supernatural exploits of the wak'as defined as their progenitors and protectors.[44]

The Incas also adapted other traditional institutions to the needs of an expanded state system. The yanas, people detached from their kin groups and assigned to the service of deities or mummies, or the Inca rulers, are one example.[45] These people, fed and maintained from the goods of the group, deity, or kuraka to which they were attached, were not necessarily of low status. The state also took young girls from the local community to be raised in the *aqllawasi*, or "house of the chosen women." These young women were given to kurakas, members of the royal lineages in state service, military leaders, or others as a mark of particular favor. To have more than one woman in a household was both a mark of high status and a source of wealth, for the women were important members of the household productive unit. As Polo de Ondegardo noted, "he who had many wives was richest . . . because the women . . . make cloth and prepare fields for the husband."[46] Some *aqlla*, as these women were called, were housed in the provinces, where they wove fine cloth from the state stores of wool, prepared chicha, and served at the feasts and drinking-fests regularly offered by the state.

One of the institutions that has been regarded until recently as an Inca innovation was the mitmaq, under which resident colonists were sent to cultivate or exploit particular resource areas by their communities.[47] It is not always easy to find mitmaq from particular regions; the state resettled colonists throughout its territories. On the basis of scattered bits of data, the presence of mitmaq from the communities of Huarochirí and Chaclla has been noted in Jauja, in Huánuco, in the area of Lima on the coast, and in Cajamarca far in the north; all of these are in addition to the colonies working closer to home.[48] According to the testimony of witnesses in the sixteenth century, the mitmaq from Huarochirí in Jauja remained part of their communities, sending produce back to their kuraka and following the "archipelago" pattern outlined in Chapter One. These mitmaq seem to have been an expansion of the traditional pattern of resident colonists whose primary function was to extend the access of their communities to valued goods and resources.

But the presence of mitmaq far from their home communities, in Huánuco and Cajamarca on the frontiers of the Inca state, argues for another explanation than the simple expansion of the productive capacity of the local community—even if such expansion was ultimately for the benefit of the state. These relatively distant areas were the sites of regional Inca capitals, one of which, Huánuco Pampa, has been the subject of a detailed research project directed by Craig Morris.[49] Tentative results of the excavations at Huánuco Pampa, together with the quipu records reported to Spanish authorities in 1567, suggest that people were sent to the regional capitals for both military and support functions. Men and women accompanied the Inca warriors as cooks and cargo-bearers, and they cultivated fields in the areas to which garrisons were assigned in order to support those garrisons. Inca armies were organized on highly traditional lines, at least during much of the lifetime of this Andean state. People served in the Inca armies as part of their mit'a service to the state, fighting in local units under their own kurakas with their own arms, military tactics, and identifying clothing. Their exploits were remembered as the assistance rendered the state by their wak'as, who symbolized the whole community, not merely its living, currently active members.[50] I suspect that the mitmaq from Huarochirí recorded as located in Huánuco and Cajamarca represent a case of military groups assigned to distant areas, probably with other members of their communities who supplied the foodstuffs and other goods they needed on lands assigned them by the state.

But if the function of these mitmaq was primarily military, there was little that they could remit to their home communities in the form of actual goods or produce. Distance undoubtedly weakened their ties to their home communities, particularly if the mitmaq received at least part of their economic support from the lands they cultivated in their new territories (undoubtedly supplemented by the gifts of prestige foodstuffs and cloth periodically distributed to warriors by the state, which thus maintained the fiction of its "generosity"). But mitmaq far away were remembered by their communities, which did receive a return for their services in the form of the additional treasure and awards given the community's wak'as by the state in return for their services in war. Though adding specifically to the wealth only of the wak'as and the priests and yanas assigned to them, such rewards did mean additional prestige for the community, whose myths note the "fear" felt toward the victorious wak'as by the Inca and his obeisance and service to their deities.[51] These mitmaq, far from their home communities with no real exchange to reinforce and maintain the social relationships that linked them to their kinsmen, were representative of new and different needs—despite the name that linked them to the traditional institutions of local society—the needs of a state system in process of evolving an effective machinery of coercion and police power. Had there been no Spanish invasion, it is quite possible that the mitmaq could have been the leading edge of a phenomenon that has until recently been assumed to have been the origin of the institution itself as used by the Incas. With time, the links to traditional ethnic groups might have dissipated, leaving a society of local groups integrated directly into a state system that they supported and from which they received support in turn without the mediation of ethnic loyalties and ties between the local community and the larger state.

The transformation of traditional institutions in the process of their extension to fit the demands of a state system also applied to the physical infrastructure that was elaborated to buttress and maintain the elite and the political structure. The surplus that maintained the Inca elite and fed armies and wak'as alike was extracted through the same mechanisms that ordered the flow of labor time from household unit to the kuraka. The social obligations that enforced cooperative labor for the community became the basis of more extensive political relationships and obligations that bound the elites of regional ethnic groups to the Inca elite and enforced their cooperation in mobilizing the labor time of their people for the benefit of the state. The kurakas, the ethnic elite of the local communities, were for the most part absorbed into the state, retaining their authority and their position. Their authority was expected to be used to administer and distribute the labor demands of the state, and they did receive gifts and prestige goods—cloth, jewelry, additional women, and yana retainers—from the Incas in return. The famous Inca decimal system permitted the *quipucamayoq*, or specialists in keeping accounts with knotted cords, to keep a detailed record of the labor services demanded by—and granted to—the state.[52] Nearly a century after the Spanish conquest, a member of the Andean provincial elite, Huaman Poma de Ayala, bragged that "with these cords the entire kingdom is governed."[53]

But even the most efficient system of organization and administration also demands a physical form. Though it appears that in the provinces for which we have records the traditional pattern of access to multiple ecological niches was preserved and even extended by the Incas, the state did concentrate people in some cases, as earlier Andean states had before them, constructing new centers or extending older ones to serve as local or regional administrative centers.[54] The Inca presence left few obvious remains in most parts of Huarochirí; the rough, largely unpainted local pottery did not change greatly, and even local imitations of the thin, finely painted Inca ware are rare in highland sites. But the presence of Inca fields cultivated by community members on mit'a turns was a constant reminder of the presence of the state. And there are other physical remains that bear witness to changes in the region introduced by the Incas. According to Diego Dávila Brizeño, the high valley at the headwaters of the Mala River, site of the colonial village of Huarochirí and core territory of the Huaros, was the capital of the Inca province of Yauyos and the residence of the principal kuraka, Ninavilca, when the Spaniards entered the Andes.[55] Archaeological remains near Huarochirí on a low hill above the contemporary village of Sangallaya today have been identified on the basis of surface pottery collections as dating to the Inca period. The site consists of a complex of buildings made of fieldstone set in mud and gravel mortar. There are several groups of buildings, some with walls that rise up to seven feet high with rounded corners, covering most of the hilltop. Some of these are rectangular rooms with defined interior spaces of twelve by fifteen feet. These may have been storehouses, or residences; the stones today are too scattered over the site to reconstruct the pattern of building and open spaces.[56] In any case, the presence of Sangallaya suggests that the Incas did add to whatever complex of buildings existed in the valley before the area became part of the state—a pattern of construction familiar from Inca traditions and eminently practical for the business of administration and state organization.

It is not at the local level, however, but at the regional scale that the physical infrastructure of integration became truly magnificent and imposing. The state was bound together by a system of communications that has become a legend. The Spaniards who traveled on them marveled at the roads that ran from Quito to Cuzco and on to Chile—all constructed and maintained by the labor of the people through whose lands they ran. Two highways ran the length of the empire, one along the coast and the other through the highlands, crossing the mountains along causeways built along the steep slopes and stairs cut into the cliffs. The main roads were connected by transverse roads from coast to highlands, of which Cieza de León wrote in 1547, "those who read this book and have been in Peru should look at the road that goes from Lima to Jauja through the steep mountain slopes of Huarochirí and by the snow-capped mountain of Pariacaca, and they will understand, those who hear it, whether what they saw is more than I can write of."[57] Fragments of that road system still remain to be seen from the modern roads today, a marvel of engineering that Cieza himself said could not be duplicated in his time. Along these roads waited runners [*chasquis*] provided by the local people as part of their labor services to the state. Stationed in huts every mile and a half to two miles along the road, they could relay a message from Lima to Cuzco in three days. In this way, information vital to the maintenance of the state could be carried to the Inca with almost no delay. "And in this way the lords were informed of everything that happened throughout their kingdom and dominion and determined what appeared to them most to their benefit."[58]

But it increasingly appears that most of the information that needed to be received, as well as the major administrative functions of the state, were dealt with not in Cuzco but in one of the provincial capitals located along the road system. There were many such regional or provincial centers; Cieza said that they were established in each provincial center.[59] Where populations were concentrated in urban or semiurban centers before their incorporation into the Inca state, the Incas apparently located their own administrative centers at the earlier focus of local authority, constructing only what was necessary to modify existing buildings according to state specifications.[60] Other centers were built from scratch, with no previous occupation of the site.

Recent work on the articulation between the state and the local areas has laid increasing emphasis upon the role of these provincial centers, indicating a degree of decentralization that is far more congruent with what we know of the real level of development of the productive forces of the Inca state than the earlier image of a thoroughly centralized system in which all goods flowed to Cuzco and all decisions emanated from that center. Recent archaeological investigation of the system of regional centers suggests the importance of the Inca governor, or *toc'ricoq*, noted in the sixteenth century by Spanish authorities who both admired the Inca political system and sought to adapt it to their own objectives. Juan de Matienzo defined the toc'ricoq in 1567 as a judge and administrator, responsible for the settlement of disputes and the collection of tribute.[61] Though most sources state that the Inca appointed a governor or toc'ricoq in each province, local sources do not always support such an assertion. What data we do have, from Huánuco, from Chucuito, and to some degree from Huarochirí, refer to the Inca governor in relation to the provincial centers—Huánuco Pampa for Huánuco, and Jauja for Huarochirí. The toc'ricoq had to be of noble blood, "brothers, grandchildren, or great-grandchildren of the kings," although Huaman Poma de Ayala stated that they were drawn from the people whose ear holes had been torn or broken—lowering their status—or whose feet or hands had been damaged in war.[62] He, as well as the Spaniard Matienzo, called them judges, for they decided issues that involved a penalty of death or complaints against kurakas; they were also responsible for investing a new kuraka with the *tiana* or stool of office upon which he sat.[63] As the local representative of the Inca, the toc'ricoq was accorded the special privileges reserved to the Inca and granted to those he favored, such as the right to travel in a litter. The governor also received "as a wife a princess of Cuzco or of his [the Inca's] lineage, or one of those called *yucanas*, who are important ladies; and with her he gave him a hundred or a hundred and fifty Indians to serve her from those who were in the houses of safe-keeping [aqllawasi], or from those who had been captured in war, and the husband was given 600 Indians to serve him in his house and fields."[64] The governor was also assigned lands in the region he administered for his maintenance.

Given the simple fact of the size of the Inca state, it is to be expected that the provincial center played a major role in the normal administration of the ethnic groups that made up the state. For Huarochirí, the provincial capital was in Jauja, said to be one of the largest and most important in the Inca state. There is little of the Inca state that remains there today, for the Inca center was almost totally destroyed or buried beneath the modern city, but the storehouse complex alone, whose ruins still stand on the surrounding hills, bears witness to the importance of that capital. Craig Morris counted some 683 storehouses, or *qollqas*, directly above or very near the modern town of Jauja, and estimated that about 550 additional storehouses were once part of the complex. Morris has estimated the capacity of the extant storehouses at 38,500 cubic meters, and with the destroyed qollqas has come to the conclusion that the original volume of goods stored in Jauja probably exceeded 50,000 cubic meters and may have been as high as 75,000 cubic meters.[65] During the civil war over the succession to Huayna Capac, which was in progress when the Spaniards entered the Andes, the Inca governor in Jauja sent for coca and ají to the valley of Quives, cultivated by mitmaq from Chaclla, and this fact suggests that the goods produced by the people of Huarochirí and Yauyos on lands appropriated by the state were stored in Jauja.[66]

Jauja, largely destroyed, is not likely to yield much more information on the structure or organization of the provincial centers in the Inca state, but work now being done at the provincial capital of Huánuco Pampa, located on a high puna plain left largely undisturbed since the fall of the Inca state, has yielded some of the most detailed information we have on the internal organization and functioning of these provincial centers.

Huánuco Pampa, a planned complex built from scratch by the Incas, undoubtedly functioned like other provincial centers—although if the decentralization of the state was as great as some are beginning to suggest, we may well find considerable variation between these centers. On the basis of its storage capacity, Huánuco Pampa was probably a somewhat smaller center than Jauja—an assumption that is supported by the fact of Huánuco Pampa's location on the state frontier, facing the unsubdued tribes of the Amazon Basin, in contrast to Jauja's location in the very center of what was, according to Inca tradition, the richest and most advanced quarter of Tawantinsuyu.[67]

Huánuco Pampa is a huge site, daunting to the archaeologist armed only with his shovel and his wits. The site is dominated by a large central plaza with a platform of dressed stone 200 by 250 feet in the center. To the east of the plaza is a complex of finely constructed buildings, a stone-lined bath, and artificial pools. Thirteen long halls are arranged around two smaller plazas nearby, connected by the typical Inca trapezoidal gateways of dressed stone with carved lintels. On the northern side of the main plaza, a walled compound with only one entrance encloses a series of fifty buildings to which entry and egress were tightly controlled. Long narrow buildings open onto the plaza. South of the center, hundreds of rectangular and circular qollqas stand in lines that follow the curve of the hillside above. There are 497 of them, with a storage capacity of about a million bushels of potatoes, maize, and other foodstuffs. (See Figure 2.) The buildings to the east provided elegant facilities for the Inca on his travels, or perhaps for the provincial governor responsible for the region. The long buildings provided communal housing for travelers, or for the people serving their labor turn at the capital. Cieza noted that over 30,000 people "served" the center, whose ruins cover an area of almost two square miles.[68]

Excavations of the storehouses have indicated that they were used for foodstuffs, principally maize and potatoes. No remains of cloth or luxury goods have been found, suggesting that these goods were transferred to Cuzco for sacrifice or redistribution to favored people by the Inca. Many fragments of large cooking pots and spindle whorls were found in the northern compound, together with other instruments used in weaving, which suggests that a part of the population of the center consisted of aqllas, the "chosen women" appropriated by the state. Huaman Poma de Ayala described their role as weavers of fine cloth and brewers of ritual beer or chicha for the state. They served "the royal tambos and served in the festivals," and "were taken from these communal houses to distribute the agricultural plots and clothing for the benefit of the community and

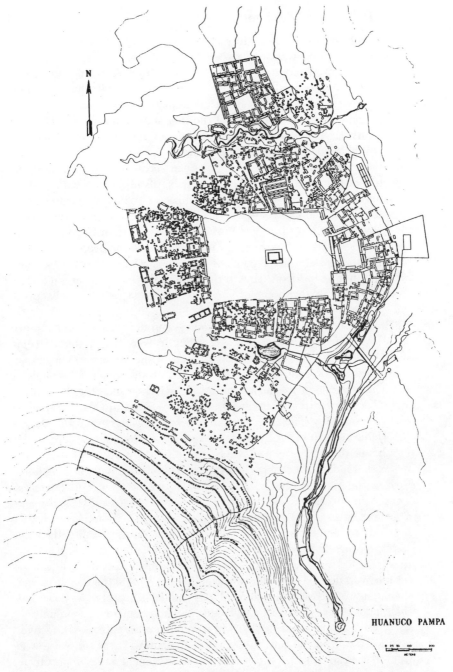

HUANUCO PAMPA

Figure 2. The Inca provincial center of Huánuco Pampa. Map courtesy of Craig Morris, American Museum of Natural History.

community stores."[69] Craig Morris has suggested that Huánuco Pampa, a large part of which was dedicated to the great plaza and the compounds used for the preparation of food and chicha, provided feasts and "hospitality" by the state to all people who worked for it.[70] All who worked for the Inca "were invited to eat and drink in place of payment."[71]

By looking at the organization of the Inca state in terms of a collection of regions, each supervised by a governor chosen from the Inca elite with substantial freedom of action and considerable authority, much of the traditional picture of the state that has been reconstructed from the perspective of Cuzco as recorded by the Spaniards in the sixteenth century can be reinterpreted in a more meaningful way. We do not have to assume that the massive amounts of labor extracted by the state from the people under its rule were all directed and administered from Cuzco, nor that the great festivals, or the chiefly generosity that fed the people while they worked for the state, involved all of those on state labor turns. We know that storehouses were distributed throughout the Inca territory; it is thus not at all unlikely that much of the contact of the state with the people it ruled occurred at the provincial level.

The first destination of products produced on state lands by community labor was the provincial capital. According to Polo, the product of community labor on state lands "was gathered in the storehouses made for that purpose."[72] Goods of all kinds were sent to the provincial capitals in the course of the year—maize for chicha, potatoes and other foodstuffs, wool that was distributed to the population to weave into cloth, and other products made by specialized artisans working in wood or metals. On the basis of an analysis of the quipu records of service to the state kept by the kurakas of the Chupaychu in Huánuco, John Murra has presented estimates that indicate that slightly less than half of the people serving labor turns for the state actually traveled to Cuzco for their work; the rest worked in the region, cultivating crops, hunting, guarding fields, and transporting goods to the qollqa at Huánuco Pampa.[73] If the Huánuco area provides any indication of the relationship of state and locality, then the state presence in the local areas was both wide-ranging and at the same time oriented more to the provincial center than to Cuzco itself. That center received the goods produced within the territory of the region, stored them, and provided the ceremonial food and drink expected by people on their labor turns. The provincial center probably represented the authority of the state for most people within the boundaries of Tawantinsuyu, save for those people sent to Cuzco on their mit'a turns, or those who went to the capital as yanas to guard and serve the mummies of past Incas or as sacrifices to important wak'as.

Direct contact between Cuzco and the local regions was probably lim-

ited largely to the kuraka elite. The Incas kept the sons of provincial kurakas at Cuzco, where they were taught the Inca traditions and narrative
poems as well as instructed in the behavior expected of a loyal servant of
the state and a member of its aristocracy-by-privilege. The provincial
elites, which remained in charge of the people they had governed, were
trained as far as possible in the ideology of the Inca rulers. The young
heirs to the chieftainships of the provinces went to Cuzco together with
the members of their own groups sent as mitmaq to guard the mummies
of past Incas or serve the wak'as that were brought to Cuzco for long
stays. It has been noted that the presence of the provincial wak'as in Cuzco, as well as of the sons and heirs of the kurakas, made both past and
future leaders of their communities hostages to the good behavior of their
people, despite the honors with which both wak'as and young people
were loaded. And the stay in Cuzco was clearly calculated to affect not
only the ones honored, but also the mitmaq in the capital for their work
turns. The obvious show of splendor and might exhibited there to awe the
subject peoples (who could be expected to pass on their experience to the
other members of their communities) was graphically described by Cobo.
He noted that "there were always Indians from all the provinces of the
kingdom living in that city [Cuzco] and court, occupied in guarding and
serving their idols, where they learned the manners and customs of the
members of the court; and when their *mitas* and turns changed and they
returned to their own lands, they kept and taught to their own people
what they had seen and learned at the court."[74]

The descriptions of the function of Cuzco, in fact, clearly make of the
capital less an administrative and political center than a ceremonial complex. It could well be argued that the function of the capital was to impress and to overawe by the exhibition of wealth and piety involved in
the daily destruction of huge volumes of goods and finery sacrificed to the
wak'as regarded as the guardians of the state and its ruling elite. The layout and the architecture of the city themselves indicate its ceremonial
function. Cuzco was rebuilt and decorated as a fitting background to the
power of the state and the Inca deities. Its plan and construction were
credited to Pachacuti, also remembered in Inca tradition as the organizer
of the administrative structure of the state system. The rivers that ran
through the city were canalized and their channels faced with cut stone.
Buildings of finely cut stone housed the images and wak'as honored by
the state as well as the palaces of current and past Inca rulers. The most
dazzling of these structures was the Temple of the Sun, or Coricancha,
famous for its walls covered with sheets of gold hammered paper-thin and
for the finely worked gold reproductions of growing corn and llamas that
filled its plaza.

Fine cloth and other luxury items produced throughout the empire were carried to Cuzco each year and stored in qollqas on the valley slopes above the city. The Spanish conquerors were impressed by the large number of these storehouses, observing that "it seemed to everyone that they could never be emptied."[75] The goods in these storehouses were used to maintain the elite, to sacrifice to the wak'as, and to feed the people in the great feasts that were held in the city. Ceremonial offerings were also characterized by public exhibitions of the largesse of the state. Huaman Poma de Ayala described the great feasts held by the Incas every month of the year, such as the ceremonial of Inca Raymi in April, when the Inca "had a great feast, inviting the great lords and principales; and the other leaders and the poor Indians ate and sang and danced in the public square . . . and the people of the kingdom drank and feasted at the cost of the Inca."[76] This constant cycle of feasting and ceremony seems to have been the major function of the city. According to Inca traditions, no poor lived in the capital. Priests, important members of the elite and the royal lineages, and the women housed in the aqllawasi who wove, prepared chicha, and served in the feasts and ceremonies made up the majority of the population.

Though feasts were important, they were subsumed in the ritual and ceremony that were an integral part not just of the superstructure but of the very character of this Andean state. Ritual sacrifices and "gifts" to the ancestors and to the wak'as made up the social investment that, according to Andean belief, maintained and increased the resources upon which the state depended. Enormous amounts of cloth, coca, foodstuffs, llamas, and even young men and women were offered to the wak'as regarded as crucial to the continued success of the Inca armies and the prosperity of the state. Feasts were held to ensure the health of the llama herds, to plead for rain, and to protect the fecundity of lands and people. The Inca himself initiated the agricultural cycle, breaking the ground with a taclla or foot-plow richly ornamented with precious metals and then laying the instrument aside for the feasts and drinking in which the elite participated while the rest of the people continued to work. Regular ceremonies were held to ward off illness and prevent the fever that regularly decimated the llama herds.

The Inca lineages living in the city were charged with organizing and performing the ceremonies, each one responsible for particular wak'as or shrines that tradition said they were assigned by Pachacuti. Juan Polo de Ondegardo, one of the few Spaniards who perceived the enormous importance of ceremony in the conduct of the state, described the ceremonial organization of Cuzco in a famous passage: "From the temple of the sun went out, as from a center, certain lines that the Indians call *ceques*;

and these make up four parts like the four royal roads that lead out of Cuzco; and along each of these ceques stood in order the wak'as and temples of Cuzco and its environs . . . and each ceque was in charge of the lineages and families of the city of Cuzco, from which came the ministers and servants who cared for the wak'as of their ceque and kept up the established offerings at their appointed times."⁷⁷ In these ceremonies, the goods offered to the wak'as were burned. The animals were sacrificed, their blood smeared over the shrines, and the carcasses then burned to ashes. A large proportion of the contents of the qollqas whose numbers and abundance so amazed the Spaniards was consumed in this way, neither directly increasing the wealth of the population nor adding to its productive capacity except insofar as it reinforced the human and social energies that maintained the social order. In Polo's words, once again, "the Indians expend an enormous amount in sacrifices, sacrificing to all the gods every day; they sacrifice something somewhere every day."⁷⁸

It would be a mistake, however, to assume that the capital of the state existed purely for elaborate ceremonial purposes whereas the real work of administration and extraction of surplus took place at provincial centers manned by a bureaucracy drawn from the Inca elite. Such a division of function would not be likely to last for long without the system itself breaking down. An integration of ideology and practice is part of any political structure, and, further, it is difficult to conceive of an effective ideological or belief system in which the elite is not itself enmeshed, at least in the last instance, in the structure of beliefs and practices that justify and maintain its domination. And the Inca state does not seem to have been an exception to this general pattern. The Inca himself could suffer from the wak'as' withdrawal of their favor, even if, like Atahuallpa, a slighted ruler was able to revenge himself upon the deity—and its priests—when they proved fickle.⁷⁹ The deities had to pronounce on a prospective heir to the throne, and could significantly affect the final selection of the Inca-to-be.⁸⁰

All of this indicates that the relation between state and deities was complex; indeed, the integration of the structures of local ceremonial into the state system was a complicated process in which local wak'as and their representatives could function to integrate large areas under the state and still command the awe as well as a considerable share of the gifts and resources of the Inca. Though the expansion of the Inca state meant that the wak'as and deities defined as the guardians of Inca power were introduced into new areas, the Incas did not attempt to eliminate or restrict the wak'as served by the ethnic groups they absorbed. In Huarochirí, for example, the state actively reinforced the status and authority of the principal wak'as of the region, assigning them additional lands and people for their service. Minor local wak'as in the Inca provinces were counted and a record of their possessions kept by the keepers of the quipu, or knot records. According to the tales of Huarochirí, "the Incas knew well all the wak'as from everywhere. They ordered each wak'a to be given its gold and silver, according to how it was recorded in the quipus . . . but the great wak'as were not submitted to these measures."[81]

The "great" wak'as were not directly controlled by the state. In at least some cases, there is considerable evidence that they became the focus of state-supported ceremonies, supported by architectural complexes specifically built for the storage and preparation of sacrifices and the maintenance of the people assigned to their service. A ceremonial center that has been identified as at least in part a shrine to Chaupiñamca (also called Mamaq), one of the three major deities of Huarochirí, provides a graphic example of the state's support of local deities.[82] Chaupiñamca, according to the traditions of Huarochirí, was the sister of Pariacaca, the major deity of the province and perhaps of the highlands of Central Peru. In one tale, she was also said to have married Pachacamac, the principal coastal deity, which linked coast and highlands in a unity that was not acknowledged by all of the ethnic groups of Huarochirí. The marriage, obviously in the interests of a state attempting to build larger-than-local loyalties, may well have been the work of the Incas themselves.[83] But whatever the political ramifications of her genealogy, Chaupiñamca was the fertility deity worshiped at harvest time and consulted by people throughout the region in cases of personal trouble. Her worship probably coincided with the solstice, for the narrator of the tales of Huarochirí remarked that after the Spanish conquest, her festival was hidden by associating it with the Corpus Christi feast in June. The ceremonies described by Huaman Poma de Ayala for the equivalent month were festivals that celebrated the end of hunger throughout the four quarters of Tawantinsuyu—the month called Inca Raymi quilla. "In this month they offered painted llamas to the wak'as throughout the kingdom, and in this there was a great deal of ceremony and the Inca had a great festival inviting all the great lords and principales and the other leaders and the poor Indians, and they ate and sang and danced in the public square. . . . This month the food is ripe and thus the people ate and drank and feasted at the cost of the Inca, and this month the birds of the sky and the rats [cuyes?] have enough to eat."[84] In Huarochirí, the feast for Chaupiñamca involved five days of dancing and drinking, including one dance called the "casayaco," in which men performed either naked or carrying only arms, since Chaupiñamca was said to take great pleasure in seeing the men's private parts, which was supposed to assure a fruitful year.[85]

Forty to fifty miles from Lima up the Rímac River, near the point where the Santa Eulalia River (the northern branch) and the Chaclla (the south-

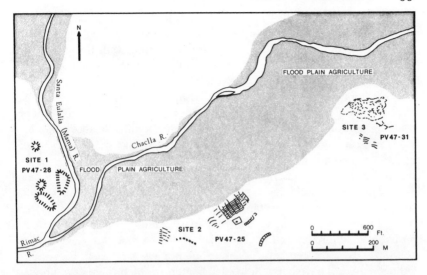

Figure 3. Ceremonial complex for the worship of Chaupiñamca (Mamaq). Survey by Thomas Patterson and Karen Spalding, 1968; map drawn by M. Armstrutz, Newark, Delaware.

ern branch) meet, are three distinct sites that together were probably part of a ceremonial complex for the worship of Chaupiñamca. (See Figure 3.) One of these three sites was described by Max Uhle at the beginning of the twentieth century as the "shrine of Mamaq," and the other two nearby are clearly associated on the basis of surface collections made in 1968. The site described by Uhle is a collection of ceremonial platforms with associated architecture and terraces; the second is a housing complex slightly upriver; and the third consists of a set of mounds, still standing in 1968 but later destroyed to build a shoe factory.[86]

Slightly upstream from the junction that forms the Rímac, on the northern bank of the Santa Eulalia, stood four mounds built on an ancient floodplain. These mounds were the collapsed remains of four straightsided platforms built of river cobbles set in adobe mortar, on top of which were rectangular rooms and stone-lined storage pits, probably to receive offerings to the wak'a. A broken mortar stone stained with red ocher from years of grinding powder was a mute witness to the offerings made to the deity. Chaupiñamca, described in the tales of Huarochirí as a "rigid stone with five wings," was probably housed in a room on one of the platforms where her priests heard the requests of her petitioners and interpreted her replies—in which, as the people of Checa irreverently noted, she "sometimes lied." Broken bits of plain cooking pots and some decorated shards were scattered around the mounds, evidence of the food prepared for the wak'a and the ceremonial associated with her worship.

Upriver along the Chaclla is another complex. This site, visited by Max Uhle in 1902, is a series of finely worked terraces faced with fieldstone laid in adobe mortar and divided by a series of stone walls that run down the slope.[87] Stone-faced drainage canals cut the terraces, which are wide and high, each standing about two to three feet above the one below. There is no evidence on the surface that they were used for ceremonial purposes, although they may well have been drying platforms for coca or other agricultural products used for ritual. On the hillside above the terraces runs an *acequia*, or irrigation ditch, that brings water from miles upriver. A line of buildings faces a flat, plaza-like area just below the irrigation ditch, and higher on the hill slope are more rectangular buildings. The lower buildings are long rectangles divided internally into rooms; the higher ones, rectangular constructions about four to five feet wide, roofed with flat fieldstones. At least some of these rooms were probably used for storing the goods of the wak'a, brought to the complex as the fields dedicated to production for her worship were harvested. Others may well have been tombs that contained the mummies of important people or kurakas. Today these structures, so carefully built, stand completely empty.

Further upriver along the Chaclla, separated from the terraces on a stony alluvial fan, is another set of structures that form a large, complicated honeycomb of rooms, storage areas, and narrow passageways— much like a housing project. One large rectangular room stands at the front of the site, with many smaller rooms behind. The complex is built of angular fieldstone set in adobe mortar, and some of the walls still reach up to six feet or more in height and have holes at the top to receive wooden roof poles. The rooms have hard mud floors, and some of the walls show traces of having been plastered. The servants of the wak'a, the people who cultivated her fields and cared for her flocks, were evidently housed in this complex. The lack of the barracks-type construction for communal housing typical of Inca-period ceremonial sites, and the separate rooms capable of housing individual families, point to this being part of the shrine complex of one of the "great" wak'as.

Pottery found on all three sites clearly date them to the Inca period. Most of it is the undecorated cooking ware characteristic of Huarochirí, but there are fragments of fine pottery imitating Inca decorations and shape in both the housing complex and the ceremonial mounds, as well as a shard with a painted design found elsewhere only at Pachacamac.[88] Since little Cuzco pottery (real or imitation) has been found at local villages clearly dated to the Inca period, the presence of some here clearly links these sites to the state, as does the shard linked to Pachacamac on the coast, one of the most important wak'as in the empire and an important bulwark of state control until the civil wars that began with the death of the Inca Huayna Capac about 1528.

The three complexes together provide an example of the physical layout of an important shrine underwritten and expanded by the state. The three are in easy walking distance of one another, and there is plenty of land in between for cultivation by the resident population for its own support, the support of the wak'a, and that of the priests. The Inca rulers apparently did their best to gain and hold the good will of important wak'as and their priests, since the predictions of the wak'as could be either an important adjunct of state control or a dangerous center of opposition.

Another example of the care the state took with important regional deities is that of Pachacamac, who as we have noted was one of the most important wak'as in the Central Andes. Archaeological evidence indicates that the worship of Pachacamac is very old in the Andean world. The oracle had considerable influence in the period before the rise of the Inca state, and was apparently in some decline when the Incas reached the central coast. Pachacamac and his priests allied rapidly with the Incas, who reciprocated by making his worship one of the major cults of the coastal areas of the state. The narrator of the tales of Huarochirí noted that "in the communities of the lowlands, people adored Pachacamac, saying 'Thus the Inca ordered me.' "[89] It was said that when Pachacamac moved his head, the earth moved, and that if he ever turned his entire body, the universe would end. The shrine received gold and silver and llamas from the lowland communities, and from some highland areas as well.[90] However, in the highlands the Incas reinforced the worship of Pariacaca, the major deity of Huarochirí (equated by some scholars with the Thunder God of the Incas), and there is evidence of some competition between the two great wak'as of coast and highlands, Pachacamac and Pariacaca, mediated through the state. As long as the power of the wak'as could be used for the purposes of the state, the Inca had a highly valuable tool of social control, one that perhaps could be made to serve the police function more effectively than any secular group. But we cannot forget that the structure just depicted was not part of a state church on the provincial level. Here, too, as in the case of the kurakas and other basic mechanisms of local society, the expanding state sought to incorporate what was there and turn it to its own purposes. Local or regional deities that had already built up considerable authority were favored, and the wealth held by their priesthood increased by the gifts and favor of the Inca. Such gifts provided real reasons for the representatives of the deities to accept the Incas; but at the same time, the fact that the entire structure of local authority and tradition was left intact meant that local society could be mobilized against the Inca readily if there was sufficient incentive.

And the incentive was apparently there—at least enough to leave a record of local rebellions and risings that periodically threatened the control and the integrity of the state. John Murra has even suggested that the rapid expansion of the Inca state and the major rebellions that threatened it were both part of the same process,[91] that the real political organization of the state, as it expanded, was to a considerable degree the product of the need to deal with rebellions—first to defeat them, and second to ensure that the defeated rebels did not simply settle back to lick their wounds and recover for another try at autonomy. The evidence for this explanation of state organization is thin, but the hypothesis makes the achievements of the Incas a product of real needs and events without diminishing the accomplishments of the Inca political system.

Much attention has been drawn over the years to developments within Andean society that suggest the emergence of new relations of production in a culture essentially oriented around cooperative labor and corporate access to the productive resources of society and the distribution of its goods. The presence of the yana and aqlla retainers, men and women detached from their communities and assigned to the service of particular individuals or groups, suggests a tendency toward private access to productive labor on the part of particular privileged groups or lineages. Land was also assigned to such groups by the state. All of this evidence is limited and general; the number of people in these statuses was never large. But there is one event associated with a particular figure—the Inca Huayna Capac—very late in the history of the Inca state that does suggest the possible emergence of new positions or statuses in Andean society that with time might have pushed it to become quite different. This event—a long, hard-fought rebellion against Inca authority in the core of the Inca territories in the high puna of the south, a rebellion that lasted for over a decade—had repercussions throughout the state, leaving evidence of its impact in the myths of Huarochirí far to the north.

The most important product of that long rebellion was the conversion of at least some of the rebels, after their defeat, into a privileged military elite of the state. The Cañaris, after their defeat, were settled in the Yucay Valley near Cuzco, where they were assigned lands for their support while not on campaign with the Inca. These people, detached from their own lands and communities and reorganized by the victors, were more directly tied to the state than other groups governed by the Incas. Their kurakas, originally given their positions by the Inca, could be and were changed at his will, which gave rise to the later Spanish contention that the kurakas were merely the creatures of the state with no standing among their people except as they were backed by Inca armies. In 1570, one Pedro Astaco, whose father was a servant of T'upa Inca Yupanqui, told the Spaniards that T'upa Inca had made his father kuraka of a community but that Huayna Capac, T'upa Inca's successor, told the man "that he had spoken with the gods and . . . it was not convenient that he nor his kinsmen in his ayllu be kurakas, . . . and so the post was taken from him."[92]

The great rebellion, remembered in mythical form by the people of Huarochirí, apparently took place during the reign of T'upa Inca Yupanqui. "Three peoples rose: Alancuna, Calancu, Chaqui—so they were called. They no longer wanted to be men of the Inca. And they fought against him with thousands of warriors, for almost twelve years."[93] In order to defeat the rebels, the Inca called upon the wak'as throughout the state for their help. Pariacaca, principal wak'a of Huarochirí, sent his son Macahuisa, who killed all of the rebels, leaving only a few of the important men alive. The Inca, grateful for his aid, gave the wak'a his own litter in which to ride to battle—a mark of high favor to a warrior in Andean society.[94] Macahuisa herded the defeated rebels to Cuzco and presented them to the Inca, receiving in return the service and the increased offerings of the Inca, who agreed to become a "huacasa," or dancer, in the ceremonies held for Pariacaca. From the perspective of Huarochirí, the help they gave the Inca made their wak'a feared even by the Inca: " 'May he not destroy me,' and so thinking [the Inca] decided to offer [Macahuisa] whatever he wanted."[95]

The rebellions—with their concomitant expansion of gifts and service to the elites and the wak'as of the Inca's loyal allies—may well have been what led to changes in the structure of Inca military organization. The organization of groups such as the Cañaris, settled near Cuzco and freed of all service to the state when not on campaign, laid the basis for a permanent state military force outside the structure of mit'a service by local ethnic groups who fought in their own style with their own weapons and their own leaders. The need to integrate the ex-rebels in some way that would prove useful to the state may have provided the stimulus for this policy, whose ultimate product may well have been the establishment of a permanent military elite directly attached to the state. And there is some real evidence that these changes were in progress when the Spaniards entered the Andes.

Huayna Capac, the last of the independent Inca rulers, seems to have been credited by his people with the introduction of large-scale innovations in the organization of the state. He followed the resettlement of the Cañaris in the Yucay Valley with a far more massive project that involved the resettlement of a large population in the Cochabamba Valley in what

is today Bolivia. These people had been deported from their home territories by T'upa Inca Yupanqui following the defeat of the great rebellion;
T'upa Inca's successor settled some 14,000 of them in Cochabamba, assigning them lands to be cultivated for the support of the warriors they
provided. These groups were defined as mitmaq whose service consisted
in military activity. Each group was fed and supported by other members
of its society who cultivated the lands of the Cochabamba Valley for its
support. The whole operation was a state project that involved the displacement of the groups previously living in the valley and their replacement by mitmaq assigned by Huayna Capac.[96]

Huayna Capac was credited with being, as his people described him, a
yacha, defined as someone who understood agriculture and the tasks of
government. "Huayna Capac was a man who governed well and created
many fields and conquered many lands."[97] He was the administrator and
organizer who understood the economic as well as the political needs of
the state and moved to place it on a more solid foundation. All evidence
suggests that he drew upon traditional institutions such as the mitmaq,
transforming them in the process into institutions whose resemblance to
their predecessors was in name only. His reach extended to areas far beyond Cuzco; he appropriated new lands in areas already integrated into
the state for the production of particularly valued goods. In Huarochirí,
he took more lands in the coca fields of Quives for the production of the
valued leaf. His efforts inevitably brought him into conflict with his own
kinsmen, the members of the traditional Inca elite who provided military
and political leaders and had become accustomed to support from state
qollqas. There is one story of such conflict that suggests that Huayna Capac was at least temporarily blocked in his efforts to build up the prestige
and the ties to the state of his military favorites through traditional practices by the resistance of the traditional Inca lineages. According to the
story, Huayna Capac, angered at the flight of the Inca elite from a battle,
began to cut down the amount of the goods issued them from the royal
qollqas, first to once in ten days, and eventually to once a month, at the
same time offering feasts and banquets to the yanas serving in the fortress
of Sacsahuaman, who were his personal clients. The Inca elite, affronted,
took the image of the sun that was under its care and threatened to leave
the campaign and return to Cuzco. Without the presence of the wak'a on
the scene of battle the fortunes of the royal armies were threatened, and
Huayna Capac was forced to buy back the favor of his kinsmen with gifts
of maize, cumbi cloth, lands, and other fine goods.[98]

But such suggestive hints of growing contradictions between, on the
one hand, an Inca elite that saw itself as the rightful holders of state power and recipients of the largesse of their ruling member and, on the other,

new sectors that derived their support and position directly from the state are tantalizingly few. There is no evidence that the people of Huarochirí, despite their boasts of prowess in war, were freed from mit'a service to the state in return for their service in war. Most of the local regions, Huarochirí among them, seem to have been but little touched by the changes that began to develop in the state at the beginning of the sixteenth century. The conflicts that may well have been the product of Huayna Capac's efforts to rationalize and reorganize the state undoubtedly played a part in the struggle for succession that split the Inca territories after his death from smallpox shortly before the Spanish armies entered the Andes. It is tempting to see the civil war as at least in part a battle for supremacy between the most prestigious and powerful of the traditional Inca corporations in Cuzco, who backed Huascar, and Atahuallpa, leader of the larger contingent of the Inca armies in Quito and backed by some of the most powerful war captains in the army. Both of the contenders were credited with remarks or projects highly subversive to the existing social order. Huascar is said to have "discovered" that the dead—the mummies of past rulers whose descendants controlled the resources they had built up—held the best lands.[99] Atahuallpa, for his part, is said to have ordered the execution of all the people charged with remembering and repeating the Inca traditions, in order to reorganize the state and its institutions. But the delineation of the tensions in the fabric of Inca society lies outside the problem of a local society—despite the fact that the existence of such strains undoubtedly contributed to the success of the Spaniards.

From these limited suggestions, it can be inferred that the Inca state at the beginning of the sixteenth century was approaching some kind of internal crisis whose resolution demanded the expansion of the productive potential of Andean society in order to continue to expand the appropriation and use of labor by the Inca elite. Yet in 1532, despite the fact that the state was torn by dissension and war, the royal corporations, as well as the provincial kurakas and the wak'as throughout the empire, had little intimation of impending doom. They took sides in a succession conflict that for the first time affected all of the people ruled by the Inca state. And as the drama unfolded, they were largely unaware of the threat posed by a band of marauding raiders from the north.

FOUR

The Age of the Conquerors

I N LESS than three years, between 1531 and 1533, a small band of men under the command of Francisco Pizarro electrified all of Europe with their conquest of the richest society yet discovered in the Americas: the Inca state. In October 1533, the authorities in Panama wrote excitedly to Madrid that "the wealth and greatness of the provinces of Peru increase so greatly every day that it is becoming impossible to believe, and in truth, to those of us who are here and see it most closely, virtually within our reach, it seems a dream."[1]

The conquest of Peru began from Panama. In 1524, the Governor of Panama, Pedrarias de Avila, gave Francisco Pizarro, a captain and veteran of the Indies who had been in the New World since 1502, authority to explore and conquer toward the south. After a first unsuccessful expedition south along the Mosquito Coast, in which the insects took all the booty that was to be had, a second expedition reached the settled area of what is today northern Ecuador. The members of the expedition, most of them hungry and ill, holed up on Gallo Island off the coast of Colombia. Thirteen remained there through the winter while the rest went back to Panama. The pilot, Bartolomé Ruiz, returned a few months later, and the tiny group explored the coast by ship, penetrating the Inca Empire as far south as Tumbez. They soon met and captured a seagoing raft with a crew of twenty people. The cargo included objects of gold and silver and finely woven cloth of many colors. Pizarro also obtained two young boys from a coastal kuraka, whom he trained to become interpreters for the Spaniards in the conquest of their own society.[2]

From Panama, Pizarro went to Spain to obtain a legal basis for further action with the evidence of the rich lands lying to the south of the territory then held by Spain. He returned in 1530 with full authorization from the Crown to establish Spanish rule over the territory he had discovered and a title of governor and captain-general of the lands he conquered.

The Spanish Crown gave him full military command and direction of the enterprise, which contravened the terms of the partnership Pizarro had formed in Panama with a younger man, Diego de Almagro, whose anger at his exclusion almost ended the partnership. But relations were patched up, and the final expedition left for Peru from Panama in January 1531, with about 180–200 men and 30 horses. They disembarked on the coast of northern Ecuador, occupying a large settlement and sending their plunder in gold and silver objects back to Panama.[3]

The expedition, with reinforcements in men and horses, entered the Inca Empire early in 1532. The first Spanish settlement in Peru, San Miguel de Piura, was founded in August. There, the Spaniards learned about the war of succession that had broken out following the death of the Inca Huayna Capac. Following rumors that Atahuallpa, the contender who was then winning the civil war, was in the local capital in Cajamarca, the Spaniards moved into the highlands in search of him. They entered Cajamarca in November and requested a meeting with Atahuallpa. After an initial delay, the Inca agreed to the meeting, and with a small force of some several thousand men, mostly unarmed, he entered the square at Cajamarca to meet an ambush from the Spaniards hidden in the long buildings surrounding the square. The ambush went according tó Pizarro's plan and the Inca was taken prisoner while his troops, unable to move within the enclosed space when the horses charged directly into them, died by the thousands.

The capture of the Inca ruler and his death a year later at the hands of the Spaniards are generally taken as marking the Spanish conquest of the Andean area. If we are to choose a date for the conquest it is not a bad one, for the capture of Atahuallpa set in motion events that resulted in the elimination of the state system established by the Incas in the Andes. From 1532 on, it becomes impossible to deal with any area of the Andean world without taking into account the European presence. The Andes became part of an expanding Europe and, more specifically, of the Spanish Empire, the most powerful European political structure of the sixteenth century. But it would be very poor history to view the events of the early decades of the sixteenth century through the focus of the twentieth century, and assume the absolute victory of the Europeans and their total control over Andean society simply because, centuries later, the relationship between European and Andean societies was one characterized by the almost total domination of the Indians by the Europeans.

From the 1530's to the 1580's, the two cultures, Andean and European, were in conflict. The Spaniards, in a series of daring moves that have captured the imagination of people through the centuries, replaced the Inca and made themselves the masters of a state structure that, by the 1530's, was itself in crisis. But the dominance of the Europeans in the Andes was a surface phenomenon, not penetrating deeply into Andean culture or social relationships for decades. The Spanish invaders were at first content to ride the surface of Andean society, supported by the local communities whom they permitted—in fact encouraged—to maintain the social relationships of production and the political structures evolved over centuries. The Spaniards did not even, in most cases, seek to interfere much with the administrative structures established by the Inca rulers. They used those structures and profited by them, absorbing the flow of labor and the products of that labor that had once gone to the Inca state.

But within a few decades of the first Spaniards' arrival in the Andes, floods of their countrymen eager for a part in the spoils of conquest joined them, and the fundamental differences in the two societies—European and Andean—began to put a severe strain on the entire system of domination. For Andean society functioned according to a pattern of social relationships that organized both productive labor and political integration. On the local level, at least, the maintenance of the Andean system depended upon a pattern of reciprocal interchange that, albeit definitely hierarchical and unequal, was based upon the acceptance of the established patterns by the great masses of the population. But though the Europeans found much in Andean society that was externally similar to their own—the emphasis upon hierarchy and status, and their close link to the exercise of authority on both the local and the state level, for example—the societies themselves were quite different. European culture, organized around commodity production and an expanding market economy, was rapidly moving toward a social structure in which social position was closely related to material wealth, which in turn was tied to the accumulation of precious metals. The role of the areas outside of Europe in the process of primitive accumulation that preceded and laid the basis for the rise of capitalism has been overemphasized, but the wealth garnered from other parts of the world from the sixteenth to the eighteenth centuries in the form of both open plunder and mercantile profits was considerable. That process was just beginning in the sixteenth century, but it expanded steadily in the centuries that followed, and as it developed it altered the entire structure of the societies of the non-European areas. And the seeds of that transformation were present in the 1530's, for the clash of the two cultures was a clash not only of productive systems but of the entire complex of law and custom that structured social relations and defined the patterns of distribution and access to goods and resources.

That clash from the conquest to the end of the 1560's is the subject of the pages that follow. These four decades constitute a clearly defined period of crisis in the Andes and in Europe as well. For the sake of definition, I have dubbed this period "the age of the plunder economy"—a period characterized by the outright expropriation of the products of the communities in which the Spaniards established themselves. Both the political and the economic relationships of this period were founded upon extra-economic forms of coercion, sometimes thinly veiled in legal rhetoric and sometimes openly revealed and even stated. The aim of the Spaniards who entered Peru in 1532 was straightforward and simple, and that of those who followed was hardly more complex, if often phrased in more complicated ways. The driving force of the rapid Spanish expansion in the Americas was the search for wealth—wealth that could be traded for rank and position in contemporary Spanish society. The Spanish conquerors were essentially pirates: organized gangs of men who, under a thin cover of legality that consisted of little more than titles of authority over the unknown drawn up in Madrid or wherever the royal court happened to be, robbed and plundered in search of the precious metals that were in short supply in the rapidly expanding European economy.

Once in control of the vast new territories they occupied, they divided up the native population and, under that same thin cover of legality, systematically built up their wealth and position on the basis of the massive exploitation of the population. Renamed "Indians" by their conquerors, the native peoples were forced to provide their new masters with goods and labor. Over the long run, they were made into a servile labor force at the command of the members of European society. But that process took a long time, for it meant much more than the short-term plunder of accumulated resources and the extraction of labor through open force. The structures and the institutions of Andean society itself, at first used by Spaniards who acted as if they could replace the defeated Inca rulers and receive the surplus appropriated by the Incas without conforming to the social institutions of Andean society, were gradually distorted, modified, and transformed. But for now, let us return to the problem of the "short run" and take a closer look at the relations of the conquest period and the economic and political sources of the crisis that emerged in the Andean world by the 1560's. The resolution of that crisis set the terms of the process of change in the Andes for the following two and a half centuries.

In the preceding chapters I have attempted to lay a foundation for understanding the reactions of the members of Andean society to the Europeans, a focus that I will return to in the second half of this book. But the relation between conquered and conqueror, or colonized and colonizer, can never be understood by looking at one side alone. And to understand the relationship between Spaniard and Indian in the conquest period, we must also take a look at the basic assumptions and relationships of the society from which the conquerors came.

The men who arrived in the Andes in 1533 were for the most part not fresh from Europe. Many had lived for years in the Americas and acquired habits and relationships in the course of years of exploration and conquest in a land new to them. Over half of the men present at the capture of Atahuallpa had been in America for five years or more.[4] Francisco Pizarro himself was in Central America by 1509, and by the 1520's had long experience in jungle fighting along the coast there. The men of the Indies were eminently practical and loyal to one another, for their lives depended upon their companions. But as has been amply demonstrated, the colonizer is at heart a conservative, living in terms of his own society wherever he is and toting the baggage of his own culture with him to new places. And the baggage of the men from Spain in the Americas was made up of the values and the motivations of Iberian society at the end of the Middle Ages and in the early stages of the growth of the modern state system. The Spain from which men left for the Indies was a highly aristocratic society, dominated by the power and the values of the great noble families built during the Reconquista, the conquest of the Spanish peninsula from the Arab principates established in the land in the eighth century.[5] The Catholic kings expanded rapidly toward the south of Spain in the thirteenth century. The conquest of Moslem territories opened vast areas of land for Spanish occupation. The monarchs assured their control over the land and the security of their new frontiers against the Moorish principates by assigning vast areas of the new conquests to the military orders organized in the course of the Reconquest.

These orders became the owners of huge territories administered in a fashion similar to the feudal tenure through which the Catholic monasteries in other areas of Europe administered their estates. The further expansion of the Catholic territories laid the basis of the great nobility of Castile, particularly in the region of Andalusia in the south of Spain. The Spanish kings assigned huge areas in lordly concessions that gave the rising nobility control of vast expanses of land. By the fourteenth and fifteenth centuries, the aristocratic families had become so powerful that they virtually controlled the royal family itself. The introduction of Merino sheep from Africa in the fourteenth century assured their power. The expansion of the wool trade with northern Europe led most of them to turn their vast estates into sheep runs. The profits from the wool trade assured the favor of the monarchy, which gave liberal concessions to the powerful sheepherders' guild, the Mesta, guaranteeing the right of way of the sheep herds across the land without regard for the devastation they brought to farms and crops.

By the late fifteenth century, two or three percent of the population of Castile owned 97 percent of the land, and over half of that 97 percent belonged to a handful of the great families. Sixty-two noble houses in the Kingdom of Castile controlled the vast majority of the lands and the wealth of the kingdom.[6] These great families were not liable to taxation by the Crown. Only the towns could be called upon for financial contributions, and without the need to participate in order to defend its wealth, the great nobility gradually lost its political influence and the representative bodies of the late Middle Ages, the Cortes, declined steadily. The growth of royal authority in the Spanish kingdoms in the fifteenth and sixteenth centuries did effectively marginalize the great nobility from political power, but the monarchy never challenged the social and economic predominance of the great families. The Spanish royal houses were themselves a part of the great nobility, tied to the noble families by kin ties that made a reality of the common form of address—cousin—used by members of the upper nobility to the monarch.

In the long process of the Reconquest, the values of the nobility became the standard of the society. The war against the Moorish principates was carried out by men who built their social and economic position on conquest; their values were those of a warrior band bent upon plunder and power over people. The traditional ideals of the feudal nobility were part of the ideals and ambitions of the members of Spanish society in the later Middle Ages. The Moorish principates, settled societies built upon skilled agriculture, with an urban culture built upon the development of skilled artisanry and some of the finest scientific and intellectual achievements of the period, were tempting prizes for those who had the strength to conquer and to hold them. The Moorish lands provided the fine steel swords that eventually conquered them; they developed the urban centers, the seaports, and the navigational techniques that were readily adopted by the expanding warrior societies from the north. For the elite of the north, it was control over the lands and the population of the newly conquered lands that made their fortunes; the values that meant success were those of land and vassals. The Black Death of the fourteenth century somewhat altered this equation. As people died and lands lay vacant, the Spanish nobility shifted from men to sheep, turning their newly vacant lands into the immense sheep runs that made their fortunes. But the ideals of the nobility remained constant: ideals that can be summarized in the Spanish term *hidalguía*—the life-style and the ambitions of the person of good family, the "son of something" (*hijo d'algo*), whose role in the system was to expand the power of the monarch as a function of his own power, founding his own fortunes on conquered lands and men in the service of the king.

Spanish society was in a process of rapid transformation during the fifteenth and sixteenth centuries, but the values of the *hidalgo* remained the principal standards of the society. The hidalgo built his fortune through his great deeds in battle, founding or ennobling his own lineage by his accomplishments. The social structure of late medieval Spain, particularly Castile, was not rigidly fixed. The nobility ranged from the monarch himself to the great families, closely tied to the monarch by consanguineal as well as affinal relations, on to the *caballeros* or hidalgos, the lower ranks of the men of good family, who themselves graded into the upper ranks of the commoners, professionals without titles or family connections. The nobility itself was by no means a rigidly defined group before the sixteenth century. The monarch steadfastly supported his allies, and as Spain moved toward a dominant position in Europe and world power as the ruler of an overseas empire, the alliance of Crown and nobility and the values of the noble class became a fixed principle of Spanish society. That alliance was reflected in specific decrees that gave fixed form to the nobility. In 1505, the Crown confirmed and extended the right of the nobility to entail its property, ensuring the immense landholdings against fragmentation. In 1520, the Spanish aristocracy was organized in a fixed hierarchy of rank, beginning at the top with the *grandes* of Spain—25 great lords from the oldest and wealthiest families of Castile and Aragon.[7] But this system, which protected the position of the great families as families, condemned the younger sons of the nobility to seek their own fortunes, since they were barred from the titles and the estates of their families by the entails.

The growing rigidity of the nobility as a class provided an inexhaustible source of recruits for the socially acceptable professions: the military, the Church, or the growing state bureaucracy. But consistent with the values of their class, members of even the lowest ranks of the nobility viewed their professional activities as service to the Crown that deserved reward. And the rewards sought were those commensurate with the position of the nobility: local power in the form of permanent membership in the town councils of their home cities; lands and income to feed and maintain large retinues of kinsmen and clients.

The lower ranks of the nobility were fed not only from above but also from below. The expansion of the Spanish wool trade from the thirteenth century, followed by the plunder that began to flow from the Americas at the end of the fifteenth century and the beginning of the sixteenth, enriched many people who were ready and willing to exchange a part of their wealth for the privileges and social position that went with a title. Ferdinand and Isabella began to create new hidalgos liberally in the fifteenth century, and by the 1520's the privileges of hidalguía were being freely offered for sale despite numerous complaints.[8]

Entry into the noble class and the right to put the coveted title of "don" before a person's name were not empty honors in the fifteenth and sixteenth centuries. The legal perquisites and protections attaching to nobility were considerable: a noble could not be tortured or condemned to the galleys; criminal charges against him could not be judged by local officials; he could not be imprisoned for debt; his houses, arms, or horses could not be seized by judicial authorities; and finally, he could not be taxed. A hidalgo enjoyed a kind of legal immunity that could be put to highly profitable use in the search for wealth sufficient to meet the demands of position. A proverb of uncertain origin but accurate insight repeated in Latin America during the period of colonial rule described a title as equivalent to a zero. Alone, it was worth nothing, but combined with money, it multiplied the value of anything placed in front of it. The cynicism of the proverb, whatever its actual provenance, fits the mood of the sixteenth century, with its inflation of titles and scramble for the wherewithal to obtain them.[9]

The values of hidalguía were predominant in the men who came to the Americas in the years following the first voyages of Christopher Columbus, as well as in the 1530's and 1540's when the Spaniards entered the Andes. Somewhat less than a quarter of the men present at the capture of Atahuallpa could call themselves "don" in 1533, and none of these came from the great families of Spain.[10] But all of them shared the values and the ambitions of the hidalgo class to which they aspired. They, and the floods of people who followed them to Peru, hoped to amass a fortune by force of arms, and trade it with the Crown for a reward that matched what they regarded as their service to the monarch in adding new lands and vassals to his patrimony. And for the first generation of the conquerors that was true: in the 1560's, the men present at the capture of Atahuallpa who were still living were indisputably the upper nobility of Peru. Moreover, members of the nobility came to Peru in increasing numbers after the first years, often as part of the household entourage of officials sent from Spain, and all of them expected to be rewarded in accord with their social rank at home. Their social position and the important positions they occupied in the new kingdom overseas firmly fixed the aristocratic values developed in Spain at the summit of Spanish colonial society.

But another important, although often ignored, figure in Spanish overseas society in the sixteenth century was the merchant-trader. Though the men who came to the Indies to seek their fortune and social position subscribed firmly to the concept of a society led by an aristocracy supported by income from land and vassals, they saw no contradiction between the values of hidalguía and active participation in commerce.[11] As the kingdoms of Castile and Aragon expanded in the thirteenth and fourteenth centuries, they gradually incorporated the thriving ports of the Mediterranean and the international commercial center of Seville. The Spain of the late fifteenth and sixteenth centuries was a society based heavily upon the trader and the merchant, but the activities of those early entrepreneurs in no way threatened the social predominance of the nobility. The merchant may have heralded the growth of capitalism, but he was neither a capitalist nor did he necessarily signify the emergence of a new class. Trade and conquest fit together neatly in the early period of European expansion.

The beginning of trade with the Americas tied Seville closely to the rapidly expanding overseas possessions of the Crown and linked merchant and conqueror in the American enterprise. Despite the alleged antagonism between nobility and traders, the great noble families took quick advantage of the opportunity to increase their wealth presented by exploration and settlement overseas. They financed at least some of Columbus's expeditions and advanced capital to merchants outfitting ships to send to the Indies in exchange for a percentage of the gains. Active participation in trade—rather than the role of the investor—was reserved for the most part to the lesser nobility, but a man who used his opportunities in America to buy and sell in the course of accumulating a fortune raised no adverse comment.[12] A fortune made in trade was frequently used to buy a title of hidalguía and enter the nobility, thus assuring social position and legal protection. The search for an income sufficient to join the nobility never impeded people from active participation in commerce, and the search for profits through mercantile activities became characteristic of the men of the Indies and Spanish society in the Americas in general. But trade, like conquest, was a mechanism for the accumulation of wealth, a means to gain the income that could be used to buy social status. Accumulated mercantile fortunes bought titles and land and entailed estates to maintain family status and position. The values of the noble class were shared by the people who dealt in merchandise; making money never undermined the predominance of the aristocracy in Spain.

In the Indies, plunder and commerce were two elements of the same search for quick wealth and social position. The expeditions that explored and took possession of the new lands in the Americas were private enterprises organized for personal gain. The men who joined an expedition "invested" their persons and equipment in the enterprise; the goods appropriated in the course of their operations were distributed among them in proportion to their initial investment and their participation. The Crown granted the right to undertake an expedition to designated leaders who petitioned for that authority, carefully reserving specific rights and incomes for itself. The agreements concluded between the prospective leader of an expedition and the Crown, usually called *capitulaciones* (capitulations), specifically reserved to the Crown the legal authority over any territory claimed in its name as well as the royal fifth—a tax of one-fifth of all plunder taken on the expedition. Since the Crown rarely provided any financial assistance to the operation, the bargaining was usually hard and the expedition leader came away with extensive authority.

In the initial period of the conquest of the Inca state, the objective was openly and frankly the appropriation of treasure. The members of the expedition outfitted themselves at their own expense, buying their horses if they joined as horsemen as well as their arms and equipment. Pizarro contracted for the ships and other supplies, paying for them from his own income or taking out loans against expected plunder.[13] The protocompany that was the expedition to Peru was financially a gamble; many similar expeditions brought little besides illness and defeat for the warrior-entrepreneurs. But Pizarro had some advance information from the earlier expeditions, as well as some real luck in the capture of Atahuallpa. That capture presented an opportunity to regain the initial investment of the company with interest. In an effort to regain his freedom, the Inca Atahuallpa offered to collect a ransom of a room filled with gold and silver as high as he could reach. The Spaniards agreed, and while Atahuallpa sent messengers throughout the state to collect gold and silver objects, respecting only the property of the mummies of past Inca rulers guarded by their clans, the Spaniards settled in Cajamarca to wait for the treasure, uncertain what to do with their dangerous and powerful captive if and when he met the ransom. His half brother and rival in the civil war, Huascar, was already dead, killed by Atahuallpa's forces at his order. The war for succession was over—or would have been if it had not been for Francisco Pizarro.

The ransom was collected and melted down into bars of gold and silver by the spring of 1533. At the same time, the Spaniards condemned Atahuallpa to death on the basis of rumors that he was organizing his forces in the field to move against the Spaniards; they thus removed a figure whose presence had become steadily more inconvenient to them. The treasure of Cajamarca totaled more than 1.5 million pesos when it was melted down.[14] After the traditional "royal fifth" was set aside for the king, the remainder was divided into shares and distributed among the men. The share of the plunder that fell to a horseman in the distribution of the treasure was some 90 pounds of gold and 180 of silver. The share of a foot soldier was about half that amount, and Pizarro himself took thirteen shares.[15] The initial investment in the expedition paid off in 1533 beyond the wildest dreams of everyone in the Americas, and sparked a rush of men to Peru in the hope of making their fortunes.

But plunder alone, no matter how great, was not the objective of the leaders of conquest expeditions. These men sought to establish new realms, new political entities under their ultimate supervision and command. In the medieval tradition, they aimed at both wealth and authority. The capitulations between the Crown and Pizarro gave the latter the rank of governor and captain-general of all territories that he conquered; he was to enjoy the full prerogatives of government, including military authority and the right to grant land and assign vassals, and he was to be responsible for organizing the institutions of Spanish society in the newly claimed lands on the model of the Reconquest and the fifteenth-century Spanish expansion into the Canary Islands. Pizarro had no intention of grabbing the plunder and running for Spain. He was not a raider, but a prospective governor whose objectives included the administration of men and women and the organization of law and justice, defined in terms of Spanish medieval tradition.

Pizarro's initial problem, however, was to win a land and people to govern, and the war of succession in the Inca state provided him with an opportunity that he used to full advantage by presenting himself as an ally of the defeated lineages of Cuzco aligned with the dead Huascar. He received delegations of kurakas while he held Atahuallpa captive in Cajamarca. These delegations, called to the presence of the Inca, seized the opportunity to offer gifts to the Spaniards, shrewdly playing both sides of a situation that might offer considerably greater autonomy and aggrandizement for themselves and their people than was possible under the Inca system.[16] Pizarro acted in the time-honored tradition of the heroes of the Reconquest, receiving the allegiance of all in this complicated game of strategy played not only by the Inca clans but by the more ambitious kurakas of the ethnic groups of the state as well.

Pizarro kept up the fiction of Spanish interest in the Inca civil war by crowning as Inca a kinsman of Atahuallpa, T'upa Huallpa, who occupied the royal *tiana* or throne for a little more than two months before he died suddenly in Jauja, perhaps from illness, perhaps poisoned.[17] From the early days in Cajamarca, Pizarro gained native allies who remained staunchly loyal to the Spaniards throughout the conquest and the subsequent wars between the Spaniards themselves. It is not easy to understand this loyalty, unless the ethnic groups that joined the Spaniards had some hopes of freeing themselves from Inca authority and appropriating lands and plunder for themselves in the service of their new allies. The Huanca peoples of Jauja, for example, who allied firmly with the Spaniards from the time of the execution of Atahuallpa, had chosen the wrong side in the wars of succession and had only Atahuallpa's revenge to look forward to when the Spaniards entered the Andes.[18]

The support of their Andean allies was crucial to the Spaniards' success. The Huancas provided Pizarro with warriors, provisions, and services of all kinds, which both groups supplemented with plunder from the state storehouses. The Spaniards left Cajamarca for Cuzco in August of 1533 in the company of over 3,000 Huanca warriors led by their own kurakas and served by additional men and women carrying supplies and provisions. The army reached Jauja in about two months, where they were welcomed and feasted by their allies, and where Pizarro declared the Andean ethnic capital a Spanish municipality—the legal basis of local authority in Iberian culture. In October, the force moved on for Cuzco, leaving a small contingent under the royal treasurer, Riquelme, to hold Jauja and guard the treasure left behind by the Spaniards. En route to Cuzco they were attacked twice by warriors who learned from earlier encounters to move against the Spaniards only after they had exhausted their horses in the high, steep areas of the Andes. The Spaniards narrowly escaped defeat on those occasions, but finally entered Cuzco on November 15, 1533, and were well received by the Inca clans inside the city. They rapidly settled in; Pizarro founded a Spanish municipality in the city and the Europeans turned to the plunder of the Inca ceremonial capital. A second melting and distribution of treasure took place in March 1534.[19]

At this distance, it is difficult to understand why the Inca clans permitted the looting of their capital and the atrocities that have been so often described in narrative histories of the conquest of Peru.[20] But looting and plunder were an accepted part of warfare in the Andes as elsewhere. Pizarro had his native allies, themselves eager for looting and revenge, and he also continued to rely upon the fiction of alliance with the Inca clans in their competition for control of the state. No longer in need of support from the factions far away in Quito that had once backed Atahuallpa, Pizarro next backed a kinsman of Huascar, Manco Inca, who had hidden from Atahuallpa's warriors and presented himself to the Spaniards as they reached Cuzco. Pizarro's choice satisfied the Inca clans in Cuzco, who received the Spaniards into the capital as allies and liberators. For them, the civil war ended in their favor when the Spaniards entered Cuzco. Manco was crowned Inca in an elaborate ceremony carried out in the traditional manner, with only the addition of a short oath of allegiance and submission to the Spanish Crown, after which Manco and Pizarro joined forces to pursue the warriors of Quito who had withdrawn and were threatening Jauja and other provinces that had allied with Cuzco on their way north. The siege of Jauja was finally raised in 1534 and the city relieved by the combined Spanish-Inca force from Cuzco.

Jauja was the initial capital of Pizarro's still nebulous territory; but seeing the vulnerability of a capital deep in the heartland of the state he meant to replace, Pizarro determined to move his capital to the coast, where ships bringing goods, news, and reinforcements if necessary could reach him easily. He sent out parties to determine a proper site, and in

December 1534 the Spaniards moved to the coast. The city of Lima, officially named "the City of the Kings," or Los Reyes, was founded in January 1535.

From the time he landed in Peru, Pizarro clearly regarded himself as the governor and supreme authority of a constituted government that only lacked a population to rule. In the context of events in the Andes in 1533 and 1534, his actions seem grandiose and out of scale, but they were the moves of a medieval leader who expected to become a great lord by conquest, replacing the Inca ruler and using the established state system as the basis of his own political authority. It hardly seems possible that a gang of only slightly more than a hundred men could have expected to exercise the enormous authority over specific groups of people that Pizarro delegated to them as part of the spoils of war in 1533, when most of the Inca state was as yet barely aware of the existence of the Spaniards, let alone of the supreme authority they claimed for themselves. And at least until 1535, Pizarro himself did not push the point with the Inca ruling class. In the early months at least, the Spaniards must have appeared to the warring Andean factions as little more than a particularly able warrior group that, like themselves, was maneuvering to gain the most it could from the war of succession that split the state. Alliance with one or another Inca faction in the hope of ultimate gain was something the other ethnic groups in the Inca state could understand perfectly, for they practiced it. The more extreme objective of shouldering aside all factions and taking over political control of the state itself might have been harder to comprehend, but to people who could remember their own conquest, the concept does not seem to have been so difficult. Years later, the Huanca kuraka of Jauja noted that his father had urged Pizarro to do just that when he met him with gifts in Cajamarca following the capture of Atahuallpa.[21]

Pizarro initially chose to maintain the fiction of Spanish support for the Inca state, backing first T'upa Huallpa and then Manco Inca for the royal throne. But the fiction rapidly wore thin, in part because the conquerors continued their search for plunder without limit, and in part because their numbers were rapidly swelled by more Spaniards seeking their fortunes in the new rich land. As the first group of the conquerors returned to Spain in 1533 and 1534, carrying immense wealth, word of their feat spread like wildfire. The first eyewitness reports of the conquest, by Cristóbal de Mena and Francisco de Jérez, were read and translated and read again. In October 1533, an official in Panama reported that "the numbers and quantity of people mobilizing to pass through these parts en route to the provinces of Peru are so numerous and so sudden that here we have not been able to provide for them."[22] Early in 1534, an authority in Panama informed the Crown that "here everyone is up in arms about leaving for Peru, and if Your Majesty does not send authority to restrain people, . . . this province will be entirely deserted."²³ A few days later, the authorities in Santo Domingo wrote anxiously that "with the enormous news of the riches of Peru, we are hard put to stop the people of this island and even of all the surrounding areas . . . because all the people are aroused with plans to go to that land."²⁴ The officials in Puerto Rico added that "with the news from Peru, not a citizen would remain if he were not tied down."²⁵ The gold rush was on.

As Spaniards seeking quick riches poured into Peru, the Andean population began to have second thoughts about its unmanageable allies. Pizarro, abundantly aware of the vulnerable position of his forces, a small band in a population of millions, ordered that the native people be respected and well treated, but his orders were ignored. Manco, struggling to reestablish state authority while the Spaniards raided and plundered, finally decided to rid himself of his onetime allies. In the spring of 1536, Inca forces rose throughout Peru in response to messages from the Inca to his kinsmen serving as governors and royal representatives in other parts of the Andes. The Spaniards estimated that the Inca force that attacked and besieged Cuzco consisted of from 100,000 to 200,000 men. The first attack was almost successful, and the Indians besieged the city for more than four months, cutting Cuzco off from all contact with the coast. Other forces were sent down to the coast to attack Lima. Pizarro sent desperate messages back to Panama pleading for help; in July 1536, the authorities in Panama reported to Santo Domingo that "the rebellion of Cuzco has spread from province to province and [the Indians] continue to rise in rebellion; rebel chiefs will soon be within forty leagues [about 120 miles] of the City of the Kings [Lima]."²⁶ The siege of Lima was not broken until August, when Manco's troops, no longer maintained by the vast system of state storehouses, began to drift off to prepare their fields for planting.

Contact between Cuzco and Lima was not reestablished until the spring of 1537, when the Indians witnessed the outbreak of civil war between the Spaniards. Diego de Almagro, Pizarro's erstwhile partner, returned from an expedition to Chile and claimed Cuzco as his share of the conquest according to the partition made between the two partners by the Crown. Outside Cuzco, Manco's warriors were treated to the sight of the Spaniards fighting among themselves as Pizarro attacked Almagro's forces in Cuzco and summarily executed his partner on a charge of treason. Even though the Andean warriors were forced to withdraw, Manco was encouraged by the dissension among the Spaniards, and sent forces north to raid and harrass the tribes who had allied with the Spaniards. Inca warriors raided Jauja, destroying wak'as and burning villages and settlements.

After the seige of Cuzco was broken, Manco and the remainder of his forces withdrew into the eastern part of the Andes, establishing a capital-in-exile in the broken jungle region that slopes gradually down to the Amazon Basin. From there, his warriors continued to harass both the Spaniards and the local population that had submitted to Spanish rule.[27] Travelers had to move about in Peru under armed guard. Villages were raided and burned by the Inca warriors on reprisal raids. In their capital in Vilcabamba, Manco and his warriors attempted to reproduce the entire panoply of the Inca court in miniature. The Spaniards, on the other hand, dropped the façade of Inca rule; Pizarro openly took control of what remained of the Inca state system, declaring Manco a rebel against royal authority. Without attempting to create a new puppet Inca, Pizarro chose Manco's brother, Paullu, as the loyal Inca now demoted to noble rather than royal status, and settled some of the Inca's estates in Cuzco on him. The members of the Inca clans became a native nobility, subject to the Spanish Crown under Pizarro's authority.

The story of the defeat of Cuzco, tragic and vivid as it was, in fact explains little more than the fate of Cuzco itself. The real consolidation of Spanish authority in the Andes was a slow process in which the leaders of distinct ethnic groups made their own choices during the short but violent period after the appearance of the Spaniards in Cajamarca. In the case of Huarochirí, which lay a little ways off the main Inca road from Quito to Cuzco, the story of the conquest does not look at all the way it looks in the capital. The pacification of the province, a traditional source of Inca warriors loyal to Cuzco, was initiated from Jauja, the Inca administrative center for Huarochirí and temporary capital of Francisco Pizarro's Spanish Peru. A small expedition of horsemen under the command of Hernando de Soto and Diego de Agüero was sent into the region in 1534, shortly before the Spanish capital was moved to the coast. The Spaniards were met by warriors from the province who, as the story was remembered years later by the Europeans, were routed by the horsemen; many captives were taken, among them daughters sent by the dead Inca Huayna Capac as wives for the kurakas of the province.[28]

The people of Huarochirí, once defeated, submitted to the traditional looting and plunder that had been part of their own history before the rise of the Inca state, and was undoubtedly as familiar to them as it was to the Spaniards. In every province the Spaniards entered in the process of establishing some control over each part of the Inca state in turn, their first objective was treasure. They seized the possessions of the wak'as and appropriated the major stores of precious metal that proclaimed social position and honor in Andean society, turning them into bars of metal that bought grants of hidalguía and pensions from the Crown.

The Spanish entry into Huarochirí was remembered by the people not so much for the Europeans' military exploits as for their greed. Stories of the Spaniards' demands for treasure and their pursuit and torture of the local priests and guardians of the property of the wak'as during the early years of the conquest were remembered and retold throughout the sixteenth century, becoming part of local traditions. According to these traditions, the priests gave the first warning of the Europeans. One of the 30 priests of Pariacaca saw danger in the entrails of a sacrificial llama and warned the people, saying, "the world is not well, nor its entrails, brothers. Not much time will pass before our father Pariacaca becomes silent and savage." The priest was reviled and attacked by the others for his prediction, but "a few days after this dispute, they all heard the notice: the *huiracochas* [Spaniards] have arrived in Cajamarca."[29]

When the Spaniards reached Huarochirí, they demanded of the priests of Pariacaca, "Where are the silver and the clothing of this wak'a?" When they found no treasure, they seized the priests, among them the man who had first given the warning, Caxalliuya. "Then the Spaniards, furious, rapidly lit a fire with some dry weeds. They decided to burn Caxalliuya. The wind rose when the fire began to climb up Caxalliuya's body. The man suffered and suffered; the others handed over to the Spaniards all that they asked, and so it was."[30] The rapid attack of the horsemen on Huarochirí and the torture of the priests of provincial wak'as had the desired effect: defeated, the kurakas of Huarochirí submitted to Spanish rule, and, according to the traditions, "after this, everyone exclaimed 'Brothers, let us disperse. The world is no longer good,' and thus they dispersed throughout all the settlements."[31]

I have argued earlier that the Inca state itself was not a monolithic, centralized structure, but a relatively decentralized system in which Cuzco stood at the head of a structure of regional administrative capitals headed by Inca governors formally appointed by the Inca and exercising broad authority. These local leaders were members of the Inca clans with political and dynastic interests of their own that were likely to emerge at times of political stress such as a contested succession. Though this hypothesis awaits confirmation or rebuttal, it makes it easier to comprehend how the state at its highest level in Cuzco could disintegrate in the short period from the coronation of Manco Inca in 1534 to the replacement of the Inca by open European rule following Manco's revolt a year later without a concomitant disintegration of the sociopolitical organization of Andean society on the level of the Inca province or the ethnic group. At the lower levels, the impact of the Spanish presence, at least initially, was largely limited to raids for plunder—the first massive expropriation of the accumulated goods of Andean society.

From the capture of Atahuallpa in 1533, the Spaniards robbed and looted freely as they moved south toward Cuzco. Plunder was as much the prerogative of Andean as of European warriors, and the native allies of the Spaniards also took their share of the goods stored by the state in its warehouses in Cuzco and elsewhere. But the values of the two societies were not the same. The Andean societies shared with the Europeans the equation of rank and position with status goods, particularly fine cloth and jewelry. Their revenge against the Inca state took the form of looting traditional status goods and, in extreme cases, the destruction of wak'as and their accumulated treasure. But war in the Andean tradition, though destructive of property and even life, was not a mechanism for unlimited destruction of goods and resources. The Spaniards indulged their tastes during the first years of the conquest by wanton destruction of the goods and resources of Andean society—for example, the llama herds protected by the decrees of the Andean state. Animals were slaughtered in huge numbers to obtain the neck and tongue, regarded as delicacies, while the rest of the carcass was left to rot.[32]

Quantitative estimates of the impact of the Europeans upon Andean society during these initial years of largely unrestricted plunder are extremely difficult to make. The looting that accompanies war and conquest in most social systems is by its nature unrecorded and unspecified. But in the case of the Andean area, the emphasis placed upon keeping a record of local resources has provided a means to evaluate the looting of these early years, in the form of a record kept by the quipucamayoq of the Huancas, the loyal Jauja allies of the Spaniards from 1533. The leaders of the Huancas kept careful accounts of their services to the Europeans, and in 1561 presented them to the Spanish courts in support of their claim for specific privileges and restitutions.[33]

Since Andean society depended heavily upon the labor of all members of the tribal groups composing it to produce foodstuffs and other needed goods, an estimate of the labor power absorbed by service to the Spaniards provides an index of the damage caused by the initial plunder of the conquest. The province of Jauja at the time of the conquest was reported to have 27,000 warriors.[34] This category, equivalent to the first group of the Inca census categories, was described by Huaman Poma de Ayala as "valiant men, soldiers," between the ages of 25 and 50—in other words, adult male heads of households. The Spaniards took thousands of these men and additional women with them in the march to Cuzco as warriors, bearers, and servants. Over 3,600 warriors accompanied the Spaniards to Cuzco, to Lima, and into the provinces between 1533 and the Inca rebellion in 1536. Some 5,000 more men and some women accompanied the Spaniards to carry provisions and booty, build fortifications, repair bridges, and otherwise maintain the fighting forces.[35] If these numbers are compared to the fighting forces available at the time of the conquest, it appears that nearly one third of the total adult male population of Jauja left the province in the company of the Europeans between 1533 and 1548. Many of these men died in battle. All but a few hundred never returned to their homes.

The great storehouses maintained by the state in Jauja also supplied the Spaniards. The Spaniards left in Jauja during the entry into Cuzco, and those who later made the area their residence, plundered these storehouses to the point that the Huancas introduced a new category into their lists of objects given the Europeans: "*rancheados*," or "plundered items." They took large amounts of fine cloth, sandals, jars, and other items. Between 1533 and 1536, the Huancas lost, according to their own records, some 22,453 *fanegas* of maize and thousands of jars and bowls.[36] In those same three years, the Huancas claimed the loss of 24,582 llamas, some 10 percent of the estimated carrying capacity of the Jauja Valley for llamas.[37] More goods, including blankets and cloth, were burned in the civil wars among the Spaniards.

But outright plunder cannot become the basis of a sociopolitical system that permits a ruling group to extract surplus from those it rules over a period of time. At a remove of several centuries, we tend to overrate the effect that new weaponry and military technology can have upon people lacking them. Terror is ephemeral, as likely to be followed by resolution as by passivity and submission. Even Atahuallpa, a prisoner who as a seasoned warrior must have been well aware that his chances of living beyond the collection of his ransom were small at best, soon overcame any fear he had of the Europeans' horses and took real interest in learning what he could about them.[38] Other members of Andean society quickly learned to ride and to handle European arms; indeed, they did so with such rapidity that the Spaniards became alarmed that their advantage might be turned against them. We must remember that the Spaniards were enormously outnumbered in the Andes. They had to adapt to the society they entered (albeit at the top) in order not only to survive but to transform their temporary advantage—the disordered political situation at the state level—into a more durable means of providing themselves with wealth and power. In general, the sociopolitical structures that emerged on the local level functioned through the traditional local elites.

I do not want to argue here that the members of Andean society, even at the elite level, understood the culture of the invaders. At least initially, each side undoubtedly interpreted the actions of the other in terms of its own values and assumptions; we need not assume that either side understood the basic culture patterns of the other. But there were external similarities that permitted the Spaniards and at least the elite groups of Andean society to assume that each understood the other, even as they failed to comprehend the implications of deeper and more basic differences until the rough outlines of a system of political domination were drawn. And in that process, the Spaniards retained their initial advantage while the Andeans were squeezed into steadily less advantageous positions. In their first two or three decades in the Andes, the Spaniards made effective use of a colonial institution developed decades earlier in the Caribbean to organize the extraction of surplus without massively altering the mechanisms through which production was organized. That institution was the *encomienda*, and it became the basic sociopolitical form through which the conquerors dealt with local society.

Adapted from the Reconquest, the encomienda was formalized and codified in the Caribbean at the end of the fifteenth century, when the native population of the islands was parceled out among the Spanish colonists for their virtually unlimited use. The first governor of Hispaniola, Juan de Ovando, regularized and institutionalized the practice, which bore a striking resemblance to the medieval tradition of frontier administration of the same name. The people of the area newly claimed for Spain were distributed among the conquerors by the leader of the expedition *"in encomienda"* as part of the division of the spoils of conquest. The grantee, or *encomendero*, received full authority to use the Indians as he saw fit. In return, he was charged with providing his people with religious instruction and the other benefits of European civilization. He was also obligated to keep a horse and arms prepared for the defense of the land, whether against outside invaders or the people under his charge. Part of that obligation included residing in the city within whose jurisdiction his encomienda fell, and housing and feeding people in times of emergency.[39]

The first encomiendas in Peru were distributed by Pizarro to the men present at the capture of Atahuallpa in 1533 and were grants of authority over thousands of people, assigned in terms of a kuraka or chieftain and all of the people subject to him. As all the Europeans in the Andes admitted openly, the wealth that could be extracted from the new territory depended entirely upon the native Andean population; the importance of the right of jurisdiction over men and women was basic to the encomienda. The encomienda altered the initial plunder of the Spaniards' first forays into the Andes, refining the practice to a more institutionalized and regular form of plunder in which the right to appropriate the goods and labor of the native population was restricted to one man alone, the encomendero. A grant of encomienda defined the legal rights of particular Spaniards—the grantees—who were authorized in reward for their services to the Crown and the conquest to assume and exercise whatever authority they could make effective over the people assigned to them. This included making virtually unrestricted use of Indian labor and goods, to the extent that they were not limited by the resistance, passive or active, of the Indians themselves.

Though the grants of encomienda define the rights of the encomendero in relation to other Spaniards, they say little about the relations expected or established between the encomendero and the people assigned to him. Those relationships were hammered out between the 1530's and the 1550's as the encomenderos' demands were accepted by the people or resisted until a modus vivendi—often an uneasy one—was reached. In the course of that often violent and brutal bargaining process, a rough political system emerged that lasted for more than three decades. Though there are common elements in all of the encomiendas on which we have information, local variations were considerable in the early years, for the particular characteristics of exploitation—the goods and labor requisitioned from the native population—depended a great deal upon the individual abilities of each encomendero as he dealt with his people. This rough, one-sided bargain settled rapidly into fixed custom, which by the 1540's had become sufficiently rooted in daily practice to make even the royal authorities cautious about attempting to alter the terms of the "agreement." That custom, even more than any formal political structure, was the basis of the society of the conquest, and the conquerors defended it even against their monarch. As one of them, a nobleman with a gift for words and fine phrases, put it in 1537, "we die and kill for our law and our king, and for the former especially."[40]

The "law" or system of justice for which the conquerors fought was essentially a set of mechanisms for the allocation of power, mechanisms that gave to certain privileged members of the society the authority to determine for others what practices were customary and "just," and what were not. This dispersed or parcelized authority corresponds to what has been defined in European terms as feudalism. Feudalism has been characterized as a sociopolitical system distinguished by the unity of property and sovereignty. Property in land was vested in an elite whose access to both the land and the productive labor of the people working that land was held by virtue of a grant from a superior—a sovereign or a liege lord. Property and sovereignty were fused, for access to land was accompanied by jurisdiction over the people living on the land. The feudal lord was par excellence the dispenser of "justice," i.e. the arbiter of custom as it evolved in a particular area.[41] Sovereignty was parcelized and fragmented, and authority was a function of the particular class to which a person belonged, for the lord was the arbiter of custom for those under his authority, whereas disputes between lords were adjudicated by the lord to whom the latter owed allegiance and submission. Such a structure was highly useful for a rapidly expanding society resting upon a productive foundation consisting of people belonging to another culture, for it permitted the adjustment of the mechanisms of rule—ultimately mechanisms for the extraction of surplus—in accordance with the relations of production in particular areas.

The encomienda system of the middle of the sixteenth century in the Andes had much in common with this structure, even though property in land and sovereignty were distinct. But in this new land, barely explored, land was cheap and apparently abundant, whereas wealth depended not upon access to land, but upon control of the people who worked that land and made it productive. For the conquerors, their control of "justice" and authority over the people assigned to them "in encomienda" was the foundation of the system, which they fought to retain even against the Crown itself. That parcelized jurisdiction, which gave the encomendero authority over the people assigned to him, was essentially feudal; but it did not last beyond the 1580's. It did facilitate, however, the relatively rapid organization of mechanisms of exploitation on the local level, adjusted to local production and to the sociopolitical organization of each region at the time of the entry of the Europeans. In the rapidly changing context of European society in the sixteenth century, the ultimate residual rights of authority over the people held in encomienda vested in the Crown were undoubtedly too weak to provide an effective foundation for the loyalty of the new rulers of Andean society to their monarch overseas, as the royal inspectors sent to Peru in the 1560's clearly perceived and reported. But at the outset, the encomienda system facilitated the rapid organization of economic activity by the encomenderos and the accumulation in the European sector of considerable wealth extracted from the Andean population.

How did the Spaniards who received encomiendas organize the extraction of goods and labor from the Andean population? Each encomendero assumed formal jurisdiction and authority over thousands of people. But how did he give orders and present demands to those people and expect them to be obeyed? On the basis of the material now available, it is amply clear that the Andean peoples were not passive sheep to be herded into pens by the conquerors. Many of the leaders of ethnic groups maneuvered skillfully in the complicated political scene engendered by the war for succession and the Spanish presence. These same leaders, at least initially, chose to accept the encomienda structure, however they defined it for themselves and their people. Without the cooperation and participation of the ethnic leaders of Andean society, the encomienda as a mechanism for extracting goods and services from the Andean population would have been worthless.

It appears that the local sociopolitical structures of Andean society were little affected by the presence of the Europeans in the early decades. The persistence of local practice and tradition is clear from the materials dating from those years that have been preserved; these materials provide us with some of the best information we have regarding traditional Andean society on the local level.[42] There were Andean institutions that could have provided some precedent for the relations between the Spanish encomendero and the kurakas under his authority, notably the Inca governor or *toc'ricoq*, who was also an outsider with extensive authority over the kurakas. The encomendero's demands for labor could be defined in terms of the state's similar demands, and the external similarities between the generosity expected of Andean leaders and the lavish table that was traditional in medieval noble households cannot be overlooked.

The case of Huarochirí illustrates the alliance between Spanish conqueror and Andean kuraka that made it possible for the Spaniards to step into the positions vacated by the local representatives of the Inca state in the provinces and use the existing mechanisms of surplus extraction in Andean society for their own benefit. The kuraka who accepted the Spanish encomendero as his local overlord often built up a relationship with him reminiscent of the ties of ceremony, reciprocal gifts, and feasting that linked the local ethnic elite to the representatives of the Inca state. The kuraka of Huarochirí, Ninavilca, apparently built up a close relationship with the Spaniards, who praised him as among the most able and acculturated of the kurakas within the jurisdiction of Lima. Ninavilca, baptized Don Antonio, was one of two kurakas assigned the administration of the Indians living around Lima, a position that brought him the title of Regidor de Indios, with power to enforce the orders of the Spaniards and supervise the affairs of the people under his authority.[43] His daughter was brought up in the household of his encomendero—a practice reminiscent of the education of young kurakas in Cuzco or in the provincial capital under the Incas—and was later married to a Spaniard.[44] All of this undoubtedly represented an extension of Don Antonio's prestige and status within his own community. On the local level, the encomendero, with his lavish table to which the kuraka was often invited, could be equated with the Inca governor. According to a Spanish official some years later: "These encomenderos each set themselves up as an Inca, and appropriated by virtue of the encomiendas all of the rights, tributes, and services granted by that land to the Inca."[45] And Huaman Poma de Ayala, also writing later, had some vivid comments to make about the encomenderos' adoption of the panoply of traditional ceremony and the marks of status of Andean society. The encomendero, he complained, "has himself carried in litters like the Inca with drums [*taquies*] and dances when he arrives at their [the people's] communities."[46]

All of this demanded the presence of the encomendero in the Andean communities, and the successful encomenderos spent a good part of their time in their encomiendas, returning to the urban centers to oversee the conversion of the goods they extracted from the Indians into merchandise for sale to other Europeans.[47] The kuraka, with whom the encomendero maintained a close relationship, transmitted the encomendero's demands to his people and organized the production of the goods he wanted. Initially, the Europeans adapted themselves to the structure of Andean society, itself well organized to produce a wide variety of goods by utilizing social relationships. These social relationships permitted the encomendero to lay claim, through the kuraka, to the goods he wanted to maintain his household and to enter the European economy with the surplus he extracted from the Indians. His legal basis for this in European terms was of course the encomienda; Pizarro clearly stated the identity between encomienda and labor in one of his grants, which assigned the people and their kuraka to a Spaniard "so that you can use them on your estates and fields, mines and farms."[48] It was possible to translate the Spaniards' demands for goods in terms of the traditional claim of political authority to labor services from the local community. It was the task of the kuraka to make that claim for the encomendero, translating the latter's demands into labor time invested in producing the goods demanded by the Europeans, generally on the lands once assigned to the state and the wak'as and appropriated by the conquerors as the successors to the Inca authorities.

The encomenderos made lavish use of the fine craftsmen of Andean society. The first buildings of Lima were erected by Huanca craftsmen sent from Jauja by their kurakas with Francisco Pizarro, and the other conquerors followed that example.[49] The members of Andean society erected the palaces of their encomenderos and sent men to plant their fields and guard their herds—both llama herds expropriated from the herds belonging to the Inca state and cattle and sheep imported from the Caribbean. The Spaniards also used considerable native labor as servants and household help. The kurakas of the Chupachos of Huánuco testified in 1549 that they sent 40 people to serve in the household of their encomendero, Gómez Arias.[50] The *cumbicamayoq*, skilled tapestry weavers, prepared the cloth that decorated the palaces of the conquerors, and skilled craftsmen carved the new coats of arms awarded by the Crown in stone over the palace doors in Cuzco.

But though the conquerors could live luxuriously in Peru on the contributions of the people they held in encomienda, they could not found a lineage and gain the wealth that assured social position without exacting goods from the Indians that could be converted into commodities: goods valued for the price they could bring rather than the use that could be made of them. The major goods sought by the conquerors were precious metals, first in the form of treasure looted from the Incas and the wak'as and later in raw form.[51] For the search for treasure soon turned into a search for mines. In every province the Spaniards entered, they demanded to know the location of mines, unable to believe that the gold and silver objects melted down in the early collections of treasure were the product of years of accumulation and in some cases were alloys that contained only the limited amount of gold sufficient to lend a great deal of glitter to the objects fashioned from them. And enough mines were found to keep the search alive. The rich silver mines of Porco and the gold mines of Chayanta were in the southern highlands, together with the fabled "hill of silver" of Potosí, discovered in 1545 and the major source of the silver ore for which Peru rapidly became famous. But silver could also be found elsewhere, including Central Peru, where mines once worked for the Inca and the local communities continued to be worked under the Spanish until the development of Potosí. Only with the steady decline in the quality of ore from Potosí in the seventeenth century did interest in these older mines resurface and a search begin for new mines. Diego Dávila Brizeño, the first Spanish administrator of Huarochirí, noted that in the province there was "a tale of a rich gold mine that used to be worked, so it is said, for the Inca, and the Indians have buried it so that no one can work it."[52] In the northern part of the province, in Mamaq, there were "many silver tunnels that used to be worked and would be worked today if there were people to do it."[53]

The exploitation of the silver and gold mines in the first years following the European invasion is one of the best examples that can be found of the use of Andean forms of production for the benefit of the Europeans. A closer study of the decades between the 1530's and the 1580's may yet yield an adequate answer to the question of how and why the members of Andean society accepted the demands of the Europeans. For it is clear that in the years immediately following the European invasion, the Andean peoples responded to the Spaniards' demands by mobilizing the productive mechanisms of their own society to produce the precious metals demanded by the Europeans as well as to feed and clothe both the Europeans and the members of their own society working in the mining centers. And in doing so, they adapted quickly to the European market system, rapidly monopolizing not only the production of ore itself but also the supply of foodstuffs and other necessities that maintained the growing city of Potosí.[54]

The kurakas of the southern highlands sent *mitayos* to mine silver in Potosí, using traditional Andean techniques of production. The friable surface ores were easily extracted and were rich in silver that could be purified by melting the silver free of the embedded ore in a wind-heated furnace called a *huayra*, fueled by llama dung. But despite the use of traditional Andean methods, the scale of the operation was far beyond that of mining under the Inca state, drawing large amounts of unskilled labor from the local communities. The laborers, working their mit'a turns under the direction of their kurakas, excavated the ore and sold it to skilled miners who reduced it according to the traditional techniques of their craft, taking a share of the metal for their services. The kuraka then passed the metal to the encomendero in payment of the tribute assigned his community, retaining any metal remaining for the community.[55]

In these early decades, the Europeans held only the mine claims themselves, returning to the Andean miners for the extraction and processing of the ores. Many of the miners sent to the mines by their kurakas remained there, paying the entire tribute assessment of their communities in silver through their labor—a clear adaptation to a new reality of the traditional Andean use of mitmaq colonists sent to exploit particular resource oases. The kurakas sent foodstuffs and other goods to the market in Potosí, trading them for silver. Cloth, maize, *chuñu* (freeze-dried potatoes), jerked meat, ají, and coca obtained from resource areas held by the communities were sent to Potosí on llama trains, where they were sold to European and Indian peddlers. The kurakas also rapidly adopted the cultivation of European products such as grapes (for wine) and cattle, which found a ready market in Potosí.[56] The trade was not a small-scale affair, for in the 1560's, when Potosí had already entered into a crisis of production and its population had begun to decline, a Spanish official noted that the trade in cloth and foodstuffs amounted to some 300,000 pesos, most of which was in the hands of the members of Andean society.[57]

In these early decades, the productive structures of Andean society could be mobilized effectively for the production of goods valued in European terms, particularly precious metals. Community reciprocity, reordered in a hierarchical structure under the authority of the kuraka, not only permitted the extraction of surplus appropriated by the Inca state; it also permitted the mobilization of skilled and unskilled labor, as well as the production of specialized goods that could be transformed into commodities in the European market. And the members of Andean society accomplished this transformation by drawing upon traditional claims to obtain the goods they later sold in Potosí. It appears that despite Spanish claims to the contrary, most of the profits gained by the kurakas from their activities went, at least initially, into the community stores or *sapsi*, to be used to meet the demands of their encomenderos and of the other Spaniards among them, such as priests.[58] We do not yet know just how the kurakas defined the process of market production in which they functioned so effectively. We need more information on how the translation from goods for use to commodities was made, for it involved a translation from Andean to European social relationships that ultimately had far-reaching consequences for the local community. But, at least initially, it appears that little of the impact of commodity production was felt by the Andean communities, for the product of their participation in the European market was transferred almost directly to the Spanish encomendero in the form of tribute.

Though in most cases the encomenderos depended upon the Indians to produce the tribute goods however they saw fit, in some cases the Spaniards became active entrepreneurs, introducing new goods and new techniques of production and using their access to Indian labor, sometimes with the participation of their kurakas and sometimes independently. Mit'a laborers assigned to an encomendero household could also be used for other purposes by enterprising Spaniards, and the conquerors found many people, voluntarily or involuntarily cut off from their own communities, who were willing to adapt to the culture of the invaders and learn the skills that helped them survive in a new milieu. It is not always possible to distinguish between a labor force that still functioned according to traditional norms and a labor force that was mobilized on European terms, but a few examples should suffice to give an idea of the variety of activities initiated by the encomenderos.

A list of the encomiendas of Cuzco prepared for Pedro de la Gasca in 1542 offers some insight into the sources of encomendero income. The document lists some 60 distinct grants, many of them originally assigned by Francisco Pizarro and later transferred, fused, or split among new holders in the course of the civil wars. It ranks the grants by estimated value to the holder, listing the number of people in each encomienda and the use made of them. The major source of income for the encomenderos of Cuzco in the 1540's was mining and coca. The encomenderos demanded a fixed number of baskets of coca from their people per season, and then sold the leaf to merchants who sent it to the mining areas. The people of Cuzco provided some 10,000 baskets of coca per harvest to their encomenderos, and some of the most highly valued encomiendas were those in which the sole source of income noted was in coca. Other encomenderos regularly sent people to mine silver in Porco, or gold in

Carabaya or Guallaripa—the latter mines within the encomienda of Francisco Pizarro. The income from ten encomiendas came solely from gold mines worked by the population in their own lands.[59] In other cases, the encomenderos drew upon Indian labor to introduce productive activities that reproduced those they knew in Europe. In 1539, Nicolás de Ribero, an encomendero and councilman of Lima, formed a fishing company with another Spaniard to provide fresh ocean fish for the city. Ribero contracted to provide eight fishermen to his partner, Juan Quintero, who agreed to run the operation and oversee the costs of the enterprise. In 1543, Doña Inéz Muñoz, the widow of Martín de Alcantara, gave a power of attorney to Ribero and a companion to use the Indians of her encomienda as miners.[60] That same year, 1543, Francisco de Ampüero, another encomendero of Lima, set up a partnership with a blacksmith, who sold the lands and the shop equipment to his new partner. Ampüero was to provide ten Indians to work in the shop and the two agreed to share all profits equally.[61] Lucas Martínez Vergazo, holder of a large encomienda in Arequipa, organized an integrated productive operation centering around the mines he controlled in Tarapacá that included a mill, a cordage manufactory, a vineyard, a ranch, and several ships that plied the coast between Quilque, the port of Arequipa, and Ilo, in northern Chile, and that probably reached Lima as well.[62]

The encomiendas supported extended households that consisted of the encomendero and his family and kinsmen who had come to Peru as well as a large group of clients, supporters, and employees: mayordomos, accountants, and specialized craftsmen who ran or supervised the often diverse business enterprises of the encomendero. In the municipalities of the early period of the conquest, these great households were the centers of European society in the Andes. The economic and social life of the colony revolved around them; the artisans, notaries, and other professionals who came from Spain generally attached themselves to one of the encomenderos, organizing his household and administering his affairs. The labor of the Indian population supplied these households with foodstuffs and other goods, and produced the goods that were turned into commodities by the encomenderos, who sent them to the merchants whose markets were in Europe or in the new urban centers established as the Spanish population grew. As the new cities were built, the encomenderos found other goods that they could appropriate from the local population and turn into cash.

By the 1550's, the plunder economy was working smoothly. The encomenderos appropriated goods produced by the Indians as tribute and turned them into profits through the intermediary of the merchants without altering the productive system of Andean society. The great majority of these goods were traditional products of Andean society that could be converted into merchandise by transporting them to the new urban centers, particularly Potosí, where they were sold to the European population and its Andean employees permanently attached to these centers. Even transportation was provided through tribute assessments, in the form of requisitions of llamas that first packed the goods to market and were then transformed into merchandise themselves for their meat. A closer look at one of these traditional Andean goods, cloth—a product highly valued by Andean and European society alike—provides insight into the commercialization of traditional goods for European profit. Andean clothing consisted of straight panels that when shorter and narrower were turned into breechclouts and sleeveless shirts for men, and when longer and wider were wrapped around the body and pinned for women. Cumbi, the fine tapestry cloth woven by skilled weavers, was a prized gift, a mark of honor and status to receive and to use. It was also prized by the Spaniards. The rougher cloth worn as clothing found a ready market in Lima, in the mining regions, and in the settlements of Chile to the south, where it was bought by the Spaniards to clothe the native people working as household servants, as miners, and in other activities. Some of the Europeans established *obrajes*, or workshops, to produce cloth, sending Indians to them to work at the looms brought from Europe. But in the decades immediately following the Spanish invasion, a far more common way of obtaining piece goods was to obtain them directly from the native peoples as tribute, relying on traditional household production.

The activities of María Suárez, wife of an encomendero in Huánuco, provide a clear picture of the transformation of Andean cloth into a European commodity. In 1567, the Indians of her husband's encomienda brought her 100 pieces of women's clothing in tribute. She sent them to a merchant, Salvador Reyes, who had contracted to give the Indians 250 pesos in a marked bar of silver for the cloth. The Indians were ordered to turn the bar of silver over to her upon delivery of the cloth to Reyes. Reyes regularly bought tribute goods from Suárez. On January 17, 1567, a few days after the transaction described above, he paid the kurakas of her husband's encomienda 375 pesos in a bar of silver for 150 pieces of tribute cloth, which the kurakas delivered to María the same day. A few days later a merchant from Geneva arrived in Huánuco and picked up the tribute clothing as well as cotton cloth and cumbi in order "to bring it from this city to the City of the Kings [Lima] and from there to the kingdom of Chile in the first ship leaving for those kingdoms and there sell it at the best prices I can obtain."[63]

An encomienda was thus a fine springboard for organizing a European productive system in the new land, for it provided the encomendero-entrepreneur with virtually everything. Capital inputs from outside the encomienda were minimal, and even then, goods and labor from the encomienda generally provided the income that was later invested in the purchase of outside equipment and labor. An accounting of the operations of the encomienda of Lucas Martínez Vergazo in 1565 provides a picture that clearly indicates the importance not only of the accumulation of surplus by the Europeans but also of the establishment of enterprises that would continue to function well into the mature colonial period. The produce extracted from Martínez Vergazo's encomienda—tribute— accounted for 69 percent of the money income of the operation and also supported the other activities he engaged in. It fed and clothed the Andean *yanaconas* working in his mines, cowboys on his ranch, slaves trained to work in the refining of precious metals, and his extensive household. The tribute included cloth, llamas, maize, wheat, ají, dried fish, wild birds, beans, and potatoes. In that list, the only product introduced by the Europeans was wheat, which in turn was consumed almost entirely by Europeans. Cloth, llamas, wheat, and ají were the most important market goods; between 59 and 99 percent of the tribute obtained in those products was marketed, primarily in Potosí.[64] In sum, over half of all of the goods received by Martínez Vergazo as tribute were transformed into commodities for sale in Potosí and other centers. The remainder maintained the other parts of the encomendero's enterprises. The Andean productive system, through the mechanism of the encomienda, supported not only the local communities themselves, but also the entire productive structure mounted by the encomendero to transform the goods of the Andean economy into commodities and, ultimately, personal wealth in European terms.[65] It is hardly surprising that the encomenderos fought tenaciously to retain their authority over the people assigned to them—and the goods they provided.

The plunder economy of the conquest period, built as it was upon the expropriation of a considerable proportion of the goods produced by the members of Andean society for their own use and for the luxury and display of the state destroyed by the conquerors, rested ultimately upon fragile foundations. The maintenance of that economic system—the continued production of goods that the Spaniards could turn into commodities in a European market—depended upon the capacity of Indian society to reproduce its own numbers and continue to meet the demands of the Europeans. But that capacity began to be undermined with the entry of the Spaniards into the Andes. The initial treasure hunt for gold and silver, the demand for thousands of people to serve as warriors and bearers of goods and supplies, as well as the extensive looting of foodstuffs and other goods from the stored supplies of the state and the local societies—

all weakened the productive capacity of a society that depended heavily upon the labor of all of its members as well as upon the careful husbanding of goods and resources. The Huancas of Jauja were a relatively small group within the Inca state, yet in a few short years they lost well over a third of their members, who never returned to take up their share of day-to-day labor.

All of these factors, as well as opposition from within Spanish society itself, undermined the viability of the plunder economy. By the 1560's, when the quarrels between Spaniards over the spoils of conquest seemed to have finally ended, and the extractive mechanisms of the encomienda seemed to be functioning smoothly to ensure the steady flow of Andean goods and precious metals to Spanish society, elements set in motion by the conquest itself were already functioning to undermine the stability of the system. By the 1560's, the society of the conquest period had entered into a clearly perceptible crisis. The bubble of the plunder economy had been punctured and was threatening to collapse. The resolution of the crisis required far-reaching changes in the political and economic organization of the new colony, which gave rise to the mature colonial system and the construction of the mechanisms of exploitation that would last as long as the Spanish Crown retained its authority in the Andes—and in some cases beyond.

FIVE

The Colonial System

THE CRISIS of the 1560's was at root a crisis of production, directly linked to a demographic disaster. The Andean economy was capable of producing considerable surplus, a fact perhaps only too fully recognized by the Spanish invaders, who assumed that it could continue to do so. The more we learn about the operation of the encomienda system in the conquest period, the more we are forced to admire its virtual self-sufficiency. As an extractive operation, the encomienda could hardly be surpassed, for it provided its holder with wealth with virtually no input of capital from outside.

But this ideal situation—for the encomendero—rested upon the productive capacity of the Andean communities that supplied the encomendero with labor and goods. And that productive capacity ultimately rested upon working people themselves, a fall in whose numbers would undermine the ability of the society to continue to provide the volume of goods and services demanded by the encomenderos. The preconquest and early colonial demography of the Andean area has been a subject of dispute since the eighteenth century, with little clarification. The evident wealth of the Inca Empire demanded a dense population—particularly in view of the limited sources of energy beyond that of the people themselves—and the miles of abandoned terraces that strike any traveler in the Andes are witness to a large population sometime in the past. But many of those terraces are difficult if not impossible to date, which only increases controversy regarding the time of their construction and abandonment. The size of the population of the Inca state in 1532 has been estimated as high as 32 million,[1] although other scholars regard that estimate as exaggerated. María Rostworowski de Diaz Canseco has pointed to the devastation of the Inca expansion, the slaughter and relocation of entire populations, and the abandoned terraces and fields noted by the first Spaniards to enter the Andes as evidence that the population of the Andean area may well have reached its maximum prior to the establishment of the Inca Empire and have declined under the rule of the Incas.[2]

War and resistance bring death, slowing or stopping population growth, and the Inca state was not built easily. But whatever the demographic cost of its building, the toll of death that accompanied its destruction was acknowledged to be devastating, at the time as well as by succeeding generations. The Spanish invaders brought with them to the Andes a companion that undoubtedly facilitated the conquest by sowing terror and dislocation but that also undermined the economic structures of the conquest period. That companion was disease. The Andean people lacked the defenses built up over millennia in the Eurasian continent, and were helpless before the arsenal of diseases that accompanied the European expansion. Smallpox, measles, and even the common cold were deadly to people who had no resistance, and epidemics spread rapidly, leaving thousands of dead in their wake. The first epidemics reached the Andes before the arrival of the Europeans. It is thought that the sudden death of the last head of the Inca state, Huayna Capac, was a result of the first of the many epidemics that swept the region.

The first epidemic, estimated to have swept through the Andes about 1525, has been diagnosed on the basis of descriptions of the appearance of people who contracted the disease as smallpox. A second major epidemic hit in 1546, originating in Cuzco and moving north. A third, again smallpox, spread through the Andes from Lima in 1558–59. Finally, at the end of the century, the area was devastated by three waves of different illnesses. The first was another wave of smallpox that began in Cuzco in 1585 and moved north, reaching Lima a year later. Then a new disease, probably either typhus or bubonic plague, came from the area of Panama, reaching Peru about 1590; at the same time, an epidemic of grippe originating in Potosí moved north through the Andes.[3]

No valid population estimates for the Andean area as a whole exist prior to the general count ordered by Viceroy Francisco de Toledo in 1572. But all sources agree that the native Andean population began to drop alarmingly from the first arrival of the Europeans. The coastal population was hardest hit. Between 1525 and 1575, it has been estimated that the population of the Andean communities fell to about four percent of its preconquest numbers on the central coast of Peru. Decimation was less in the highlands, but even there two-thirds to three-fourths of the population is estimated to have died during the first 40 years following the entry of the Spaniards.[4]

Despite the evident drop of the Andean population, however, the crisis was due not so much to the alarming decimation of the native Andean population as to the squeeze between falling Indian population and the rapidly growing numbers of Spaniards in the new kingdom. And this in turn was not absolute, for the number of Spaniards was and remained tiny in comparison to the native populations among which they moved. It was rather social—the product of the fact that the plunder economy functioned on the basis of the exploitation of many people by a few, of the assignment of thousands of people to be used by one encomendero for his own and his household's profit. From the time of the initial assignments of encomiendas by Francisco Pizarro, the total number of encomiendas changed little while the number of Europeans competing for those encomiendas multiplied. And the encomienda not only offered a promise of riches to the recipient who managed it well; it also excluded those who did not enjoy those grants from access to wealth in excess of that which they could gain by their own efforts and personal skills and labor. Save for those few people satisfied with a modest living—and they were few in the gold-rush atmosphere of the conquest period—access to an encomienda was the major (and in most cases the only) avenue to wealth and position.

In this context, the flood of Spaniards to Peru from the Caribbean, from the Isthmus, and from Spain takes on new meaning, for it put pressures upon an economy organized on the basis of the exploitation of many people by a privileged few. In 1536, there were approximately 500 encomenderos in a total Spanish population of about 2,000 in Peru. In the following two decades, the total number of encomenderos remained constant while the Spanish population grew rapidly: by the 1540's, the encomenderos accounted for only about one-eighth of the total Spanish population, and by 1555 they made up only slightly more than six percent of all Spaniards in Peru.[5] The growing volume of Spanish hopefuls was accompanied by an inflation in the social status expected of an aspirant to an encomienda or its equivalent in Peru. Men who could prove their presence in Peru during the first few years after the European invasion were generally assured of encomiendas, although those who chose the losing side in the civil wars lost theirs in the redistributions made by Vaca de Castro and Pedro de la Gasca. These redistributions incorporated newer arrivals, generally with claims to social status in Spain; also, the viceroys who came to Peru from the middle of the century brought kinsmen and clients whose social rank in Spain inflated their claims for consideration. By 1556, the only men eligible to receive encomiendas were court nobles from Spain, men who had served the Crown in the civil wars, the first conquerors, or men in Peru before 1540.[6]

The authorities in charge of the political structure of the plunder economy following the civil wars were well aware of the dangers represented by the growing numbers of ambitious and often unruly men of arms in Peru, even though they themselves brought additional kinsmen and clients with them to the new kingdom. When these people could not find employment or support from the encomenderos, they turned to raiding and plundering. The Marqués de Cañete, Viceroy from 1556 to 1560, wrote the Crown from Seville before his departure for Peru complaining, "I am informed that there are more than 3,000 men in Peru, all well armed, who expect to be rewarded for their services."[7] His sources informed him well.

The exhaustion of the surface deposits of precious minerals was another element in the crisis of the plunder economy, although probably not a decisive one. Nevertheless, it contributed to unrest, in Peru and in Spain, and ultimately to the transformation of the mining operations in the colony. The mines of Potosí were discovered in 1545, and from the end of the civil wars to the 1560's the production of precious metals rose rapidly. During the fifteen years from 1545 to 1560, approximately 180,000 pesos of silver left Peru for Spain, most of that amount from Potosí.[8] But the mining boom, based upon traditional Andean techniques of extraction and processing, began to wane after the middle of the sixteenth century. By the end of the 1560's, the surface deposits of nearly pure silver that could be easily reduced in open-air furnaces were almost gone; and as shafts were sunk, the ore brought up had a lower silver content, and the metal was less easily separated from the rock in which it was embedded. The yield of silver per unit of ore began to fall off sharply, affecting both the viceregal economy and the remission of silver to Spain.

The first boom-and-bust of silver production in Peru has been overshadowed by the later, far more sustained prosperity of the "hill of silver" in the seventeenth century. But in political and social terms that first cycle was crucial, for it coincided with a period of heavy dependence upon overseas silver by the Spanish Crown; indeed, much of the particular form of the colonial system in Peru was undoubtedly the product of the efforts of the Crown and court to ensure that the flow of silver from the Andes did not again fail. The importance of silver, not to the economy of Spain but to the economy of the court, was basic. Francisco Pizarro entered the Andes during a period in which the authority of the Crown of Spain was supreme in Europe, and the treasure from the Americas was playing a growing part in the political calculations of Charles V. The wealth represented by the early plunder and later the mines of the Americas seemed like a divine gift to the Crown. Charles won the title of Holy Roman Emperor, defender of the Catholic faith in the Germanies, as a direct result of his overseas possessions, for American treasure guaranteed the loans that funded his election. And that treasure, followed by the silver that began to reach Spain from Potosí after 1545, made it possible for Charles to fund the last European effort to build and maintain an empire on the medieval pattern, an effort that was sadly out of step with the times. Charles' rule was founded upon a political system based on inheritance and ties of vassalage and formal political loyalties that were rapidly disintegrating in the fifteenth and sixteenth centuries.[9] In the sixteenth century, when most European monarchs were locked in a struggle with their nobilities to obtain the income needed to build a centralized political and administrative structure, the Hapsburgs of Spain seemed singularly blessed. The fantastic treasure of the Inca Empire was followed by the silver and gold from the mines of Porco and Carabaya, and finally by the fabled mines of Potosí, which by the 1550's seemed to promise an unlimited supply of silver.

Charles, and his son Philip after him, came increasingly to depend upon the regular arrival of the silver fleets from the Americas, primarily from Peru. American silver permitted the Crown to leave largely undisturbed the vested privileges of Church and nobility. Rather than risk political trouble by extending old taxes or establishing new ones as his fellow monarchs were forced to do, the King of Spain borrowed against the expected income from the Americas. That income underwrote the construction of the Spanish army, the famous Spanish *tercios* that dominated the battlefields of Europe throughout the sixteenth century. With that army, well-trained and well-paid, Charles fought to reverse the rapid disintegration of the political loyalties that bound together medieval society. The reformation of a corrupt religious bureaucracy, initially supported by reformers throughout Europe and including Spain, became a political threat to the Holy Roman Emperor when the project became linked through Luther with the ambitions of German princes seeking political and financial freedom from Emperor and Papacy. The new Protestant doctrines espoused by the German princes became the rationale for the political fragmentation of Europe and the coalescence of new political loyalties that brought Charles' armies into battle in Germany. The diversity and extent of the territories he ruled forced Charles, and his son and heir Philip, to participate in virtually every armed struggle that took place in Europe during the sixteenth and the first half of the seventeenth centuries. Charles' 35-year reign saw only eighteen years of peace, and even his eventual partition of his realm, an open admission of the failure of his struggle to reestablish the medieval basis of society by force of arms, did not grant Philip much respite from military adventures.

Charles' wars spelled the end of the last vestiges of pan-European empire and resulted in the sagging finances of Castile. In 1556, he agreed to the terms of the Peace of Augsburg, which meant the end of any pretense of centralized authority in the Germanies; in the same year he abdicated the throne, leaving his realms in Castile and Aragon, Italy, the Netherlands, and the Americas to his son Philip II, one of whose first tasks was to preside over the bankruptcy of the Crown in 1557. Charles bequeathed to his son an intractable nobility, ready and eager to defend its privileges against the monarch. The Crown could not raise taxes for military action without the express permission of the nobility. It could not intervene in Italy or the Netherlands without risking rebellion from nobles and townsmen always ready to defend themselves against encroachments on their autonomy and their pocketbooks.

American treasure represented an apparently enviable solution to such difficulties. The hope of increased funds from the Americas enabled the Spanish Crown and officials to evade the hard choices facing other European monarchs, who were forced to confront their nobilities in order to gain a more solid financial basis for their military activities. From the mid-1530's, the Crown continually ordered its representatives in Peru to send money. Pizarro was initially very careful to remit the Crown's share of the treasure from Peru; the treasury officials who accompanied the conquerors informed the Crown of its share in 1533, and sent it to Spain with the first men to return home after the death of Atahuallpa. By the time more treasure was remitted to Spain in 1535, Charles' financial needs were already severe enough to incite him to seize all private shipments of specie sent back to Spain in order to prepare the royal expedition against the Turks in the Levant. Charles later yielded to complaints, but the pattern that was to continue throughout his reign was already established. [10]

In 1536, the Crown sent the Bishop of Panama to Peru to audit the accounts of the treasury officials and report on Pizarro's handling of the royal interests. Pizarro argued that he had to use the royal tax moneys to obtain men and arms from Panama during the rebellion of Manco Inca in 1535, and that remissions of specie to Spain would have to be postponed until Indian resistance had ended. [11] But Charles, fighting to preserve a European empire, continued to place the needs of state policies in Europe first, and regularly ordered his officials in Peru to audit the treasury accounts and collect all moneys owed the Crown for remission to Spain. These same orders were included in the instructions to all of the royal officials sent to Peru for the remainder of the century. The Crown's demands brought the treasury officials in Peru—directly responsible for royal interests—into open conflict with the efforts of governors and viceroys to lay a sound basis for royal authority in the Andean kingdom.

The policies of royal governors were further undermined by their monarch's efforts to obtain funds from the people bound for Peru before their departure from Spain by selling claims against royal income to be redeemed upon their arrival in the Andes. La Gasca complained to the Crown in 1548 that he had word that licenses to embark for Peru were

being offered for sale in Seville, continually flooding the new and still un-
certainly held land with more people in search of offices, perquisites, and
position.[12]

By the 1560's, the Crown's need for income was severe, and Peru's capacity to supply a part of that need was diminishing. Spain remained the
major power in Europe, but that power depended heavily upon the income the Crown could command. Philip was at war with France, and
faced a renewed Moorish offensive in the central and western Mediterranean. But in Peru, the crisis of the plunder economy constricted the surplus that could be extracted from the Andean population upon whose production the Spanish presence in Peru was ultimately dependent. Production at Potosí slowed to a trickle as a result of both the exhaustion of
surface deposits and the steady fall of available labor with the decimation
of the Andean population. Commerce dropped off, for as Peru began to
produce foodstuffs previously imported from Spain, such as wine, olive
oil, and wheat, the demand for Mediterranean products declined sharply.
Spanish commerce with the Americas was also interrupted by the appearance of pirates—Dutch, French, and particularly English—in American
waters. All of these factors combined to produce a situation of growing
crisis in both Peru and Spain.

What elements made the crisis of the 1560's a political crisis? On the
surface, it might appear that the political crisis of the conquest period was
over by the 1560's. For virtually the first time since the Spaniards entered
the Andes, open civil strife between Spaniards was absent. Yet from the
conquest itself a struggle had been set in motion over the form and, in
particular, the distribution of expropriation. Who was to get the spoils of
conquest? How much could be gotten? These were the basic questions,
overlaid by the further question of what share the Crown was to receive,
and how the organization of political order and the maintenance of local
authority were to be funded. Seen from this perspective, the problem of
the division of the spoils provides a main thread that runs through the
events of the conquest period from the 1530's to the 1560's and beyond.

Francisco Pizarro insisted upon his authority as governor of the new
kingdom of the Andes, reserving to himself the right of handing out
offices and perquisites to his personal followers. That authority was challenged almost immediately by Pizarro's onetime partner in the conquest
of Peru, Diego de Almagro, who rapidly became the focus of a rival group
composed of those who felt slighted in the distribution of the rewards of
conquest. They sought redress from the monarch, but their efforts to petition the Crown were blocked by Pizarro, who answered complaints about
his high-handedness with the reply, "What could they write him (the
king) except tell him that they want to take and usurp what I won with

such travail?"[13] The struggle for supremacy ended with Pizarro's arrest and execution of Almagro following the latter's attempt to seize Cuzco during the revolt led by Manco Inca, but the stories of battles between the conquerors had already spread well beyond Peru, prompting the Crown to send a representative to the Andes to investigate the situation. Between Almagro's death and the arrival of the royal official, Cristóbal Vaca de Castro, the local situation continued to deteriorate, as Almagro's supporters, whose fortunes were joined to those of their dead leader, turned to looting the territory claimed by Pizarro's allies and supporters. In 1539, a report from Panama described conditions in words that suggest a situation of nearly open war: "The band of Almagro continues stronger since his death. They go about in gangs robbing, nor do they want to settle until someone comes to judge them. If the person who comes is not more than a man, he will end by losing the land and the Almagrists will be insufferable with their haughtiness."[14] The climax was reached before Vaca de Castro reached Peru. Pizarro might have been able to contain the vendetta had he given up vengeance and offered the Almagrists a share in the administration and profit of the new land, but he was unable to conceive of such a policy and was murdered by twelve members of the Almagro faction. Vaca de Castro, on the other hand, was an official worthy of the new, growing bureaucracy, who expected to make his personal fortune and position through his service to the Crown. He was able to rally Pizarro's faction to defeat the Almagrists and reestablish unity among the Europeans in Peru. His wry comment on Pizarro in a letter to his wife is a penetrating judgment on a man who lost a kingdom by insisting on his right to it without regard to the realities of the situation: "It was thought that the Marquis Don Francisco Pizarro did such a great service in winning the realm from the Indians, which was winning it from lambs, that they gave him a marquisate here; and afterwards he lost it all by his own fault, and I won it back after it had been lost, and from people of our nation."[15]

Vaca de Castro used his broad power to withdraw and confer encomiendas to strengthen the ranks of those who had allied with the Crown in the recent conflict, but this patchwork solution ended neither the flood of aspirants to encomiendas in Peru, nor the acrimony about the distribution of power and authority among the Spaniards. He left Peru in 1542 to make way for the first Viceroy, Blasco Nuñez Vela, who brought with him a bomb that once again tore apart the fragile fabric that held Spanish society in Peru in one piece: the New Laws, as they have come to be called. The New Laws caused a storm throughout the Americas, for they erased the parcelized jurisdiction upon which Spanish rule was founded, decreeing the absorption into the Crown of all encomiendas by the second generation after the conquest.[16] The complicated court politics that lay behind these laws await illumination, for it is amply clear that the decrees were out of step with the real conditions of the time. Wiser and more cautious officials ignored them while they appealed them to the Crown, but Nuñez Vela seems to have had the same jealous personal definition of his authority as Pizarro, joining his honor to the execution of policy without regard to reality.

The conquerors reacted immediately, rallying around Gonzalo Pizarro, the most senior member of the Pizarro family in Peru, and demanding that Nuñez Vela suspend the New Laws until information could be gathered to inform the Crown of the damage they would cause to the Spaniards' interests in the new kingdom. All members of Spanish society rallied around the conquerors; even the provincial of the Dominican Order later testified that he had warned the viceroy not to fight the demands of the conquerors to suspend the laws until they could inform the Crown of the "state of the land"—i.e., of the damage the laws would cause. But Nuñez Vela refused to negotiate and demanded that the Spaniards submit to the execution of the laws. Armies were organized and in the ensuing struggle Nuñez Vela, hopelessly outnumbered, was killed in battle.

The victors claimed the right to act in their own defense, and for almost two years their claim was not challenged openly and Gonzalo Pizarro functioned as de facto ruler of Peru in his brother's stead. But the Crown, although it did recognize the ill effects of the New Laws and formally annulled those parts of them that eliminated the encomienda, could not permit such an open show of *lèse majesté* and sent another official, the clergyman Pedro de la Gasca, to Peru in 1547 to restore royal authority, armed with full jurisdiction and the right to punish or pardon as he saw fit. La Gasca used his authority with consummate skill, winning over almost all of the Spaniards in Peru with the promise of a full pardon for their participation in the action against the late unlamented viceroy and suspending the execution of the New Laws. The unfortunate history of the debacle was later caustically summarized by Juan Polo de Ondegardo as "the noise provoked by the Ordinances of the Indies, later revoked by His Majesty and without anyone understanding the matter."[17]

La Gasca carried out a thorough reorganization of the new kingdom, redistributing encomiendas among those Spaniards who had joined him against Pizarro. La Gasca also sought to regularize and limit the extraction of goods and services from the Indians by drawing up official tribute lists and limiting extraction to specified goods and services. But regulation, no matter how careful, could not solve the problem of how to distribute the spoils and at the same time ensure the political authority of the Crown and the flow of specie back to Europe. The royal authorities were aided by the short-lived economic prosperity brought by the first silver boom, which gave them some income to distribute among those Spaniards excluded from the redistribution of encomiendas. La Gasca drew upon potential future royal income, just as the Crown was itself doing in Spain, by creating and distributing offices and positions as notaries and officials in the Spanish cities, particularly in Cuzco and in Potosí, in order "to have some way to reward those who have served in this affair."[18] He granted pensions against royal income, and sought to defuse the growth of potential factions and further revolts among the Spaniards by organizing new expeditions of exploration and conquest into the interior.[19] Three years later, La Gasca was replaced by Antonio de Mendoza, who came to Peru in 1551 from a long and successful term as Viceroy of New Spain. But he died the following year, and the Audiencia, or judges of the royal court in Lima, constituted an interim government until the arrival of the next viceroy, Andrés Hurtado de Mendoza, Marqués de Cañete, who ruled the area from 1556 to 1560.

The last rebellion of Spaniards in Peru against their government took place in 1553, when discontented encomenderos took advantage of an interim government to press once again their claims by force of arms. During the government of Cañete, local conditions seemed relatively calm. The period of rebellions seemed definitely over, although squabbles and street violence were common enough. Cañete was followed by the Conde de Nieva, a notorious bon vivant who died suddenly in 1564, rumored to have fallen from the balcony of his current mistress. The viceroyalty was then governed by the new president of the Audiencia, Lopé García de Castro, sent out that same year from Spain to relieve Nieva, until the arrival of Francisco de Toledo, fifth Viceroy of Peru, in 1569.

The political struggles within Peru during the civil wars, although temporarily smoothed over by the redistribution of encomiendas under La Gasca, were not solved but rather displaced up to the level of the viceregal government itself, to take the form of a struggle between the royal treasury officials and the head of government in the new colony. Following La Gasca's lead, the viceroys and interim rulers used the income of the state to buy the loyalty of Spaniards seeking favors from the government. Since there were few encomiendas to distribute, the viceroys created offices and pensions funded from expected future income.

Within a year of Cañete's arrival in Peru in 1556, the treasury officials were writing angry letters to the Crown complaining that the viceroy's policies were eating up funds that could have been sent to Spain. They complained of the seed money that was offered to Spaniards to induce them to settle in the new towns founded by the viceroy. They argued that the viceregal guard organized by Cañete was unnecessary and expensive, and clearly regarded it as a threat to themselves as well as to the rest of the Spanish population.[20] They fueled their arguments with gossip, arguing that Cañete married his relatives to widows of encomenderos in order to provide them with estates, and adding that the viceroy opened their mail and countermanded orders from Spain, refusing to confirm people who arrived in Peru with offices granted them by the Crown. One official fumed that Cañete had handed out some 20,000 pesos without accounting for them to the treasury officials, throwing away the income of Peru "not as if it were his own wealth, but as if it were money discovered in a dungheap."[21]

Such letters found an audience in Spain despite Cañete's solid support by other established interests in Peru, and the viceroy was eventually replaced. He died before his replacement arrived with a further order to return to Spain to account for his actions. His replacement, the Conde de Nieva, another high-ranking nobleman, served his sovereign no better and probably much worse. More interested in lining his pockets and rewarding his clients and lovers than in the daily grind of government, Nieva quickly provoked the same complaints from the treasury officials that they had flung at Cañete. By 1561, the officials were writing desperate letters to Spain complaining that Nieva had not only handed out all of the income from Indian tribute in pensions and grants, but was moving to appropriate income from the royal fifth of all precious metals, as well as other sources of royal income in Peru that had never before been committed to internal uses. Nieva's conduct led them to have second thoughts about his predecessor. Within a year of Nieva's arrival, one of the officials wrote sadly to the Crown that if Cañete "had not been so reckless about squandering the royal treasury, it is clear that his government was not as bad as some others."[22]

The joint exercise of patronage by both the Crown and its officials in Peru soon reduced the royal treasury in the Andean kingdom to bankruptcy. In 1561, the treasury officials reported to the Crown that it was not possible to pay the awards and grants obtained in Spain for presentation in Peru, amounting to more than 200,000 ducats.[23] Nieva added his voice to the complaints in a rare example of unity with the treasury officials, writing to the Crown that "if as many pay orders are presented in this kingdom as have been granted to date, and are met, it will be impossible to send money to Your Majesty; because in five pay orders alone, [the amounts] reach 300,000 castellanoes."[24] By the 1560's, the annual deficit of the treasury in Peru was estimated at some 150,000 pesos; in 1563 alone, the Factor reported a deficit of 80,000 pesos.[25]

The penury of both Crown and local government found an echo in renewed political unrest, this time originating not in the upper levels of the new society but further down. Although these movements never reached the point of open violence, they were symptomatic of trouble. In 1561, the authorities discovered a movement of sedition sparked by leading citizens of Cuzco. In 1567, conspiracies organized by young mestizos, the offspring of Spaniards and Indian women, some of them from the upper ranks of colonial society, were discovered in Lima and Cuzco shortly before the risings were scheduled to take place. [26]

Trouble from the Spanish segment of the new colonial society was echoed by trouble from the larger Andean majority as well. To some degree, dealing with that trouble was a constant element in Spanish policy from the conquest period. The Inca rebels who maintained a state-in-exile in the jungle lowlands below Cuzco after 1536 remained a continual threat. From the fortress of Vilcabamba in the Urubamba Valley northwest of Cuzco, the Inca intensified his raids into the neighboring Huamanga and Jauja districts. But in the 1560's, a new threat emerged from among the people who had apparently submitted to and accepted the domination of the Europeans. In 1564, a Spanish priest reported a subversive religious movement among the Indians of his parish in the southern highlands. The Taki Onqoy, as it became known, was a messianic movement that preached total withdrawal from Spanish settlers, customs, and goods, and predicted the elimination of the Spaniards by an alliance of the wak'as against the invaders. The movement seriously alarmed the Spanish population, and the viceroy sent out a priest to investigate the movement and stop its activities. A year later, in 1565, the acting viceroy received warnings of possible native risings from the authorities in Cuzco, Huanuco, and Huamanga. Arms caches were discovered in Jauja, Andahuaylas, and elsewhere. [27]

Under the surface turmoil lay the bald fact that the Andean people could no longer meet the massive and growing demands of their new masters and still survive. At least some members of Spanish society in Peru perceived this, and a torrent of proposals, memorials, accusations, and counteraccusations flooded not only the authorities in Peru, but the Crown in Spain as well. Churchmen and other reformers accused the encomenderos of destroying the native population. The accused replied in kind, asserting that they, as conscientious property-holders, cared for and conserved their property, which was exploited and wasted by people who, holding no vested rights to Indian labor, sought only to extract a quick profit and run.

Beneath all of this wrangling, the fact remained that the economic, social, and political institutions that sufficed for the maintenance of a small occupying force profiting from the goods and labor expropriated from the native population were not sufficient to ensure the survival of a society that had become considerably more complex.

The new Spanish society that took form in the decades between the 1530's and the 1560's was not a society of conquerors alone, but one of nobles, professionals, merchants, entrepreneurs, and artisans. The only group that does not appear in the catalogue drawn up by careful scholars is that of the manual laborer, for manual labor remained for all practical purposes the sole responsibility of the members of Andean society. Indian labor built the Europeans' homes and stores, carried their mail, transported their goods, and produced their food and clothing. And the Indians mined the precious metals remitted to Spain. It was that basic reality, combined with the effective monopoly over the native population held by a small group of encomenderos, that lay behind the political disputes and conflicts of the 1560's. For Andean society did not operate according to the calculations of a mercantile society; its communal organization facilitated the organization and realization of tasks that, by the market-oriented calculations of the Europeans, did not bring sufficient gain to be worth the undertaking. And in the conquest period, the benefits gained from such labors went to the encomendero, whose monopoly over Indian labor gave him a competitive advantage that the other members of the new Spanish society in Peru found very threatening.

By the 1560's, there was a substantial Spanish population in Peru that not only did not live from the surplus extracted through the encomienda system, but was also in open and often antagonistic competition with the members of traditional Andean society. In Lima, there were only 32 encomenderos in a Spanish population of 2,500 in 1569—between one and two percent of the total population. In Potosí, the second-largest urban center in Peru, there were none at all.[28] And Lima and Potosí together contained more than half the total Spanish population of Peru in 1569, offering a market for goods and services that was greater than all of the other centers combined. The people who sought to make their living by producing for that market were not part of the conquest elite. They held no encomiendas and could hope for none. They were settlers of all kinds: small farmers, peddlers, merchants, professionals, and even priests trying to make enough to support their families and kin and retire in comfort.[29] And by the 1560's, they were finding it very difficult.

It would be hard to define these people as a class separate from or opposed to the encomenderos, who were clearly the elite of the new colony. They made up a motley group that stood between the encomenderos and the mass of the native Andean population that served the encomenderos, and they felt squeezed between the two and understandably resentful of their situation. They came to Peru to make their fortunes; the anger they felt at the difficulties they were having by the 1560's became focused in their opposition to the encomiendas, whose operations undercut their own livelihoods. And that opposition had a chance to surface during the 1560's, when in response to a combination of factors in Spain and in the Andes the question of the encomienda and its persistence became the political question of the day, brought up and debated at all levels in the colony by order of the Crown itself. The immediate circumstances behind this situation lay in the financial troubles of the Crown and its efforts to resolve them. One of the first preoccupations of Philip II on assuming the throne in 1556 was to search for ways to increase the flow of income from Peru. In 1554, during the revolt of Hernández Giron, a group of loyal encomenderos had petitioned the Crown for legal confirmation of full feudal rights of jurisdiction over the Indians. They sent a representative to Madrid with a promise to pay a "service" to the Crown of some 7,600,000 pesos if they were awarded full civil and criminal jurisdiction over the population of their encomiendas.[30] The promise was initially very attractive to the Crown, then on the verge of bankruptcy, and immediately after his accession Philip sent a group of four commissioners to Peru to investigate the situation and recommend action. The financial needs of the Crown were to be a major consideration, for as Philip noted in his instructions, the commissioners were to justify and explain any recommendation against the confirmation of feudal privilege, "because you must keep in mind the fact that our needs are great, particularly in these times in which we receive so many affronts from the King of France, and if we do the Indians native to said provinces the great favor of not alienating them perpetually from our royal crown, it is only just that they do us a service according to their capacities."[31] In other words, political jurisdiction over the native Andean population was to be put up for auction, and the members of Andean society quickly understood the principle and responded as Philip had specified. In 1560, a group of kurakas authorized their champion, the friar Domingo de Santo Tomás, to offer the Crown 100,000 ducats more than the highest offer presented by the encomenderos.[32] The arguments presented by the encomenderos and their supporters, as well as by the faction (considerably swollen in numbers by the 1560's) that opposed the consolidation of feudal authority in Peru, are somewhat muddled by the fact that the whole affair was largely an auction in which the Crown and its representatives were calling for bids on which way its decision should go. But despite this atmosphere, the arguments presented to the commissioners and to Philip II permit a relatively clear reconstruction of the conflicting class positions at issue in the organization of a political system in Peru.

The encomenderos and their supporters argued from the basic assumption that every society depends upon an aristocracy that organizes production and defends the society against attacks from outside or inside its territory. They argued that trade with Spain depended upon the market they provided, for the encomenderos supported not only themselves and their immediate families, but all who cultivated their lands and estates and all of the clients they maintained.[33] Without their presence, the new realms would be destroyed by pirates from without or by the rebellion of the conquered Indians from within. One of their most able exponents, the lawyer and jurist Juan de Matienzo, expressed the aristocratic argument succinctly and clearly. His position was that without a hereditary aristocracy founded on the right of the conquerors, a Spanish society could not survive in Peru: "there would not remain a man in this Kingdom, as is well known, since it is obvious that the encomenderos maintain the land, and without them there can be no republic, nor can it be kept, because the merchants do not intend to remain here, but to get what they can and leave with it for Spain."[34]

The pro-encomendero faction also presented the classic position of the property owner, arguing that only the owner of property cared for and preserved it for the future, whereas a temporary occupant got what could be squeezed out of the property in a hurry, heedless of later consequences. The equation of feudal parcelized jurisdiction with private property may seem slightly anomalous, but in the context of the modernizing sixteenth century and the growing equation between agrarian production and national wealth, the encomenderos sought to present themselves as a responsible productive class whose efforts to increase its wealth were the foundation of the wealth of the kingdom as a whole. They argued that the Indians "would be governed and treated better by perpetual lords than by temporary ones. This [argument] is based on the whole of natural reason and law, since the first differs from the second in the same way as the lord and owner of a vineyard differs from he who merely rents it, because the lord and owner treats it carefully as a thing of his own, whereas the renter uses and exploits it as something not his, since he will not keep it."[35]

The opponents of the encomenderos' petitions made their opposition known in a flood of memorials and petitions and letters to the Crown and its representatives in Madrid as well as to the commissioners in Peru. They denied the basic assumptions of the encomenderos' argument, insisting that the elimination of the encomiendas, rather than denuding the land of its Spanish population, would do just the opposite. Some among this group, among them priests, friars, and Crown lawyers, argued for a form of indirect rule derived from medieval principles governing the relations between victorious and vanquished lords. They argued that the Inca was a "natural lord," in the medieval tradition of the "señor natural," who could be defeated and converted from an independent ruler to a conquered prince subject to tribute levied upon his people by the victors, but who according to the principles of canon law could not be eliminated.[36] The advocates of this position argued that Andean traditions should be respected and accepted insofar as they were compatible with Catholicism and the legal and nominal supremacy of the Crown. This argument, which reflected much of actual practice in the relations between the Andean people and their Spanish conquerors in the conquest period, was used by many on both sides of the battle over the encomienda.

Others argued more specifically from fears that the fragmentation of royal jurisdiction that would result from the confirmation of feudal authority would eliminate the Crown's ability to rule its new kingdom. Jurisdiction—the authority to decide disputes and arbitrate quarrels—is one of the most fundamental attributes of power. The encomenderos had exercised that authority in fact since the conquest, establishing in that way practices that by the 1560's had become established custom and tradition. The confirmation of that jurisdiction would have meant the effective alienation of the Crown's right to determine accepted practice through the exercise of justice. According to some, such as Domingo de Santo Tomás in 1562, any legal acceptance of the jurisdiction of the encomenderos meant the loss of royal control over its new subjects, and with it the elimination of royal authority in the new kingdom: "even when the encomenderos had no more right than that of collecting the tribute, they were so convinced of their own authority that they became absolute lords who made peace and war as they wished, and the King, holding everything by right, had nothing in fact."[37] It was jurisdiction rather than income alone that was the foundation of the real power the encomenderos sought to confirm. They made their offer to the Crown contingent upon the grant of jurisdiction over the Indians in their encomiendas, and Santo Tomás, who based his opposition on the same grounds, insisted to the Crown that "any jurisdiction . . . would be a total loss of the Indians and the kingdom."[38]

There were also those among the opponents of the encomienda who argued that the elimination of the institution would enable the economy of the new kingdom to grow and develop free of the fetters of feudal institutions that hindered the incorporation of the native Andean population into the labor force of the new society. But this incipient bourgeois argument was flawed and undermined by the fact that many among the Spaniards in Peru found themselves unable to compete with the Indians, who drew upon the productive power of their local communities for the goods and labor that they offered in the European marketplace at a price far below what the Spaniards could afford to meet. Most of the Spaniards in Peru thought of economic activity in terms of special privileges and monopolies that limited loss in a situation of constricted and fixed markets. These assumptions distorted their efforts to fight the encomienda on the grounds that the Indians' submission to their encomendero gave him an unfair advantage over a market all sought to reach, for it is clear that the Spaniards who lacked encomiendas were eager to find a way to cut themselves a piece of the pie that would free them from competition from the Indians, whether as representatives of their encomenderos or as free agents.

These Spaniards sought to enlist the authorities on their side, demanding legal restriction not of the encomendero himself, but of the Indians whose participation in the European market brought them a substantial share of that market, which in turn went to the encomendero in the form of tribute payments. Though their petitions were not directed against the encomendero as such, the thrust of their arguments, in the context of the encomenderos' effective monopoly of the products of Indian labor, was directed against the Indian-encomendero relationship that hurt their own activities. An anonymous memorial to the Crown written by a treasurer in Potosí in the 1560's expresses both the difficulties of the members of this group and the remedies they proposed for them.[39]

This shrewd individual shared all the attitudes and prejudices of the incipient class he represented, whose members were squeezed between the encomenderos and the aristocratic plunder economy on the one hand and the Andean system of production built on cooperative labor and reciprocity on the other. Totally contemptuous of the Indian population, which he described as lazy, slothful, and given to all kinds of vices, he accepted completely the assumption that the production of the mines depended entirely upon the Indians, whose methods of extracting and refining silver according to traditional practices he described in detail.[40] But, he continued, though the Indians produced only a few bits of pure silver a day, they were content with that amount, whereas a Spaniard could not produce sufficient metal with the same technology to purchase his food and clothing.[41] Only where the native Andean miners enjoyed the support of their communities and were not forced to feed and clothe themselves from the products of their labor could they produce the silver demanded by the Europeans. But that same community support also made it possible for the Indians to obtain the silver demanded by their European masters by selling a portion of the goods they produced to the urban centers. As the memorialist pointed out, more than 20,000 fanegas of wheat and maize were consumed yearly in Potosí, where a population of 800 Spaniards together with 15,000 transient Indian miners made up a considerable urban market for foodstuffs. The use of oxen, plows, and European agricultural techniques permitted the Spaniards to produce wheat for that market, but the farmers found their prices driven down by the crops sold in Potosí by the Indian communities, whose members were willing to sell their goods at low prices in order to obtain the silver they needed. In effect, the silver had no value in their own society, nor was the cost of the goods they offered in the market calculated in terms of the cost of its production in silver.

In desperation, the small producers turned to the Crown for help. Our anonymous memorialist begged the Crown to give the Spaniards a monopoly over the provision of foodstuffs for the new urban centers in the kingdom by barring the Indians from participation in those markets. He argued that the Indians should be confined to mining, "since it causes them no more work or harm, and [they] should leave the business of providing bread and foodstuffs to the Spaniards who can do it more easily and without so much work, since they cultivate with oxen and the Indians do it by their own efforts."[42] Small farmers, bureaucrats, and officials represented a combination of interests that could not prosper under an aristocratic society dominated by a new nobility with its extensive control over the labor of the Indian population, labor that represented for them the defeat of the incipient commodity production in which they were engaged.

The arguments presented by the opponents of the encomienda constitute the first efforts of members of European society to present the interests of colonists whose social attitudes and aspirations differed sharply from the medieval framework of an aristocratic feudal system. These people did not regard the members of native Andean society as sources of labor and surplus. On the contrary, many of them saw the Indians as competitors in the struggle for survival and economic prosperity. They joined priests and friars in vocal protest against the encomienda system, although their opposition was not generally motivated either by high moral values or by their piety and generosity toward the Indians. They expressed their opinions both in writing and in vocal and even violent protests to the commissioners, who complained to the Crown that in Peru, "the people . . . live with more liberty than is convenient."[43] The strength of their position lay more in the threat of renewed violence that they represented than in the logical coherence of their arguments. In at least one case, protest threatened to turn into a riot when low-level professionals together with "plebian people of Spain" caused a public scandal in Cuzco.[44]

The forces opposed to the encomienda system, however, were fragmented and in conflict. They were united only in their efforts to prevent the confirmation of seignorial rule in Peru. Beyond that, no coherent position was developed. Conservatives such as Domingo de Santo Tomás, dedicated in his efforts to prevent the destruction of native Andean society, joined for the moment with small farmers, artisans, low-level bureaucrats, and professionals in a fight to eliminate the aristocracy of the new kingdom. But this short-lived alliance for a specific limited objective did not last long. Ultimately, the interests of those who sought to preserve Andean traditions clashed with those who saw the Indians only as a source of labor and goods and who sought to block the encomenderos' petitions in order to gain access to that population for their own ends.

The commissioners, faced with this situation, set the financial needs of the Crown against the limited means of all but the most prosperous encomenderos, and offered Philip II a compromise solution that reflected all the problems of adapting a feudal structure to ruling a distant land. They recognized clearly that the confirmation of jurisdiction for the encomenderos threatened to leave the Crown in a weak position, similar to that of a feudal lord whose vassals were greater than he in both lands and subjects. What was to prevent the encomenderos, once confirmed in their authority, from breaking loose from their allegiance to Spain? The 1560's were a decade of revolt in Europe that amply confirmed such fears. In the Netherlands, growing aristocratic discontent with Spanish rule merged with popular revolt to lead in 1566 to secession and war.[45] Italy— the commissioners' example of the benefits of aristocratic rule through their analogy of the greater prosperity of a vineyard cultivated by its owner as against rented out—was also brought up as a warning against the dangers of separatist sentiments in a nobility whose position no longer depended on its monarch.[46] As they pointed out in a prophetic passage, which did not bear fruit until nearly 300 years later, "if all were perpetual, then the sons and grandsons of the encomenderos would not be beholden and loyal to the King of Spain, but would acquire a loyalty to their country of birth, as has been shown in Italy in the Kingdom of Naples, where sons of Spanish fathers respond to the call of their country of birth rather than to Spaniards among whom are numbered their fathers and from where they originate. This has been seen increasingly in seditions and risings after the deaths of their parents."[47]

On the basis of this reasoning, the commissioners proposed that the Crown only grant some of the encomenderos' petitions, granting perpetual seignorial jurisdiction to a third of the encomenderos in Peru. This would create a stratum of grandees of the new realm, a legally constituted nobility upon which monarchical rule could rest secure. Another third of the encomiendas were to be reserved as grants to be awarded for the lifetime of the recipient in reward for services rendered the Crown—a form of nobility of the robe. The last third of the encomiendas were to become estates of the Crown, the income from which could be used to grant pensions and benefits to deserving claimants to royal favor without alienating the properties of the monarch.[48] Potential separatist tendencies among the upper nobility thus constituted would be restrained by the continual addition of new members to their class, whose access to the nobility would be only for their lifetimes and was the direct product of their service to the monarch. Thus the commissioners hoped to prevent the breakdown of ties to a distant monarch that could be seen in Europe, and with it the fragmentation of political entities. "With perpetuity, in thirty or forty years the descendants of those born here—or at least one may suspect it of them—will become foreign to our nation and enemies of it. And if all are confirmed in their authority, they will be united in a single body, which since it will be the nerve and strength of these kingdoms can rise easily and not obey the kings of Castile, hating, as is natural, to be governed by a foreign kingdom, as they will then view Spain."[49] An elite in the new kingdom was regarded as essential to political order, but if it were kept fragmented and if its membership were rotated regularly and renewed by new nobles created by the Crown, control by Spain over its overseas kingdoms could be maintained.

The argument presented by the commissioners was both articulate and convincing, and although the proposal to create a feudal system in Peru was somewhat anachronistic, the expansion of feudal relationships in conjunction with the growth of powerful monarchies in Eastern Europe at about the same time leaves open the question of whether or not such a project was possible, despite the strong opposition of a large and growing group of Spaniards in Peru. But the question needs no answer, for the commissioners, together with the viceroy, the Conde de Nieva, exceeded the limits of past practice in their greed for personal enrichment and brought down the hopes of the encomenderos with them. The Crown discovered that they all had accepted bribes, had sold encomiendas and offices on a vast scale, and further, had attempted to smuggle their new fortunes back to Spain piecemeal to conceal them. The commissioners were arrested as they left their ship in Seville, and orders were given for the arrest of the Conde de Nieva in Peru, who conveniently died at this point.[50]

The exposure of the commissioners' activities effectively wrecked any chances that their proposals for the confirmation of feudal jurisdiction in Peru might be acted upon. The petitions of the encomenderos were also shelved. The Crown did not entirely lose hope of obtaining some income from the encomenderos, but though the question of perpetuity remained alive for some years, the issue of parcelized jurisdiction died, and with it died the possibility for the creation of a feudal aristocracy in Peru. The encomienda gradually became little more than a guaranteed source of income, a mark of status that made its holder a member of the elite of the viceroyalty. The holders of encomiendas became equivalent to a nobility in Peru, a nobility that, like its European counterpart, lacked the authority over men and the right to dispense justice that defined a feudal society. The elite founded on the encomienda was enlarged by officials and bureaucrats, whose service to the Crown constituted another measure and source of prestige that put them at the top of colonial society.[51]

But the problem of the organization of a system of government remained, and with it the conflict between the needs of local government and the financial demands of the Crown. The development of an effective state structure and bureaucracy meant that the Crown either had to find the means to pay those who worked for it or had to provide rewards by granting its officials a share of the surplus obtained from the colonial enterprise. Juan de Matienzo, who regarded the creation of a feudal aristocracy as the most effective solution to the problem, made a gloomy calculation of the costs of government without the encomienda. "If the repartimientos [encomiendas] were to fall into the royal crown, there would need to be at least 100 men in the cities to maintain the citizenry, and they would each have to be given at least 1,000 pesos a year, and these could not maintain a tenth of the people who are now maintained."[52] The factors of the equation did not change between 1540 and 1570. The Crown in Madrid needed money. For another generation Spain fought to maintain her supremacy in Europe, until Spanish power and the Spanish treasury went down together in bankruptcy and Spain entered into the long decline that lasted until the eighteenth century. If Spanish authority was to be maintained in Peru, either the representatives of the Crown had to be rewarded with incomes that met their expectations, or the Crown had to turn a deaf ear to what, three centuries later, would be defined as corruption and share both its authority and its income with those responsible for enforcing its rules.

The fifth viceroy of Peru, Francisco de Toledo, was given the task of organizing the political structure of the kingdom so as to meet the demands from the Spanish population for a share of the labor and goods of the members of Andean society while generating sufficient income for the royal treasury in Peru to pay the costs of government and still remit something back to Spain. Toledo has gone down in Peruvian historiography as the great organizer, the architect of the colonial system, but neither the man, nor the class he represented, nor the structure he built emerges clearly from the few biographies of him or studies of his period that exist.[53] We sorely need a good study of the construction of the colonial regime from the mid-sixteenth century through the administration of Toledo that would bring to light the competing interests in Peru and in Europe that contributed to the organization of the colonial system of European absolutism.

Toledo himself is a prime example of the modernizing aristocrats of the absolute monarchies, the members of the great nobility who identified their personal ambitions with those of their monarch and devoted their efforts to creating a powerful centralized state whose summit and center was the Crown. Toledo's vision of the state and his concept of social order was on a par with that of the state-builders of Europe, and a close study of his life and times would make a significant contribution to our understanding of the European system just prior to the transition to capitalism.

European absolutism has been described as an instrument for the protection of aristocratic wealth and privilege in a situation of rapid commercial expansion through the creation of a centralized state and the consequent displacement of the parcelized jurisdiction characteristic of feudalism up to the state level. The Crown protected the real supremacy of the nobility by appropriating its powers of jurisdiction and using them to reinforce the control and subordination of the peasant masses, and to maintain the flow of surplus from below to the aristocracy.[54] Much of this argument can be applied to the Andes in the 1570's and the 1580's, when the organization of the colonial state and the mechanisms for the extraction of surplus from the native population were given the form that they would retain for the next two hundred years. The battle over the confirmation of feudal jurisdiction in Peru was fought and lost before Toledo arrived in the Andes in 1569: feudal jurisdiction was denied the encomenderos of Peru; and the right to set the terms and the limits of exploitation—to exercise justice—was centralized under the viceregal authorities. This made the state a central factor in the expropriation and distribution of the surplus obtained from the native Andean population. It gave the representatives of the state the authority to set the terms and define the mechanisms of interaction between the native Andean population and the members of Spanish society in Peru.

The levies paid by the members of Andean society and distributed by the state among those with claims upon its favors were an important part of the productive system of colonial society. These levies paid the costs of Indian administration, principally the salaries of civil and religious authorities in the Indian provinces, and they transferred to members of European society a portion of the Indians' labor and the products of their labor. With the decline of the encomienda, the state apparatus in Peru and its representatives—the bureaucracy, civil and religious—became the principal agents of the extraction of surplus in its various forms. The system of control that existed in the decades between 1533 and the 1580's was modified to exclude the conquerors and encomenderos from direct access to the Indian population, replacing them with royal officials responsible for the execution of the state's demands. The levies paid by the members of Andean society, in one form or another, represented a direct transfer of surplus generated within their society to the bureaucracy, which in turn distributed it among the members of the Spanish colonial elite. This system preserved, in a modified form, the system of claims upon the state in return for service to it that was the basis of the Crown's authority over the Spaniards in Peru. The ability of the Crown and the royal authorities to distribute a share in those levies preserved the power of patronage upon which the state rested.[55]

The patronage powers of the state consisted of the right to assign to favored individuals the privilege of access to the goods and labor of members of Indian society, through an elaborate set of extraeconomic mechanisms of surplus extraction. These mechanisms began to take form from the 1540's, alongside the feudal structures of the conquest period, but the system was not fully elaborated and codified until the viceroyalty of Toledo (1569–82), after the ephemeral attempts to build a feudal system in Peru had failed. In the following pages, I want to define the major levies through which goods and labor were extracted from the native Andean population by the colonial state or its representatives, and suggest some of the ways in which those levies functioned to distribute the labor, and the products, of the members of Indian society among a relatively large group of Spaniards and their descendants in Peru.

The Europeans never intended to carry out any fundamental changes in the socioeconomic structures of the Andean local community, and the entire apparatus of colonial Indian administration as it was organized under Toledo was founded on the principle of retaining the traditional Andean system of production as the economic underpinning for the extraction of surplus from the Indians. Andean society was legally defined as a distinct "republic," whose internal customs and relationships were to be respected and maintained by Spanish colonial courts and authorities.[56] Andean communities were concentrated or "reduced" by Toledo in a massive resettlement program in the 1570's that forcibly moved people from their dispersed settlements—often more dispersed by flight and dislocation during the conquest period—to new villages where they could be more easily counted and assessed by the Spanish authorities assigned to oversee them.[57] Traditional Andean forms of production, which had produced the immense surpluses that maintained the Inca state, were expected to continue to produce the surplus that was to fuel and propel the colonial economic system. The Europeans introduced little in the way of new techniques or products into the Andean local community, whose stock of tools and goods—even agricultural goods—remained essentially the same as before the Europeans entered the Andes.

The ordinances defining relations between Spanish and Indian societies introduced during the Toledan administration on the one hand guaranteed the productive resources and relationships of traditional Andean society to the degree that the Europeans understood Andean definitions of them, and on the other hand established the levies that either channeled goods and labor directly to members of European society or else forced the Indians to offer their goods and their labor time on the European market in order to meet the demands imposed upon them. The latter tactic provided a general subsidy to the members of European society who were unable to obtain a direct subsidy from the royal authorities. From the 1540's, the Crown regularly ordered its officials to gather information on the quantity and the value of the surplus extracted by the Inca state from the local Andean communities. The information produced by those Europeans with considerable experience among the Indians not only provided later historians with some of our best data on the operation of Andean society during the life of the Inca state, but also gave royal officials a basis for calculating their own levies. Toledo made it his business to collect information on the nature and volume of the surplus extracted by the Incas. On the basis of the information received, the Spanish authorities assessed the Andean population with the expectation that they could regularly milk the local community without exhausting its productive resources, human and material.

The basic levy paid by all members of Andean society, save for a selected few—kurakas and the members of the old Inca elite—was tribute, regular payments assessed every male household head as a vassal of the Spanish Crown. The whole concept of tribute represented a major change for the members of Andean society, accustomed as they were to the assignment of levies or tasks that were then divided among the members of kin groups by the kurakas, and they fought it accordingly. Spanish officials who understood the principle of labor service in Andean society, such as Polo de Ondegardo, supported their protests, arguing that tribute should be levied by community rather than by individual, leaving the kuraka to work out the distribution and preparation of the levies according to traditional norms. He insisted that "if we want to impose a new order, they will lose their own, by which they understand one another and we understand them, and they would end with nothing."[58]

The Crown paid little attention to these protests, despite the authoritative sources from which they came, insisting from the early years of the conquest period that the Spaniards inspect and count the Andean population and forward the figures to the royal authorities. Francisco Pizarro was ordered by the Crown to prepare such a census, which he finally ordered in 1540, under protest, naming inspectors from among the conquerors to carry out such an investigation in the provinces then under Spanish control. His orders make it clear, however, that the men sent out were to rely upon the numbers provided them by the kurakas, and then add a personal assessment of what they felt the people could provide.[59]

Each succeeding official sent to Peru carried similar orders, but the first general effort to prepare a count of the Andean population and to regulate the amounts that the encomendero was to be permitted to extract from the people under his authority was the work of Pedro de la Gasca. Preparatory to his general reassignment of encomiendas, La Gasca named two men from each of the Spanish cities founded by 1549, usually themselves encomenderos, and sent them to various parts of Peru with instructions to report on land resources and population, crops and other products of the local communities, and the goods and labor provided to the Inca state before its demise. One example of the reports prepared for La Gasca, describing the Chupachu of Huánuco, survived to become one of the earliest widely known local sources on the Andean population.[60] The reports followed the general form of the instructions prepared by Pizarro in 1540. Each pair of inspectors provided an estimate of what they thought the people could pay and forwarded their reports to La Gasca, who retired with two clerics who had been deeply involved with the Indians and with the members of the first Audiencia of Peru (who came to Peru with him) to a hideout chosen to escape from the constant flow of petitioners and claimants. There they prepared the tribute assessments that would become part of the privileges and the limits of the encomiendas distributed by La Gasca.

La Gasca, true to his main objective of restoring peace in the land, basically ratified the existing volume of goods and labor appropriated by the encomenderos. *Oidores* (lawyers) of the Audiencia and clerics who had participated in the preparation of these first legal assessments later stated flatly that the tribute lists ratified current practices. Twenty years later, Fernando de Santillán, one of the lawyers of the Audiencia who participated in the first assessments, informed the Crown that, "if the assessments had been put at a just level the first time around, it would have been insupportable to the encomenderos, and given the liberty of the past, to avoid this they did not adjust affairs all at once."[61] The original tribute assessments prepared by La Gasca and his assistants were modified under succeeding viceroys as a result of protests and objections by both the kurakas and encomenderos, but not until the administration of Toledo was there any general overhaul of the system.

One of Toledo's first actions after reaching Peru was to embark upon a five-year personal tour of the viceroyalty, lasting from 1570 to 1575. He was later bitterly criticized for his action by royal officials in Peru, particularly by members of the Audiencia who insisted that he was engaged in amassing personal authority rather than attending to his official duties. Toledo defended his tour as the only effective way to impose royal authority throughout the viceroyalty, insisting that without his presence and the direct information he obtained, it would have been impossible to ensure the obedience of both disgruntled Europeans in Peru and the Indians.[62] In many ways, the tour seems to have met his purpose very well, for its similarity to the general tours of Tawantinsuyu by the Inca could not have failed to be noted by the Indians.

The part of the *visita general*, or general inspection, organized by Toledo that dealt specifically with tribute was carried out by inspectors named by him and responsible for particular areas of the viceroyalty. They were ordered to count the native population and ascertain current payments to the encomenderos, much as previous inspectors had done before them. Upon Toledo's return to Lima in 1575, the tribute assessments were recalculated and distributed. These lists provided the basis for further modifications and assessments for the following two centuries.[63] Prior to the Toledan reassessments, tribute was collected in both silver and goods, a situation that permitted the encomenderos to adjust their demands either to the capacity of the people to meet them, or to their own market speculations. As noted earlier, the market activities of the encomenderos provoked opposition from other sections of European society because the encomenderos' access to the products of the Andean economy provided them with marketable goods at a cost below what non-encomenderos could obtain. In this case, Toledo, one of whose major charges was to increase the flow of specie to Spain, aligned with the non-encomenderos and reduced many of the tribute assessments to a fixed sum in silver, although a number of provinces, among them Huarochirí, continued to pay their tribute in kind until well into the eighteenth century.[64]

From Toledo on, tribute was legally defined as a head tax paid by all able-bodied adult men between the ages of eighteen and 50. A selected number of people were exempted from the payment of tribute for specific reasons, ranging from their definition as members of the native elite— kurakas or descendants of the Inca rulers—to personal infirmity and congenital illness.[65] Tribute assessments were based upon periodic counts of the population of a province, repartimiento, or waranqa performed by the local representative of Spanish authority, the *corregidor de indios*. Such a count could be legally requested by the encomendero, the royal attorney-general, or the kuraka in the name of the Indians themselves, in order to adjust the tribute figures to changes in population.[66] Until a new count was completed and remitted to the Contaduría de Tributos in Lima, and a new assessment prepared and issued to the provincial authorities and the royal treasury officials of the district in which the province was located, the people were expected to pay the tribute assigned them on the books, however much the actual population of the province might have changed in the interim. Despite the legal definition of tribute, therefore, the assessment in practice became a levy upon the community as a whole.

From the 1550's, the state took over the collection and distribution of tribute, barring the encomendero from direct access to the Indians. Tribute was collected twice a year, in June and in December, and delivered to the regional treasury officials. Salaries for provincial administrators assigned by the state, for priests, and for kurakas were taken out of this, as well as special assessments for the Church. The remainder went to the encomenderos in cases where the province was held in encomienda, and to the royal treasury in provinces held directly by the Crown. As encomiendas relapsed to the Crown in the course of the seventeenth century, those not reassigned to members of European society then paid their tribute to the state rather than to the encomendero through the state until the formal legal abolition of the encomienda early in the eighteenth century.[67]

Despite the control that the state exerted over the surplus that the encomendero obtained from the Indians, the value of an encomienda in the last two decades of the sixteenth century was still considerable. The mitmaq of Huarochirí and Chaclla paid between one-fourth and one-half of their tribute to their encomenderos according to the assessments made by Toledo, and though these people were few in number, it is probable that the proportion of tribute income that went to the encomendero was the same for the larger home territories of the people of Huarochirí and Chaclla, for whom detailed assessment figures are not available.[68] In both areas, in addition, a considerable part of the encomendero's share was paid in kind: the mitmaq of Huarochirí gave 21.4 percent of the goods they paid to their encomendero, and those of Chaclla sent their encomendero all of the goods they owed in tribute. The cloth and maize collected in Huarochirí, both easily marketable, were probably sold by their encomendero. But what about the goods collected by the state, not only in the 1580's but later in the colonial period? How was the value of tribute in kind realized by the state, and did the goods provided by the members of Indian society in the form of tribute provide a subsidy to the members of European society?

The available evidence on this point comes not from central Peru, but from the south. It consists of records of the sale of tribute in kind kept in the city of Cuzco, the site of a regional treasury, in the middle of the seventeenth century.[69] After the distribution of a certain proportion of the goods to the hospitals and beneficent institutions of the city for their sustenance, announcements of the goods offered and the fixed values assigned them by the Contaduría de Tributos were posted by one of the attorneys of the treasury, together with the provincial official of the province from which the goods were collected. The goods offered for sale in Cuzco consisted largely of maize, wheat, potatoes, and fowls, usually chickens. Essentially the same variety of goods, as well as cloth, was collected as tribute in central Peru. In Cuzco, residents of the city bid upon the goods of a province, offering to pay the assigned face value of the goods in assayed silver.

If the state found bidders for all of the goods, it would realize the full official price of the tribute in kind, and the goods would become the property of the buyers, apparently local merchants who dealt in such goods. But in the particular case described here, the bidders did not immediately come forward—a situation that probably happened increasingly in the course of the seventeenth and eighteenth centuries. After nine announcements and only two responses, the remainder of the goods were sent to auction to be sold off in item lots to the highest bidder. This practice, necessary as it may have been for the state, which did not deal directly in the provision or sale of foodstuffs, effectively subsidized the Spanish buyers of these goods and the merchants who put them into circulation, probably the same people. How did this happen?

Harvests vary widely in the Andes, where crop failure is an omnipresent possibility and the regular alternation of good and bad years is common. But tribute in kind was not a percentage of the harvest; it was a fixed amount, collected no matter what the size of the crop harvested by the Indian farmer. And that fixed amount went on the market each year within a few weeks after the harvest. The amount collected from the Indians bore no relation to either the harvest or the market price of the crops, and it was offered on the market at fixed prices, set by the state well ahead of the harvest and probably varying little from year to year. But the amounts actually sold by the state undoubtedly responded to market conditions, rising in years of poor harvests and falling in years of plenty. So in effect the state's sale of tribute in kind constituted a kind of buffer not for the farmer, whose burden rose in bad times relative to his total harvest, but for the dealer in grain and other foodstuffs, the merchant and middleman who was protected from shortages in his stock of goods by the regular supply of commodities provided by the state through its auctions of tribute produce. And at least in Cuzco, these middlemen were members of European society, as the names of the purchasers of tribute goods in Cuzco in 1647 indicate. So, save for a few significant exceptions in regions where kurakas operated actively in the European market, the benefits from this system went to the Europeans, although they were both less secure and far more widely distributed than the direct subsidies enjoyed by people who held encomiendas and other pensions based on Indian tribute.

The second major levy assessed by the colonial state in Peru was the *mita*, or labor draft, derived from the preconquest mit'a, the labor "turn" through which the Inca state drew upon people for its various projects and tasks. The mita, as it was formalized and given legal form by Toledo, was conceived primarily as a mechanism for lowering the costs of production of the silver upon which Peru depended. Together with the supply of mercury from Huancavelica provided to Potosí for the refinement of ore, the mita was Toledo's solution to the crisis of production in Potosí. It assured a regular, cheap supply of labor to the mines, which made it possible for Spanish miners to sink shafts, to introduce mercury refining (also subsidized by the royal authorities), and in general to invest in the extraction and refining of silver over the long term. The mita also consolidated the control of the Spanish mine owners over the native Andean producers, who until the 1580's continued to mine with traditional Andean techniques, retaining considerable control over both their own labor and the ore they produced. The mita ended that, providing the Spanish mine owners with an assured supply of unskilled labor that largely replaced the skilled miners of the earlier period and reducing the Andean miner to a forced laborer working under dangerous conditions for a legally assigned wage that was often not paid.[70]

The mita, like the tribute based upon the population statistics filed in the Contaduría de Tributos, took between one-sixth and one-seventh of the adult male population for six-month periods of service at tasks defined as essential by the state.[71] The economic function of the labor draft, at least in its conception, related more to the production of Peru's main export goods than to the internal economic structure of the viceroyalty. By providing a substantial labor force from all of southern Peru and the area of present-day Bolivia, Toledo ensured the mines a regular supply of labor to prevent the shortages they had experienced since the 1550's and to maintain a regular flow of silver to Spain. The *mitayos* were legally supposed to be paid according to a wage scale first established by Toledo, and revised at the end of the seventeenth century by the viceroy Duque de la Palata.[72] Not all of the Indian population was subject to labor service in Potosí or in the mercury mines of Huancavelica, but all had to do mita service. Mita allocations were granted by the viceroy on the grounds of the importance to the state of the activity for which mitayos were requested. The mita was explicitly conceived by Toledo as a source of patronage, since "the major wealth in this country is to have Indians with whom to carry on business."[73] The Crown's centralization of jurisdiction was effective, in that it gave the viceroy the means to assign temporary control over the labor of other people—as Toledo said, the source of wealth—to claimants upon the favor of the authorities. Such claims, according to Toledo, should be rewarded on the basis of the "common good," or in other words, the benefit that would be obtained for the viceroyalty and the Crown from the labor granted to the petitioner. Virtually all mita assignments other than the mines underwrote the production of foodstuffs for Lima, the second major urban market in the viceroyalty after Potosí, and the provision of services and luxuries for the colonial elite, including transport and mail service.

The Indians of Huarochirí were not subject to mita service in the mines of either Potosí or Huancavelica, but their labor was drawn upon heavily for the benefit of Lima. Most of the mita labor to which they were assigned was within the province or on its boundaries, either on the coast or in the high puna, the site of silver mining from the seventeenth century. There were three types of mita service to which the people of the province were subject. The first, the mita of the sierra, assigned on the basis of one-seventh of the tributary population, provided labor for the mines of Nuevo Potosí and for the cutting and transport to Lima of glacial ice, used as a food preservative and cooler. The second levy, the mita of the plaza of Lima, based on one-sixth of the population, sent men to the coastal haciendas within the jurisdiction of Lima, providing a temporary labor force to supplement the Negro slaves used by the coastal hacendados. The third, the mita of the tambos, or way stations on the route from Lima to Cuzco and on to Potosí, again assigned on the basis of one-seventh of the male population, sent people to maintain the road and hostel service along the route followed by the mails, by soldiers and officials, and by private travelers.[74]

The economic function of the mita requires little explanation. It was a simple expropriation of labor for the benefit of the silver mines and for other activities that had to be subsidized by the state in one form or another. Its impact was massive. Since the mita draft was assigned only on the basis of the population native to the province in which it was counted, and thereby assumed to have access through its kin groups to lands and resources for its own maintenance and reproduction, a migrant to the province, as an outsider without access to land, was not liable for mita service. Thus the labor draft was in effect a push factor stimulating migration. By the eighteenth century, 40 to 60 percent of the population of the archbishopric of Cuzco, subject to the mita of Potosí, were migrants from other provinces.[75] Outside the area subject to the mining mita, migration between provinces cannot be attributed to that cause, and indeed, the proportion of outsiders in the archbishopric of Lima in the mid-eighteenth century was only about 23 percent of the total tributary population.[76] The mita could still be a heavy burden, and there is little doubt that it did stimulate migration, since a person could escape the levy merely by moving to a place other than where he was born. But the decision to forfeit access to lands and resources—in other words, to cut all claims to the security of kin and tradition—was a heavy one. At least for people not subject to the mining mita, such as the people in Huarochirí, it probably meant a choice to trade the social relationships of traditional Andean society for a more European pattern, in which survival was a matter of wage labor or the personal ties of clientage characteristic of a precapitalist European system.

There were other levies, legal and extralegal, through which the members of European society in Peru extracted goods and labor from the Indian population. The representatives of royal authority in the Indian provinces (the *corregidores de indios*, the civil authorities, and the parish priests assigned to the Indian provinces) commonly extracted a variety of levies from the Indians to which the Crown turned its back, aware that its only alternative to providing a salary that would attract people to such positions was to ignore the extra demands they laid upon the people under their authority. When the exactions exceeded the level set by custom and the limits of tolerance of the Indian population, the people's protests in the courts, as well as outside them, usually forced the state to apply the laws forbidding extralegal exactions; but such occasions were the exception rather than the rule.

For the most part, the official levies of the state—tribute and mita—permitted the royal authorities to appropriate a considerable proportion of the surplus generated by the native Andean population. Throughout the colonial period, the income from tribute was second only to the income from the royal fifth of all production of silver in the viceroyalty.[77] This income provided a financial basis for the exercise of patronage by the Crown. Further, the distribution of provincial offices as rewards for claimants to the favors of Crown and viceroy also added to the patronage powers of the state. The Crown and the viceregal authorities disputed one another's right to the exercise of this patronage throughout the colonial period, with the Crown, despite its own laws and regulations, gradually absorbing from the viceroy the authority to appoint provincial officials in Peru. It used that authority to obtain income by selling the right to hold the offices.[78] But whether the appointment originated in Lima or in Madrid, the reorganization of the colonial system and the centralization of the authority of the Crown provided a resolution of a kind to the political crisis of the 1560's.

But the solution brought consequences of its own. It made the colonial state and its representatives the agents through which the surplus of the Indians was funneled to the European population in Peru. This in turn meant that access to the viceregal authorities—and better yet, to the Court in Madrid—became the basis of privilege and wealth. The power of appointment, together with the authority to assign access to the labor and goods of the Indian population, became a major determinant of social and economic position for members of European society in Peru. Access to the colonial bureaucracy was a springboard to upward mobility and eventual membership in the colonial elite. But by making the state the major source of access to the surplus generated by the Andean population, in a system with a limited development of productive activity for both the external and the internal market, the colonial system gave to the political sphere an extreme degree of control over the development of the economy of the viceroyalty. The exercise of patronage by the authorities did not create the colonial elite, but it certainly played a major role in its orientation and character during the colonial period. And further, the direct and active participation of the state in the appropriation and distribution of the surplus generated by the Andean population set the terms of the colonial relationship.

SIX

The Shrinking Web

THE VICEROYALTY of Francisco de Toledo (1569–86) marked the definitive organization of a colonial system in Peru based upon the extraction of surplus in labor and goods from the Andean people for the benefit of their conquerors, broadly defined as the members of European society resident in the Andes. For the members of local Andean society, the impact of the Spanish presence took a while to be felt, for conquest is a great deal more than catastrophic violence, than armies and plunder and disrupted homes. On the local level, the conquest of Peru was also a long, slow process of adjustment and struggle through which the members of Andean society sought to reach a *modus vivendi* with their conquerors. In that slow process, the traditions and culture of local society were distorted, changed, and restructured day by day in a multitude of small individual adjustments as people sought to survive, and even prosper, under new conditions. The result of this process was a society whose fundamental relationships were very different from what they were when the invaders first appeared, although much of the external forms and practices appeared to have changed little from the sixteenth century. But the imposition of the Spanish state, and with it the constraints and mechanisms through which surplus was extracted from the members of Andean society, set new conditions and a new framework for the evolution of local society that in the course of the seventeenth and the eighteenth centuries fundamentally changed its internal relationships.

Through the examination of the changing character of access to the resources and means of production in Huarochirí, I want in the course of this chapter to illuminate some of the fundamental changes in the economic structures of local society under Spanish colonial rule. Those changes were not spectacular. They did not involve the imposition of European relations of production such as those characteristic of the mining economy of Potosí, the great landed estates, or the *obrajes* (textile manufactories) of the Spanish colonial world. But though slow and almost imperceptible, the changes in the relations of production in Huarochirí over the long run fragmented and eroded the fundamental relationships that bound the minimal units of Andean society into larger entities that, by organized cooperation, could build and maintain the material basis that meant the difference between real (if limited) prosperity and poverty.

The majority of the data upon which the following discussion is based are drawn from the latter part of the colonial period—essentially from the 1650's to the end of the eighteenth century. The sources available to me did not permit me to trace the process of change in detail from the sixteenth century to the eighteenth; my data are scattered and fragmentary, permitting the establishment of a baseline in the latter part of the sixteenth century that cannot be picked up again until nearly a century later. Hence the early stages of the transformation of the productive structures of Huarochirí are extrapolated from the data available. I do not have data permitting the elaboration of quantitative indices of change. In fact, the data do not permit the construction of either a narrative or a quantitative history of the process of change in the province as a whole, or in any one particular portion of it. They are far too varied, as well as too fragmentary, to permit such an effort, useful as it would be. But the very diversity of the data permits other approaches, one of which is the use of materials drawn from different areas within the province for the reconstruction of a process that did not affect all of the areas of the province at the same time. The often episodic quality of the data is itself a test of the reconstruction, for when material drawn from widely different sources, prepared for different purposes, validates the same interpretation, the hypothesis advanced to explain the material merits consideration.

Although Huarochirí bordered on the metropolis of Lima, capital of a territory that reached the length and breadth of a continent, until the latter part of the eighteenth century the region was not integrated into the European colonial world. The province lay across the main travel route from Lima into the highlands, but although the members of European society passed through in large numbers, they stopped only at the tambos or rest stops on their way to the highland valleys, to Cuzco and to Potosí. Members of European society did not settle in the towns of Huarochirí; the total European population of the province never amounted to even 3 percent of the total population, even including the parish priests.[1] Descriptions of the province noted its benign climate, free from both the heat of the coast and the harsh cold of the high puna areas, but the steep valley slopes with their few relatively level pockets of land offered little to a European looking for agricultural land. Agriculture in the province was—and is—vertical in the extreme. Land is farmed in tiny plots scattered over the slopes. I have even seen a farmer anchored to his plot, partway down a steep slope, by a rope tied to a tree several yards above at the crest of the slope.

All of these factors contributed to making Huarochirí a relatively isolated area despite its proximity to one of the two most important urban centers of the viceroyalty. This relative isolation was magnified by the fact that the colonial state did not dislocate the people of this region as it did others. As we have noted, Huarochirí was never subject to the mining mitas that sent thousands of men to work in the mines of Huancavelica and Potosí. Instead, the mitayos of Huarochirí served their labor turns inside the province or on its boundaries, manning the rest stops and maintaining the heavily traveled route into the highlands, working the farms and chacaras bordering Lima, or, from the early decades of the seventeenth century, working the mines of Nuevo Potosí on the eastern edge of Huarochirí. All of this made this area, so close to the center of the Spanish colonial world in Peru, a relatively closed system whose internal dynamics reflected the response of traditional Andean society to colonial rule. It was not even particularly subject to the impact of other members of Andean society. Though migrants from distant provinces did settle in Huarochirí, they were few in number. Most people lived and died within a few days' journey of their birthplaces. This relative stability makes Huarochirí a good area for the study of social transformation from within. Though the stimuli for the kind and direction of social transformation came from outside the local system—from the demands and the relationships imposed by an overseas metropolis—the process of change was the product of the response to those demands on the part of the local communities as they sought to survive and to prosper within the new limits imposed upon them.

The incorporation of Huarochirí into the structure of the conquest society did not bring rapid changes in the region as a whole. Despite the initial plunder of the treasure of wak'as and mummies, and the subsequent division of the people of the region into three encomiendas, the internal organization of local society continued much as it was before the European invasion. Though people supplied their encomenderos with foodstuffs and other local goods, the products of even a diversified agricultural society were hardly what the conquerors, eager to find commodities that could be the basis of the fortunes they hoped to amass, were seeking. Some products of Andean society, such as coca, the mildly narcotic leaf chewed largely as part of ritual and ceremonial activities before the conquest, found an immediate and highly profitable market among the Andeans working in the mines. The coca trade that enriched the encomenderos of the area around Cuzco, who took much of the levies they imposed upon the Indians in the leaf, found an echo in Huarochirí, where the encomenderos of Canta and of Chaclla intervened in a conflict over coca lands between the people of their encomiendas in the 1550's. But the coca lands of Quives, although highly valued by the Indians, were not valued so highly by their encomendero, who collaborated in their loss. Coca, highly valued in the south, does not seem to have found such a ready market in Lima, center of a European rather than an Andean population.

From the 1540's to the 1560's, those Spaniards who sought to obtain wealth in Huarochirí shared in the search for gold and silver common to the Americas in general in the early decades.[2] The first Spanish administrator of Huarochirí, Diego Dávila Brizeño, noted that there were mines in several parts of the province that had been worked in the early decades after the Spanish invasion and abandoned by the 1580's. Gold was mined in the low hills near Mamaq at the juncture of the Rímac and Chaclla rivers, and there were mines upriver above the village of Matucana that were abandoned for lack of labor.[3] At the southern boundary of the province, in the repartimiento of Mancos y Laraos in Yauyos, Dávila Brizeño described a silver mine that was closed up by the Indians when the Spaniards entered the area. The mine, worked before the conquest, was reopened and worked with Indian miners, who were offered a sixth of the ore for their labor. They "responded eagerly," but the work stopped when the mine fell in again.[4] The growing crisis of the plunder economy and the civil wars that erupted between the Spaniards meant that many workings were abandoned despite the willingness of the Indians to work for the specie that they could use to pay the levies of their encomenderos. By the 1580's Dávila Brizeño reported that despite rumors of rich deposits throughout the region, existing mines were no longer worked and prospecting had been abandoned.[5]

The civil wars of the 1540's and 1550's between the Spaniards drew many people into the warring forces, both as soldiers and as service personnel who carried goods and foodstuffs. Not only did the Spaniards impress people, but as Dávila Brizeño noted, the people of the province, who prided themselves on their skill as warriors, eagerly joined the Spanish forces.[6] After the end of those struggles and the organization of the European population, the people of Huarochirí did not return to the mines. For whatever reason, they turned instead to the rapidly growing Spanish urban center in Lima. Fernando de Santillán noted in the 1560's that the people of Huarochirí, together with those of Yauyos and Huaylas, went down to the coast to obtain their tribute by hiring themselves out to Spaniards.[7] Twenty years later, Dávila Brizeño gave that as the reason why the mines in the province were not being worked: "the people are occupied in the City of The Kings in the service of that city, where they obtain their tribute and other benefits by the dealings and activities that they have there."[8]

Thus the members of the Andean society in Huarochirí adapted to the demands of the Spaniards, as they did in other parts of the Andes during the decades from the 1530's to the 1580's. In the case of Huarochirí, the sources do not indicate whether the people who offered their labor to the Spaniards did so on an individual basis, or as part of a community for which they provided a "turn" or service in order to obtain the goods (in this case, specie) needed by the community to meet outside demands. But it is probable that, like the people of Chucuito who sent specie back to their communities from the mines of Potosí,[9] the people of Huarochirí also adapted the traditional principle of sending mitmaq from the home community to a specialized resource area—Lima—to obtain a good— specie—needed by the community. The specie that people received in return for their labor in the city and its surrounding countryside was then returned to their encomenderos in the form of tribute. The well-known reluctance of the Indians to use their own fields and resources to produce goods for an outside authority may have also played a part in the reorientation of their labor toward service in and around Lima at tasks set for them by the Europeans. Such outside service could be more easily assimilated to the traditional Andean concept of mit'a service for the Inca state. Tribute goods that the Indians had to produce on their own lands, rather than on the lands of the state, were regarded as a double assessment that was resisted as unfair and excessive.

During the first decades of the seventeenth century, a Spanish presence in Huarochirí was marked by the existence of obrajes, or textile manufactories, as noted by Antonio Vásquez de Espinosa. This writer also mentioned "good mines of silver," undoubtedly referring to the mines of Nuevo Potosí on the eastern border of the province between Huarochirí and Tarma that made that place the second-ranking producer of silver in the viceroyalty by the end of the seventeenth century.[10] But, despite these pockets of European economic activity in Huarochirí, the coast continued to be a major source of specie for the people, who came down to the area of Lima both to serve their mita turns in the gardens and farms that supplied the city with foodstuffs, and to earn money to pay their tribute at the same tasks. In the 1650's, Bernabé Cobo listed the mita labor draft from Huarochirí at 357 people, or about 39 percent of the total mita draft for service in Lima from the central highlands. And in addition, Cobo added, "many come down voluntarily" to earn a wage of three to four reales a day—almost twice the legal wage of the mita laborers.[11]

Whether people went to the farms around Lima, to the city itself, or to the mines to earn the specie demanded of them as part of their tribute payments, the evidence indicates that most sold their labor rather than the goods they produced. Hence their capacity to obtain additional specie, in the absence of technological improvements that might increase the productivity of labor, depended upon their numbers. As miners, they might work for a share of the ore they extracted, but the technology of amalgamation with mercury, introduced in the 1580's, rapidly undermined native Andean mining techniques and left not only legal control of the mines themselves but also effective control of the work process in the hands of the Spaniards.[12] European technology, such as that introduced in the mines or in obrajes, generally meant European relations of production and usually European control, save for the limited number of cases in which communities or kurakas undertook to operate an obraje or an agricultural unit with Spanish techniques. But even in such cases—and there is no evidence of them in Huarochirí—the European technology of the sixteenth and seventeenth centuries was not saving of labor, and the absolute numbers of people available set a limit upon the productive capacity of the local group.

Thus the demographic curve of the native population during the colonial period offers some insight into the changing capacity of local Andean society to reproduce itself and to meet the demands placed upon it. Throughout the seventeenth and early eighteenth centuries, the Andean population appeared to be gradually but definitely losing the battle for survival. If we accept Dávila Brizeño's estimate of approximately 6,000 household heads in Huarochirí in the 1540's, shortly after the entry of the Europeans, then the province lost more than 1,700 tributaries, or almost 30 percent of its adult male population, in the quarter century between 1545 and 1571.[13] The decline did not stop there, nor did it even slow by much in the remaining years of the sixteenth century. Antonio Vásquez de Espinosa, whose figures record official population counts (including recounts only when such were made between 1571 and the years 1616–19, when he was in Peru), gives a tributary population of 2,886 for Huarochirí in 1619.[14] There was a recount of the population by the tribute office in 1729, and another in 1751, immediately following a bloody rebellion. The 1751 count recorded a low of 1,704 tributaries. A count made in 1780 listed a tributary population of 2,264, showing a recovery almost to the level of 1619.[15]

The general curve of the population in Huarochirí is not much different from the estimates offered to date for the demographic history of the Andean population as a whole during the colonial period. The low point of the native population in Peru as a whole was reached sometime in the middle of the eighteenth century, a full century later than the nadir of the native population in Mesoamerica to the north. The phenomenon has been noted and commented on since 1946, when George Kubler published his estimate of the demographic curve of the colonial Andean population.[16] The variation in the two areas has been used to argue that worse conditions in the Andes must have impeded the recovery of the population there following the epidemics of the conquest period, but in the present state of scholarly work on the demographic history of the Andes it would be unwise to go beyond speculation. We lack data on living conditions, dietary patterns, and the fluctuations in the production of basic grains and other foodstuffs. And we need such data not for the European population, but for a peasant population whose produce entered the market, and was therefore registered in some form, primarily as a result of expropriation by the encomendero or the state.

In the case of Huarochirí itself, there are a number of factors that undoubtedly contributed to the slow recovery of the local population, factors that are not significantly different from those that can be cited for other parts of the Andes. According to the first *corregidor* (administrator) of the province, the area lost large numbers of able-bodied men in the conquest period, for the warriors of Huarochirí either joined or were taken by both sides in the civil wars between the Spaniards.[17] But from the 1570's on, there is no evidence that the province suffered any more than the rest of the Andes from that grim triumvirate of overwork, insufficient food, and disease—complicated of course by the slow process of building up resistance to the diseases introduced from Eurasia.

Another factor that must always be taken into account in reconstructing the demographic history of any part of the Andes is migration. The Andean population, quite probably for centuries before the arrival of the Europeans, was a transhumant population. The nature of Andean agriculture made seasonal migration a basic part of productive activity; in the south in particular, with its extensive puna pastures, migration, both seasonal and for longer periods, made it possible for communities to obtain goods from an extensive area ranging from the Pacific coast to the Chaco region on the eastern slopes of the Andes. Again, the specific weight that must be assigned to migration in the case of Huarochirí is difficult to determine, for although the proximity of the province to Lima made it relatively easy for people to go to the coast or the capital in search of work or a different life, the push factors that stimulated many people to flee the southern provinces to escape the mining mita were absent. As noted earlier, Huarochirí was not subject to the mining mita, and as might be expected, the proportion of *forasteros*, or migrants from other areas, in Huarochirí was relatively small. What movement took place was primarily within the province, or from neighboring provinces such as Tarma and Jauja—areas with which the people of Huarochirí had maintained relations prior to the arrival of the Europeans.[18]

Mamaq, the repartimiento that did lose its population more rapidly than the rest of the province, faced (or suffered from) some rather special conditions. The repartimiento was primarily in a low area, and most of its villages were located at an altitude of from about 500 to 1200 feet. This warm, lower slope of the coastal range was subject to the dreaded *uta* (*Lesmaniasis tropicalis*), a disease carried by a mosquito that feeds upon a wild plant that thrives only in this area. Uta produces ulcers that gradually rot away the soft tissues of the nose, producing the kind of disfigurement graphically shown in portrait vases from the Moche culture to the north. This region was regarded as dangerous and disease-ridden in the colonial period, and this fact coupled with the pull of both better land and higher wages on the coast in the Valley of Lima undoubtedly accounted for the rapid and continuous depopulation of the region, as well as its resettlement by migrants who were themselves in the process of moving slowly, perhaps over generations, to the coast.

Since the household unit was the basic productive unit in Andean society, and the Spanish administrators continued to calculate tribute in terms that approximated that category—a young man became a tributary when he married, whether or not he had reached the official tribute age of eighteen—the numbers of tributaries can be assumed to have a rough relation to the productive units of the society. But that relation was not only rough; it varied considerably in the course of the colonial period. Figures on the total population of the province are available, but for more widely scattered dates than those recording tributaries alone. Although the first available data on total population are from 1571, 40 years after the Spanish invasion, they indicate that the demographic picture of total population in Huarochirí is roughly equivalent to that of tributaries alone. The ratio of tributaries to total population does vary, from 1:5 to 1:6 in the 1570's to 1:3 to 1:4 by 1751. (See Table 6.1.) Given the sharp downward curve of population already well under way by 1571, the high ratios of that period suggest not large families but broken ones, in which the remnants of households that have lost their paternal head have joined with other kinsmen, sharing in the labors of that household in exchange for their own survival. That ratio remains high in the repartimiento of Huarochirí into the early years of the seventeenth century, whereas in other parts of the province (particularly the repartimiento of Mamaq, where the kin groups of the conquest period virtually disappear altogether) it drops to 1:3.9 by 1619, indicating that the population was failing to reproduce itself.

Huarochirí, though in many ways an extensive area, was a relatively small part of the Andean region, and it is clear from the census figures that the population could be heavily affected by a single epidemic, or even by political events and their aftermath. The sharp drop in tributary

TABLE 6.1. *Population Statistics for the Province of Huarochirí from the Sixteenth to the Eighteenth Centuries*

Population	1571	1619	1729	1751	1780[a]
REPARTIMIENTO OF HUAROCHIRÍ					
(1) Tributary population	1,812	1,481	1,050	848	1,054
(2) Total population	12,057	9,097	—	3,365	—
(3) Ratio of (1) ÷ (2)	1: 6.65	1: 6.14	—	1: 5.53	—
REPARTIMIENTO OF CHACLLA					
(1) Tributary population	1,386	854	500	472	728
(2) Total population	6,880	4,561	2,588	2,094	—
(3) Ratio of (1) ÷ (2)	1: 4.96	1: 5.34	1: 5.18	1: 4.44	—
REPARTIMIENTO OF MAMAQ					
(1) Tributary population	1,026	551	275	384	482
(2) Total population	5,675	2,177	—	1,794	—
(3) Ratio of (1) ÷ (2)	1: 5.53	1: 3.95	—	1: 4.44	—
TOTAL PROVINCE					
(1) Tributary population	4,224	2,886	1,825	1,704	2,264

SOURCES: The data for 1571 are from "Relación de oficios," p. 191; those for 1619 are from Vásquez de Espinosa, p. 648; those for 1729 and 1751 are from the ANP, Sección Histórica, "Derecho Indígena," Cuaderno 287; those for 1780 are from "Razón de los tributarios de la provincia de Huarochirí, 1779–80," in "Libro primero de los cargos y distribución del Ramo de Tributos de las provincias de la jurisdicción de este virreinato de Lima segun las últimas matrículas de cada uno de ellos (1781)," ANP, Sección Histórica, sin clasificar.
[a]The 1780 figures record only tributaries, and in view of the considerable variation in the ratio of tributaries to total population over time I have chosen not to extrapolate total population as a multiple of tributary population here. The population for the province as a whole does not include figures from Yauli, a new repartimiento carved out of Huarochirí and Canta in 1751 to separate the region of the mines of Nuevo Potosí.

population between 1729 and 1751 amounted to some 7 percent of the adult male population of the province. Most of that drop, however, a numerical total of 121 persons, can be traced not to the failure of the population to reproduce itself, but to something much more specific and violent: the rebellion of 1750. The census taken immediately afterward lists many men killed in the rebellion, executed in retribution, or sent to the prisons of San Fernandez in Lima.[19] The lists of dead and executed far exceed 121 people, making it clear the rebellion was probably the event that pushed, for a two-year period only, the number of deaths above their replacement by young men approaching maturity. The trough of the demographic decline in Huarochirí was thus apparently reached by the 1730's, after which the population began a steady recovery.

Perhaps a clearer idea of the devastation of local society that was part of the steady decline of population over the two hundred years from the 1540's to the 1740's can be seen by looking more closely at one particular census: a 1711 count of the population of the waranqa Checa, one of the five waranqas of the repartimiento of Huarochirí, largest of the three repartimientos making up the province. This count was annotated by provincial officials later, perhaps over a period of years.[20] Internal evidence makes it clear that the marginal notes cannot have been made after 1729, the date of the next recount made in the province as a whole, and I have tentatively placed the later notations at 1725, or fourteen years after 1711, on the basis of marginal notes that particular children had reached tributary age. Whereas all people, female as well as male, are recorded in the census of 1711, almost all marginal notations refer only to men, the tribute-payers, so my evaluation will be based upon the fate of the men of the province only.

In 1711, there were 116 tribute-paying men in the waranqa, and a total male population, including children and old men past the age of tribute, of 376. Fourteen years later, 52 percent of that population was dead. Of the men between eighteen and 50 in 1711, only 42 survived, and many of the boys died before reaching the age of eighteen. The picture for Checa in the 14 years between 1711 and 1725 is devastating, but perhaps not reflective even of the province as a whole. Though the long-term decline of population was massive, the decline seems to have slowed toward the eighteenth century. The decline between 1545 and 1571 was some 30 percent, or about 1.15 percent per year. In the following interval (1571–1619), a period of 48 years, the decline was about 32 percent, or .67 percent per year. And in the 110 years from 1619 to 1729, the date of the next census of the entire province, the decline was 37 percent, or .34 percent per year.[21] The case of Checa makes it clear, however, that disaster did not strike evenly in all areas at the same time, that one region could be decimated by disease, by famine, or (more likely) by the dismal combination of the two. Nor was recovery an even, smooth process. It is clear from conflicts between communities that some populations survived or began to recover while others continued to decline well into the later years of the eighteenth century. Communities whose lands were concentrated in more heavily traveled areas—such as the repartimiento of Mamaq, astride the main route from the central highlands down to Lima—disappeared entirely, and their population was replaced by migrants from other provinces or from other communities of Huarochirí. In general, the communities of the repartimiento of Huarochirí, concentrated in the upper reaches of the Lurín and Mala river valleys, whose original population was denser than that of Chaclla and Mamaq, as well as more isolated, survived somewhat better.

The impact of this protracted demographic decline upon the resources of production in Huarochirí—in particular upon the lands and productive oases held and cultivated by the extended kin groups of the society—is difficult to determine. Few analogies can be drawn between the case of the Andean area and the picture of European landholding in periods of declining population, since the overlapping rights to land characteristic of societies such as that of Huarochirí tended to limit the abandonment of lands. As the population declined, not only households but entire kin groups, ayllus, and even larger entities disappeared. The remnants merged with their kinsmen, the groups from which, according to tradition, they had originally split. By the mid-eighteenth century, the component ayllus of villages had disappeared altogether in some areas, whereas in others the numbers of such groups had been reduced by half.[22]

Even the disappearance of an entire ayllu did not always mean the abandonment of the land held and cultivated by the members of that group, for the larger group to which extinct ayllus belonged retained residual claim to the lands as kinsmen and could occupy it on those grounds. Still, as the numbers of people declined, marginal lands were left fallow, terraces that demanded maintenance were forgotten, and the remaining people concentrated their efforts upon the most productive land, unable to keep up resources that required a continual input of labor for their maintenance. For without labor, land had little value, especially in this region where the steep inclines and the scarcity of level land provided few incentives for European occupation or settlement. Throughout the seventeenth century, despite residual claims to land, it seems that lands were abandoned or at least not maintained as population declined. This tendency ended as the population decline slowed and then stopped. Testaments dating from the early eighteenth century make it clear that people were by then attempting to bring abandoned lands back into cultivation. Testators noted having inherited lands gone to brush and shrub and cleared "by my own efforts."[23] Resource oases distant from the main village of a group were also more vulnerable, and more likely to be occupied by rival groups or by Europeans.[24] But the land of Huarochirí was broken and jagged, and of little interest to the Spaniards, who entered the province as officeholders, priests, traders, or miners, but seldom as settlers seeking land to farm or to ranch. As the population of Huarochirí declined, lands were abandoned for periods of time, and terraces were left uncleared and irrigation ditches uncleaned; but the people did not forget their claims to these lands and came forward quickly to assert them when it appeared that their tenure was threatened. They might lack the people to farm the lands, but in the idiom of the Andes, land was a grant held in trust from the ancestors who claimed it, protected it in death, and would avenge its loss with crop failure and starvation.[25]

The forced resettlement and congregation of the multitude of tiny hamlets in the province into 14 large villages in the 1560's and 1570's, though it represented a real attack upon traditional ritual practices and was meant to make it easier for the representatives of the colonial bureaucracy—corregidor and priest—to collect state levies and control the population, did not affect the landholding patterns of the social groups to any significant degree—despite laws that seem to indicate the contrary. The Toledan regulations permitted the kin groups to retain their traditional lands as long as the distance between their new settlements and the lands did not exceed one league, or about three miles, a distance that Spanish authorities expected would make it possible for the members of Andean society to cultivate their fields and still reside in the new villages.[26] But at the same time, Spanish law also specifically ordered that the Indians be permitted to retain their traditional lands without challenge.[27] The courts heard claims to lands on the basis of their antiquity. Established practice and custom were the basis of the common law of the people in the Andes as well as in Europe, and claims to lands that could be traced back at least to the period of the Inca Empire were respected.

The kin groups of Huarochirí continued to hold the lands they had cultivated at the time of the Spanish invasion even when they had to travel for days to reach their fields. As they did in their own words "from time immemorial," they traveled to their more distant fields to break the ground, to plant and cultivate, spending weeks and more away from the villages to which they were moved by the Spaniards. The fact that it has been possible to reconstruct as much of the pattern of landholding prior to the European invasion as appears in Chapter One on the basis of documentation from the seventeenth and eighteenth centuries is in itself evidence of the persistence of traditional patterns of land access.

The fragmentation and dispersion of the original *reducciónes*, or Toledan villages, organized in the sixteenth century is further evidence of the maintenance of traditional patterns of land access and cultivation. The Checa people, who belonged to the repartimiento of Huarochirí, were settled along with other, smaller ayllus in the Toledan foundation of San Damián de Urutambo, capital of a parish and of the waranqa Checa. The lands held and cultivated by the Checas ranged from the headwaters of the Lurín River north to the banks of the Rímac and south to the high puna pastures between the Lurín and the Mala rivers.[28] These lands were not distant oases, cultivated by resident colonists or *mitmaq*, but part of the core holdings of the group. In 1713, the testament of a member of this group, born in another part of the waranqa that had by then become a village, left his heirs *tablas*, or plots of land scattered throughout the agricultural area held by the Checas.[29]

Many of the fields scattered over this large area were far from the new settlement of Urutambo, and people working in the more distant areas soon returned to old tradition, remaining for long periods in or near their fields. As this happened more and more, the Spanish authorities eventually gave up and tried to make reality fit their administrative models by officially founding a new village in an area occupied by a sufficient number of people. The history of the village of San Bartolomé de Soquicancha, officially recognized at the beginning of the seventeenth century, is an example of this phenomenon. At the end of the sixteenth century, people who had been resettled in the village of Urutambo were found in the lands called Soquicancha, on the banks of the Rímac River more than fifteen miles from the official settlement. The Indians remained in their fields most of the year, effectively deserting the reducción of Urutambo. Archbishop Toribio Mogrovejo, on a visit to Huarochirí, recommended that the existing situation be recognized and religious control maintained by officially founding a new town on the site. The corregidor did so, naming the new settlement Bartolomé after himself and Soquicancha in recognition of the name it already held for the native occupants.[30]

But even then the problem was not solved, for the Spanish authorities soon discovered that the new village of San Bartolomé was often deserted (or nearly so) as people moved on to work lands that they also held in a lowland area, Cocachacara. Cocachacara did not become a recognized village in the colonial period, but it appears on maps of the region by the 1950's.[31] Indeed, by the 1950's the original 17 Spanish settlements had given way to 44, as ayllus gave their names to settlements: Lupo, Yambilla, Sangallaya, and Quiripa, for example, which had all been ayllus of the village of Huarochirí in the 1580's. And just as in earlier times, many of the houses in the small cluster called Yambilla today stand empty and padlocked for much of the year, occupied only when someone comes to prepare the fields for planting or to harvest the crops.[32]

The traditional Andean pattern of land access was respected in practice, but in theory ultimate authority over the land and its resources—"fields, hills, waters, and pastures"—was claimed by the Spanish Crown by right of conquest.[33] The legal argument was based upon the Toledan interpretation of the Inca Empire as a total despotism that reserved all land to itself and allotted portions of that land to the Indians to work. Since the Spanish Crown had freed the Indians from the Inca tyranny, the lands once held by the tyrant became the property of his successor, to be disposed of as he saw fit. Despite the dubious history that underlay this argument, it was used as the legal precedent for the Crown's right to dispose of land and other resources in the new kingdoms, a right first exercised by the local authorities and reserved by the Crown to itself late in the sixteenth century.

Since the Andean people were in possession of the land and cultivating it when the Spaniards arrived in the Andes, the Crown recognized their right of access to the lands they worked. What they did not have was the right of ownership, or the ability to dispose of or alienate the lands. The Indians were to retain "all that belonged to them, both individually and in community, as well as the waters and irrigation systems; and the lands in which they had constructed irrigation systems or any similar improvement. The lands they had made fertile through their own labor should be reserved for them first, and in no case may they be sold or alienated."[34] The colonial courts, defining Indian tenures as *posesión precaria*, contended that the Crown assured the members of Andean society access to land sufficient for them to meet their needs and pay the levies demanded of them; lands in excess of what was sufficient for their sustenance were defined as vacant lands, or *tierras baldías*, that reverted to the Crown to be disposed of as the monarch and the colonial authorities saw fit.

From the latter years of the sixteenth century, the Crown found in this legalism a ready source of income to meet its steadily growing needs for money to fight the European dynastic struggles in which Spain was inextricably involved. From the time of the conquest, lands had been distributed to members of European society by the *cabildos*, or town councils, of the Spanish cities in Peru or by the viceroy. Ambitious men had expanded their holdings by moving into lands adjacent to their legal holdings, occupying large areas *de facto*. But now in 1589, the Crown claimed the sole right to grant lands, annulling all grants previously made by the local authorities in the Americas. This left many Spaniards illegally occupying land that they had received from those authorities.[35] The Crown resolved the problems of these people, as well as of those who held land by virtue of occupancy alone, and made a profit by permitting all these people to purchase title from the Crown.

From the 1590's, royal officials in Peru as well as in other areas of the Indies were periodically ordered to throw lands defined as vacant onto the market in land sales called *composiciónes de tierras*. The commissioner, or person in charge of the operation, was named by the Audiencia and held authority throughout the territory of the court. He was ordered to announce the sales in each region of the Audiencia, passing from one to another in turn, so that all those who held land without title or sought land declared vacant could pay a price set by him to regularize their titles or purchase vacant lands in open auction.[36]

The first composición took place during the last decade of the sixteenth century, the second in 1615; 38 more had taken place by 1646, when in reaction to protests against land-grabbing the Crown ordered that no titles be confirmed to lands held for less than ten years, adding that "the Indian communities are to be granted composiciónes in preference to other individual postulants, giving them every advantage."[37] Such a law suggests strongly that members of Indian society were concerned about retaining

their lands as their numbers fell, although I have no record of composiciónes of community lands in Huarochirí prior to the eighteenth century.
The lack of evidence regarding land purchases in Huarochirí may be the
result of any of a number of factors. It may simply mean that the data are
lost or destroyed, as many local records have been. Or (and this seems to
me quite likely) it may indicate that the communities of Huarochirí did
not attempt to use the state to confirm or secure their possession of lands
until the eighteenth century. We must remember that the Spanish laws
regarding land were not part of the Andean tradition; although the local
people probably knew how to use the European laws when they had to do
so or when it was to their advantage to do so, it is unlikely that they would
turn to those laws unless a need arose. In the absence of conflict, actual or
impending, why spend money to assure a tenure still unchallenged? Thus
the appearance of land purchases by communities may be an indication of
real or foreseen threats to land, whether from Europeans or from other
communities. In other words, land purchase may be an indication of conflict or of growing insecurity of tenure.

In the case of Huarochirí, there was little need for assuring tenure in a
situation of declining population and abundant land. The composiciónes
of the first half of the seventeenth century probably consolidated the European landholding structures of the coast, the major food-producing area
for the population of Lima. In the 1630's, the Viceroy Conde de Chinchon
even appealed an order for a new composición, arguing that after salaries
and costs were deducted, the composición would produce no financial
benefit for the Crown, and would further harm the Indian communities.[38]
In 1695, again in need of money to meet war costs, the Crown sent out
another order to undertake composiciónes de tierras in its American kingdoms, and the order was implemented in the Audiencia of Lima in 1710.[39]
The commissioner's instructions specified that the lands to be sold included those "that have belonged to the Indian communities and, through the
depopulation of the villages, have reverted to the possession of the
Crown, since the Indians do not possess lands, but only their usufruct,
save for lands purchased with their own money in the fashion of the Spaniards."[40] These orders served notice that the Indian communities—whose
populations had declined steadily throughout the seventeenth century,
and who by the end of the century obviously held lands far in excess of
what the state was likely to define as necessary for their survival (and in
some cases in excess of what they could even cultivate)—stood to lose at
least a part of their lands if they did not pay for them in exchange for a title of ownership from the colonial authorities. Such a title legally defined
land as private property, albeit private corporate property, officially separate from the graded series of rights-to-land that bound increasingly larg-

er groups of people to one another through their common access to the lands of the group as a whole.

This difference was not just a legalism, for it permitted one component group of the society of Huarochirí to separate itself out from the rest as an autonomous unit, with its own resources to which its kinsmen at more extensive levels were barred from access. Though the Indians were forced by the laws of the colonial state to participate in this process or else risk losing access to their lands entirely, such participation also inserted a wedge into the nested hierarchy of rights-to-land that integrated large groups in Andean society despite local quarrels. The purchase of a title by one social group, at any level, legally separated it from its erstwhile kinsmen, making it an incorporated entity and excluding the rest from access to its resources.

A number of the larger social units of Huarochirí purchased title to their lands in the composiciónes of the first decades of the eighteenth century. The repartimiento of Chaclla bought title to its pasture and maize lands. The waranqa Chaucarima paid to obtain title to pastures that its members were afraid of losing because of the extinction of many of its component ayllus since the sixteenth century. Smaller social units—ayllus and the villages gradually formed of such ayllus in the century of dispersion since the Toledan concentration—also bought title to the lands they cultivated. The communities of Chauca and Otao, both components of the waranqa Casta, each bought title to their lands, as did Concha and Sunicancha, ayllus in the Upper Lurín Valley and part of the waranqa Chaucarima.[41]

The Andean communities seem to have been willing to invest money in two kinds of lands: lands that were disputed or at least coveted by a rival community, and lands that did or could bring them in income that could be used to meet some of the claims upon them. The lands purchased from the state in the composiciónes of the eighteenth century were lands that could be used to produce goods for the European market. The members of Andean society in Huarochirí, long accustomed to offering their labor to the Europeans in return for the specie demanded of them by the state, found in their own resources by the eighteenth century additional sources of income that could be used to meet the demands upon them, and at least some of them used their lands for that purpose.

The entire apparatus of colonial Indian administration organized by the 1580's was founded on the principle of retaining the traditional Andean structure of production as the economic underpinning for the extraction of surplus from the members of Indian society. The role assigned the Indians in colonial Peru was twofold: they were to maintain and support themselves, and they were to provide a regular surplus to the European sector. As we have seen, that surplus was extracted in part by the state through tribute and mita levies and in part by known but unsanctioned forms of extralegal compulsion used by both official and private individuals.

Initially, the extraction of surplus from the Indians was assigned to the colonial state and accomplished through tribute and labor services. But the steady decline of the native Andean population undercut the ability of the state to maintain the flow of Indian labor to members of European society at the same time that the European economy was expanding, placing an increasing demand upon the Indians for labor. In any precapitalist system, particularly one with the limited technology characteristic of the colonial Andean communities, there are absolute limits upon the time that productive members of the community can be pulled away without endangering the survival of the group. The people of Huarochirí continued to work in and around Lima, some as seasonal field hands in the farms and ranches of the coast and some as servants or artisans in the city itself. A count of the Indian population of Lima made in 1613 reported 45 people from Huarochirí, or slightly more than 2 percent of a total Indian population of 1,914 permanently resident within the walls of the capital.[42]

But many people did not choose to leave their communities and had to find other ways of meeting the levies demanded of them. The communities' purchase of their lands at the beginning of the eighteenth century meant that, at the low point of the long-term population decline, people were determined to retain lands that, though they might not be consistently occupied and used, were clearly potentially valuable in producing goods for commercial exchange. Rather than risk losing their lands, groups were willing—and able—to find money to pay for title to them.

Data are not available to permit a calculation of the distribution of wealth or of productive resources among the members of Indian society in Huarochirí, but we can still calculate an average of the total volume of the demands that weighed upon the people of the province. Extrapolating from that, we can construct an estimate of the levies borne by an "average" Indian, a procedure that should provide a valuable background for evaluating the changes in the internal organization of local Andean society in Huarochirí under the colonial system.

Let me name this "average Indian" Juan Runa (*runa* means "man" in Quechua). Juan was a married man with small children in the mid-eighteenth century. He paid levies to both secular and religious authorities. Juan's basic levy was tribute, assessed upon all adult males who were neither members of the Indian elite nor crippled or infirm. In 1705, the men of the repartimiento of Chaclla were assessed about five pesos, six reales apiece. The censuses of both Chaclla and Huarochirí in 1752 assessed the

Indians about six and one-half pesos per man.[43] We may take the figure of five and one-half pesos as representing the minimum tribute assessment of the Indians during the eighteenth century, at the population represented by the census count taken when tribute was reassessed by the Contaduría de Tributos. With a steadily if slowly declining population, the tribute assessment per man rose between recounts by a peso to a peso and a half; in 1726, just prior to the first recount since 1705, the Indians of Chaclla were paying about seven pesos apiece.[44] And it must be remembered that this estimate is based upon average population decline; the residents of a waranqa with a greater loss of population would have to pay much more tribute than the members of another with less loss.

The mita or labor draft was the second major levy in Huarochirí. Service in the mines was not regarded by the Indians as unduly hard. Mitayos formed only a small part of the mining labor force in Huarochirí, and though the workers complained that they were not paid on time, they said that they received the full legal wage when they were paid.[45] The snow mita, as it was called, was much more widely hated by the Indians. The monopoly on cutting and transporting glacial ice down to Lima was sold to the highest bidder, and the purchaser, or *asentista*, was alleged to use any means possible to get a maximum of work out of his laborers with a minimum of personal expense. The mitayos had to guard and care for the mule trains on the way up to and back from the ice, and once at the glaciers had to cut the ice and pack it in straw. All this was done under the supervision of black overseers. For all this work, only nine people were assigned in 1706, and the Indians complained that the asentista took many more Indians than his assigned quota and forced them to serve for one-year periods instead of six-month turns.[46]

The mita of the tambos, or road service, was regarded as a heavy duty as early as 1580, and by the mid-eighteenth century it was described as a major burden upon the Indians.[47] Four Indians each were assigned to four tambos along the route through the province for six-month periods, and they kept the rest stations stocked with provisions, served as guides, and performed other services for those journeying from Lima to virtually any part of the central or southern highlands.[48]

If the actual population had corresponded to the census figures, an Indian would serve a six-month turn every six or seven years. Actually, as the population declined, the Indians had to serve far more often. For example, in Chaclla in 1726, the Indians were found to be serving one mita at least every four and a half years. The complaints of specific areas show an even greater disparity between law and practice in the mita. In 1745, the ayllu Concha petitioned for a new visita, alleging that the population had declined from 26 tributaries to eleven, of whom five had moved away.[49] The original "seventh" of the population, or not quite four Indians, now represented nearly half the effective residents, forcing the Indians of Concha to serve a mita every other year. The law specified that the loss of mitayos in one portion of a repartimiento was to be made up by an increase of mitayos in another, but if the population was declining everywhere, as was the case here, the Indians just had to bear the extra load.

The situation was alleged by provincial authorities to have been even worse in some communities, forcing the Indians to serve every year.[50] In view of the more general figures, however, I will assume that in the eighteenth century Juan Runa could expect to serve a mita turn at least once in every four to six years.

The regular levies paid to the ecclesiastical authorities by the Indians were the tithe and the parochial fees for services rendered by the priest. By law, the Indians owed a tithe of one-twentieth upon the increase of all animals of European species raised, consumed, or sold by the Indians, and upon the produce of all lands held by virtue of purchase or rent, except for lands rented by the Indians from Spaniards, in which case the tithe was one-tenth, as in Spanish society. The Indians were not to be held liable for payment of the tithe on the produce of community lands granted them by the government. All tithes were to be paid in kind, and fractions of the twentieth were to be excused.[51]

Collection of the tithe was farmed out by the Church to individuals who bid for the privilege, and as might be expected under such a system, tithe farmers seeking to realize a profit substituted other practices, which varied from province to province. In Huarochirí, the tithe was reduced to a monetary sum. The tithe on agricultural products was made a head tax, the *diesmo de personas*, which amounted to one peso for nobles and mestizos, four reales, or one-half peso, for married commoners, and two reales for single persons, whether unmarried or widowed. Sheep and goats were assessed in the 1770's at a rate of five pesos for each hundred females, and cattle at a rate of two reales for each calf born during the year.[52]

The parochial fees the priests could assess were determined by the bishop in each diocese. In the archbishopric of Lima the tariff established by Toribio de Mogrovejo at the end of the sixteenth century was maintained until Melchor de Liñan y Cisneros published a new one in 1704, which remained unchanged throughout the eighteenth century. It forbade the priests to charge fees for weddings, baptisms, or burials. The priest could charge two pesos, two reales for performance of the mass commemorating the wedding ceremony, and six and one-half reales for the proclamation of the bans. He could charge four reales for a burial mass.[53]

The fees legally permitted the priest in Huarochirí were far below those that prevailed in the bishoprics of Cuzco and La Paz during the latter part of the eighteenth century, although evidence relating to fees actually charged closes the gap somewhat. In 1721, the priest of the *doctrina* of San Pedro de Casta was charging the legal maximum for the burial mass, with an additional four reales for each response chanted. Marriages and the wedding mass were charged at four and one-half pesos, and the proclamation of the bans at twelve reales. No fees were levied for baptisms, but the celebration of a holy day mass brought the priest five pesos, five reales.[54] A further indication of the way fees could be multiplied can be seen in the bishoprics of La Paz and Cuzco, where the basic rates for services were not much greater than those permitted in Lima but where extra charges added for each embellishment could bring the cost of a burial mass up to some 27 pesos.[55] Such practices in all probability occurred in the archbishopric of Lima as well, even if they were not officially permitted by the authorities.

The Indians paid further levies to maintain the ecclesiastical arm of Spanish society. The Church received a portion of the tribute revenues to pay the salaries of priests, and additional sums were levied to maintain religious and charitable facilities for both Indian and Spanish societies. A permanent levy added to the tribute was the *tomín ensayado*—about one and one-half reales—assessed each tributary for the support of the Indian hospital in Lima. In addition, special taxes might be added to the tribute for limited periods of time, as was done for about 50 years during the eighteenth century to help pay for the construction of the Cathedral of Lima.[56]

In addition to these regular, calculable levies owed to the Spanish government, the Indians were faced with a wide variety of demands for goods, labor, or money from the members of the provincial power group. The demands of the corregidor and priest were most extensive and direct, but other people added demands that were less regular and more difficult to trace. Perhaps the largest proportion of these extralegal burdens resulted from the economic activities of the corregidor, who gradually became more famous as an entrepreneur than as a minister of justice.

In the sixteenth century, the economic activities of the corregidor were as varied as those of the encomendero he replaced, and a quantitative estimate of the burden they represented to the Indian is correspondingly difficult. The corregidor requisitioned or commissioned cloth woven by the Indians, which was sent to the urban markets for sale. He used Indian labor to mine gold or silver, gather and transport coca, and guard sheep and cattle. He requisitioned a portion of the produce of his province or imported articles from other regions, and used the Indians to transport these goods to the rapidly growing urban centers for sale.[57]

By the eighteenth century, the expansion of the European economy in the viceroyalty undercut the activities of the corregidor, limited as he was by his term of office. Increasingly, the provincial administrator was reduced to the role of middleman between the Indians and the members of European society, using his authority and his police power to supply labor, often through coercion, to European enterprises, and to distribute the products of his own culture to the Indians. He became a merchant, dealing in goods that he forced the people under his authority to purchase. This activity, known as the *repartimiento de mercancías*, was widely accepted and practiced not only by the corregidor but also by the local priests or Spanish residents in the provinces, and even by members of the Indian elite. The mercantile activities of the corregidor were forbidden by royal ordinances, but all Europeans, up to and including the Crown and the Council of the Indies, were well aware of the practice and condoned it in practice as inevitable, even to the point of taking the expected profit from the repartimiento into account in estimating the purchase price of the office of corregidor, which was sold openly from the seventeenth century to the 1780's.[58]

In the 1750's, the Crown, anxious to increase the flow of income from the Americas, opted to legalize the repartimiento in the hope of obtaining the sales taxes from an operation that authorities viewed as necessary, if regrettable. In his report on this legalization, the Viceroy Conde de Superunda expressed the widely accepted rationale for the mercantile activities of the corregidor. In his words, "since it is well known that the provinces cannot maintain themselves without a distribution, nor would there be anyone who would administer justice in them, these [the repartimientos] have come to be tolerated."[59] In other words, the Indians needed the articles they were forced to accept, but since all Indians were defined as lazy, they had to buy the goods they needed from someone in a position to compel them to pay their debts. Thus, in the process of filling his own coffers the corregidor performed a valuable economic service by providing the members of Indian society with the goods produced by the Spanish sector.

The repartimiento was legal for 30 years, from 1752 to 1782, and the published schedules of the goods permitted to be distributed and their prices permit an assessment of the value of this business to the corregidor—and conversely, the weight of his activity upon the Indians under his authority. The only merchandise that the corregidor of Huarochirí could legally sell to the Indians in 1753, as recorded in the price schedules of the repartimiento, was 3,500 mules, which at 40 pesos each amounted to 140,000 pesos during a three- to five-year term of office.[60] On the basis of the population of the province in 1751, the corregidor could distribute about two and a half mules per household head, for a total of 82 pesos, two reales per household head over a five-year period, or about sixteen pesos, three reales per year.[61] (See Table 6.1 above.) This minimum, however, seems to have been a theoretical sum, and many corregidores managed to carry out two repartimientos during their term of office. In 1750, before the legalization of the repartimiento de mercancías, the corregidor in Huarochirí had managed to distribute mules worth 200,000 pesos, or some 117 pesos, three reales per tributary (on the basis of the population in 1751) during his term.[62]

This figure may seem high, and in general Huarochirí was assigned a repartimiento in excess of its share of the population of the viceroyalty in the eighteenth century. On the basis of the official lists and the population of the province at the end of the century, the cost per household of the repartimiento to the Andean population on the average was nine pesos, five reales per year, in contrast to Huarochirí's sixteen pesos.[63] The province received more mules than any other area of the viceroyalty save one, and unlike most other regions, it was assigned no other goods in the official lists. The reasons for both the abundance of mules and the lack of other goods are not clear, but some suggestions can be made. Huarochirí was, by the eighteenth century, despite its steep and jagged slopes, the "throat" through which passed much of the goods and merchandise destined for the interior of the viceroyalty. As a result, one source of income for the people of the province was in transport; the tambos had to be staffed and mules made available to transport people and produce through the province, for those animals were traditionally supplied by the communities whose members were responsible for servicing transport. This need for transport animals may explain at least in part the larger number of mules assigned to Huarochirí, just as the proximity of the province to Lima may be at least part of the reason for the lack of other goods in the repartimiento. Communication with Lima was regular—the kuraka of Huarochirí even maintained a house in the capital for those on community business in the city—and the flow of such small goods as were needed and sought by the members of Andean society into the province was probably taken care of through local petty commerce.

The local priest also frequently ran his own repartimiento de mercancías within his *doctrina*. One practice was to requisition a supply of foodstuffs, such as bread, chickens, and other items, as well as Indian carriers to send the goods to Lima or to Nuevo Potosí for sale. Or the priest might choose to monopolize one profitable item, as when one priest took over the sale of liquor within his doctrina, distributing it to certain of the

Indians in the village for sale and collecting the proceeds. The priests also tended to absorb for themselves the usufruct and the produce of the lands set aside for Church and cofradía maintenance, requisitioning Indian laborers to work the lands.[64]

In addition, both corregidor and priest demanded daily provision of foodstuffs such as chickens, bread, fruits and corn, as well as firewood, for their personal consumption. The Indians also had to assign members of the community—both men and women—to cook, serve, clean, and otherwise care for the often extensive household of the corregidor or priest.[65] By the eighteenth century this informal requisitioning of members of the local community as unpaid servants, or *pongos*, was general among the European population in provincial areas.

With this information, we can calculate the levies that Juan Runa had to pay to members of European society in a nonexistent average year in Huarochirí in the eighteenth century. Juan owed a minimum of five and a half pesos, and a maximum of about seven pesos per year in tribute. He owed the Church a tithe of four reales as his *diesmo personal*. In addition, let us assign him a herd in which five or six cattle had calved during the year, for which he owed a tithe of two reales per calf. There would be a minimum of three holy days a year: Christmas, Easter, and the festival of the patron saint of his village. If he lived in an average village of about 40 families, that meant that he owed three reales as his share of the priest's fees for the holy day services. The only extralegal levy that can be estimated with any precision is the repartimiento de mercancías of the corregidor. The lowest possible amount he could owe the corregidor—the amount permitted by the legal repartimiento—was sixteen pesos, two reales per year in the 1750's. More probably, however, he would owe 23 and one-half pesos per year, the actual repartimiento in 1750. Thus far, Juan owes a minimum of 23 pesos, three reales to various sectors of the Spanish superstructure, and a maximum of 32 pesos, two reales.

There were more levies that came up over the course of the years. If one of Juan's children had died that year, he would have had to pay an additional five and one-half pesos minimum for the burial, raising the maximum estimate to 37 pesos, 6 reales. In addition, although his mita turn, which he served from once every seven to once every three or even two years, was legally supposed to be paid at the same rate as that set for free wage labor, the law was often ignored. If Juan was not paid for his mita service, and the other debts incurred during his mita turn had to be made up by his earnings during the period between labor levies, that would add an additional sum to his yearly debts. If, for instance, his yearly debts totaled 32 pesos, two reales, the distribution of one year's debts over a six-year period between mitas would add about six pesos, six reales a year, bringing the total to 39 pesos, without attempting to assign any monetary value to any additional debts that Juan might incur as a member of his community.*

Where did Juan get the money to pay these levies? He might, as noted above, go down to the coast to seek work on the farms and ranches around Lima or up to the mines of Nuevo Potosí on the eastern boundary of the province. The wages that an Indian was legally owed for his labor throughout the eighteenth century were established by a tariff promulgated by the Viceroy Duque de la Palata in 1687. A muleteer in Huarochirí was to receive four reales, or one-half peso, a day, and an assistant or *peon* three reales. Indians working on a hacienda, whether as mitayo or as free labor, were to receive four reales per day, and this wage applied as well to anyone working at other tasks within the city of Lima or its jurisdiction. A miner, depending upon the specific tasks he performed, was granted a daily wage ranging from four reales for work in the shafts to two and a half reales.[66] This was the law, but in Peru in the eighteenth century it tended to represent an infrequent maximum, rather than a minimum wage. The man who held the ice monopoly in Huarochirí contended that the official wage was an absurdity.[67] The wages paid on the coastal haciendas varied from one to two reales per day.[68] In order to calculate possible income, we need to know how much time a person could dedicate to wage labor. In assigning the term of the mita, the Spanish administrators assumed that the Indians needed six months a year to care for their crops and herds, leaving six months free for other activities in addition to subsistence. The legal work week was six days; even if the actual work time was longer, pay would probably have been based upon a six-day week.

Now if Juan spent six months a year at wage labor in the vicinity of Lima or in the mines, he could have earned on the basis of four reales a day 78 pesos. He was more likely, however, to receive from one to two reales a day, which would have left him at the end of the season with only 20 to 40 pesos. Further, the shortage of currency led hacendados and miners to pay their laborers whenever possible not in cash but in goods: wine, cloth, foodstuffs, or other such items, which were credited with an excessively high value in the exchange.[69] In addition, living expenses on the job would have to be deducted from earnings.

Now if Juan were not an average but a particular individual, he could have been one of the few who found a ready source of income through wage labor in the mines of Nuevo Potosí. From the sixteenth century to the eighteenth, three-fourths or more of the tribute from Huarochirí was

---

*If the wages Juan received were two reales per day, or 12 reales for a six-day week, in six months he would earn 39 pesos (312 reales = 12 reales/week × 26 weeks).

levied in silver rather than in goods, and the presence of the mines on the boundaries of the province offers a ready explanation of how people got at least some of the silver they paid in tribute. The mines of Nuevo Potosí, named after the famed Hill of Silver in hopes that the new workings would rival the old, were in operation by the early years of the seventeenth century. In the course of the century, both Indians and Spaniards moved into the mining area, located on the crest of the western range of the Andes on the frontier zone between Huarochirí and Tarma. For some years the area was administered as a separate entity under the authority of a mine administrator appointed by Lima, but in the mid-eighteenth century the authorities made it into a new repartimiento, called Yauli after its principle settlement, which they joined to the province of Huarochirí.[70]

Reports in the 1750's make it clear that the population of Yauli, whether Indian or Spaniard, was there only because of the mines. The Indians, according to their own testimony, devoted all their time to the production of silver and were no longer involved in agriculture at all.

They become excellent workmen and become so imbued with their greed that some live by working for their bosses, the Spanish miners, and others who neither serve nor work for wages work for themselves in the mines scattered throughout the hills and in claims abandoned by the Spaniards, which number more than a thousand; and breaking down and destroying old buttresses and supports and finding new sites and directions, they take out very fine metals, to make their fortunes with them or to sell them; and they also work in the mines of the Gentile Indians.[71]

As at Potosí, the entire focus of the population was on the production of specie, and the lure of silver attracted foodstuffs and other goods to the markets of the cold puna region. In the words of the report on Yauli drawn up by the Contaduría de Tributos, "everything is abundant and nothing is lacking because there is silver . . . in the mines of Nuevo Potosí, and the same happens in the mines of Lipes, Potosí, and Huancavelica, which is that there is abundance in them because there is wealth."[72] The mines thus became a market that drew merchants, mine owners, and Indian farmers who sold foodstuffs and other goods to the miners. Their market consisted of Indian miners, the resident Spanish or mestizo population, and even the rebel Indians in the jungle area to the east, led by Juan Santos Atahuallpa from 1742 until his death sometime in the latter part of the eighteenth century.[73]

With a ready source of specie on the boundaries of Huarochirí, we need not explain the source of the silver paid by the Indians to members of Spanish society in terms of the integration of the Indians into the economic organization of the colony as a whole or their direct participation in the far-flung commercial circuits that brought cloth from Quito south to Lima and on to Potosí, or mules and pack animals from Salta in northern Argentina as far north as Cajamarca. The number of people from Huarochirí who moved to the mines of Nuevo Potosí for work was limited. The mitmaq system of the sixteenth century, by which a few members of the local community in permanent residence in the mines paid the tribute of the larger group, receiving foodstuffs and other goods from their kinsmen in return, was not present in the eighteenth century. We must also look for other sources of income to pay levies within Huarochirí, and for that, we can return to the lands of the local communities—lands they valued sufficiently to be willing to find silver to pay the Crown to obtain full title to.

By the eighteenth century, the people of Huarochirí were producing commodities for the European market in order to obtain the levies demanded of them by the colonial authorities, and the Lima markets were provisioned with fruits and other crops from Huarochirí and Canta to the north, as well as with sheep, goats, and some cattle brought down from those same provinces to fatten on the lomas outside of Lima before sale to the city butchers. Cattle, sheep, goats, and llamas were raised on the pastures of Chaucarima and Chaclla, purchased by composición in 1711. The fields of Otao, Chauca, Concha, and Sunicancha, bought at the same time, included good lowland areas that produced fruits for the Lima market: guavas, avocados, apples, and peaches, as well as ají (chile peppers), a valued condiment.[74] Descriptions of Huarochirí from the beginning of the seventeenth century emphasized its good climate and abundant harvests, but none depicted the province as a regular supplier of foodstuffs to Lima until the eighteenth century. The account of Peru by a Dutch buccaneer in 1615 described Huarochirí as "temperate land where it rains and where potatoes and wheat and maize and other goods are harvested."[75] And though the description of the provisioning of Lima by Fray Buenaventura de Salinas y Córdoba in 1630 provides a list of highland provinces that send cattle and other foodstuffs to Lima, it does not include Huarochirí.[76] But Cosme Bueno's geography of Peru, prepared 130 years later, says of Huarochirí that "in its valleys the climate is benign, and seeds, vegetables, and fruits are harvested in abundance and taken to Lima when they are scarce there because of the changes in the seasons. And thus throughout the year, avocados, *granadillas*, strawberries, guayabas, palillos, chirimoyas, and other fruits can be found in [Lima's] plaza."[77] Between the seventeenth century and the middle of the eighteenth, the communities of Huarochirí turned to the Lima market as an outlet for their crops. The foodstuffs from the province sent to Lima came not from large haciendas owned and run by members of Spanish society, but from the small plots cultivated by household labor or by members of the village communities. Disputes over land among the communities of Huarochirí in the eighteenth century indicate the reorientation of land use to the production of agricultural commodities. At least initially, this reorientation probably did not threaten the basic self-sufficiency of the local community. Given the steady decline of population and the extermination of entire lineages and kin groups, lands were available to the community without cutting into household resources.

The history of a particular dispute between two communities of Huarochirí is a good illustration of this reorientation process. In the 1740's, the communities of Chauca and Otao, both belonging to the waranqa Casta in Huarochirí, went to court over competing claims to agricultural lands. Both communities were located at the headwaters of *quebradas*, or small river valleys created by streams tributary to the Rímac River. They probably shared rights to land as distant kinsmen at a more extensive level at some time in the past, for the populations of the two villages were intermingled: people from Chauca held access to lands within the fields of Otao by inheritance through their wives or mothers.[78] This mixing of access rights between villages initially led to no difficulties, for the people of Otao, following the traditional custom of permitting access to lands to people who married into the minimal kin group in exchange for their assumption of the duties of kinsmen, recognized the tenure of the people who married into the group in exchange for community labor.

All our ancestors simply and in good faith permitted them to work some *chacaras* with the condition that they help in the tasks of repairing roads, bridges, irrigation ditches, and such light jobs, and this was the basis upon which they entered [the lands], where in the course of time they pressed their claims with pleas and obsequiousness to our elders, who in good faith and conformity with this [tradition] permitted them to work the *chacaras* that they asked for, and this has gone on until the present day.[79]

But the people of Chauca, rather than using the fields they obtained to produce foodstuffs for distribution within the community—as those fields had been used for centuries—began to turn them to other purposes. They cleaned the fields they held and spread into neighboring fields, cutting down maguey plants, turning maize lands into fruit groves, and sending their mules into the Otao pasturelands. Finally, in 1741, the elders of Otao charged the Chauca farmers with invading their lands and destroying the fields they used for wood and pastures.[80]

High court costs finally forced the two villages to get together and agree to a division of the lands, but the basis of the conflict is clear. Nor was this an isolated case. By the eighteenth century, disputes between communities over lands were increasingly common, as people began to produce for the European market. It was not even necessary to use the lands. From the sixteenth century, Spanish administrators rented lands claimed by the Indians to outsiders—Indian, mestizo, or Spaniard—for rent to be paid into the community treasury. The larger and more important properties were supervised by the Contaduría de Tributos. The repartimiento of Huarochirí, for example, held lands in Chaclacayo, in the warm lowlands of the Rímac River valley, which according to the encomendero were rented in 1741 for 300 pesos a year.[81] The encomendero made this claim in an action to gain his share of the income, but the Indians insisted that their repartimiento had no community funds, and the Contador de Retasas supported their statement. The encomendero may have been technically correct, however, for the administration of the rental income from Indian community lands by the Contaduría de Tributos left much to be desired. Such rents often went unpaid for years while the holder remained in possession, until the weight and authority of long-term tenure led to the properties being lost to the Indians altogether.[82]

Given such circumstances, the local communities understandably tried to bypass the colonial authorities and rent out their lands on their own. In the mid-eighteenth century, a lieutenant of the corregidor complained that much legal wrangling between communities over boundaries was the product of the wish to obtain income from renting lands, either to one another or to outsiders. In the 1730's, the four villages composing the parish of Chaclla got into a court fight over lands assigned to the support of the religious festivals. By that time, the share of the festival owed by each village had been converted to specie, and the wrangling was finally ended by assigning the task of renting the lands and supervising the collection of rent to the kuraka of Chaclla. The settlement lasted until the early nineteenth century, when in the disorder of the independence struggle Chaclla tried to take its lands back in order to rent them to someone else, and one of the other villages involved, Jicamarca, rented the lands it held to the village of Olleros.[83] Communities rented lands to individuals as well as to other communities. In the mid-eighteenth century, some twenty families moved into the northern boundary of Huarochirí, renting lands from the communities of Chaclla and Larao.[84] *Forasteros*, or migrants from other provinces, also had to apply to their new communities for lands to work, and those communities found in the migrants an additional source of income. In the eighteenth century, the community of Huarochirí rented pastureland to a migrant whose widow was still resentfully paying rent at the time of the rebellion of 1750.[85] The miners who settled in the mining region to the east of Huarochirí also had to rent pastureland from the kuraka of Tarma, who claimed the lands.[86]

The rental of lands by the local community signified a major change in the definition of land in Huarochirí. The conception of land as a source of income in itself—as rent—signaled the disruption of traditional relationships between people with respect to productive resources in Andean society. The idea of land as a source of rent and private property broke the traditional balance between land and labor, for when rights of access to land could be bought and sold within the community, the process of separating the productive resources of the group from the obligations of group membership had begun. Those people who controlled access to land could accumulate wealth through the disposal of that access, whether they did so as individuals or as a corporate group. This step, insignificant as it may appear on the surface, was essential to the institutionalization of unequal access to resources within the community, and thus to the stratification of society into rich and poor.

But for the process of social differentiation to get under way, there were needed not only resources for the production of commodities, but a market in which to dispose of those commodities. Lima provided that market, and the provision of foodstuffs to the capital, rather than being part of the large-scale commerce dominated by the great merchant houses of Peru, remained for the most part in the hands of the producers themselves. The most detailed description of the structure and organization of the Lima market is that of Salinas y Córdoba in the 1630's. The description is highly reminiscent of the market organization of Peruvian towns of comparable size in the 1950's—which suggests that, in the absence of data from the eighteenth century, it provides a fairly reliable guide to the market organization of Lima later on. The population of the capital city was estimated by Salinas y Córdoba in 1614 at 25,450.[87] It grew to about 40,000 by 1630, and in 1700, in the aftermath of the great earthquake of 1683, it had fallen slightly to 37,200. By 1746, though, it had fully recovered and grown to about 60,000.[88]

In 1630, this population was fed by the farms and ranches around the city, and by the people who brought their crops down from the highlands for sale. Spanish preserves and sweets brought from throughout the viceroyalty were available, but local fruits and vegetables were sold by black, mulatto, mestizo, and Indian women, who spread their wares on mantas or shawls on the ground or on wooden tables. The Indian women came into the market daily with earthen jars and pots with prepared food for sale. "Others sell the fruits and root crops that they sowed in ancient times, from which they live today: yucas; sweet and green potatoes cooked and dry; maize; peanuts; corn; beans; . . . dried meat; . . . lucumas; ocas; giguimas; yacomas; many kinds, odors, and colors of ají; many kinds of vegetables; and various kinds of wild fruits."[89] Further, the climatic differences between coast and highlands meant that Lima could be supplied with fresh fruit and vegetables throughout the year.[90]

The people of Huarochirí also sent animals—sheep, goats, llamas, and some calves—down to Lima for slaughter. According to the tithe farmer of the province in 1773, sheep and goats brought five to six reales a head in Lima, and cattle could be sold for two to three pesos apiece. Data on the prices of agricultural crops are limited, but the evidence available indicates that in Lima during the latter part of the eighteenth century maize brought one peso, one reale per fanega, and potatoes six reales per fanega.[91] The Indians did not always get these prices, however, for a protest prepared for the Crown in 1722 complained that blacks, mulattos, mestizos, and Spanish middlemen met the Indians bringing their goods down to Lima for sale at the outskirts of the city, forcing them to sell at a lower price so that the purchasers could make a few pennies by reselling the goods in the plaza.[92]

Small as the profit from the sale of foodstuffs to Lima seems to have been, agricultural production for the market permitted some members of local society in Huarochirí to accumulate lands and goods far in excess of other members of their society. There is evidence that the accumulation of individual wealth by a few accompanied the gradual redefinition of land as the private corporate property of particular kin groups or even as private individual property in the province. The sources indicate that the accumulation of private lands in Huarochirí began in the seventeenth century. In the 1660's, the village of Otao protested against the occupation of some of its lands by an elder and elite member of the community of San Pedro de Mamaq, part of a separate repartimiento. In the village of Huancaire, part of the repartimiento of Huarochirí early in the seventeenth century, a woman left a chacara of maize and another of potatoes to her daughter, together with some woollen cloth, her *llicla* or shawl, and a piece of *cumbi*, or fine tapestry cloth—her total worldly goods.[93] A half-century later, in 1667, her male descendant left to his son seventeen and a half chacaras of potatoes and fourteen of maize. His son, who died only three years later, left not only fourteen maize fields and some twenty fields of potatoes in his will, but also a record of considerable market activity. He had purchased one potato field and five maize chacaras—some of them from his co-heirs, members of his family—for prices ranging from five to seven pesos. He passed on three houses, two of which he had purchased, and left jewelry and silver vases valued at sixteen pesos. All in all, he had invested some 55 pesos in property and in loans to other Indians, although he died owing some 90 pesos to a variety of people.

Two points emerge clearly from this evidence. First, it is obvious that, royal prohibitions notwithstanding, people in the Andean communities by the eighteenth century bought and sold land among themselves. Such activity would have been unlikely to attract much attention as long as the land did not threaten to pass out of the control of the community itself. The accumulation of land within the community could take place; the land could even be passed on to heirs and increase over the course of several generations. But—and here is the second point—there is no evidence that this accumulation of land was directed toward the consolidation of an estate. The fields accumulated by the heirs of the woman from Huancaire were scattered plots distributed over a large area, from the high puna to the lower, warmer reaches of the sierra slopes. Such a pattern of accumulation was consistent with the Andean ideal of access to plots at a variety of altitudes, a protection against crop failure and local climatic variation that was still a basic part of community agriculture at the time of the Agrarian Reform in Peru in 1969.

Another testament witnessed in the village of Tuna in 1713 draws a profile of a prosperous peasant farmer who devoted his life to the accumulation of property and left a large amount to his children and heirs. This man, José de la Cruz, inherited lands from his own family and from his mother-in-law throughout the core territories of the waranqa Checa to which he belonged. He inherited lands in the communities of Tuna, Tupiococha, and Soquiacancha, and added to them in a variety of ways. Some he bought openly; others he acquired for small sums and invested his labor and time in—clearing the overgrown, abandoned fields or repairing fallen buildings. He bought some chacaras from the cofradía of his village and others from his neighbors. He even held one field as payment for serving as executor of the estate of another family member. A good family man who assumed the costs of family funerals, he also profited by them to obtain full title to the fields they left their heirs. At his death, he left over 100 separate pieces of land, 55 of them planted in marketable fruits such as peaches, avocados, and guavas. He had invested some 227 pesos in lands, and sold other lands for 130 pesos.[94]

But the fragility of the landed wealth accumulated by men like José de la Cruz is evident from his history. This man can be located in the census of the waranqa Checa taken in 1711 and annotated again about 1725.[95] In 1711, de la Cruz was living in Huarochirí, capital of the province, and had four children. He returned to his village, Tuna, to die at the age of 33 in 1713, dividing his estate among his two sons and two daughters, one of the latter newly married. Between twenty and thirty plots, several with springs or rights to the community irrigation system, were inherited by the daughter and her husband. But within twelve years, the married daughter was the only survivor of this wealthy peasant family. The rest were dead, perhaps from an epidemic, along with half of the rest of the population of the waranqa Checa.

By the eighteenth century, there was clearly a group in Huarochirí that monopolized much of the wealth and the resources of local society. Some of these people seem to have held no special positions in their communities, but others—probably the majority—built at least part of their wealth on the basis of their special status as part of the native colonial elite, which gave them greater access to lands and other resources by virtue of their political position. Particular elite families in the province, such as the Cajahuaringas, who included the kuraka of Langa in the 1730's, not only owned large herds of cattle and sheep but also effectively controlled their village.[96] The surnames of kuraka lineages in the colonial period—the Cuellars, Macavilcas, and Cajahuaringas—were still important in Huarochirí in the 1930's.[97] The wealth of such elite people in the eighteenth century consisted essentially of land and personal possessions. The list of the belongings of Francisco Julcarilpo, former acting kuraka of the waranqa Chaclla, 50 years old in 1730 when he was investigated by the church for idolatry, provides a detailed picture of his movable wealth. Julcarilpo's goods were not strikingly different from those of his less prosperous neighbors and kinsmen; he just had many more of them. He had a large collection of clothing—mantas, ponchos, dresses, shirts, and breeches, stored in large trunks. He had a variety of agricultural implements—an adze, a hammer, an anvil, a vise, and a chisel, as well as iron stirrups, saddlebags, and a pack saddle. He had sacks full of junk and papers, and sacks containing stored corn and potatoes in one of several houses. He also had a good deal of silver jewelry—women's pins or *topos*, as well as several small *tembladeras* and silver-inlaid *mates* and their spoons, together with small sacks of silver coins.[98] He owned over 300 head of sheep and goats, and over 400 head of cattle, as well as fourteen llamas, probably used as pack animals, and five mules, probably for riding. He asserted that his estate was worth more than 3,000 pesos, and friends testified that his houses had been looted of much silver jewelry, at least some of it received as security on loans he had made to other members of the community.[99]

Francisco Julcarilpo is a far cry from our hypothetical average Huarochiriano, Juan Runa, struggling to meet levies of twenty to 40 pesos a year. But Juan, the average man, is a useful reminder that though we may find information on the rich and powerful, even on the limited scale of a small and not particularly wealthy area, much of our image of the mass is gained by inference and the construction of averages like him. And for every Francisco Julcarilpo in Huarochirí in the mid-eighteenth century, there had to be many people whose economic position was worse than Juan's in order to make the average possible. The contrast between Francisco Julcarilpo, a historical figure, and Juan Runa, a hypothetical average, is evidence of the development of considerable social differentiation between the rich and poor in Huarochirí by the middle of the eighteenth century. Wealthy families monopolized lands; they may well have even engineered the purchase of community lands in the composiciones de tierras for their own personal benefit, charging the cost of title to their communities. They bought and sold land and hired outsiders or other members of their communities to work for them. At the beginning of the eighteenth century, a tightly knit lineage in Langa—the Cajahuaringas— hired a migrant from the neighboring province of Jauja to care for their herds of cattle, sheep, and goats, and later charged him with sorcery. Their employee insisted that the charge was designed to enable them to avoid paying his wages, and the colonial authorities tended to agree with him.[100]

The private wealth of some members of the communities of Huarochirí was the product of their activities in the Lima market—albeit on a scale far below what would attract the European merchants of the viceroyalty in the seventeenth and eighteenth centuries. It was the long-term product of the slow but steady destruction of the ties of reciprocity and kinship that determined access to labor and to productive resources in native Andean society, and of the conversion of the remains of that system into private property to be bought and sold. Thus the market for foodstuffs represented by the European society of Lima, despite the small quantity of goods offered by each seller, was sufficiently large to undermine the basic principle of community self-sufficiency that was an essential part of the role assigned to Indian society by the colonial state. The end product of this process was a society of individual peasant farmers, an evolution that, as noted above, was far from complete by the end of the colonial period.

But though commerce from the bottom, initiated and carried on by the Indians themselves, enriched some and furthered the social differentiation of Indian society into rich and poor, another part of the commercial activity of the province steadily absorbed a considerable proportion of the surplus generated in local society that contributed to the growth of a native economic elite in the Indian provinces. The commercial circuit in which the people of Huarochirí sold their goods was limited and local, despite the fact that its major terminus was the capital city of the viceroyalty. But the province, like the others of the viceroyalty, absorbed goods from the larger commercial networks of the European economy, interregional as well as international, through the repartimiento de mercancías, or forced distribution of goods by the corregidor.

The corregidor was the terminus of a commercial system that reached from Spain—and beyond Spain, from the other countries of Europe—to the Americas. The international trade that supplied Peru, and through Peru the rest of South America, reached its apex at the end of the sixteenth century. The incursions of French and later Dutch and English privateers into first the Caribbean and then the Pacific put Spain on the defensive and led to the organization of the *flota* system, by which the Spanish galleons, loaded primarily with trade goods on their trip to the Americas and with silver bullion on their way back, traveled in fleets escorted by warships. The flota system, cumbersome but effective, protected the Spanish treasure fleet from pirates throughout most of its lifetime, although the volume of the trade began to decline in the 1620's, undercut by competition from contraband traders as well as by the short-sighted tendency of the Crown to sequester cargoes of specie in its need for money to meet its increasingly pressing debts.

During the second half of the seventeenth century, trade between Spain and Peru declined as the fleets, harried both by buccaneers and by war between Spain and her European competitors, sailed less and less often. But the decline of trade with Spain did not mean the constriction of commerce as such. Peruvian merchant houses moved actively into intraregional trade, investing their profits in the construction of fleets in the Pacific and the expansion of a trade that reached from Central America to Chile. By the 1640's, at least 40 percent of the ships plying the Pacific had been built in Guayaquil.[101] They carried copper, wheat, and hides from Chile to Lima, cloth from Quito to Lima, and foodstuffs and other goods from point to point along the long coastline of Peru and Chile. Overland trade also expanded, stimulated by the presence of rich and landlocked Potosí. Foreign goods entered Buenos Aires through the Portuguese contraband entrepôt of Colonia do Sacramento to be carted overland across the pampa to the eastern foothills of the Andes and from there up to Potosí.

The flota system, by which goods were brought from Europe to be sold at the Portobelo fair in Panama for shipment down to Lima, effectively ended around the beginning of the eighteenth century. The War of the Spanish Succession (1701–14) cut off contact between Spain and its American kingdoms, and the flota system was officially ended in 1740. The costly fleet system was undermined by cheaper goods brought around Cape Horn or shipped inland from Buenos Aires, and the Crown sought to meet that challenge by licensing single trips from any port in Spain to particular destinations in the Americas. The activity of the *registros*, or registry ships, as they were called, threatened the monopoly of trade within Spanish South America previously held by the Lima merchant guild, to the point that the Viceroy Conde de Superunda, who stood on the side of the Lima merchants in the struggle for the control of trade within (if not beyond) the viceroyalty, complained to the Crown in 1756 that the flood of goods into southern Peru from Buenos Aires meant that prices were often lower in Cuzco than they were in Lima, which had once reigned supreme as the point of distribution for the internal trade of the viceroyalty.[102]

It has often been assumed that the reorientation of the commercial routes that took place in South America during the eighteenth century undermined the merchant houses of Lima, leaving them poor and weak by the end of the century in comparison to the rising mercantile interests of Buenos Aires.[103] But though the shift is undeniable, and though there is considerable evidence that the Lima merchants were put on the defensive by the loss of their monopoly, there is also some indication that they fought back, moving into local commerce within the viceroyalty and taking an active interest in the stimulation of production and the development of closer trade links between the provinces of Peru. The Lima merchants took part in the active trade in mules between Salta, in northwestern Argentina, and Peru, regularly attending the great fairs at which the animals were purchased for later sale in Potosí or in the provinces of the northern kingdom.[104]

I suspect that the great merchant houses of Lima lay behind the mercantile activities of the corregidor in the Indian provinces—activities that by all evidence grew steadily in the eighteenth century. At the start of his term of office the corregidor had to purchase the goods he intended to sell from the merchants, often on credit. It was generally agreed that a fair sale price for the goods was 100 to 150 percent over the purchase price. Mules bought at the fair in Salta for thirteen to seventeen pesos a head were sold by the corregidores for 34 to 50 pesos per head in the 1770's.[105] The official schedules for the repartimiento de mercancías during its short two decades of legal operation specified prices of from 30 to 70 pesos a head, and the Church in 1741 officially recognized the right of a corregidor to charge 100 to 150 percent over the purchase price for mules in the repartimiento.[106]

The official lists assigned each Indian province a quota of mules, the principal good favored by the repartimiento. The other common items were iron, steel, local cloth, *guano*, knives, and other imported goods such as French linen from Rouen and Brittany, thick woolens and beaver cloth from England, and silk stockings.[107] All goods were priced at 100 percent over their purchase price. The forced sales of the corregidor undoubtedly stimulated intraregional trade. The goods distributed were paid for either in specie or in local products, at a reduced valuation to permit their later resale by the corregidor. A list of the provinces that yielded the best profits to the corregidor prepared in the 1780's provides a good example of the importance of the trade. Four provinces—Conchucos, Huaylas, Lampa, and Tarma—received the highest valuations, all

listed as "first class." Both Conchucos and Huaylas were marked high because, as the compiler stated, they were major producers of the light
woolen cloth and baize that was widely used in the viceroyalty. Cloth had
a ready market, although, as the report added, the value of this good in
Lima had fallen, making it harder to sell. Huarochirí was also ranked in
the report as "first class; the repartimiento is easy to collect."[108] As we
have seen, the province received only mules—3,500 of them, the largest
number assigned any province save for Sicasica, near Cuzco, which received 4,000.[109]

The repartimiento may have been easy to collect in Huarochirí because
the nearby Lima market for their agricultural surplus provided them with
specie that could pass, in many cases, directly into the hands of the provincial official in payment for the mules they had to accept. But whether
or not the province owed its rating to the fact that the corregidor could
realize his profit without the additional step of selling merchandise received in payment for his goods, the office of corregidor in Huarochirí
was profitable enough to attract the interest of some of Peru's more important members of the elite, Spanish as well as local. Indeed, the importance of the repartimiento to the European elite is borne out by the
intensity of the protests that accompanied its official abolition in the wake
of the massive Indian rebellion led by Túpac Amaru II in 1780–82 and
the subsequent reorganization of the viceroyalty the following year. One
of the most vocal protests against the abolition of the repartimiento came
from the Spaniard Alonso Carrió de la Bandera, friend and associate of
the most powerful men in Lima and corregidor of the province of
Chilques y Masques in southern Peru in the 1730's. The legal repartimiento in that province amounted to 84,500 pesos, and Carrió himself
estimated that a corregidor "without injury to the Indians" could realize
50,000 pesos in a five-year term.[110]

The active interest of the Lima merchant guild in the repartimiento
was underlined by one of the proposals for the reorganization of the commercial system submitted to the viceroy in 1784. In it, Jorge Escovedo y
Alarcón argued that the suppression of the forced distribution of goods
would ruin the economy of the viceroyalty and proposed that the repartimiento be assigned directly to the merchant guild, who would be responsible for the distribution of their goods in the provinces together
with the state, without the local provincial authority as intermediary.
Thus, he argued, the provinces would be supplied with the goods they
needed at a lower price than had been the case when the corregidor had
also taken his cut of the commerce. Escovedo's plan was rejected, but his
proposal is evidence of the importance of this trade, whose returns per
unit of goods distributed were probably small but whose aggregate value

was important to the merchant houses of Lima, struggling to maintain their profits from a commerce whose geographical extent had already been seriously reduced.[111] The total value of the official repartimiento as published in the distribution lists in 1753, at the time of its legalization, was 5,831,826 pesos, which divided by the five-year period over which the goods were expected to be sold meant a gross value of 1,166,365 pesos a year—a considerable sum.[112]

The extraction of the surplus generated by the members of local Andean society in Peru by the European sector took place in essentially two ways: through the levies, or open requisitions, of the state apparatus, and through the more indirect but effective channels of commercial exchange. And even in the latter area the role of the state loomed large, for the officially prohibited but openly recognized mercantile role of the corregidor was a major factor in the distribution of goods throughout the viceroyalty. The Indians constituted a forced market for the goods sold by the European elite. And the complaints of the members of European society in Peru that the forced sales of goods were a mainspring of the economy of the viceroyalty have merit despite their obvious bias. As noted above, the Europeans argued that the elimination of force in the sale of goods to the native Andean population would mean the end of commerce and the destruction of provincial economic structures. It is not easy to test their assertions, since despite the official abolition of the forced distribution of goods in 1783 and the replacement of the corregidor by other provincial officials, these new officials rapidly took on the same activities as their predecessors. The forced sale of goods to the Indians decayed with the constriction and decline of internal commerce after political independence, in the disturbed years of the nineteenth century. But legal or not, the forced participation of the members of Andean society—always the majority of the population of the viceroyalty—in the network of intraregional and even international trade was a basic part of the economic structure of colonial Peru, and remained largely intact until the state that depended on that forced market was itself eliminated.

But though the colonial state shied away from disturbing the forced-commerce system, there are indications that in the eighteenth century it intervened directly in the internal organization of production in Andean local society. In the latter part of that century, the colonial courts, through their decisions on land cases, moved actively to limit and even to reverse where possible the process of internal differentiation within local Andean society. The impact of the Enlightenment and of "enlightened government" in Latin America has been the subject of much study and research, most of which seems to suggest strongly that the reforms introduced by the Spanish Crown in its overseas kingdoms were aimed principally at increasing the flow of income to the royal coffers. Where "reforms" meant a reorganization of local power structures, proposals for changes tended to drown in local intrigue and factionalism.

But there is a clearly perceptible trend in the orientation of the colonial bureaucracy in Lima regarding land disputes among the Andean village communities in the second half of the eighteenth century. There was no fanfare and no bureaucratic reorganization accompanying this change. The courts hearing land disputes between Indian communities simply began to apply different criteria in deciding cases. In cases heard toward the end of the century, appeals to the antiquity of land access disappear from the arguments presented to the court. The judges were no longer willing to admit such claims, and people knew it and rephrased their cases. Two disputes from this period make the point graphically. The first is one that lasted throughout the eighteenth century, a dispute over pasturelands in the high puna between the headwaters of the Lurín and Mala rivers between members of the waranqas Colcaruna, Checa, and Chaucarima in the repartimiento of Huarochirí. In the 1780's, Chaucarima claimed the lands as private corporate property purchased in the composición de tierras of 1711. Checa, in its reply, argued that the lands in question were not included in the title sold to its opponents, and went on to argue its case on the basis of need, alleging that Concha and Sunicancha, the two villages of Chaucarima involved in the dispute, had fewer than 50 people between them, whereas the village of San Damián de Checa had nearly 100 people and the waranqa Checa 400. It is clear from the case that the population of the waranqa Chaucarima had declined steadily, forcing the waranqa to purchase lands in order to retain them. But even that purchase does not seem to have assured their retention of the lands, for the people still lacked the ability to hold them against incursions from others. The court made its final decision in 1799 on the basis of need, redistributing the lands in question between Concha, Sunicancha, and Checa in proportion to the population of the contending groups. Concha and Sunicancha thus lost the fight—and the lands.[113]

A second case dealt with the lands rented by one community to another.[114] Sometime prior to 1725, the ayllus of Huarochirí and Yambilla rented out pasturelands to Calahuaya. In mid-century, the people of Calahuaya claimed that they should be adjudged the lands without paying rent on the basis of their greater need. They won the case and were assigned the lands, but their rent was not suspended. The peoples of Huarochirí and Yambilla lost the lands, although they still received an income from them. Then in 1786, the governor of the province ordered the suspension of the rent that Calahuaya had been paying on the grounds that the fact that Huarochirí and Yambilla had rented the lands proved that they held lands in excess of their needs. So Huarochirí and Yambilla lost their lands entirely, and in their later efforts to regain them based their appeals entirely on the principle of need, arguing that their populations were greater than that of Calahuaya. This time they won, but that may not have been the end of the matter—the documents do not take us beyond 1807.

The courts were quietly but effectively carrying out a kind of piecemeal agrarian reform limited to the lands of the Indian communities. There is no evidence of any *cedula* from Spain ordering that the distribution of lands among the communities be readjusted, but the regularity with which the lawyers applied the principle of need to disputes indicates that a policy had been laid down that revived the old laws specifying that members of native Andean society were to be granted land sufficient for their subsistence needs. In the late eighteenth century, with rising population and pressure on existing land from the native communities, the colonial authorities interpreted the law to mean that communities had no legal right to claim more than sufficient property to meet their needs, and asserted the right of the state to take land from them and give it to their neighbors. The Contaduría de Tributos removed all doubt by ordering in 1796 that "those who have held [lands] in the form of precarious possession have no right to be reaffirmed and maintained in said possession when it does not correspond to the number of tributaries and people composing their respective population, and it is because of this that the laws and ordinances of the Kingdom specify that the territorial judges are to reassign the lands every three years so that all are equalized."[115]

This principle was also applied to forasteros, people who moved into a province from elsewhere and rented lands from the communities. The application to them of the principle of need gave them access to lands, but the lands they gained were at the expense of the existing communities, and undermined the ability of those communities to obtain income through land rentals. Over the long run, the application of this principle meant the elimination of the process of internal differentiation taking place within local Andean society and the equalization of poverty, as fixed resources in land were divided, again and again, among the members of a steadily growing population. One last example illustrates this process. As noted earlier in another context, a number of forasteros in Huarochirí settled in Yauli, where they rented lands from the kuraka of the neighboring province of Tarma, and in the upper Rímac Valley, where they rented lands from the villages of Chaclla and Larao. In the latter part of the eighteenth century, both those groups were settled by the colonial authorities in new villages. The authorities assigned them the lands they cultivated, which meant the loss of those lands to their previous owners. In the case of the Rímac Valley settlers, the process accompanied the le-

gal establishment of a new village, San Antonio de Quilcamachay, founded by the colonial authorities in 1808. The communities of Larao and
Chaclla refused to recognize the expropriation of their lands, and a fight
began that showed no evidence in the court records of ending. Larao and
Chaclla sent their animals into the lands and the new village appealed to
the courts again and again—until documents cease at the end of the
1830's. [116]

It is difficult to evaluate the action of the colonial courts at the end of
the eighteenth century. Levies and the demands of the colonial state
stimulated the participation of the local communities in the European
market and the allocation of traditional resources and labor to the production of commodities for sale. A process was thus initiated that tended,
in the long run, toward the stratification of provincial society into a
wealthy class that monopolized landed resources and a poor, increasingly
landless class forced to sell its labor to its neighbors to gain the means of
survival. There is nothing admirable about that process, as will be clear
to any who have traced the penetration of commodity production into a
rural area. The end product of that process is the monopolization of the
means of production by a few and the creation of the conditions for the
genesis of a landlord class.

Given the direction of change clear in the eighteenth century, should
we not applaud actual evidence of the colonial state's action in favor of the
poor members of Indian society? And yet such action did little beyond
equalize poverty. Without touching property relations beyond the limits
of the local Indian community, the authorities moved against the emerg-
ing stratification of native Andean society, denying the pretentions to
wealth and status of the more fortunate members of the Indian communities. The state gained by such actions, for the more people who were
given full status as community members, the more tribute-payers were
available to pay the state's levies. But such decisions also institutionalized
conflict, for the organization of a new village by expropriating lands belonging to one community for the benefit of a new one automatically
made villages into bitter enemies. The penetration of commodity production into rural Andean society stimulated conflict between kin groups
over access to resources, and the efforts of the state to reverse the process
exacerbated that conflict.

By the late eighteenth century the disintegration of traditional relations of production within Andean society had gone a long way in Huarochirí. By devoting a portion of their resources to the production of agricultural commodities for the European market, the communities of the
province met the levies imposed upon them, and some individuals even
prospered, accumulating land far in excess of the minimum allotment

calculated by the state, and monopolizing community lands and pastures as well. Though everyone participated in the European market as purchasers of goods, frequently under duress, these privileged few were buyers as well as sellers. Inventories of their possessions include iron tools, luxury items, and clothing imported from Quito and even from Europe.[117]

By the last decades of the eighteenth century, the wealthier members of provincial Indian society were essentially small-scale farmers who stood on the boundary between Indian and European societies. Most of them continued to participate in their local communities. To gain and hold their positions they not only drew upon the economic opportunities available to them, but also sought to turn to their advantage the political structures of colonial Indian society. Some won and some lost in this risky operation, for the colonial state apparatus was not structured in their favor. But the socioeconomic transformation of provincial Andean society in the seventeenth and eighteenth centuries is as much a question of power as it is of the more purely economic problems of production and commerce. And for a clearer understanding of the power relations of local Andean society in Huarochirí, and their relation to the larger political system during the two centuries following the organization of the colonial state apparatus in the sixteenth century, we must turn to the next chapter.

SEVEN
The Cutting Edge

C ONQUERORS cannot become rulers without using some of the people they conquer to execute their demands. The only alternative to that axiom is for the conquerors themselves to become part of the society they conquer, so that as rulers they know the traditions and the culture of the people they rule. For no political system can hope to last unless its rulers are able to gain the support of some people who not only ensure the flow of surplus from the producers to those who live on that produce but also maintain the authority of the ruling class sufficiently to minimize the need for that class to resort to open force in order to maintain its rule. On a day-to-day level, whether through fear, conviction, or greed, this intermediate group of brokers plays an important part in maintaining the existing political system.

Who were those brokers in colonial Andean society? During the conquest period, for approximately a half-century after the Spaniards entered the Andes, the traditional Andean elite saw to it that the demands of the conquerors were executed by their people. But by the 1560's, the erosion of the foundations of Andean society and the evidence of rebellion and reaction against the Spaniards among the Indians stimulated Spanish suspicion and mistrust of the traditional Andean elite and led finally to the reorganization of local Andean society under the fifth viceroy of Peru, Francisco Toledo. The Indian provincial elite that was the product of this reorganization was drawn both from the traditional elite—the kurakas and those close to them—and from other members of Indian society whose primary qualifications rested in their association with the Spaniards. The share of the members of this group in the benefits of the colonial system was more nominal than real, consisting largely of freedom from some or all of the levies paid by the other members of Andean society. But added to the authority that went with their positions as the executors of the orders of the colonial state, these benefits were sufficient to attract people to fill those positions.

The kurakas, the traditional elite of Andean society, were not eliminated by the Spaniards. They were essential to the conquerors in the early decades, for only through them could the Spaniards gain access to the labor and the products of the Indians. And even though the architects of the colonial state did their best to minimize the authority of the kuraka among his people, they were not willing to erase it completely, for the kurakas were equivalent in their minds to a local nobility, which they regarded as part of any organized political society. As we have seen, the kuraka was quickly equated by the Spaniards with the *señor natural* of medieval conception—the natural and hereditary lord whose authority derived from his long tenure and his acceptance by his people.[1]

The local elite confirmed or created by Spanish colonial legislation can be likened to a blade finely honed to slice into the body of traditional Andean society and cut out elements that threatened the domination of the state and the flow of surplus from the Indians. The laws and regulations that defined the members of this elite were designed to create an efficient arm of the colonial state, an arm whose value lay partly in the authority its members could command in their own society as a result of the traditional relationships of Andean society before the invasion of the Europeans. As long as the native elite were willing to use their traditional authority and their knowledge of the values and standards of their own culture in the service of their European rulers, they represented a sword whose blade was at the service of the colonial state. The cutting edge of that blade was the elite's membership in and knowledge of the culture they were expected to turn to the service of the conquerors. That edge cut into the values and the relationships that held Andean society together, furthering its fragmentation and disintegration, and its submission to colonial rule.

But if the local elite was of value to the Europeans, it was also a danger to them. For the members of the elite were themselves part of Andean culture and society, and no matter how hard the Europeans strove to transform them into imitation Spaniards, their ability to serve their masters depended upon their continued membership and participation in their own society. If they were a blade, it was a double-edged one. The Indian who broke entirely with his own culture and tried to become a European was an isolated and ultimately pitiable figure, an orphan who in the effort to trade in his own values and assumptions for those of a foreign culture often got lost in the space between the two. It was dangerous to attempt to move too far into the society of the conquerors, for one risked repudiation by one's own people, which in turn damaged one's value to the Europeans. Felipe Huaman Poma de Ayala, who claimed descent from the kuraka elite of the region of Ayacucho, and who was the author of a massive treatise on the reform of colonial government submitted to the Crown early in the seventeenth century (our only example of an early evaluation of the colonial system by someone who spoke from the perspective of Andean society), provided in his own life an example of the member of Andean society who attempted to join the ruling class and in doing so lost his claim to authority and position in his own world.[2]

Huaman Poma spent much of his life as a petty functionary of the Spanish colonial bureaucracy. He participated in the campaign against the messianic anticolonial movement called the Taki Onqoy that swept Ayacucho in the 1560's. He served as a minor functionary in the *composiciones de tierras*, or sale of lands, carried out by the Crown in the 1590's, and attempted to obtain a post as lieutenant to the corregidor of the province of Lucanas at the end of the century. But his own efforts to obtain title to lands whose possession he disputed with the Indians of Chachapoyas failed completely. When the lands were formally assigned in 1600, Huaman Poma failed to appear. No Indians would recognize him as their kuraka, and the land judge accused him of harboring "malicious intentions and tricks with which he has always pursued offices."[3] Having lost his social base in his own society, he was unable to use his knowledge of his own culture to build a place for himself in Spanish colonial society.

The members of the colonial Andean elite could do a great deal to bar the Europeans from access to the internal structure of their society and protect the relationships, practices, and traditions that provided strength and cohesion for that society. But that choice was not easy, for the local elite walked a narrow road in the thin and always shrinking space between European and Andean cultures. They could not hide in the crowd. If they chose well, they could protect their communities and still amass wealth and status for themselves. But if they made the wrong choices, they could be thrown aside by their European masters, losing their offices or even their lives—or they could be repudiated by their own people, sometimes also at the cost of their lives.

In the decades immediately following the conquest, the kurakas were incited to join their interests to those of the Europeans by the medieval panoply of honors and privileges that were both the marks of status and the means to wealth in European society of the sixteenth century. The kurakas, themselves part of a culture that laid heavy emphasis upon hierarchy and position, responded eagerly to the bait. The kuraka of Huarochirí, who served as an administrator of the native population in the area of Lima, was a prime example of the rapid construction of ties between the conquerors and the elite members of native Andean society. Don Antonio, as he was baptized, married his daughter to a Spaniard, and himself took a Spanish wife after his daughter married.[4] One young kuraka who was active in the support of the Spaniards even petitioned the Crown successfully for a coat of arms.[5] Many of the Spaniards, impressed by the efficiency of local administration under the Inca state, proposed adapting the institutions of that state to the needs of the European conquerors. Juan Polo de Ondegardo argued persuasively in the 1560's that the settlement of conflicts among the Indians should be left to the jurisdiction of the kurakas, who understood the institutions and practices of their own society as the Spaniards could never hope to do, and his arguments even swayed Francisco de Toledo, who was hardly a proponent of anything derived from the Inca state.[6] Juan de Matienzo, who viewed the kurakas as a bad influence upon the Indians in general, recommended that the Spanish state adopt the Inca system of provincial governors, or *toq'ricoq*. The *tocoricos*, as he called them, were to be acculturated Indians chosen by the state to serve as subordinates or lieutenants of the corregidor de indios in each repartimiento. They were to supervise the execution of the demands of the state and the settlement of disputes within their provinces, much as their Inca equivalents had done; and like the Inca governors, the *tocoricos* were to be drawn from distant areas so that they would have no ties to the provinces they administered that might affect the discharge of their functions.[7]

These proposals were aimed at modifying or amplifying orders emanating from the Crown as early as the administration of Francisco Pizarro to settle the native Andean population in villages with local officials chosen from among them who would be responsible for the settlement of minor disputes and the execution of the orders of the Spanish authorities.[8] Some efforts were made to found Indian towns, particularly on the coast, in the 1550's and 1560's, but there was no concerted effort to alter the traditional structure of authority in native Andean society before the government of Francisco de Toledo. And the disruption of the new kingdom, the growing resistance to the Spaniards among the Indians in some areas, and the economic crisis that set in from the middle of the sixteenth century stimulated considerable suspicion of the kurakas among the Spaniards. Many members of European society in Peru were envious of the kuraka's ability to call upon the labor of the people under his authority, and his use of that labor to amass wealth and goods either for his encomendero or for his own—or his community's—purposes.[9] Despite the fact that many of the Andean elite took an active part in the civil wars among the Spaniards on the side of the Crown, the rebellion of Manco Inca and the attacks of the Inca-in-exile upon Spaniards and Indians who had accepted the conquerors from his retreat in Vilcabamba also reminded many that they remained in Peru in large measure on the sufferance and through the continued support of the Andean elite.[10] And the loyalty of the elite was increasingly forgotten in the tense climate of the 1560's, when Manco's assaults upon Spanish commerce were combined with the threats of Indian rebellion represented by the messianic Taki Onqoy movement, which spread a doctrine of total withdrawal from all participation in Spanish society pending a general war of the Andean deities against the European God and the expulsion of the Europeans from Peru. Memorialists began to argue that the kurakas' access to European military technology should be controlled and their privileges limited. The Europeans were clearly pulled in contradictory directions. One anonymous memorial from the 1560's suggested that the kurakas be made corregidores in their regions, since they knew the customs of their people far better than the Spaniards, referring to Juan Polo de Ondegardo's successful experiment of using the native elite as judges in Cuzco.[11] Yet the same writer voiced concern at the kurakas' rapid adoption of European ways, in particular their skill in the use of Spanish arms and horses. "Many caciques [kurakas] have acquired oxen and horses and mules, and many have become horsemen and good hunters, and have fine horses and harquebuses in their houses, and this custom could increase to such an extent that in time it could threaten the peace of the land."[12] He went on to propose that the kurakas be forbidden to have horses or harquebuses, thinly veiling his real concern under a hypocritical show of concern for the health of the Indians, "so that they do not fall [from the horses] and kill themselves."[13]

Francisco de Toledo arrived in Peru in 1569 with his own concept of how to solve the problems of the new kingdom and renew the flow of surplus to Spain. Toledo was convinced that political turmoil was the source of the declining fortunes of the Crown in the Andes. He argued that the manipulation of the fortunes of the Crown in the interest of private enrichment had stripped the monarchy of its resources and undermined its abilities to reward those who supported it and maintained peace in the land.[14] Toledo was a true representative of the sixteenth-century state; for him the purpose of the new kingdom was the aggrandizement of Spanish power. But the increase of state power demanded wealth, so Toledo's primary objective was to restore the production of the flagging mines of Potosí. And to do that he had to have a steady flow of labor from the conquered population. The role envisaged for the Andes in Spain's empire was clear, but to accomplish it Toledo had to be prepared to reorganize the pattern of Spanish control and the relations between Spaniards and Indians in the Andes. He was prepared to do just that, and complained bitterly on his arrival in Peru of the tendency of the conquerors to adjust to the society they had conquered, extracting their profit by inserting themselves into the places vacated by the Inca ruling class. For though that solution might permit private profit, as Toledo pointed out acidly, it did not serve the needs of state power. He complained later of this, insisting that "it seemed to the governors, and they persuaded the people to the same opinion, that it was not appropriate to interfere, because it would offend and anger the natives."[15]

As Toledo argued, in order to get native labor for the mines on the massive scale needed to restore the earlier production of Potosí and if possible to increase it, Andean society had to be fundamentally reorganized.[16] Toledo's objective was to restore the Andean kingdom as a producer of silver, and he achieved that objective by organizing the Huancavelica mercury mine to produce mercury for the amalgamation of the silver ore and by mobilizing native labor for both the silver and the mercury mines. In order to mobilize native labor, the Andean population had to be brought together in large groups from which labor gangs could be drawn without destroying the capacity of the society to survive and reproduce its numbers. The concentration of the native population was essential for another purpose as well, for as Toledo took pains to point out, the continuing raids of the Inca pretender threatened commerce—particularly the transport of silver from the mines. Toledo also feared the potential participation of the rapidly growing mestizo population in rebellions and raids.[17] Toledo's remedy for all of these troubles was the forced resettlement of the natives in large settlements where they could be supervised and controlled. In his own words, "the reduction of the Indians to villages and parishes makes them easier to manage, to be governed and given religious training."[18]

The Toledan regulations ordered that the Indians be grouped into as few settlements as possible.[19] The form of the villages was specified in detail.[20] They were to be laid out in the grid plan that had become increasingly popular in Europe since the Renaissance, with straight streets running from a central plaza on which faced the Church, the priest's residence, the buildings of the municipality, and the jail—the symbols of the European Catholic conception of society. Each ayllu was assigned its own sector of the village. Each family was to have a separate house on its own plot with an entrance to the public street and no passageway to another house, a decree evidently meant to eliminate both the polygamy that was a mark of high status in Andean society as well as the more general kinds of sexual relationships formally barred by the Church and common in virtually all societies. Land under cultivation was relegated to the area outside the village; only fruit orchards were permitted within the village limits.

The Spanish authorities made every effort to ensure that the people moved to the new foundations and remained there. The villages were to be constructed first, and once they were completed the people were given a limited time to move in. The sites they left were burned to guard against abandonment of the new village. Although the people were at this time legally declared to be free subjects of the Spanish Crown—free to travel and move as they wanted—later regulations forbade them from leaving the new villages and decreed that any who left were to be brought back by the local authorities.[21] The Indians resisted their "reduction" into villages. The kurakas even attempted to bribe Toledo to abandon the project, offering him 800,000 pesos if he would leave the Indians where they were.[22] Many people managed to evade the move or fled the settlements once they were installed there. The Toledan official responsible for the resettlement of the population of Huarochirí left before his work was completed, and the people promptly returned to their traditional lands. Ten years later, the corregidor of the province repeated the resettlement, preventing the people from deserting the new villages by his presence.[23] The corregidor "reduced" Huarochirí from over a hundred small population clusters into seventeen villages. The northernmost repartimiento of Chaclla was pulled into five villages, and the village of Santa Eulalia, which had particularly good lands nearby, was made the capital. The repartimiento of Mamaq was also reduced to five villages, and San Pedro Mamaq, the site of the temple of the wak'a Chaupiñamca, was made the capital. (The corregidor was thus able to use the stone from the temple for the residence of the local corregidor, for the hospital, and for the jail; and the maintenance or renewal of traditional ceremonies was prevented by the presence of Spanish authorities on the spot.) The repartimiento of Huarochirí became several towns, with Santa María de Jesús de Huarochirí, probably on or near the original site of the community, as the capital of the repartimiento and of the province.[24]

Toledo's orders for the resettlement program were that the Indians be grouped into as few settlements as possible. We do not know the size of the *reducciones* in Huarochirí, but some calculations can be made from the total population of the province at the time that Toledo's appointee, Lorenzo de Figueroa, began his work. The average population per village in the three repartimientos in 1571 varied from about 200 to about 250 tributaries or household heads, with the largest average population in the repartimiento of Huarochirí. The total population per town thus averaged between 1,000 and 1,700 people of all ages.[25] Undoubtedly, the population of all villages was not the same, but there was clearly a desire at the official level to make the settlements at least approximately the same size, which suggests that the average population was probably not far from the actual one at the time of the foundation of the villages.

The structure of village and parish was basic to the Toledan plan. The Church was assigned a major role in the conversion of the native Andean population into a docile labor force, as will be discussed in greater detail in Chapter Eight. Ideally, each village was to constitute a single parish, with a resident Catholic priest to teach and train "these barbarians," as Toledo dubbed them, to respect a God whose representatives on earth were chosen and deployed by the Spanish state to aid in the maintenance of its authority in this world. Juan de Matienzo, a major supporter of Toledo's programs, insisted upon the role of the Church in his argument for the necessity of the resettlement of the native population, "because they can neither be instructed in the faith nor can they become men if they are not gathered together into towns."[26] Concentration also made it possible for Toledo to organize the diverse regulations sketching the vague outlines of a native political structure into an organized local political system. Village and parish were each given their native officials under the supervision of the Spanish provincial bureaucracy, the corregidor de indios and the priest.

The model for village government was European, although it was probably drawn more from Renaissance plans for ideal states than from actual practice in the towns of rural Castile. Toledo maintained the Spanish offices that had been held by Indians in their communities since the 1550's, adding other positions and preparing a general structure that became the official form of Indian civil government for the next 200 years.[27] The key figure in the Indian town council (*cabildo*) was the village *alcalde*, or mayor, in charge of general administration. Toledo originally specified two alcaldes per settlement, but later legislation modified his order, calling for two alcaldes in villages consisting of more than 80 households and one in villages of 40 or more.[28] No formal provision was made for any further dispersion of the native population, although court cases brought before the Audiencia in the eighteenth century indicate that even villages consisting of a few families were represented by an alcalde from among their number.[29]

The alcalde was given legal authority over the distribution of village lands and was expected to supervise the conduct of the Indian villagers. He functioned as the most minor official on the ladder of justice, with civil and criminal jurisdiction in disputes or crimes committed within the village. The alcalde was also charged with carrying out the colonial plan for "civilizing" the members of Andean society. He was to serve as guardian of the orphans of the village, and was also assigned the supervision of the hospital and of the market that the authorities ordered built in each parish and each village, respectively. He was further responsible for the roads, bridges, and tambos within the jurisdiction of his village. The elder alcalde held one of the two keys to the village treasury, or *caja de comuni-dad*, where community funds obtained from the labor of the villagers or the sale of their goods or resources were kept, to be disbursed to meet the levies of state and Church. The alcalde was even enjoined to inspect the homes of the Indians to make sure that they used the appurtenances of civilization prescribed for them, such as beds and tables, and he was expected to uphold the dictates of the Catholic religion and report any evidence of the practice of traditional ceremonies or rituals. Finally, he was responsible for collecting the tribute levies of the state, and for exe-cuting the orders of the Spanish provincial official, the corregidor. As de-picted in the laws laid down by Toledo, the alcalde was the "right arm" of the colonial state in his society, wielding the sword directed by the state against the traditional relationships of native Andean society. [30]

The other Indian officials of the cabildo were primarily the administra-tive assistants of the alcalde. The laws provided for one or two *regidores*, or councilmen, who assisted the alcalde in such duties as inspections, land distributions, and the general supervision of the village. The cabildo was also to include an *alguacil mayor*, or constable, responsible for making ar-rests and patrolling the streets of the town after curfew. All of these offi-cials were to be replaced yearly, and none was permitted to succeed him-self. Provision was also made to prevent monopolization of office by a sin-gle ayllu by specifying that both of the alcaldes could not be members of the same ayllu. [31]

The only permanent member of the cabildo was the *escribano*, or no-tary, the heir of the Inca *quipucamayoq*, who as late as the seventeenth century still retained his Inca title in some areas. In addition, the cabildo included several minor positions filled by the alcalde and his colleagues. The laws provided for a *mayordomo*, or village overseer, who also served as *procurador*, or attorney, in the village's formal dealings with the Span-ish authorities. Laws also created the posts of mayordomo of the hospital and its properties, *progonero*, or crier, and *verdugo*, or executioner. [32]

If the alcalde was one arm of the colonial state, the structure of local authority in the parish under the control of a Spanish priest was the other. The Catholic priests charged with "civilizing" the Andean people rapidly set about building their own set of officials to support their authority among the Indians. And that authority was exercised as much in the inter-est of personal gain as religious conversion or even civil authority. As a cynical but practical memorialist in the 1560's pointed out, "nothing has worth and virtue among us that is not well paid in the temporal sphere." [33] In the early years after the conquest, the priests gathered around them large numbers of Indian assistants charged with the care of the church and the execution of priestly orders and demands. The numbers of these assistants multiplied to the point that a corregidor newly arrived at his post in the 1560's complained that the local priests had appointed some 63 constables to ensure that the people came to church on Sundays—far more than necessary.[34] The representatives of the Crown in Peru eventually set strict limits on the size of Indian religious officialdom: in each village of 100 or more Indian parishioners, there was to be one *sacristan*, or sexton, in charge of caring for the church, two or three *cantores* to lead the choir and the responses, and a *fiscal*, or constable, to ensure attendance at mass.[35] In addition, each repartimiento was to be provided with a school to teach the Indian children Spanish and the catechism.[36] By the seventeenth century, the Church expanded the number of schools, requiring one in each parish under the supervision of the priest.[37] The Indian schoolmaster, responsible to the priest, had to be Spanish-speaking and literate. The Church took its educational duties seriously, enjoining the inspectors sent out periodically to check the activities of the priests in the diocese to make sure that the school was operating satisfactorily, and penalizing the local priest when they found him negligent; we can thus be relatively sure that the office of Indian schoolmaster provided for was actually filled in at least some parishes.[38]

There were incentives offered for participating in either the civil or the religious offices established by the colonial system. Most were indirect, consisting not of salaries but of exemptions from some or all of the levies imposed by the state. The only exception was the Indian schoolmaster, who was assigned a salary out of the community funds of the villages he served.[39] In the sixteenth century, most of the members of Indian civil government seem to have been free of both tribute and labor services.[40] Such largesse could not long survive the combination of declining Indian population and expanding demands for surplus from the state and the members of European society. Exemptions were increasingly limited until by 1618 only the alcaldes were free from both tribute payments and mita service during their terms of office. The other principal members of the cabildo were liable for tribute payments but relieved of labor service during their terms. All of the major religious offices—sacristan, cantor, and fiscal—carried exemptions from both tribute and labor service for the term of the office, which was at the discretion of the priest and often in practice was for life. This was no boon for the fiscal, since he was supposed to be chosen from among Indians above the age of 50—i.e., past the age of labor service and tribute. Nor do the census lists, whose exemptions provide the proof that individuals were in fact freed of specific levies for their services, record any such dispensations for people on the grounds of serving as fiscal.[41]

The institution of new officials whose power in their communities derived from the authority of the conquerors alone led to numerous complaints in the decades following the conquest. In 1565, the lawyers of the Audiencia of Quito complained that the Indian cantores and musicians, raised and instructed in the monasteries, had become a scourge of the Indian communities and "in many villages . . . attempt to shake off their obedience to their leaders."[42] The new power structure imposed by the Spaniards cut directly across the traditional Andean hierarchy based on age and inherited position. The contradiction between the place of the new officialdom in its own society and the role assigned its members by the Spaniards led to considerable trouble and conflict. Felipe Huaman Poma de Ayala, in his evaluation of colonial rule at the end of the sixteenth century, pointed to the new officials' lack of status in their own societies, arguing that it made them unable to exercise authority.

The first alcaldes were not obeyed or respected by the Indians, and they called the alcalde *michoc quilliscachi* [young clown or liar]. They say that if there is a quarrel between two alcaldes the town crier arrests an alcalde and whips him in public; . . . they say that the reason [for the crier's authority over the alcalde] is that they name despised young boys as alcalde and honored old men as crier, and the law that [the Indians] keep and maintain is to obey the elders and not a boy.[43]

Developments such as these made it clear that the Spaniards could not attempt to create their own hierarchy of authority among the Indians without risking the loss of access to and control over Indian society. Traditional values, such as respect for age and experience in the community, could not be overturned by fiat. In the face of Indian resistance, the Spanish authorities were obliged to incorporate the traditional Andean hierarchy into the model of local government defined by colonial laws and regulations. Most importantly, this meant that despite their suspicions they had to deal with the traditional Andean elite — the kurakas.

The representatives of the Spanish state in the Andes all agreed that they could not dispense with the kurakas altogether. Even those who argued that the kurakas exploited their own people and had to be controlled and limited by the state were not willing to attempt to destroy a pattern of native authority that they could interpret in terms of their own culture. Juan de Matienzo, despite all his comments about the kurakas' uselessness and exploitation, argued that "the *cacique* [kuraka] should not lose the authority and jurisdiction that he has over the Indians as a natural lord."[44] Toledo himself disagreed completely with the idea that the kurakas could be regarded as a legitimate noble class and did his best to prove that the kurakas were merely appointed officials of the Inca state who appropriated power following the conquest. Following that argument, he went on to insist that the position of kuraka should be made an office filled by the state and responsible to the colonial authorities.[45] But despite his efforts, Toledo was unable to convert the kurakas into a nobility of the robe whose members exercised authority by virtue of their nomination by the Spanish state. He settled in the end for a nominal formalization of the kuraka hierarchy and a regulation that a kuraka could not legally succeed to his position without confirmation by the Audiencia, which provided a measure of state control over the members of this class. The kuraka hierarchy as recognized by Toledo was an orderly ladder of authority that was often not reflected in actual practice in the Indian provinces.

There are many kinds of caciques [kurakas]. There are some who are most important and have greater authority than the rest, whom Don Francisco de Toledo differentiated by calling them *primeras personas*. There are also others somewhat less important, who preside and govern in the village in the absence of the first, called *segundas personas*; these two ranks of caciques command and hold authority throughout the repartimiento. There are others of lesser degree, who are called *principales*, who serve as chiefs in each division, which divisions are called there ayllus, so that if there are ten divisions or ayllus in a repartimiento, there are ten chiefs or ten principales whom each division or ayllu obeys and respects, and all these respect and obey the primera persona, who is the principal cacique of all. [46]

The closest that the colonial state came to making the position of kuraka an appointive office, however, was to dicker over the form of succession. The respect of the Crown for the principle of nobility, even in a conquered people, proved greater than that of Toledo, and the kurakas were confirmed in their legal status as a hereditary nobility equivalent to that of Spain, whose incumbents succeeded to their positions by virtue of birth, the position passing down in the male line where possible, and otherwise in the female line.

The Spanish authorities also sought to tie the kurakas to the colonial state by transforming the native elite's traditional access to the labor and goods of the members of their communities into grants from the state. The services that the kuraka was empowered by custom and tradition to "beg" from his people were codified and written into the levies imposed on the members of native society. The kuraka principal, the segundas, and the kurakas of the largest villages received small monetary salaries that were paid out of the tribute moneys. The Indians were also ordered to cultivate four *fanegadas* of corn, four of potatoes, and two of wheat for the kuraka principal. In return, the kuraka was ordered to give the Indians seed for sowing and food and drink during the time they worked for him. The community was also required to provide eight Indian men and eight women past the age of tribute, plus six boys, for his personal service, a task that was rotated among the villagers each year. These people were to receive food, drink, and woolen clothing in return for their services. The *segunda persona* was granted half of the labor and household service assigned the kuraka principal, and the kurakas of ayllus that met a minimum size specified by Toledo had four *topos* of potatoes, the most basic food item, cultivated for them by the Indians.[47] The justification for this formalization of the traditional relationship between kuraka and community was that it would limit and control kuraka excesses, but an additional purpose was clearly to attempt to embed the relationship between kuraka and community in the colonial system. Custom was rephrased as a grant from the state that would in time be seen as such by all parties to the relationship, thus converting the kuraka into a part of the colonial state apparatus, his privileges dependent upon his relationship and service to that state.

In accordance with their role as a provincial nobility, the kurakas were exempted from the control of the provincial corregidor de indios, and legal disputes involving them were referred directly to the Audiencia, on the model of noble privilege in Spain.[48] Their access to the lands and resources of their community was also confirmed and respected by the state. The idea behind all this seems to have been to gradually convert the kurakas into a provincial *hidalguía*, a minor nobility whose members would seek to increase their wealth and status through service to the colonial state in their provinces. Again, the model for this was Castile, where the *hidalgo* ideal was to amass sufficient wealth to permit the purchase of lands, herds, and a seat in the provincial cabildo, with the attendant honors—all to the benefit of the centralizing state.

The kurakas initially responded eagerly to the lure of participation in the colonial system, actively seeking offices and privileges in the same fashion as their European counterparts. Members of the native elite served as lieutenants or subordinates of the Spanish corregidores in the provinces from the 1550's, and the kurakas continued to compete for positions in the Spanish colonial bureaucracy after the reorganization of native Andean society under Francisco de Toledo. In the 1580's, the Viceroy Martín Enríquez dealt with both the needs of the state to maintain communication within the viceroyalty and the demands of the kurakas for access to office by creating a new position for the native elite, the *alcalde mayor de quipucamayoq y contador de los chasquis*.[49] The holder was given jurisdiction over three provinces, within which he was responsible for the maintenance of all facilities necessary for communication, was authorized to carry the staff of a member of the royal court of justice, and had the power to appoint subordinate officials to execute his orders. The position was reserved to the upper ranks of the kuraka elite, and appointees were required in addition to be both Christian and *ladino*, or Spanish-speaking. Appointment to the office rapidly became a mark of prestige, and the kurakas who obtained it were quick to protest to the Audiencia if they felt that a new appointee did not have the proper social rank. In line with the usual trappings of office in Spanish society, the position carried access to both the service of personal retainers and extensive lands and herds that could be used to amass personal wealth.

The first kuraka to hold the position was the son of the kuraka of Huarochirí at the time of the conquest and heir to the leadership of the province, Don Sebastián Quispe Ninavilca. Don Sebastián was well thought of by the Spaniards in Peru. He helped the first corregidor of his province, Diego Dávila Brizeño, in the resettlement of his people in new villages, and he eagerly supported the Jesuit priests who arrived in the province to convert the Indians to Christianity in the 1570's.[50] In 1587, Don Sebastián was named alcalde mayor de quipucamayoq of all the roads and tambos of Huarochirí, Yauyos, and Jauja.[51]

On the local level, the kurakas also participated in village government, initially with the active support of the Spanish colonial authorities. In his instructions to the corregidores he placed in the Indian provinces in 1565, acting Viceroy Lopé García de Castro recommended that "it would be suitable if the alcaldes, at least now at the beginning, were 'indios principales,' because in addition to the other Indians being very poor and untrained people, the upheaval among people who have had and continue to have so much respect for the caciques would be great if suddenly common Indians began to command the caciques."[52] Toledo altered this recommendation, stipulating that only one of the two alcaldes in a village could be a member of the traditional native elite, whereas the other had to be a commoner.[53] But deference to the traditional elite remained strong, as shown in Matienzo's suggestion in the 1560's that the commoner alcaldes be chosen yearly by the elite.[54] Matienzo's recommendation was not followed in this case, however, and the laws that laid down the structure of the Indian cabildo specified that the officials were to be elected yearly by the community as a whole. Still, the influence of the traditional elite remained predominant: Huaman Poma de Ayala, in his proposal for the reform of Peru, pointed out numerous cases in which the close kin of the kuraka occupied the major positions of importance in the colonial officialdom imposed by the Spaniards, as in Huarochirí, where the son of one of the kurakas of the province served as an alcalde and then as a cantor.[55]

The forging of links between the kurakas and the members of Spanish society, however, demanded in Andean terms the exchange of gifts and feasting that bound donor and receiver to one another. We have already seen that the maintenance of the traditional relationship between a kuraka and his community required this kind of reciprocal largesse, just as the maintenance of the relationship between the kurakas and the Inca state did. But in the decades after the conquest, the skew in the relationship became pronounced, and the drain on the resources of the kurakas (and through them on the resources of their communities) resulting from their efforts to establish ties with their encomenderos and other members of European society such as corregidores and priests undoubtedly contributed to the erosion of the kurakas' authority among their own people. The major kurakas of the province of Chucuito reported to the Spaniards in 1567 that they no longer received the services they once commanded from their people.[56] Huaman Poma de Ayala complained of the loss of respect for the authority of the kuraka in Andean society, attributing it both to condescension on the part of Spanish officials and to disdain on the part of the people because the kurakas were no longer "true lords, nor did they do good works . . . , they did not serve well nor offer hospitality."[57] The cost of establishing ties with the conquerors—valuable as those ties might be in the long run—ran high, and provided an additional spur forcing the elite into more extensive commercial activities among the Europeans in order to obtain sufficient income to retain their traditional position in their own communities.

The kurakas' efforts to obtain office and social position within the new colonial regime commensurate with what they had held in the Inca state suggests that they moved rapidly toward participation in European colonial society—or would have done so if there had been no barriers to their full absorption by the society of their conquerors. The drawings of members of the native Andean elite done by Huaman Poma de Ayala depict people who rapidly adopted the dress and external manner, at least, of their conquerors. The kurakas of provinces, legally defined by the Spanish colonial regime as equivalent to European nobility and freed of sumptuary restrictions, adopted all the panoply of the European nobility. (See Figure 4.) And though there is little evidence that the Europeans accepted their pretensions—save in the cases of some in the upper ranks of the Inca nobility of Cuzco—many were quite willing to build their fortunes on the basis of alliance with the Andean provincial elite, from whom they received lands and goods that could be used to build estates for themselves and their descendants.

In at least some areas of the Andes, the mingling of Indian and Spaniard began very soon after the conquest. Rather than the casual rape or temporary union that accompanies invasion and conquest, this was a less dramatic but steady intermarriage between members of the Indian elite and their conquerors that lay the basis for a provincial elite with ties to both cultures. At the beginning of the seventeenth century, a Spaniard petitioned the Crown to eliminate the law barring Spaniards or people of mixed descent from living among the Indians on the grounds that the law discriminated against people born and raised in the Indian provinces. In

Figure 4. Andean adoption of European dress in the sixteenth century. On the left is a high-ranking kuraka; on the right, a *principal* points to an Indian tributary. Adapted from illustrations by Huaman Poma de Ayala in *Nueva Corónica y Buen Gobierno*.

Cajamarca, an Indian province into which Spaniards had moved and settled on a large scale late in the sixteenth century, a landowning provincial elite had formed from the merger of the two societies, Spanish and Indian. The members of this group, according to the petitioner,

> . . . have their estates in those same towns and lands that belonged to the Indians in the past, and have erected luxurious and costly homes in which to live in those same towns; and they possess their lands by reason of grants, purchase, or *composicion* with His Majesty, and have acquired others from the Indians themselves through purchase and dowry. . . . [The] majority of them were born and reared in those same towns and provinces, [and] many married Spanish or *criollo* women from the same areas, and quadroons, mestizas, and Indians, daughters and granddaughters of those same Indians and criollos. [58]

Huaman Poma, as might be expected, did not look so favorably upon the development of this group of mixed ancestry, complaining that "the mestizos are worse [than criollos, i.e. Spaniards brought up by Indians], for they are wild and disdainful to their uncles and aunts, mothers and sisters and brothers and Indian kinsmen." [59]

From the middle of the sixteenth century, the Crown barred Spaniards other than priests and corregidores from living among the Indians. The decree, ostensibly aimed at protecting the Indians from unrestrained extortion and open pillage by the Spaniards during the troubled decades following the conquest, placed the state squarely in the middle and made its representatives the sole intermediaries between Spanish and Indian societies. Some among the royal authorities saw the danger of giving the representatives of the colonial bureaucracy the power to expel Spaniards from the provinces and urged that the prohibitions on the intermingling of the two societies be revoked. Toledo himself urged this course, arguing that "the danger . . . with respect to the natives is the little love they hold for our nation, and in order to stop this, a good route is exchange and intercourse with one another, and marriage between the children of one nation and the other, so that we draw them to us and make them capable of our esteem as much as possible, since we call them to our Faith."[60] He went on to insist that the presence among the Indians of not only Spaniards but people of mixed descent would "civilize" the Indians and inspire them to embrace the Catholic faith despite the "bad customs" and poor examples that could be expected from criminal elements.[61]

But despite repeated recommendations to erase the legal barriers erected in the decades of the conquest between Spaniard and Indian, the Crown consistently refused to change the existing order.[62] The law did not stop the growth of provincial elites tracing their descent from both Spaniard and Indian, but it did keep those elites vulnerable and subordinate to the Spanish provincial officials, who could always draw upon this ready and repeated prohibition to make themselves petty lords of the provinces they administered.[63]

The legal structure of local Indian government erected primarily under the authority of Francisco de Toledo lasted throughout the colonial period, but Toledo's plans for the creation of an Indian peasantry that would provide a regular labor force for the mining of silver to support the military might of Spain were distorted and changed by the Indians themselves. Neither the "reductions" of the 1580's, nor the structure of village and parish parallel authority, nor the ladder of kuraka authority endured. The concentrated villages began to disperse within a few years after their foundation. Less than twenty years after the resettlement, the Crown sent a *cédula* to the viceroy, then Luís de Velasco II, noting that the Indian villages were rapidly losing their population and ordering that the people be returned to their settlements.[64] Further *cédulas* on this subject in 1601, 1609, and 1618 bore witness to the continued dispersion of the village population.[65] The need to carry out a new reduction and concentration of the Indians into large villages became a leitmotiv of official correspondence between the Crown and its viceroys well into the eighteenth century, although no real action was ever taken to carry out such proposals.

The census records from Huarochirí clearly show the dispersion of the population. In the 170 years between 1580 and 1750, the seventeen original villages grew to 49, and the average population per village dropped from some 1,500 to some 160. But by 1750 averages had little meaning, for the villages ranged from relatively large concentrations of people to tiny hamlets. A few of the more active and important centers such as La Asención de Huanza, near the mining region, or Santo Domingo de Olleros, a pottery-making center, neither of which were among the original sixteenth-century foundations, boasted populations of 3,000–4,000. At the other extreme, Urutambo, one of the original reductions, was occupied by only about twenty people in 1750, and other places were ghost towns. Santa Eulalia, another of the original seventeen foundations, was empty by 1705.[66]

The structure of local authority in Indian society, and the purpose to which it was put also look very different by the middle of the seventeenth century from what the Spanish authorities hoped to bring about at the end of the sixteenth. In some ways, Toledo's plan for a provincial minor nobility integrated into the structure of colonial administration was successful. The kurakas in the central Andes, at least in Huarochirí and nearby regions, did form a tightly knit elite whose members were outwardly much like the Spaniards and people of Spanish descent among whom they moved and lived. The kuraka of the repartimiento of Huarochirí in 1660, Alonso Quispe Ninavilca, was the son of a mestiza and brother-in-law to a Spaniard. His family associated closely with the Spaniards in the repartimiento, particularly the parish priest and the lieutenant of the corregidor, who lived in the village. Alonso's younger brother, Don Sebastián, was a young hothead who not only wore Spanish arms and knew how to use them but had childhood friends among the Spaniards, generally traders, resident in Huarochirí. This was a proud family whose members were highly conscious of their social position, to the point of defying even officials with inquisitorial authority sent out from the Archbishopric—something most members of Spanish society would hesitate to do.[67]

Did people like these constitute a separate class in colonial society? To a considerable degree, yes. Yet there were kurakas of all levels and ranks, from the powerful elite at the provincial or repartimiento level down to the petty village headman who spent his days in his own fields and had little more wealth than his non-noble neighbors. Just as the petty *hidalgo* of Spain could often claim little more than his legal rank and his poverty, so the kuraka hierarchy at its lowest levels was effectively part of the local community, with only the advantage of freedom from labor services as a result of legal recognition of nobility.[68]

Had the kurakas performed their tasks as the laws specified, they would have been the ideal representatives of colonial authority on the local level, eliminating traditional practices and allegiances and transforming the Andean population into a European peasantry. The kurakas were certainly carefully trained for their function: they were educated in *colegios* originally founded by Francisco de Toledo in Lima and Cuzco,[69] were fluent and literate in Spanish, and probably had essentially an education equivalent to that of most members of European colonial society. And yet there is evidence that behind the façade of loyalty to colonial authority, the kurakas could and did provide a buffer behind which they not only helped maintain local Andean traditions but actively participated in them.

The principal kuraka lineage of Huarochirí, the Quispe Ninavilcas, provides a fine example of the active role played by the kuraka in protecting local tradition. The kuraka of Huarochirí in the 1640's, Don Sebastián, appears in the documents of his time as the perfect native representative of Spanish colonial authority. He was literate in Spanish, and served as interpreter in local investigations into the practice of traditional rituals. We can presume that he was at least formally a practicing Catholic—required of all kurakas—since he was buried in a habit of Saint Francis. In 1642, he appeared as interpreter and translator in an investigation into the ritual activities of a kinswoman by marriage accused of having a llama sacrificed in an attempt to save the life of a dying relative. Throughout the testimony, Don Sebastián gave no sign that he was not totally allied with the priest-investigator and the cause of the colonial Church. However, when the order was sent out for the accused's arrest twelve days after the initial testimony, the woman had disappeared, and the records give no sign that she was ever located.[70] Sometime before 1660, Don Sebastián died, and when the idolatry investigator returned to Huarochirí his son Alonso had succeeded to the *kurakazgo* of the province. This time the net of anonymous accusations drew in one of Alonso's own kinswomen, a member of his ayllu and household as she had been of his dead father's. Under interrogation, she told a very different story of Don Sebastián's role in his community.

According to this woman, Don Sebastián had known about sacrifices performed in their lands by the members of different ayllus to ensure good harvests and, like his grandfather before him in the 1580's, had said nothing about them to the priest. When a woman was denounced in an early inspection—perhaps Sebastián's kinswoman Isabel—Don Sebastián had "negotiated for her, and hid the papers." He himself had consulted ritual specialists for prognostications about the coming year, and he had taken an active part in keeping information about traditional ceremonies from reaching the Spanish authorities. Indeed, before the 1642 inspection he had "said nothing should be mentioned about witchcraft and everyone should keep everything in their hearts."[71] Don Sebastián was obviously well aware of how the expression of even petty grievances through accusations of witchcraft could ricochet, providing an opening wedge to pry apart the bland Catholic edifice behind which the community hid its traditional ceremonies and rituals. And he seems to have used his considerable authority to stop leaks during his lifetime.

Kurakas also used their personal estates to buffer their communities from the excesses of the system. The kuraka of a community in the Bolivian highlands in the 1670's claimed land in his testament that members of his community used as pastureland until the middle of the eighteenth century, and left money for the purchase of lands whose produce was to be used to help his community meet the levies of the colonial state.[72] But not all of the provincial elite viewed their position as a responsibility toward their communities; some used their influence with the colonial authorities to avenge petty grievances and win personal quarrels. An example of this in Huarochirí is provided by the actions of the Cajahuaringas of the village of Langa in 1700, who brought charges of sorcery against their hired shepherd, an outsider from Jauja.[73] The Cajahuaringas were hereditary kurakas of the waranqa Langasica. In 1700, the kuraka was Don Cristóbal Cajahuaringa, whose widowed mother still took an active part in family affairs. The members of the family pastured their animals together, and the herd was guarded by a shepherd from Jauja named Gerónimo Pumayauri. Sometime before 1700 a young man of the Cajahuaringa family married the shepherd's daughter, but relations between him and his father-in-law were not good: he accused Pumayauri of hating his daughter and attempting to turn her against the Cajahuaringas. The anger festered, finally blowing into the open in a fight over a dead calf that the Cajahuaringas accused Pumayauri of losing by neglect. While drunk (apparently a fairly frequent state for him), Pumayauri openly threatened the matriarch of the family outside her house, so that when a daughter of the family took sick and died the Cajahuaringas accused Pumayauri of bewitching her and called in the Spanish colonial authorities, claiming that Pumayauri was planning to kill them all so his daughter might inherit their wealth. They presented witchcraft bundles that they claimed to have found in the house of the dead woman and in the houses they had up in the puna pastures where their animals were kept. They produced witnesses who swore that Pumayauri was a sorcerer, and the accused was duly arrested. But all the witnesses the family presented in support of their case were kin either by blood or by marriage, and even the alcaldes serving in 1700 did not contradict the story presented by the family. Pumayauri's witnesses, who included other members of the provincial elite outside Langasica, pointed out how the closed character of the community gave him little chance of disproving the accusations against him. And Pumayauri himself insisted that the Cajahuaringa family had framed him in order to avoid paying him the back wages they owed him. The authorities seemed to agree, but nonetheless the family ultimately had its way: Pumayauri was removed to a hospital in Lima for further interrogation, and no action appears to have been taken against the family, whose members were clearly still in power in Langa a half century later.

A kuraka might also detach lands from the community and appropriate them as personal property to form the basis of a landed estate. This tendency of kurakas to separate themselves from their people and form a separate landed aristocracy has been noted by many scholars,[74] but traditional relationships, although distorted and transformed, also continued to function, and the kuraka and his lineage remained an important force in many local communities. The buffer role of the kuraka as protector and guardian of his community became more and more assimilated to the concept of a local nobility whose position was associated with some responsibility for the minimal welfare of its subjects.

Kurakas were often responsible for the administration of the property of their communities and the disbursement of the funds collected, and their authority gave them an ideal opportunity to appropriate the proceeds of the rental of community lands or to absorb the lands as their own property, taking advantage of the legal procedure by which lands were claimed in the name of the community and of the kuraka as its representative. A land dispute in the waranqa Chaclla in the eighteenth century provides a good example of how community lands could be gradually detached by an elite lineage whose own ties with its community changed in the course of the century.

The repartimiento of Chaclla claimed pastures in the highlands above the Rímac from the time of their resettlement in the 1570's. In 1711, they purchased those same lands in a *composición de tierras* to assure their continued possession. The lands were rented and the proceeds used to pay for community festivals. For 40 years competition among the various component groups of the community gave trouble, until the lieutenant of the corregidor assigned the rental of the lands to the kuraka, probably confirming long-standing tradition in the Andean community. The income from the rental was to be used to pay the tribute for the dead, absent, and injured members of the community.[75] The kuraka, too, used some of those lands—also apparently by long-standing tradition. The overlapping property rights apparently caused no lasting difficulties until the kuraka died without direct heirs and the position passed to one Silvestre Cisneros, whom the people of Chaclla subsequently accused of being a mestizo outsider with no legitimate claim to his office. Cisneros recruited an ally, Juan Clemente Julcarilpo of the waranqa Carampoma, a member of the traditional elite, and the two of them rented the lands to the man who held the monopoly on the provision of ice to Lima. This was a direct affront to the people of Chaclla, for the "snow monopoly" was generally hated. By this act, Cisneros and Julcarilpo openly allied with the worst representatives of colonial exploitation, and the people fought back, insisting that since the lands belonged to the office and through it to the lineage of the Macas Sacllapomas, now extinct, they should be returned to the community. The dispute began in 1771 and dragged on for more than twenty years without resolution.

By the eighteenth century the native Andean nobility had become a tightly knit group, with ties that reached beyond to include members of European society as well. The wealth of the native elite varied widely: at the top, the testament of a kuraka of the Bolivian highlands in 1673 detailed an estate that included 3,590 llamas, 5,100 sheep, 1,060 mules, and over 40,000 pesos in loans due; in the middle, the property of a kuraka in Huarochirí sequestered in 1730 was valued at about 3,000 pesos in silver and silver objects (an undervaluation, since much was collateral for larger loans, but still far below our first example); and at the bottom, another kuraka in Huarochirí had only 720 head of sheep and cattle, 14 llamas, and 5 mules.[76] At its upper levels, the native nobility merged into the elite of colonial society, members of wealthy families who lived in Lima and Cuzco from their lands, their business activities, and the wealth extracted from the Indians under their authority. At its lower levels, it merged into the local communities, whose leaders were officials of the village or the Church who might or might not hold the legal rank of noble but whose positions in their communities depended primarily upon their personal status and prestige rather than upon their wealth.

The urban Indian upper nobility set its sights upon the same goals as its European counterpart and had political ambitions as inflated as its fortunes. In 1678, a wealthy noble of Jauja petitioned the Crown to establish an order equivalent to the military orders of Spain for members of the Indian nobility descended from the Inca and Aztec rulers. The Crown agreed that the Indian nobility should be favored, but turned down this petition on the grounds that it was politically unwise to emphasize the memory of the defeated Inca or Aztec states.[77] Two decades later, in 1691, the Crown responded to petitions of the Indians by ordering that qualified members of Indian society be "admitted to the religious orders, educated in the schools, and promoted according to their merit and capacity to ecclesiastical positions and public office." The order was repeated in 1725, but it had still not been promulgated or enforced by the 1740's, when two official visitors to Peru reported that the Spanish aristocracy there was determined to protect the rights to enter the Audiencia, to wear a judge's regalia in the streets, and to occupy the places of honor in the choir of the Cathedral reserved for the judges from being demeaned by their extension to "individuals of mixed blood and other disabilities." The order was not finally promulgated until 1767.[78]

Some of the Indian nobility did obtain at least honorific positions. Military service was unpopular with the members of European society in Peru, and the militia forces were swelled by people from other social strata.[79] Service to the state was a credit that could be presented by a person ambitious for other offices, and that may have been what drew the members of Indian society in Lima to the militia, where they had their own companies of both infantry and cavalry, with Indian officers. In the middle of the eighteenth century, Viceroy Superunda reported that there were eighteen Indian infantry companies totaling 900 men and three mounted Indian companies of fifteen men each, all with their own officers.[80] And military service did bring rewards: the first Indian to be appointed to the Audiencia, Mateo Pumaccahua, had served in the militia.

Though Pumaccahua was intensely loyal to the colonial state—to the point of taking the field against his own people in the great Indian rebellion of 1780–82—not all members of the Indian elite were willing to accept the contempt of members of European society for people defined legally and socially as Indians, whatever their wealth and their manners. Discrimination against Indians apparently grew in the eighteenth century, for the two official visitors to Peru in the 1740's, Jorge Juan and Antonio de Ulloa, noted that the sons of Indian nobles were treated with contempt by Spanish and even mestizo children. The officials recommended that noble Indian children be sent to Spain for their education, since in Peru "it [was] enough for them to be Indian for everyone, including even mestizos, to regard it as demeaning to teach them."[81] At least some people, rejected by the society they sought to join, attempted to reassume at least the accoutrements of their own culture. Their links with the Inca Empire were real; their noble rank and their positions as kurakas depended upon their ability to trace their ancestry back to the Inca state. From the mid-seventeenth century, portraits of Indian nobles in Cuzco reveal a tendency to reassume elements of Inca dress, abandoning the finery of the Spanish aristocracy that had become normal among the Indian elite in the sixteenth century.[82] (See Figure 5.) In the parades commemorating the coronation of Ferdinand VI in 1748, the Indian nobility prepared a pageant depicting the Inca rulers and their courts. Some were so moved by the resurrection of past glories that they cried when the Inca insignias were torn down in the reenactment of the conquest.[83]

The eighteenth century brought difficulties for members of the Indian elite at all levels, for the major shifts in international commerce resulting

Figure 5. Portraits of an Indian noblewoman (above) and an Indian nobleman (right) from the mid-seventeenth and eighteenth centuries, showing the return to elements of Inca dress. Photos by Martín Chambi of originals in the Cuzco Art Museum, courtesy of John Rowe.

in the loss of the monopoly over the South American continent once held by Peru's commercial elite forced the great mercantile houses to turn to their own immediate hinterland for recovery. The effort to extract still more from the provinces stimulated reform projects and sparked some of the first capable reporting on provincial economic conditions and structures since the *relaciones geográficas* of the sixteenth century.[84] But the provincial elite at all levels felt growing pressures. The kuraka, liable for the tribute of the Indians under his authority, was often forced to borrow the money necessary and hope he could recover it from his people before the tribute again came due. But his people also had other debts and obligations—for example, to the corregidor for the goods distributed to them in the repartimiento de mercancías, goods that the corregidor often himself got on credit from the Lima merchants, so that he was likely to press the people for his payment and even force the members of the Indian cabildo to do the collection for him. Such pressures made participation in village government a liability rather than an advantage. The letters written by a corregidor of Yauyos to the Indian alcaldes in 1702 ordering them to distribute the goods he sold illustrates not only the pressures upon the alcaldes, but also the contempt that suffused the relationship between corregidor and Indian in the eighteenth century. The corregidor wrote:

Hijo Pedro Sánchez Moscureño:
   It has come to my attention that not a single mule has been distributed in this village, and I order and charge you, as soon as you receive this note, to make sure that everyone takes a mule, you yourself setting an example for the others . . . and do all of this like a good boy. . . . God keep you,
                          your corregidor who values your services,
                                              Oquendo[85]

Another note in the same vein warned the alcalde of another village to "mind, do not delay, or else I will send for you."[86]

   Under such conditions, the acceptance of a position of ostensible authority in the Indian community became a source of potential impoverishment rather than gain, and people avoided local office. The community was forced to elect people or the Spanish authorities to appoint them, and observers complained of the Indians' lack of interest in achieving honor and respectability, of the Indians' laziness and lack of ambition in seeking neither prestige nor advancement. The Indian, they argued, was "as content to be town crier as alcalde."[87] The parish officials also became largely the servants of the priests, being frequently charged with carrying out forced distributions of goods for the priest, just as the alcalde was made to do for the corregidor. A few did benefit by running the taverns through which the liquor often imported by the priest was sold to the Indians, but their wives complained that they drank up any potential profits and ended up even more in debt to the priests. [88]

The lower levels of the kuraka hierarchy were squeezed until they virtually disappeared into the body of the rural peasantry or those fleeing to the cities in the hopes of improving their fortunes. In 1663, the Archbishop of Lima, Pedro Villagómez, warned that the practice of collecting tribute for the dead and absent carried the risk of driving the kurakas to abandon their positions, and his warning was well-founded. In 1711, for example, the kuraka principal and tribute collector of the village of Tupicocha gave up his position and left to seek his fortune in Lima. [89] By the middle of the eighteenth century, the position of kuraka principal was held by Indian commoners and carried few privileges and almost no power. A community officeholder who did not rank as noble was legally exempt only from the mita during his term of office, and in practice even that privilege seems to have been denied him. The notes to the census of Chaclla in 1752 warned that "the tributary Indians . . . who are noted as principales and who do not have noted at the foot of their entry their reservation from mitas and personal services are not so reserved, because they are elected and the community changes them whenever it wishes."[90] By 1750, the only kurakas listed in the census of Huarochirí were kurakas at the level of waranqa or above. Even the upper levels of the kuraka hierarchy in the provinces came under attack from the late seventeenth century. A royal order of 1690 decreed that kurakas be given a residencia, or investigation of their conduct in office, in the same form as that prescribed for viceroys, priests, and corregidores, every two years, and that they and their descendants be denied the office if their misdeeds warranted. [91] Such a law, if enforced at all, could only increase the pressure upon the kurakas to yield to the corregidor and aid his efforts to extract a profit from the Indians.

Does all this mean that the Indian provincial elite disappeared in the latter part of the colonial period? It does not. There was still a considerable group of people who could claim the legal rank of noble in the Indian provinces in the eighteenth century, as well as a still larger group of officeholders or people who were held in sufficient respect by the Spanish officials to merit the honorific title "don" in the province of Huarochirí in the middle of the eighteenth century. A house-to-house census of three of the four repartimientos of Huarochirí taken in 1751 permits an estimate of the numerical size of the local elite and the relations among its members. [92] The census-taker made a clear distinction between people designated as noble on the basis of descent from the pre-conquest elite, and those listed as alcaldes or principales or given the honorific title of "don." There are some limitations on the use of these categories:

a designation as a member of the Indian nobility could also mean that a person claimed partial Spanish ancestry and could show a certificate from the colonial government testifying that he was not legally defined as an Indian; and the title "don" by the eighteenth century bore little or no connotation of nobility among Europeans and meant only a person of some social position and prestige. Hence the actual nobility may have been somewhat smaller than our figures indicate, and the honorific "don" may indicate only a person of prestige rather than a member of an elite defined by law or tradition. But it undoubtedly signified a person of accepted social position in the eyes of the people themselves or of the census-taker. For that reason, the "dons" of the community are included as part of the provincial elite.

The nobility of the repartimientos of both Huarochirí and Chaclla in 1751 consisted of a relatively limited number of lineages whose members had intermarried with one another. There were 22 households designated as noble in Chaclla, concentrated primarily in the waranqas Chaclla and Carampoma, and within those in about six ayllus. In the repartimiento of Huarochirí, 28 households enjoyed noble status, through either the male or the female line. Five percent of the total number of households were designated noble in Chaclla in 1751, and three percent in Huarochirí. If we include in our estimate of the provincial elite the alcaldes and principales and persons designated "don," the proportion of the households rises to 21.5 percent of the total population in Chaclla, and 12 percent of the total households in Huarochirí.

In each of the villages in which the native nobility appeared, it made up from 5 to 10 percent of the population. As might be expected, the "dons" were more widely distributed throughout the repartimientos. But it might be more to the point to talk of elite villages rather than elites in villages, for the effective reach of the native nobility was much greater than the boundaries of the particular village in which its members were living at any particular time. Even in the eighteenth century, the village was in large measure an administrative fiction. People moved from village to village in the course of a lifetime or of a year without such movements actually showing up on any census records, since the people continued to pay their tribute to the same kurakas.

The reach of the kuraka lineages was extended even more by intermarriage among the elite families. The kuraka of Huarochirí, José Quispe Ninavilca (d. 1746), had married the daughter of the kuraka of the waranqa Colcaruna, Gregorio Dávila. One of his sisters had married into the waranqa Quinti, and another was married to the kuraka of the waranqa Lahuaytambo, Andrés de Borja Puipuilibia, who assumed the interim leadership of the repartimiento of Huarochirí after his brother-in-law's death.[93] The major surnames of the kuraka lineages of the province were Dávila (of Checa), Inca (of Quinti), Cajahuaringa (of Langasica), and Puipuilibia (of Lahuaytambo)—in addition to the Quispe Ninavilcas, the first lineage of Huarochirí. In Chaclla, the elite lineages were far more fragmented, for male heirs died out and the position of kuraka was passed down through the female line, becoming hopelessly confused and contested in the process. But at least one of the surnames of these elite families, the Cajahuaringas, is carried by one of the more important families in the village of Huarochirí today.[94]

The Indian nobility on the provincial level in 1750 showed considerable reluctance to become involved in the structure of civil or religious government, in contrast to the pattern of the sixteenth century. Few of the people listed as noble in the census of 1751 held community or parish office. Those offices had become essentially positions of servitude under the control of priest and corregidor, and the Indian elite withdrew to exercise what authority it still commanded in the local community outside the structure of colonial government. The Indian revolts of the eighteenth century hardened the growing prejudice against the Indians in colonial society. In 1793, following the defeat of the rebellion led by Túpac Amaru II, the Crown officially eliminated the position of kuraka and with it the special status and privileges of the Indian nobility, retaining in office only those kurakas who had distinguished themselves by their loyalty to the government during the rebellion.[95] The decree did not automatically eliminate the Indian nobility, for custom is tenacious, and many of the elite families continued to occupy the offices that had been in their families for generations down to the end of the colonial period. The last of the line of the kurakas of Huarochirí, Don Ignacio Quispe Ninavilca, is an example of this phenomenon. Don Ignacio became a guerrilla leader in the wars for political independence from Spain—wars in which few of the people who remained part of Andean society took much interest. An ardent supporter of José de San Martín, Ignacio's prestige in and knowledge of the local communities made it possible for him to play an important part in organizing and leading guerrilla forces against the Spaniards, and he later served for a short time as a representative to the first Constitutional Congress, in 1827.[96]

But despite his successes, Don Ignacio was himself an example of the disappearance of the Indian nobility—at least as a class surviving in the interstices between Indian and European in colonial society. With independence, the wealthier and more powerful members of the class merged into the elite of the newly independent state. The others were ground under, fading into the mass of the rural Indian population. For the class itself gave way in the face of the principal contradiction of colonial society, purified and sharpened through centuries of colonial rule: the dichotomy between Indian and Spaniard that merged with political independence into the republican dichotomy between Indian and citizen, between the rural peasants, laborers, and peons who provided the goods and labor appropriated by the ruling class, on the one hand, and the citizens who constituted that ruling class and structured the new state in their image, on the other.

EIGHT

Belief and Resistance

COLONIAL control depended heavily upon the cooperation of the conquered. I do not refer here to the people who are always willing to ally with their conquerors in the hope of personal survival or even advancement. There is another kind of acquiescence, less censurable but just as real, that consists of a people's surrender to their conquerors of the power to influence their vision of themselves and their society. Every society has such a vision, which can be defined as a system of shared values and practices through which people explain their world to themselves and give themselves an explanation or rationale for the inexplicable events of daily life—illness, defeat, or accident. The Europeans had such a set of beliefs and the Andean peoples had another, and each was both an expression and a support of the social relations of their respective societies. In sixteenth-century Europe, the Catholic faith was gradually being separated from the productive structures of society, but the close links between the political structures of Europe and the faith held by the people remained to play an important part in the reorganization of state structures that was part of the Reformation. In the Andes, the set of beliefs expressed in local histories and in ritual and ceremonial, and given form at the state level in the complicated ceremony and ideology of the Incas, was a closely woven cloak that gave form to the rules and regulations governing social interaction.

Much of the struggle of conqueror and conquered in the Andes was phrased in terms of the conflict between two opposing ideologies, world views, or religions—however we want to call them. An important part of the conquest—both the initial defeat of the Inca state and the gradual transformation and fragmentation of the relationships of Andean society that followed—was the battle between the Andean deities and values and those of their conquerors. For both European and Andean societies shared a common basic assumption that social order and survival depended ultimately upon forces beyond their own direct control, forces that could be entreated or appeased but that had a will and a logic of their own. Many explanations of the success of the Spanish conquerors in the Americas have laid great weight upon the alleged "fatalism" of the Americans in contrast to the confidence of the Europeans in the strength and invincibility of their own God. But explanations of success are constructed by the victors and as such are suspect—as indeed are the explanations of those of us who are to some degree products of the European belief system, notwithstanding our pretensions to objectivity. For the purposes of the analysis that follows, we need only concede the proposition that the members of the two societies, Spanish and Andean, shared the assumption that their political systems depended upon the favor and support of beings or forces beyond themselves. The construction of the colonial system therefore involved a battle to replace one set of beliefs by another— Andean traditions by those of European Catholicism. For as the members of Andean society conceded to the Europeans the power to define belief—to provide the accepted explanations of the events of their lives— they gave them control over their actions as well, and became accomplices in their own control and exploitation.

The close relationship between the Spanish state and the Catholic faith has long been a commonplace of European historiography. But though it is easy to link Spain's decline and the religion professed by most (though not all) Spaniards, it is more difficult to comprehend the relationship between Catholicism and state policy or nationality in Castile in the sixteenth century. The Spaniards in Castile and in Peru were hard practical men whose political choices and decisions can often be explained with little or no reference to religion. But sixteenth-century Spain—or Europe—was not part of the twentieth century. The expansion of the Christian kingdoms of Spain to the south during the centuries of the Reconquest was a struggle for land and vassals between opposing medieval states, but it was framed in terms of a Catholic crusade against the infidel. In medieval Spain, Catholicism became fused with the interests of the state, and the faith was the predominant and perhaps the only definition of nationality in the kingdoms finally linked under the rule of the Catholic Kings, Ferdinand of Aragon and Isabella of Castile.

Faith became the principal element of membership in a community for the members of Spanish society. The conquerors fought for themselves, but they also fought for king and faith. Though the finer values of religious practice may seem far removed from the pillage of conquest, the conquerors were not entirely forgetful of the universal protestations of the faith they professed, even if they remembered them only on their deathbeds.[1] Even at a remove of more than 400 years, the culture in which we are imbedded is in many ways too close to the medieval Catholic world to gain perspective on the influence that the basic assumptions of Catholic ideology had over the actions of the people who professed it. We are too likely either to accept without question both the assumptions and the cynicism by which people adjusted ideals to ambition, or to reject all protestations as hypocritical pretense. But action is the product of a framework of meaning held by the person who acts, and that framework as a whole can be defined as belief.

The faith of the Spaniards and their conviction that their God favored their efforts gave them an additional weapon in the conquest of the Inca state. The state structures of the fifteenth and sixteenth centuries were built upon the unity of the monarchy and the Catholic faith, particularly in Spain. The expansion and consolidation of royal authority in Spain was based heavily upon the Church, for at the end of the fifteenth century that great bureaucracy was a society within a society, whose wealth and political power were essentially equal to that of the state with which it was linked. The power and the annual income of the Archbishop of Toledo was second only to that of the king himself.[2] The Church held immense landed estates with full medieval jurisdiction over the people who lived within them. The bishops were medieval lords in the full sense, with castles and armies that they used to take an active part in the political conflicts of the time. In the course of the Middle Ages, the more important ecclesiastical benefices gradually gained *de facto* independence from Crown and Pope alike. The Catholic monarchs, Ferdinand and Isabella, fought to consolidate their right to appoint bishops to these important positions, thus converting potential foci of opposition to their policies into bulwarks of royal authority. They carried on the same struggle with the powerful military-religious orders of Santiago, Calatrava, and Alcantará, which had amassed huge territories and immense authority in the course of the Reconquest. The heads of these orders were great magnates, and their positions gave them command over resources and men on a grand scale, thus posing a threat to the centralization of royal authority. By the end of the fifteenth century, Ferdinand and Isabella succeeded in making the Crown Grand Master of all three orders; and in 1523 a papal bull incorporated all three permanently into the Crown of Castile, thus transforming a potential threat into a major asset of the Crown. Membership in the military orders became a source of royal patronage, a mark of social rank for which aspirants would readily pay; and the income from the lands and estates of the orders not only brought in revenue but could be used as security for loans from bankers.

Royal control of the assets and the allegiance of the religious bureaucracy, however, cut both ways. The Crown placed itself at the head of the military orders; it did not eliminate them or transform them into civil institutions. The ruler assumed legal responsibility for assuring the proper performance of the duties of the Church. This increasingly fused Crown and Church, as the state became the arbiter and guardian of belief as well as of secular relations. The Inquisition was first established in Castile in 1483 under Crown control to investigate and punish backsliding to Judaism by *conversos* or converted Jews, many of whom had become quite wealthy and influential. The close link between the struggle for power between rival factions at court and the faith was part of the Inquisition from its inception, and the Holy Office, with its broad powers and the combined threat of both corporal and spiritual punishment that it wielded, played an important role in Spanish politics in the sixteenth century.

Catholicism provided not only a justification for but also a real stimulus to political expansion in the fifteenth and sixteenth centuries. The campaign against Granada, the last Arab territory in the Spanish peninsula, was a holy war in which Ferdinand and Isabella both prompted and were led by the fervor of their people. The crusade against Granada, a highly popular enterprise, united the people behind their monarchs. But it would be naive and mechanistic to think of the rulers as using the belief of their people to obtain their own political objectives, for the European elites were also part of their societies, sharing the basic assumptions expressed in part through the tenets of the Catholic faith. The Inquisition— actively sought by the monarchs but maintained by the classes who found it both useful to them in their struggle for rank and position and necessary as well to justify their struggles for power in terms of a larger cause—is an example. The Holy Office became more and more important in the years between the death of Isabella of Castile and the accession to the throne of her grandson Charles. By the first decades of the sixteenth century, there were many accusations from high quarters of corruption and misuse of authority against the Inquisition. But repressive institutions that can be turned to the advantage of one or another party have a tendency to survive in a period of social crisis and transformation. The sixteenth century was just such a period, as the unity of Christendom, the umbrella of faith that during the Middle Ages provided a common identity and framework of assumptions for the societies of Western Europe despite their diversity, gradually fragmented, giving rise to mutually hostile factions that merged firmly with local state entities to play an active part in the consolidation of centralized states whose struggle for supremacy was the leitmotiv of the transition to the modern world.

The growth of Lutheranism, adopted by the German princes seeking to eliminate their subordination to Rome and to the tottering structure of the Holy Roman Empire, gave the Inquisition a new reason for being and consolidated its authority in Spain. Charles was elected Emperor shortly after his accession to the Crown of Spain, and he was thus immediately drawn into the challenge thrown out by the German princes ranked behind Luther. By the time he was able to remain in Castile long enough to hear the complaints against the excesses of the Inquisition, the threat of Lutheranism seemed more important than the petty excesses of local bureaucrats, civil or religious. The jurisdiction and authority of the Holy Office were not disturbed.[3] As the schism of Christendom widened and the lines between the two competing faiths hardened into settled warfare, the identification of Spain with Catholicism became general and the Spanish Crown assumed the role of defender of the Catholic faith. Concepts and practices that had once coexisted comfortably—or at least with a minimum of conflict under the broad umbrella of a Catholicism whose basic supremacy went unchallenged—became irreconcilable. Elements within Spain such as the Erasmian circles, whose members were eager to reform the monastic orders, made enemies. It was not difficult to identify such reformers with others whose ties with the Lutherans were closer, and by a careful use of spies and denunciations, and a skilled manipulation of the popular xenophobia that is easy to incite in a period of social crisis, the juggernaut was set in motion. The campaign to preserve the faith led by the Inquisition in the 1520's and 1530's even affected people close to the monarch himself.

By the middle of the sixteenth century, the inability of the Spanish armies to crush the protestant sects was clear, and the pattern of the struggle between the European states over the next two centuries acquired its basic outlines. Adherence to a particular sect—Catholic, Lutheran, or Calvinist—became a matter of social identification in which actual beliefs and practices were far less important than the political allegiance for which religious doctrine was only a shorthand. Doctrine became a matter of geography and birth, an incipient form of national identity. And for the states in conflict with one another in the sixteenth and seventeenth centuries, religion became a justification for policy—in particular the mercantilist dogma that the function and objective of state policy were territorial aggrandizement. Internally, religious identification became a basis of community, providing a convenient and ready explanation for the acts of other people. The Black Legend, the vision of the perfidy of the Spaniards that became a commonplace of the Anglo-Saxon concept of the role of Spain in the Americas from the sixteenth century to the twentieth, is perhaps the most vivid example of the process through which such ready explanations are constructed, and then become themselves part of the body of assumptions from which people draw their explanations of events.

The early decades of the Spanish presence in Peru coincided with the rapid definition of orthodoxy in Spain. Pizarro reached Cajamarca in 1533, when both the war against the Lutheran princes in Germany and the attack upon the relatively open and tolerant Erasmians were in full swing. These factors gave a cast to the temper and the actions of the Church in the Andes that was lacking for much of the first decades of the Spanish presence in Mesoamerica, where the climate and attitudes of the Renaissance and the missionary fervor of the reformers among the monastic orders dominated the projects and the activities of the Church. By the 1560's, the period of the organization of a state system in the Andes, the revolt of the Netherlands was on the horizon, and French pirates eager for a share of the treasure flowing to Spain appeared in the Caribbean. The Catholic bureaucracy in the new Andean kingdom was an arm of a state at war, and much of the formulation of the role of the Church among the conquered Andean peoples, at least on the official level, reflected that situation. The new kingdom was beset by enemies from within and without, and the men who built the colonial state regarded the Church as an essential arm of the colonial system.

The justification for conquest advanced by apologists for the Crown, civil or religious, was the bringing of Christianity to the Indians. This was the foundation of the papal grant that gave Ferdinand and Isabella authority over the Americas beyond the line of Tordesillas, and the souls won for Christ in the lands beyond the line were often presented as God's compensation for the loss of souls to protestantism. This justification followed conquest; it did not precede it. The conquerors brought priests with them to the Andes and gave at least lip service to the principle of conversion, but until the 1550's at least, political considerations took first place over missionary zeal and there was no systematic attack upon native rituals or ceremonies. The Incas retained the ceremonial state calendar without interference by the Spaniards. A description of the harvest feast of Inti Raymi in Cuzco in 1535 makes it clear that the ancestor-mummies, wrapped in fine cloth and gold medallions and circlets, symbols of the power of the Inca state through time, played a prominent part in the festivities. The ceremonies lasted for eight or nine days, at the end of which time the mummies were returned to their palaces and the first earth was broken to mark the onset of the planting season.[4] But the rituals and ceremonies dedicated to the maintenance of the Andean state structure could not be long tolerated by the conquerors, particularly in the climate of growing uncertainty and rebellion of the 1540's and 1550's. By the 1540's, the members of the religious establishment in Peru who were dedicated to replacing the wak'as with the Christian pantheon found a hearing among the royal authorities, who agreed to lend their support to the destruction of the Inca state through the elimination of the rites and ceremonies that were an integral part of the social relationships upon which it was built. The first orders to proceed against native beliefs, however, were careful and cautious, for the conquerors were well aware of the dangers of provoking unified opposition among the natives, who vastly outnumbered them.[5]

In the 1540's the Archbishop of Lima, Gerónimo de Loayza, issued the first *Instrucción* to guide the priests assigned to Andean communities in the conversion of the Indians to Catholicism. The local priests were urged to involve the Indians in the destruction of the old deities, on the assumption that their participation in the destruction of their wak'as would bind them to their new faith. But the tenor of Loayza's instructions was still timid in comparison to what followed—the first Conciliar Council of Lima in 1551. In part the Council's decisions simply affirmed basic Catholic dogma, but in part, too, they represented a declaration of war against the conception and definition of social relationships in Andean society.[6] One of the objects of the attack mounted by the Council was the body of ritual surrounding the ancestors.

Whether or not to condemn those who had died before the Spanish conquest to the Catholic Hell was a theoretical point that was much debated in the early years after the entry of the Europeans into the Americas. In Peru, the first Conciliar Council of Lima resolved the question in 1551, deciding that all the people who had lived in the Andes before the Spaniards brought Christian salvation were in Hell.[7] Whatever its theological underpinnings, the political advantage of this decision is obvious. The ancestors' condemnation to Hell was a statement that they were defeated and impotent before the Catholic God. The Church was intent upon convincing the Indians that the ancestors' spiritual power was the product of an alliance with the Devil—whose reality the Europeans were quite convinced of—and so any member of Andean society who sought relief or improvement in this life by appealing to the aid of his ancestors must pay the price of eternal damnation. The Church formally denied the power of the ancestors, but the intensity of its efforts to destroy the mummies and the wak'as indicates that it eagerly accepted what it perceived as a challenge from the wak'as and declared war on the Andean traditions.

The objects of the Church's efforts were of course not the long-dead ancestors against whom the decrees of the Council were directed in 1551, but the people who trusted and respected them. The vision of the Hell to which the ancestors were confined was explicitly spelled out by the Council with all of the graphic imagery for which the Counter-Reformation was justly famous. Hell was a house of demons who carried the souls of those who died to a dark place, where the dead burned in an eternal fire, devoured by thirst, by hunger, by illness, and by suffering. The text puts it clearly: "They want to die to put an end to their torment, but God wants them not to die, but to suffer there forever for their sins."[8] This essentially orthodox depiction of hellfire could be used to threaten members of the conquered society who yearned for the past and maintained the old ceremonies that reinforced the cohesion of the local group. The Indians, the Council ordered, were to be told that "all their ancestors and lords are now in that place of pain [hell], because they did not know or adore God, but [worshiped] the sun and stones and other creatures."[9] Priests prepared printed books of sermons for parish priests whose imaginations did not lend themselves to the task set for them. In one of his printed sermons, Hernando de Avedaño offered a text to convince the members of Andean society of the fate of their ancestors whose words still have the power to chill over a distance of 400 years:

Tell me, then, where are the souls of your *malquis* [ancestors]? Tell me, where are they? If you do not want to say it, I will tell you, clearly. Know, my sons, that they burn in Hell. . . . Tell me now, my sons, of all the people born on this earth before the Spaniards brought the Holy Word, how many were saved? How many? How many are in Heaven? None. How many of the Incas are in Hell? All. How many of the queens, the princesses? All.[10]

The attack upon traditional beliefs mounted by the Church did not go unanswered. The counterattack was formulated in the same terms: as a war of the deities in which the wak'as, defeated once, rose again to challenge and defeat the gods of the Spanish conquerors. The form taken by the counterattack is itself an index of the massive impact of the conquest and the Spanish presence upon Andean society, for the wak'as themselves were transformed, adopting new characteristics in the struggle to reestablish the old traditions and relationships. During the 1560's, at the height of the crisis of the plunder economy, the Central Andes were swept by a millenarian movement, the Taki Onqoy.[11] The movement was centered in the province of Huamanga (modern Ayacucho). It reached as far north as Lima, as far east as Cuzco, and over the high puna of the south to La Paz in contemporary Bolivia. As word of this "heresy" began to reach the Spaniards, a priest-inspector was sent to investigate the movement and locate and punish its leaders. The testimony gathered in the process of that investigation provides what information we now have on this Andean reaction to the Spanish invasion.

The "heresy" was disseminated by native "preachers" through whom the deities spoke in a kind of spirit possession. According to the testimony gathered by the investigator, members of the movement believed that the wak'as, defeated by the Christian deities, had come to life again now free of the fixed sites from which they once spoke to their people. "When the Marqués [Francisco Pizarro] entered this land, God defeated the wak'as and the Spaniards defeated the Indians. However, now the world has turned about, and this time God and the Spaniards [will be] defeated and all the Spaniards dead and their cities drowned; and the sea will rise and overwhelm them, so that there will remain no memory of them."[12] The wak'as, abandoned by the people who turned to the Catholic faith, had grown hungry and vengeful toward their descendants. They sent the unfamiliar illnesses that devastated the people, for they were known to bring disaster and bad fortune to those who did not feed and serve them well, just as they favored those who maintained the traditions. In order to end the illness and death, the representatives of the wak'as argued that the people had to return to the old traditions and remove the discord and disunity sown by the Spaniards.

The remedy was as traditional as the explanation, for it was the expected and normal response of the Andean ritual specialist to conflict within the social group. Death or disaster came because a person had angered a wak'a, who had to be propitiated and fed in order to prevent the disaster from spreading to others.[13] Those who did not return to their own traditions would be punished as the wak'as traditionally punished those who angered them—they would be turned into animals commonly hunted or pursued by men. "And if they did not adore the wak'as and perform the ceremonies and sacrifices . . . they would die and go about with their heads on the ground and their feet in the air and others would turn into guanacos, deer, and vicunas and other animals and throw themselves over the cliffs like the wild things they were."[14] In order to escape from the epidemics and survive, the Indians must reject the Christian faith and avoid any adoption of the trappings of European culture. The wak'as, through their spokesmen, ordered the people to avoid eating European foods and drinking European beverages, to reject European clothing, and to avoid entering Christian churches and taking Christian names. If they rejected the European world altogether, "there would be no illness or death but health and the increase of their goods."[15]

The Taki Onqoy movement drew upon traditional roots, modified and adjusted to a new situation. The myths of Huarochirí indicate that the wak'as were regarded as having had human form in the past, but that they turned to stone to guard their works and receive the service of their people after they performed their exploits. Even spirit possession was conceivable in terms of traditional practice, for the wak'as were also oracles who responded to petitions through the priests who served them and interpreted their answers.[16] The "preachers" of the Taki Onqoy movement were not necessarily part of the traditional native priesthood, drawn from particular kin groups that held a monopoly on the skills and ritual knowledge related to their tasks. They were often "tapped" by the wak'as in the same way as local curers and ritualists had been designated before the conquest—by a birthmark or defect, or by a cataclysmic personal event such as being struck by lightning. The most striking break with tradition that emerges from the testimony on the Taki Onqoy is that at least some of the preachers apprehended by the Spaniards had taken on the names of two of the most popular and gentle saints of the Catholic pantheon—Mary, mother of Jesus, and Mary Magdalene—in a curious violation of the prohibition against adopting Christian names that was part of the movement.[17] Nathan Wachtel has proposed that the development of the Taki Onqoy in the 1560's fits the cyclical vision of history contained in Andean tradition. Four creations and destructions of the world and its people had, according to tradition, preceded the Inca Empire. The Inca Empire formed the fifth cycle, whose end had begun with the defeat of the Inca wak'as by the Christians and their gods. Now the mita, or turn, of the Christians was ending and "the wak'as would create another new world and other people."[18]

The implementation of the wak'as' commands to withdraw from all contact with the Europeans was hardly a military threat, though the discovery of arms caches in Jauja in 1565 that were said to be hidden in preparation for a rising gave rise to concern.[19] But without the Indians there would be no colonial system; and despite the lack of any further evidence that the Indians planned to take up arms against the Spaniards, the Taki Onqoy was viewed as a direct threat to the presence of the Europeans in Peru. The state gave full authority to its representatives to stamp out what it defined as heresy and apostasy, which were virtually treason in an age when loyalty to political authority and to professed beliefs were regarded as essentially equivalent. The priest-inspector charged with the investigation centered his efforts in Huamanga, Arequipa, and Cuzco, and the representatives and leaders of the movement caught in his net were beaten, fined, or exiled from their communities. By the 1570's, the threat to the Catholic faith and through it to the Spaniards seemed to be over.[20]

The revival of the wak'as and the continued presence of the Inca state-in-exile on the frontier of the Amazon undoubtedly influenced Francisco de Toledo in his determination to construct a justification for the Spanish presence in Peru that was solidly founded upon the latest theological and political doctrines. Toledo, himself a high official in the lay religious order of Santiago, regarded the destruction of native ceremonials and rituals, together with the destruction of the claim of the Inca state to any legitimacy, as essential in the establishment of order and royal supremacy in the new lands. He organized an elaborate investigation of the Inca state whose objective was to enable him to present the Incas as tyrants and representatives of the devil who had taken all the lands and possessions of the people, and who had reduced the people to virtual slaves existing on the sufferance of their conquerors.

The theory of Inca tyranny was carefully built upon what was known of that Andean state from the testimony of its own elite. The mitmaq, or resident colonists, were presented as people forced to move from their homes by the state. Mita labor was another example of tyranny, a tactic for forcing people to exhaust themselves in unnecessary labor so as to keep them submissive and quiet. The massive engineering feats of the Incas were seen as evidence of forced labor. The rebellions against the state, the lack of centralized, formal laws of government, and the conflicts over succession among the Inca lineages were all part of the brief presented by the Spaniards in their attempt to convict the Incas of tyranny and oppression. Toledo's indictment could be applied, point by point, to the Spaniards themselves, but it was used to see the Andean state not as similar to the Spanish one but as evil, so that the memorialists could present a moral that justified the conquest. "Therefore, although these Incas were natural lords of Peru, they can be called tyrants, since they combine all the signs [of tyranny], which is that the true king becomes a tyrant by his own evil behavior."[21]

The final proof of the tyranny of the Incas was their rejection of the Catholic faith, which provided the justification for the destruction of the Inca state and its replacement by a civil power that would facilitate rather than impede the work of God by freeing the Indians to adopt the True Faith.[22] And if the destruction of tyranny were not in itself sufficient justification, the Spaniards could always fall back on the divine charge given them by God and the Pope to bring salvation to the Indians, thus winning back to God souls to compensate for the success of the devil in the Protestant lands of Europe. All of this contributed to the fusion between state policy and religious orthodoxy. Toledo left this objective in no doubt, informing the Spaniards charged with the inspection of the new viceroyalty that their aim was "the extirpation of idolatries and sorceries and the neutralization of the dogmatizers so that the doctrine of the Evangel can be planted in earth prepared to receive it."[23] Christianity was the legal justification for the presence of the Spaniards in Peru, and as the memorialists argued, the material support of the Europeans was a small price for the Indians to pay for their eternal salvation.

The Church in the Americas was an integral part of the Spanish overseas bureaucracy. In 1508, the Spanish Crown had obtained from the papacy full authority over the Church in the Americas in exchange for its support of the pope's Italian designs. The monarch filled all ecclesiastical offices and even held veto power over the promulgation of papal bulls within the American kingdoms.[24] With that security, the Crown could apply its own criteria to the appointment of clerics, and religious office became another source of income and position for members of European society in the Americas. The parish priest, or *doctrinero*, was in many ways the key local functionary of the colonial state in Peru; priests were far more numerous and better informed about local conditions than the corregidores de indios, whose territories were more extensive and who were likely to spend their time in the nearest urban center, leaving lieutenants in the provinces to supervise their affairs and collect tribute. In 1572, there were approximately 451 Indian parishes in the Viceroyalty of Peru (excluding Upper Peru, or modern Bolivia), serving a native population of just over 800,000 people. With almost 1,800 people to each priest, we can see that even the religious bureaucracy was spread thin—although the proportions improved slightly in the course of the colonial period, largely owing to the decline of the native Andean population. In 1792, the viceroyalty's 483 Indian parishes served a population of 608,894 people, so that there were 1,261 people per priest.[25] It is obvious from these statistics that the priests could not hope to know the actions or the intentions of most of the people they instructed in the Catholic faith. Though the concentration of the Andean population into large settlements made their task conceivable, if still enormous, it is obvious that only the most dedicated or perhaps fanatical priest could even attempt to investigate the day-to-day activities of his parishioners outside his immediate locale in search of backsliding or disloyalty to the faith. Disloyalty to the state was of course something else. To the degree that the Andean people did accept the priests and the Catholic faith, they opened a wedge into their communities, for the priests did not hesitate to ignore the sanctity of the confessional when they received word or rumor of revolt or plots against colonial authority.[26] That wedge was further broadened by the contacts that the parish priests established with the native elite in the villages. The relationships between priest and kuraka or elite lineages were inevitable, since the alternative was isolation; and in some cases close ties were built between the community elites and the priests, ties that could prove very useful in cases of trouble.

Nor was trouble such a distant possibility, for the parish priest stood in the middle between Spaniard and Indian. His official responsibility was to his parishioners, for their spiritual guidance and their protection. But he was also expected to inculcate in his parishioners if not love for the colonial regime, at least the conviction of its inevitability. Resignation to exploitation has always served the interests of ruling classes, and the Spaniards were well aware of the importance of inducing the Indians to resign themselves to conditions as they were. Printed sermons prepared for the use of priests working among the Indians preached total acceptance of the social role assigned the Andean people by the colonial state, the usual position taken by official religion in fulfilling its role of enlisting the exploited as active participants in their own exploitation. But in the case of Peru, the religious authorities became even more explicit, using the confessional as a means of checking on the Indians' acceptance of their exploitation by the members of Spanish society. In printed confessionals for priests to use among the Indians, the ten commandments became the vehicle for interrogations of the penitents that went into considerable detail about any infractions of the rules established by the Europeans for their Indian laborers. The commandments "thou shalt not steal" and "thou shalt not covet thy neighbor's goods" were spelled out in questions whose import could not be missed.[27] The questions asked if the penitent had taken anything from priests or other Spaniards for whom they worked, if they had hidden part of the ore they mined—and the places on the body where such ore might be hidden were enumerated—or if they had failed to care for the ornaments of the church.

The importance of the local priests to the structure of colonial rule explains why Indians were not generally admitted into the priesthood. In the early years after the conquest, people of mixed Spanish and Indian parentage (mestizos) did enter religious orders, some becoming famous for their sensitive understanding of Andean culture. But though some members of the upper ranks of the Andean elite did join monastic orders throughout the colonial period, occasionally becoming dedicated fighters against the exploitation of their people, I have found no evidence that a person of Indian descent ever served as a parish priest in an Indian province. Given the clear role of the parish priest as watchdog of the colonial system, the idea of creating a native Catholic priesthood, advocated by some in the early decades after the conquest, was rapidly forgotten.

The efforts of the Spanish colonial authorities to replace the traditional beliefs of Andean society with the European dogma of the Catholic religion seem to have had only indifferent success before the seventeenth century. From the 1550's to the end of the century, priests and civil administrators carried out limited campaigns against the wak'as and the mummy bundles guarded and cared for by the members of Andean society. They burned those mummies they found and destroyed the wak'as they could (they placed crosses on the stones that were too heavy to move or destroy), but then they left and the people returned to their traditional practices. The pattern changed at the beginning of the seventeenth century when the Archbishop of Lima, Antonio de Arriaga, threw the authority and support of the Church hierarchy behind a campaign to expose and eliminate all vestiges of Andean religious beliefs and practices, a campaign that continued sporadically until the eighteenth century. The first investigators were sent out from Lima in 1619 in a campaign that lasted until 1621. Systematic investigations were not renewed until the 1630's, when a new campaign began that lasted until 1638. The accession of a new archbishop, Pedro de Villagómez, in 1641 stimulated yet another campaign that lasted until 1671. Though the records of investigations continue until the 1730's, evidence of centrally organized and directed campaigns fades out by the latter years of the seventeenth century.[28] The records of these campaigns contain valuable information on the efforts of the members of native Andean society to preserve the traditions upon which the social relationships of their communities were built against the concentrated efforts of the Catholic bureaucracy to destroy them.

The Church records credit an ambitious if somewhat obscure member of the Catholic bureaucracy with the discovery that the Indians did not always forsake their wak'as and their ancestors when they gave formal allegiance to the Catholic faith. People no longer abjured openly as they had in the 1560's, but they remained dedicated to their traditions nonetheless, even if they did not openly challenge the Church. It is clear from the evidence that many local parish priests were aware of the maintenance of traditional beliefs among the Indians and chose to ignore it, closing their eyes to practices that presented no direct threat to the presence of the Spaniards—or of their priests—in the Andes. But one priest, Francisco de Avila, found such a comfortable *modus vivendi* with his parishioners impossible to accept, and a closer look at this man, the revered "extirpator of idolatry," can provide a glimpse into the character of the religious bureaucracy of the early colonial period.

Francisco de Avila was an orphan, abandoned in Cuzco as an infant by unknown parents in the early 1570's. Later in his life he gave his birth date as 1573. He was adopted, was trained at the Jesuit school in Cuzco, and went on to Lima to the University of San Marcos in 1592. Six years later he was ordained as a priest, a canon lawyer, and an exorcist, and he went on to win the competition for a position as priest of the Indian parish of San Damián in Huarochirí. A year after he began his work in San Damián, he was named vicar and ecclesiastical judge of the province.[29] His promising career was interrupted in 1600, however, by a series of accusations against him brought by the Indians of his parish. He was cleared, but in 1607 he was again charged by the Indians with forcing them to provide him with goods and to work for him without pay. He was brought to Lima for trial. In August 1608, while his conduct was still under investigation (though he was functioning once more in his parish), Avila was invited by the priest of the neighboring village of Huarochirí to participate in the Feast of the Assumption, a particularly brilliant festival there. As Avila later recorded the event, a pious Indian told him that the festival was in reality a camouflage for the celebration of the feasts of the wak'as Pariacaca and Chaupiñamca. When Avila delivered his sermon, he attacked the Indians for their idolatry and heretical practices. Later, the inspector investigating his conduct was given a tour of the parish in which Avila exposed the wak'as and mummies hidden by the Indians. He was cleared of the charges against him in 1609 and spent the rest of his life in the vanguard of the campaign to eradicate traditional Andean beliefs and ceremonies.

Avila apparently knew a great deal about local ceremonies and beliefs well before he began his campaign against them. Our best source on the traditional beliefs and ceremonies of the Andean world is a collection of myths, descriptions, and stories prepared for him around 1598, a year after he assumed his post in San Damián, the reducción of the Checa peoples. Yet it was some ten years before Avila enlisted the machinery of the colonial state in the holy war against the beliefs of his parishioners. Why? What were the motivations of this zealous priest who was willing to destroy all chance of any peace in his parish for his cause?

It is perhaps too tempting to search for extraneous motivations for a crusade such as Avila's, but his own origins are a fine example of the social problems that faced Andean-born members of European society eager to make a name for themselves. European society in colonial Peru was highly conscious of rank and position; the insistence upon purity of blood that became law in Spain a few decades before Avila began his career was also part of colonial society. At bottom, requirements such as that demanding a candidate for office to provide proof that his blood was free of the taint of Judaism or non-Catholic elements was an insistence upon lineage and descent. Family lines were in their own way as important to a member of European society as the kin groups of Andean society were to the Indians. Without kinship identification, a person's chances of finding either a position or a patron to help him obtain a position were severely limited. Avila had no lineage; his parents were unknown, although there is some indication that he knew who they were, at least later in his life. There were even rumors that he was descended from the Indian nobility; but to claim such would be to admit that he was a mestizo, a member of a social group whose members came under a growing cloud of suspicion and mistrust in the latter part of the sixteenth century. Mestizos were felt to be a security risk to the new kingdom, capable of turning against their Spanish in defense of their Indian side, and a number of decrees at the end of the century sought to protect the state against potential sedition by ordering careful vigilance of mestizos and other people of mixed descent, and by barring them from holding some offices. [30] Avila was quite probably a mestizo, although as an able lawyer he always claimed the legal right of an "*expuesto*," a child of unknown parents, to hold any office or position of which he proved himself capable. But his clouded birth followed him even in his own time. The Viceroy Marqués de Montesclaros (1607–15) wrote of him that "although there are those who say his parents are known, he presents himself as an orphan [*expuesto*], and in either case he is most probably a mestizo." [31]

People like Avila, whose ancestry and social position were in doubt, were totally dependent upon their abilities. Avila's contemporaries emphasized his ability, which in a man of proven ancestry and family might have eventually won him a bishopric. But he did not have that ancestry, and was in fact suspected of links with the native Andean population. The resistance of the Archbishop Toribio de Mogrovejo to the ordination of mestizos was known, [32] and Avila must have felt himself to be in an uncertain position. I do not think it is far-fetched to assume that Avila's total dedication to the elimination of traditional beliefs and practices among the Indians stemmed in good measure from the fact that his identity as a member of European society was totally dependent upon his own actions. He could point to no ancestors, no established lineage either in Spain or in Peru, as proof of his membership in the European community in the Andes. The self-made man, of which Avila is a prime example, was not unknown in the colonial world. But the very circumstances of his existence made it particularly important for him to declare his allegiance and make it clear that he was a loyal Spaniard before all else, dissociating himself from any taint of association with the society of the conquered.

Such people would be likely to be more European than those who had the easy security of lineage and established ancestry to protect them from any suspicion of becoming too close to members of native Andean society. The colonial state was built upon men like this, as well as upon men of established lineage born both in Spain and in the Andes whose self-identification centered around their membership in European society. Despite antagonisms and resentments born of competition for favor and position between those born in Spain and those born in the viceroyalty, in any crisis those people who identified themselves as members of European society stood together against the "other," whatever or whomever that might be. This basic division between those who considered themselves Europeans and those who did not was at the heart of the colonial system. That system was European, functioning in the interest of those who identified themselves and were identified as European. Its survival depended ultimately upon the submission and the acquiescence of the people defined as Indian. The members of European society in the Andes knew well that they were a minority living on the backs of a society that far outnumbered them. Even when the large population of mixed or uncertain ancestry is counted in with the Europeans—an artificial device that does not reflect actual practice except in limited cases—the Indians accounted for some 60 percent of the total population of the viceroyalty of Peru at the end of the eighteenth century. Moreover, the people defined as Spanish, both European- and American-born, made up less than three percent of the total.[33]

These factors undoubtedly had a good deal to do with the intensity and persistence of the investigations into native beliefs and ceremonies in the seventeenth century. A closer look at these investigations can provide us with an insight into both the response of Andean village society to the colonial system, and the function of these investigations as part of the mechanisms of control brought to bear by the colonial state. Let us look first at the impact of such an investigation upon local Andean society in Huarochirí. The village of San Damián de Checa was Francisco de Avila's first parish, and the region from which the idolatry investigations of the seventeenth century spread.

Avila's first report on idolatry in Huarochirí, written in 1611, summarized the structure of nested kin groups with their deities and ancestor guardians.[34] The first major investigation, from 1619 to 1621, produced a guide for investigators written by Pablo José de Arriaga, who was both a participant and a careful recorder of the reports of others. His summary of the practices of the Indians provides a graphic picture of the maintenance of native beliefs and traditions with only minor changes in Huarochirí and elsewhere almost a century after the Europeans entered the Andes.[35] The third campaign, which began in 1660, brought the priest-inquisitor Don Juan Sarmiento de Vivero into Huarochirí for several months, and the records he left offer an unparalleled insight into the behavior and attitudes of local village society toward the religious authorities at the time.

Sarmiento was a canon lawyer charged with investigating and rooting out traditional ritual. He arrived in the parish of San Lorenzo de Quinti in the repartimiento of Huarochirí in January 1660, where he remained for five months.[36] He began according to the instructions on how to conduct an investigation left by José de Arriaga in 1621, reading the edict against idolatry and preaching a sermon against traditional rituals in the village church. The investigation began with a secret denunciation supplied by an anonymous informant, naming a number of people as idolaters, witches, and priests of the traditional ceremonies. These people were brought in for questioning and then locked up for the duration of the investigation. They were periodically brought back for further interrogation to the cabildó, or town council, where the inquisitor had established himself. People were threatened and some were even tortured to elicit confessions and full descriptions of traditional ceremonial practices. Rumors that some people had broken began to fly about the village. Friendships and longtime associations crumbled under the threat of torture or betrayal. Finally, on May 28, sentence was pronounced on 32 people from Quinti and neighboring villages in the two parishes of Quinti and Huarochirí. The sentences ranged from public humiliation to lashings and even to exile and imprisonment in the House of Santa Cruz, the Lima prison for people regarded as the most unregenerate of the priests of the native beliefs discovered by the inquisitors.

The people sentenced were brought into the public square in Quinti. They were placed upon mules or donkeys, with wooden crosses about six inches long hung around their necks. They were ordered to wear these marks of humiliation from that day forward. On their heads, the religious authorities put a medieval *corosa*, a cone-shaped hood made of pasteboard, that was the European Catholic mark of infamy and disgrace. Beneath these hoods the hair was cut off—an Andean mark of humiliation. Those who had been condemned to receive lashes had their backs bared. Ropes were put around their necks. They were paraded slowly through the streets of the town with a crier ahead of them reading out their crimes against the True Faith in a loud voice. After this spectacle, the people were brought back, some with their backs bleeding from the 20, 40, or 100 lashes with the cat-o'-nine-tails wielded by the village executioner or jailer. At the edge of the village, Sarmiento had a huge fire built, into which were thrown all the ritual objects collected in the course of the investigation: 17 painted shirts, 32 tiny drums, 30 *queros* or carved wooden goblets, and assorted bones of ancestors collected for the burning.[37]

The crimes of idolatry elicited by the inquisitor in the course of five months of interrogation and torture in 1660 were a far cry from the rejection of European beliefs and values represented by the Taki Onqoy movement almost exactly a century earlier. The people charged with idolatry and witchcraft confessed to a series of rituals and procedures related to the day-to-day miseries and preoccupations of village life. People went to them to find lost goods or to get a prognosis on their chances of returning from a dangerous journey. They sought help in getting an errant husband to return, in finding a lost animal, or in improving their harvests and their herds. The most common "criminal" activity was curing, which involved a variety of herbs, potions, and rituals. In general, the evidence of idolatry obtained in the course of the interrogation was thin at best; Sarmiento had to content himself with punishing people not for crimes or invocations to the ancestors to aid them against the colonial state or Church, but for the use of local practices and rituals that expressed an often forlorn wish for small pleasures, for security and comfort on an extremely limited scale.

Sarmiento was skilled in what might be called the psychology of interrogation. He kept husband and wife, mother and child, or friends apart from one another and asked them the same questions about their movements, using discrepancies in their testimony to confront them and demand information.[38] Both kin ties and friendships crumbled under the pressure of the investigation. A son whose mother was jailed as a suspect provided the inquisitor with information about people who consulted his mother while she, isolated and unable to communicate with him, stoutly denied any knowledge of the people.[39] The use of minor lies and bits of information to destroy people's confidence in one another and to lead them to fear that friends would eventually betray them was a tactic recommended in the instructions for investigators, and Sarmiento used it with considerable effect in Quinti in 1660.[40] An example of the destruction of one such friendship provides a vivid example of the danger to the Indians of permitting themselves to be drawn into angry confrontations with their fellows in the presence of the inquisitor. María Huanico, a mestiza woman, was a friend of the kuraka's aunt, María Pomaticlla, at whose request she carried out a divining ritual at the beginning of the idolatry investigation to determine if she would be safe from denunciation. But María Huanico gave way under the combination of imprisonment and repeated interrogation, and gave the inquisitor information about her friend. On April 20, after María Huanico had been in jail for almost three months, during which time she had become terrified of both the priests and her fellow villagers (whom she said had threatened her for giving information to the investigator), the priest brought the two Marías together. In the exchange he provoked between the two—one angry at her betrayal and the other defensively angry at the friend she had betrayed—Sarmiento obtained still more grist for his mill.

[He] asked María Huanico how she knew that María Pomaticlla had an idol of white stone, and María Huanico said that María Pomaticlla told her, to which Pomaticlla answered, "since you've talked, I will tell them how you told me that you have two idols dating to the time of your father, one of which you kept and the other you gave to me, and you must hand over the articles that you have together with the two stone idols." To which María Huanico replied that she had given one stone to the inquisitor, and she had no more. María Pomaticlla continued to threaten her, saying that she would be sent to the Cercado [the house of detention for idolaters] and that she must hand over the coca, llama fat, and beads that she had, and demanding to know why she had not done so before. María Huanico answered that she had already said that she would hand them over. And with that, the inquisitor ordered the interrogation suspended until María Huanico handed over the materials that had just been mentioned.[41]

The tactics of divide and rule, of suspicion and vengeful anger provoked in people and then turned against them worked in Huarochirí in 1660. They are the same tactics that have worked through the ages, for unless people are very well prepared to meet their interrogators, a small crack in anyone can be quickly widened to provide information that can lay open an entire community or group of people.

In the course of the five months of interrogation in 1660, did lines of fission within the community emerge that indicate changes in the structure of the community? The idolatry investigators could not have gotten anywhere without at least the initial cooperation of members of the community. Again, this was well known by the investigators, whose manuals told them that their "first goal is to win over some reasonable Indian by offering him rewards in secret and by telling him that no other living person will find out what he has said."[42] As the dragnet of secret denunciation, accusation, and counteraccusation spread in Quinti in 1660, a general picture of the kind of people who were drawn into the net and the people who sent them there emerged. The people accused of divination and curing, and particularly those accused of worshiping the ancestors and the wak'as, tended to be among the older members of the community, often closely associated with the traditional native elite.[43]

The kurakas were traditionally responsible for maintaining community norms and practices, and many of them continued to fill that role despite all the efforts of the Europeans to transform them into compliant servants of colonial authority. Most of the people convicted in the investigation of 1660 were women (28 of 32), although the men were among the most important of the "doctors," as the specialists in the performance of local ritual were called. The average age of the people convicted was 47—not particularly aged, but certainly older than the average in the Andes in the seventeenth century. More striking is the fact that virtually all of the people accused of maintaining the old beliefs spoke through an interpreter during the interrogations; this contrasts strongly with the fact that most of the people associated with the Spanish authorities, whether as informants or as part of the police apparatus, understood and spoke Spanish. This latter group was younger (average age 32) and almost exclusively male, and included several principales, or younger members of the traditional elite, and a notary known in the community for his antagonism toward the people who kept the old ways. There were no other clear distinctions; members of the same kin groups or ayllus were in both groups. The difference in age and acculturation between the people who held to community ritual and those who opposed it suggests a conflict, latent if not open, between the traditional community elite, among whom respect for the ancestors and for the elders was an important value, and the younger, all-male group whose ambitions and activities were linked to their relationships with the Spanish authorities. But even these people did not shake off all of the old traditions. They were not above turning to the doctors or ritual specialists when they were in need, as even highly educated and "modern" people do today. Though the notary of Huaro-chirí openly associated himself with the Spanish investigators and was de-nounced as an informer and openly threatened by the kuraka's Spanish brother-in-law, the notary's brother turned to a specialist to recover lost goods.[44] And there were also many people in village society who had no great stake in the battle between the two traditions; they answered the questions that were put to them and fled from the field of battle as quickly as possible. They used the ritual specialists in their community when they were ill or needy and abjured them when the priest-inquisitor arrived. Confronted, they confessed and faded back into the day-to-day life of their villages.

But not all of the members of village society—even the curers and doc-tors caught in the net spread by the Catholic investigator—gave way be-fore the Spanish authorities and told all, hoping only to be left alone to return to their fields and their homes. Some fought the investigation, re-sisting interrogation and even torture in a display of resistance that com-pels admiration despite its futility. On February 1, 1660, the inquisitor ordered the arrest of a middle-aged couple, Lorenzo Llacsayauri and his wife, Juana Tantamallao. The couple fled and were traced to the province of Yauyos before the officials of the investigation could arrest them and return them to Quinti for interrogation.[45] Both Juana and Lorenzo were repeatedly questioned and finally tortured. Juana, when confronted with the testimony of neighbors who had broken and given information about her husband's performance of rituals, gave way little by little, always ad-mitting only what was already known from other testimony. Lorenzo, de-spite three months of repeated interrogation, denied everything, even written confessions shown to him by the investigators. But unlike his less controlled fellows, he never argued with a witness who informed on him in the presence of the inquisitors nor accused anyone else of performing rituals. Faced with the testimony of other people, Lorenzo admitted that he had performed cures but insisted that he had confessed to all of his sins in Lima in an earlier investigation and had given up all of his idols to the priests. The formal language of court records seldom reveals emotion, but here the intensity of the antagonism between Lorenzo and the priest-in-quisitor emerges clearly from the testimony. When threatened with

torture, Lorenzo insisted that he had already confessed his sins and had
no more idols. He added that the inquisitor should not wear himself out,
since he no longer had any idols or any knowledge of the sites of wak'as
or community ceremonies.[46] Faced with Lorenzo's contempt and open de-
fiance, the inquisitor ordered him returned to jail and, later, tortured. On
April 2, Lorenzo was submitted to the rack, after being told that if he died
in the course of his interrogation it would be his own fault for refusing to
confess. At each stage of the torture, as the officials turned the screws that
stretched first his arms, then his legs, the officials stopped, repeated their
warnings and waited for him to confess. Lorenzo was tortured twice, once
on the rack and once with cords twisted around his arms and tightened;
but each time he confessed only to information that his interrogators already had.

Lorenzo also did his best to prevent others from giving information
about the wak'a of his ayllu, warning both his wife and his kinswoman,
María Huanico, that they should not admit to possessing idols or com-
municating with the wak'a of their community.[47] María Huanico, who by
April was completely broken by the investigation and ready to give any
evidence the investigators wanted of her, told the authorities of his efforts
to prevent the disintegration of his community. The records of the investigation of Lorenzo and his wife are incomplete, but as far as they go they
depict Lorenzo as a strong, determined individual, a skilled ritual leader
or doctor who tried with all the limited means at his disposal to protect
himself, his people, and the ancestors from the attack of the investigators
who had occupied his village.

Lorenzo did not fight alone. He was supported in his struggle to with-
hold information from the Catholic investigators and to persuade his fellows to do the same by the traditional elite of the parish, at least some of
whom were themselves caught in the net spread by the priest-investigators. The kuraka's aunt, María Pomaticlla, was apprehended, as was Pedro
Solis, regarded as one of the leaders of the old ceremonies, who bore the
honorific title of status "don." Solis, like Lorenzo, attempted to prevent
the people imprisoned with him from giving information. According to
María Huanico, hated by all of the village for cracking under pressure,
"Don Solis said that they were talebearers and should not talk."[48] In the
village of Huarochirí early in the investigation, a group of people broke
into the cabildo building while the inquisitor was interrogating a witness.
The people were led by three of the principales or minor leaders of the
community, including one Don Pedro Cajavilca, who was reported to
have "addressed the *visitador* in a loud voice, asking him if the inspection
of his villages was finished."[49] The confrontation between the inquisitor
and the village leaders rapidly developed into a near riot, the threat of

which was ended only by the arrest of the leaders by the alcaldes, who at least this time responded to the orders of the Spanish authorities. The Spaniards could hope to retain control of the community only as long as the loyalty of the village officials held: when the investigation also clashed with the kuraka of the province through his family, eventually provoking further violence,[50] the unified resistance on the part of the traditional elite may have stimulated the investigator and his retinue to shift their head-quarters to the neighboring parish of Quinti, where there were fewer members of the traditional elite (this is a hypothesis, for the sources do not record reasons for the shift).

A unified front was the best defense against the Church's assault upon the beliefs and ceremonies that people felt protected them from destruction. The failure of the investigators to obtain any information from an earlier visit to Huarochirí in 1642 was later proven to be due to the strength and leadership of the kuraka, Don Sebastián Quispe Ninavilca, who not only supported the traditional rituals and participated in them, but managed to convince his people to say nothing to the investigators.[51] But Don Sebastián died sometime before 1660, and his son and heir, Don Alonso Quispe Ninavilca, could not prevent the petty jealousies of village life from providing the investigator with the clues he needed to begin his investigation and to carry it through despite the open antagonism of the native elite and their European allies, and the more covert efforts of the accused to stop the leaks whereby the priest-investigator obtained information about the maintenance of the old beliefs and practices.

And what form did those beliefs and practices take, nearly a century and a half after the Spanish conquest and about five decades after the initiation of the colonial Church's intensive campaign to eradicate native beliefs? Despite the fact that most of the practices uncovered by the Spanish authorities in Huarochirí in 1660 dealt with curing, finding lost goods, and the other forms of what might be generally called village "witchcraft," enough bits of information emerged in the course of five months of interrogating many people to show that the ancestors and the wak'as retained their importance in the Andean community despite the concentrated campaigns of the colonial Church. In the view of the community, the good will of the ancestors and the wak'as continued to be essential to their survival and prosperity. Pedro Solis, the ritual leader in the parish of Quinti, was alleged by a witness to have told another member of the community who consulted him that the latter's poverty and illness were the fault of his community. People no longer followed the law of their ancestors, Solis said, and for that reason the man's entire ayllu would die.[52] One of the women tried for idolatry told the Catholic investigator that her grandfather taught her to offer food to the ancestors each year because they were the owners of the chacaras she farmed and the houses she and her relatives occupied, and because they were hungry and needed to eat. To feed the ancestors, her community assigned a chacara to their support, spending the proceeds of the harvest from the plot on coca, chicha, llama fat, and maize that was burned in a huge bonfire to feed the deity.[53]

The treatment of illness also involved the ancestors as well as the social group to which the sick person belonged, for personal illness was the manifestation of a disease that affected the social group and had to be treated as such. A curer rubbed the body of the person he or she treated with a sacrificial *cuy* or guinea pig, and then killed the animal and offered it to the wak'a or ancestor felt to be the cause of the affliction, saying "*chechia*," "father, cure me of this illness."[54] A cure performed by Lorenzo Llacsayauri upon a kinsman involved the man's entire family. Lorenzo had the sick man, his wife, and their two children lie down on a mat and massaged them all with a white cuy, saying, "with this, you will live well with your children and your wife, and you will not die like the other person who has died, and you will find enough to eat."[55] After the treatment, Lorenzo slit the throat of the animal with his fingernail and told the sick man to throw the carcass into the river outside his village, saying that he would have two or three more years to live with his family.

The most striking difference that emerges from the investigation of 1660 in the form of community ceremony from that of the preconquest period is the loss of group participation and celebration. The festivals of community deities were traditionally occasions for drinking, storytelling, dancing, and games. People competed with one another to show off their finery; they danced, feasted, and drank for days on end. But in 1660 the ceremonies were performed in secrecy and silence, according to Lucía Suyacargua, a witness from the village of Quinti who described the ceremony for the wak'a of her ayllu, Hualcaraya. Lucía told the priest-investigator that people slipped out of their houses at night, alone, to go up to the flat, high pampa within sight of the idols. They built a solitary fire, threw in their offerings of coca leaves, cuyes, red maize, chicha, llama fat, and potatoes, and spoke in a low voice to the idols in their mother tongue so that they would not be heard, saying "you see that the times are all in reverse and you take no heed of us, and we give you all this because you are the owners of the chacaras, because we are persecuted and in another time."[56] And then they ran back to their houses in the dark, silently, so that no one would know where they had been.

The testimony from Quinti in 1660 paints a picture of a community in which the old traditions were giving way under pressure despite the struggles of the members of the community to maintain them. The persecution of native ceremonial seems to have achieved at least part of its objective. Traditional beliefs and ceremonies were not erased, but at least some members of the community repudiated the old ways and chose to ally with the Spanish authorities, denouncing their fellows to the priest-investigators when they appeared in the native parishes. The presence of potential spies and informers among them had to feed the suspicions and divisions that were part of this kin-based competitive society. Some of the testimony from 1660 suggests that people were caught between the implacable Catholic God and the hungry ancestors, afraid to reject the old beliefs for fear of the vengeance of the ancestors, not to mention the anger of their fellow villagers. [57] If the investigations did not succeed in destroying group ceremonies, they certainly can be credited with contributing to the fragmentation of local society that was an important factor in the control exercised by the colonial state over the Andean population. By the end of the sixteenth century, the people of Huarochirí no longer gathered in large groups to worship the major wak'as of the region. In the 1590's, the people of the region celebrated the major festivals in smaller groups, probably at the level of the waranqa. But the festivals continued. [58]

The evidence of the Church's investigations in the seventeenth century indicates that community gatherings and offerings to the wak'as and the ancestors no longer took place. Can we assume because of this evidence that the warnings of the kuraka, Don Sebastián, to his people to say nothing about their beliefs to the inquisitor-priest in 1642, or the similar orders to keep silent about wak'as and idols by the ritual specialists in Huarochirí and Quinti in 1660, were intended only to protect individual specialists, and that group ceremonies had indeed disappeared? Both in 1642 and in 1660, the testimony of witnesses interrogated by the priests was limited to the description of individual acts of curing or worship. Even when the wak'a of an ayllu is mentioned, all insist that worship was individual, performed by one or two people who sneaked out to the fields in the dead of night to perform their rituals. The community as a group does not emerge.

Here, however, we are faced with a typical colonial situation, unfortunate perhaps for a historian but a useful reminder of the limits of our sources. For our data are the records of the Spanish colonial authorities, and a lack of data may mean that there was nothing to be found—or else it may mean that the Indians were successful in hiding the extent of their practice of their own customs and beliefs. Evidence from the eighteenth century, between 1723 and 1730, suggests the latter. The information emerged in the course of two cases against men charged with idolatry in the waranqa Carampoma, in the repartimiento of Chaclla in the Rímac River drainage, two valleys to the north of Huarochirí. Two men were accused of serving as ritual specialists, with responsibility for maintaining the shrine of the idol of their ayllu and leading sacrifices and ceremonies for their kin group.[59] In the course of the first investigation, the interim kuraka of the waranqa, Francisco Julcarilpo, was called for questioning. Julcarilpo, clearly preferring to ally with the Spanish authorities against the Indian villagers, told a story of ceremonies in which the entire population participated, and claimed that the villagers would stone their kuraka to death if he tried to interfere. According to Julcarilpo, the people of the village of Carampoma went out each year to worship the wak'a of their ayllu on the feast day of Santiago, patron saint of their village. The old home site of their ayllu, still remembered in the eighteenth century, was located in the mountains high above the village. Before the trek to the ceremonial site, the people gathered at a cross above the village of Huanza to dance. Then they moved on to the lake above the village, also called Carampoma, source of the group's water. There they spent the night in sacrifices, returning the next day to Huanza where they slaughtered a llama and had a feast and a grand celebration.[60]

The continued existence of the ritual specialist in charge of the ceremonies of the kin group also emerged from Julcarilpo's testimony. The accused in the investigation of 1723, Juan de Rojas, was clearly a person who had taken on the responsibility of caring for the idol of his kin group. His brother testified that the idols had been passed down within the family since the preconquest period, although he insisted that he did not have the care of them and knew nothing about the ceremonies. Juan de Rojas received the idols from his mother after his father's death and kept them in his house, where the men of his kin group gathered to sacrifice and to drink.[61] There is also evidence that by this time the position of ritual specialist was a "cargo," a community responsibility rotated among those members willing to assume it in return for the prestige that accompanied performing the task. Again according to Julcarilpo, one person was reserved by the community as the *mascayoq*, or "seeker of food" (from *mazcani*, "to seek," and *mazca camayoq*, "diligent in earning food").[62] The village paid his tribute and protected him from retribution by the priest for his failure to attend mass "because it is said that if he goes [to mass] the harvests will fail."[63] The *mascayoq* led the ceremonies to beg for rains, organizing the children of the village to parade in a tearful procession, beating on tiny ceremonial drums or *tinyas*. He was also responsible for the sacrifices that were offered to placate the ancestors when the rains were too heavy and threatened to ruin the crops.

The Spanish authorities insisted from the sixteenth century that the kuraka was responsible for the difficulties and the failures of the campaign to eradicate native beliefs and ceremonies. But by the eighteenth centu-

ry, the kurakas—at least those at the community level if not higher—
were part of their societies and could be overruled, intimidated, or even
silenced by the people they allegedly commanded. The kuraka who, like
Don Sebastián of Huarochirí in the 1640's, could juggle Catholicism and
traditional ritual to present a good front to the Spaniards while protecting
the ceremonial practices that, as far as the people were concerned, ensured them good crops and good health, was respected and commanded
a hearing. But the man who made the mistake of thinking like the Spaniards and attempting to use his position to change community practices
might be met with a brutal reminder of the limits of his authority. When
the kuraka in Carampoma at the beginning of the eighteenth century surprised the people returning from sacrificing to the wak'a of their ayllu and
threatened to inform the Spanish authorities of their practices, the people
stoned him so badly that he died of his wounds. And when his successor,
Francisco Julcarilpo, did tell the authorities about the village ceremonies,
which brought one man 50 lashes for his role as caretaker of his community's idols and another perpetual exile from the village, the community
used the state to rid themselves of him in turn. The Spanish authorities
were told by the usual anonymous informer than Julcarilpo himself sacrificed to idols in his own home. They investigated and found stone objects smeared with the blood of cuyes in the home of his sister-in-law.
Julcarilpo protested that the people were trying to frame him for his rev-
elations of community ritual, but despite his protests he was taken into
custody, tried, and convicted.[64] It is difficult to avoid the conclusion that
the community thus rid itself of an unwanted member in a position of
authority. Julcarilpo undoubtedly had at least family idols whose task it
was to protect and preserve his own household, whether or not he shared
in community ritual. And the community, knowing this, could easily use
the knowledge to put him in the wrong, get him out of the village, and
invalidate his testimony.

From the early years of the sixteenth century until the 1670's, the campaigns against native beliefs and ceremonies carried out by the Church in
the central Andes were orchestrated, brutal affairs that were essentially
medieval autos-da-fé mounted in the small highland villages of farmers
and peasants that huddled on the steep slopes of the western Andean
range 8,000 to 12,000 feet above the sea. The idolatry campaigns were
exemplary rituals, didactic theater-pieces directed to the audience as
much as to the participants, much like a public hanging in medieval Europe. Their objective was to intimidate those who might think of following the same practices as the people who were publicly beaten, exhibited,
and humiliated for the edification of the rest of their communities. But it
is difficult at first to comprehend the meaning of the massive expenditure

of effort and time by the Church in trying to ferret out and destroy all of the practices and beliefs that were basic to the social integration of traditional Andean society. The whole process takes on the ugly face of fanaticism, of the destruction of people's basic assumptions and beliefs merely for the sake of destruction unless we can place the campaigns of the Church in Peru in the broader context of the colonial state and beyond that, the Spanish empire of which Peru was but a part. At that remove, the brutality and fanaticism, though still real, become explicable in terms of the basic assumptions of Spanish society, and in particular the basic identity between professed religious belief and loyalty to the Crown that was characteristic of the sixteenth and seventeenth centuries.

By the 1560's, as I noted earlier, Spain faced the attacks of French and Dutch pirates who began first to enter the Caribbean and then to move into the Pacific around Cape Horn. After Magellan's circumnavigation of the globe, the route to the Pacific from Europe, though dangerous, was a ready alternative to the standard route across the Isthmus of Panama and down the Pacific Coast to Peru and points south. From the time of the opening of the Pacific to foreign ships, the colonial state became increasingly concerned about pirate attacks upon coastal shipping, and their concern was justified on several occasions. After open war began between Spain and the Netherlands, the fear of piracy and contraband was fused with the fear of attack from Spain's enemies. War made the former European possessions of the Spanish Crown into bitter enemies, and religion gave both sides a ready explanation for the hatred generated by political conflict. The Dutch were depicted as the Protestant heretics lost to the True Faith through the machinations of the Devil, the people who enlisted in Lucifer's army as part of the struggle to defeat Catholicism and return Europe to barbarism.

The fear of invasion was linked to the fear of heresy that was expressed in Spain in the growing strength of the Inquisition, the expulsion of the Jews and, in 1609, the expulsion of the Moriscos, the people of Moorish descent who became part of Catholic Spain as the Reconquest incorporated their lands into the Christian kingdoms of the peninsula. The Moriscos were regarded as a fifth column, a potentially dangerous and rebellious force within Spanish society, because their dubious loyalty to the Catholic faith defined them as potentially disloyal to the Crown as well. The same fears that made the expulsion of the Moriscos popular in Spain were present in Spain's Andean colonies, and as Pierre Duviols has pointed out, were drawn upon to mobilize support for the campaigns against native Andean beliefs and ceremonies throughout the seventeenth century. The Indians, who far outnumbered their Spanish masters and whose antipathy toward the Europeans among them could not help but be known, were ready suspects for the role of a fifth column that would unite with Spain's enemies to destroy Spanish power in the Andes. A scenario developed in which the Dutch or British were expected to ally with the Araucanian Indians in southern Chile to invade Peru by both land and sea while the Indians in Peru rose at the same time to slaughter their Spanish rulers.[65] Francisco de Avila himself played upon these fears to convince the authorities to support his campaign to eliminate native beliefs. He described the Dutch as "evil people, heretics and enemies of God who come as messengers to warn us by their presence that we must guard our way of life, to warn us that we must believe in God and not offend him because if we do offend him God will permit them to make war on us, to take our houses and our goods and even our lives, as the Romans did to the Jews, and the Spaniards to the Incas."[66]

The fears of the members of Spanish society in Peru, whether born in Spain or in the colony, were fed by their awareness both that the Indians among whom they lived far outnumbered them, and that they were in an exposed position on the frontiers of the Spanish empire. The defense of the viceroyalty from attack from within or without ultimately rested upon the colonists themselves. The ships that patrolled the Pacific Ocean against raiders and pirates were built in Ecuador, financed by contributions from members of Spanish society in Peru.[67] In this context, it is hardly surprising that the Spanish authorities, given to regarding belief as essentially equivalent to loyalty to the Crown, would be willing to listen to demands to eliminate beliefs that maintained and reinforced the loyalties of the conquered Andean peoples to a precolonial past. To the degree that the Spanish authorities in Peru believed in their own justification for colonial rule, they were also caught in the corresponding assumption that their failure to inculcate Catholic beliefs and values in Indian society was evidence that the Indians were potentially dangerous to the survival of the colonial state and the European society it served.

But these convictions did not survive. By the eighteenth century, the energy devoted to the campaigns to eradicate traditional Andean beliefs and ceremonies faded and died. Although accusations of idolatry and witchcraft continued to be made into the eighteenth century, there is no evidence of organized, centralized missions sent out from Lima after the 1670's. The evidence of the continued maintenance of traditional ceremonies and the solidarity of local Andean society in preserving its customs that emerged in 1723 was never followed up by the religious authorities. The accusations of idolatry in the waranqa Carampoma in 1723 were forwarded to the local parish priest, who punished the two men directly accused of witchcraft and sent his report on to the Archbishop, in whose office it was filed and apparently forgotten. The accusation made in 1730 against Francisco Julcarilpo, the kuraka who had informed on his community, was investigated by the lieutenant of the corregidor and the interim priest of the parish. Though the accused was convicted, there was no further investigation of Julcarilpo's descriptions of organized village worship. It is hard to imagine Don Juan Sarmiento de Vivero, the priest-inquisitor who put the parish of Quinti and Huarochirí through five months of interrogation in 1660, failing to follow up the evidence offered in 1723 and 1730. The only conclusion I can draw from this is that by the 1720's and 1730's the state was no longer particularly interested in the maintenance of traditional beliefs and was willing to let the local communities be unless accusations stemmed from within them. And action once taken was kept to the minimum necessary to restore order in the community.

The eighteenth century is generally described by historians as an age of increasing rationalism, a time when the fierce conflicts stemming from the Reformation faded and conflict between countries became part of the open competition for trade and territory in which war was but one more weapon in the diplomatic arsenal of the European states. The Age of Rationalism, or the Enlightenment as it is also called, is most often described in terms of the scientific laboratories and theories of a small group of savants, or the projects of political and economic reform originated by educated gentlemen eager to increase production and with it the fortunes of the state. But the struggle between the conquerors and the conquered in Peru, expressed through the battle between the colonial Church and the Indians over the maintenance of traditional Andean beliefs and ceremonies, also faded with the changing temper of European society. A fight can only take place when both combatants share a contest. As the European states—and the society they ordered—became increasingly secular in the course of the eighteenth century, the official view of traditional beliefs as an arm of the Devil's organized effort to destroy the Spanish state also faded. The ceremonies and rituals of daily life were shunted to the sidelines and the colonial authorities withdrew from the battle of conflicting beliefs, leaving the Indians to carry on what ceremonies they would, as long as they met their levies and did not directly threaten the Spanish authorities.

As the state increasingly left faith to the choice of the individual or group—a process that had only begun in the eighteenth century—it shifted the terms of the conflict between conqueror and conquered. Conflicting beliefs are the foundation of active conflict, but the battle cannot be joined unless both sides in the struggle view the beliefs of the other as an open challenge. The traditional rituals of the local Andean society remained, to become part of the distinguishing characteristics of Indian as

against European society. But the struggle between conqueror and conquered, the basic dichotomy of the colonial system, moved to the openly
political plane. By the middle of the eighteenth century, there were clear
signs that for Indians as well as Spaniards, their definition of themselves
was an increasingly political one. And many members of Indian society
went on to see themselves as belonging to a separate society oppressed
by its colonial masters. The step from there to revolt was not a large one.

NINE

The Challenge to Colonialism

F ROM THE middle of the seventeenth century, some members of native Andean society began to turn from reliance upon the ancestors and tradition and to take charge of their resistance against their Spanish rulers themselves. The planned revolts against the colonial regime that the Spanish authorities detected from the 1660's on were a measure of both the hatred for the colonial system harbored by the Indians and the growth of new relationships or the reorientation of older ones that were products of the colonial situation. Every colonial regime breeds new attitudes that are eventually used to destroy it, and the Spanish colonial regime was no exception. The Spaniards were well aware of the threat represented by the people they ruled. An anonymous author, in a letter to Spain describing a revolt that took place in Huarochirí in 1750, graphically illustrated the specter provoked in the minds of the members of Spanish society by any sign of open rebellion against their authority. It was essential to stop the rebellion, he wrote, not only for its own sake, "but to stop the contagion aroused in the other provinces, for if it reaches to Tarma, Jauja, and Cuzco it will be the end of the kingdom for the Spaniards, because the revolutions that this portends cannot be reversed."[1]

The colonial authorities were thoroughly frightened by any sign of organized resistance to the system they maintained. The cycle of revolt that began in the viceroyalty of Peru within a century after the construction of the colonial state apparatus eroded their security and their fortunes. By the eighteenth century, Spain was on the defensive against the growing power of England on land and sea, and an increasing proportion of the income of the colonial state went to construct and maintain the military defenses of the far-flung territories under the distant authority of the viceroy in Lima. Until the 1780's, the security of Spanish rule in South America depended upon the local population, organized into battalions of citizen-soldiers responsible for defending the state with their arms and their persons.[2] The appearance of pirates or even foreign warships off their shores was a danger the authorities and the European population could comprehend, even if they could not always defend themselves against it. But the possibility of attack from within, of an Indian rising, was something else again, and from the 1660's on the antennae of the state were more and more sharply tuned to receive any sign or rumor of Indian revolt.

These fears were not entirely fanciful. In 1666, the Spaniards discovered a plot to cut off Lima, set it afire, and eliminate the Spanish population.[3] Nine years later another plot was discovered in which a group of Indian artisans planned to incite their people to revolt and then seek aid from England, with whom Spain was then at war.[4] The most famous and long-lived Indian rebellion was the organization of a rebel community led by Juan Santos among the Campa Indians in the jungle area behind Tarma. Santos, educated by the Jesuits in Cuzco and fluent in Latin as well as Spanish, Quechua, and Campa, together with his Campa followers expelled the Franciscans from the missions they had established in the region in 1742 and then managed to hold off the Spanish authorities until the 1760's.[5]

Another rising was planned in Lima in 1750, aimed at being the first spark of a general rising that would include the rebels in Tarma led by Juan Santos. It was discovered and most of the plotters were caught and executed, but the people of Huarochirí did rise in revolt, killing about sixteen members of Spanish society and holding out for almost a month before they were defeated. Three decades later, the entire state apparatus was threatened by the massive rising known as the revolt of Túpac Amaru, in reality a series of revolts that shook the entire southern area of Peru and what is today Bolivia from 1780 to 1783. Túpac Amaru II led a revolt in 1780. He was captured in April 1781 and executed the next month, although fighting continued for some time. The rebellion was effectively over by the middle of 1783, but an echo of the rising was heard in Huarochirí in 1783, when an Indian named Felipe Velasco, who took the name of Túpac Inca Yupanqui, attempted to spark a revolt in that province.[6] All of these revolts failed. The Indian rebellions against the colonial system did not merge into the wars for political independence, which were the product not of the dichotomy between Indian and Spaniard but rather of the struggle for supremacy within European society in the Americas between those who identified with the American lands and fought to found a political system independent of ties to Spain and those who identified with the motherland and sought to prevent the political fission of Spain's American empire.

But the failure of the Indian rebellions does not make them less worthy of study. They were the product of the basic dichotomy of the colonial system. The rebels confronted that dichotomy and attempted to eliminate it through political action, and the organization and structure of their efforts throw the colonial regime into sharp relief. In this chapter I want to stop and take a close look at one of these revolts in order to obtain a clearer picture of the product of two centuries of colonial rule. How did the members of Indian society structure their opposition to the colonial system and how did the members of European society respond to their challenge? It is a truism that people participate in their own oppression, and the truism holds here as well. But it is made true by the active intervention of the oppressors, who had to learn to understand and manipulate the values and the relationships of the people they ruled in order to prevent the coalescence of unified resistance. The examination of rebellion—and of defeat—is important as part of the story of people's efforts to take charge of their own destinies. The study of a situation of crisis brings out the basic alliances, the social relationships and values that made it possible for people to trust one another enough to act together. It also brings out the lines of fission that were part of the foundation of colonial rule, and constituted the weak links in any effort to organize and structure a unified struggle against oppression.

The revolt I will examine took place in 1750. It was planned to begin in Lima as the first stage of a general rising that would free the Indian population of its Spanish masters. But that plan failed, and the rising was limited to Huarochirí, where it was violent but eventually suffocated. The rising was the object of much concern in Lima, provoking documents of all kinds, from viceregal correspondence to bad doggerel.[7] But in addition to sources that speak entirely from upper levels of the viceroyalty, there is an invaluable source from within the province, though written from the perspective of a member of European society. Sebastián Francisco de Melo was a Spaniard who emigrated to Peru as a young man to make his fortune. According to his own testimony, he became a merchant (sometimes prospering and sometimes losing), married, and finally went to the mining region of Yauli to try to make his fortune as a miner. He was raised and trained for a military career before he chose to go to America, and boasted of his tactical abilities in contrast to the local European-American population. Melo was in the mining region of Yauli when the revolt broke out in 1750, and he took part in defeating the Indians. According to him, the defeat of the rebellion was largely the product of his own efforts, as he pointed out in great detail to Viceroy Amat y Junient in 1761 in a day-to-day diary of his actions in Huarochirí in 1750 in support of his plea for aid and assistance from the viceregal authorities.[8] Melo's account of the rebellion and his part in it substantially contradicts the sources emanating from Lima, but although he may well have been guilty of special pleading, the bare outlines of his narrative fit the information we have on the revolt from other sources. The contradiction lies in his account of how the revolt was broken, and here his version is more comprehensible in terms of the structure of local Andean society. He may not have been responsible for all that he credits himself with, but I suspect that his is a fairly accurate account of what actually happened in the villages of Huarochirí during the months of July and August 1750.

The events of the abortive movement of 1750 are essentially similar to those of the other movements detected and smashed by the colonial authorities before 1750. On June 21 of that year, in Lima, a friar asked Viceroy Superunda for an audience. The friar told the viceroy that he had learned through the confessional of a plan among the Indians of the city to attack the viceregal palace at midnight, kill the royal officials, and lead a general rising of the Indian population of the city. The friar refused to name names, arguing that a public attempt to deal with the threat on the basis of such vague information would only serve to warn the plotters rather than to apprehend them. The next day, the warning was repeated by a parish priest who was told of the planned rising by a freed slave in his household who was recruited by the Indian organizers of the rising, eager to attract the black population of Lima to their movement. The viceroy handed the matter over to a lawyer of the Audiencia, who after interrogating both the friar and the ex-slave, persuaded the former to provide further information and the latter to continue meeting with the Indians and report the progress of the plans back to the authorities.[9]

The plotters used the habits of the city as a cover for their plans, disguising their meeting by gathering in public on the feast day of San Juan in the Hills of Amancaes, a favorite Lima gathering place for holiday celebrants of all ranks and classes. Through the black informer who attended that meeting, the authorities learned the names and addresses of the organizers, and shortly before dawn on June 26, five days after the authorities first received word of the plot, they arrested as many of the people involved in the planned rising as they could, extracted further names from them, and pulled in more people—eleven in all.[10] Some of the plotters escaped—one to Huarochirí, where he raised the standard of revolt.

According to the viceroy's subsequent report, the organizers of the revolt began to work out their plans more than two years before they were apprehended. There was a mystical content to the plot. One of the organizers, noted for his religious devotion, held that Saint Rose foretold the return of the Inca Empire to its legitimate masters in 1750, thus making the organizers of the revolt the instruments of divine will. The plotters also made capable use of the religious calendar to cover their plans—as Indian villagers did to protect the ceremonies and festivals of the wak'as and local deities of traditional Andean society. The rising was set for the feast day of Saint Michael the Archangel.[11] One of the traditions of that day's festivities was a procession in which the Indians carried weapons as part of their costumes. The plan called for the rebels to borrow shotguns, pistols, swords, and daggers from the Spanish residents for the procession, which would at one and the same time arm the rebels and disarm their enemies. Then at midnight they would set fire to the thatched huts at the edge of the city, driving the people out into the streets. According to a drawing of the center of the city that was captured with the plotters, the rebels planned to attack the viceregal palace, posting a group of men at each corner of the plaza to bar Spaniards from access to the palace while a fifth group stormed the palace and killed all of the Spanish authorities inside. The plot called for all Spaniards in the city except priests to be eliminated.[12]

The rebels did not limit their plans to Lima. They had begun to recruit in the provinces when their plans were discovered. They actively recruited blacks and mulattos and offered freedom to all slaves who would join them in their move for liberty. They also sought contact with Juan Santos, still successfully holding off the Spaniards in the jungle area east of Lima, and some argued that Santos, who claimed descent from the Inca, should be crowned king of the empire they hoped to restore. Others among the rebels argued for an interim government of the most important members of the native Indian elite pending later choice of a ruler.[13]

The rebels were sentenced and their punishment carried out on July 22, a little less than a month after they were captured. Four of the men were sentenced to perpetual hard labor; one, a mestizo who was the notary of the group, to 200 lashes; and six to hanging and quartering. The city population, frightened and angry, apparently attacked Indians in Lima at random, causing many to flee the city.[14] The sentences were carried out in the main plaza of the capital in the presence of a company of 400 Indian nobles and militia to underline the assumed loyalty of the majority of the Indian population of the viceroyalty to Spain and the colonial authorities. The severed hands and heads of the dead men were fixed on the walls of the city as a reminder and a warning. The meaning of the event to the Spaniards was expressed by one of them in a letter to Spain, in which the writer noted that the aim of this exemplary punishment was to assure "that they [the Indians] can never arouse the entire kingdom as has happened, with all of the Indians arrogant and refusing to quiet down until they learn of the justice done here. [Our] objective is to ensure that we Spaniards live carefully and refuse to loan the arms we have to anyone, keeping them always ready for the defense of the Crown and our persons, in accordance with our obligations; for all of the Indians and blacks bear us no good will."[15]

But by the time this exemplary punishment was carried out, word reached Lima that the province of Huarochirí was in revolt. One of the plotters in Lima, Francisco Jiménez Inca, a captain of the Indian potters' guild, was in his home province when the plans for the revolt were discovered. He used his return to the village of Lahuaytambo in June for his wedding to the daughter of the interim kuraka of the waranqa Chaucarima and the feast day of the village to convince his new kinsmen to join the projected revolt. Don Andrés de Borja Puipuilibia, interim kuraka of the repartimiento of Huarochirí following the death of the hereditary kuraka, his brother-in-law, and Don Juan Pedro de Puipuilibia, Don Andrés's brother and father of Francisco Inca's bride, were both sufficiently angry at the colonial regime and the debts they had accumulated for back tribute and labor services to consider calling upon their people to join the rising. When news of the capture of the plotters in Lima reached Huarochirí as Francisco Inca was preparing to return, both kurakas responded to their new kinsman's call for revolt. The people of Lahuaytambo followed their kuraka's lead and organized their forces, naming captains, sergeants, and other officials to lead them. Some of the leaders were members of the provincial elite, among them Don Andrés and Don Juan Pedro, though others held no official positions. Some of the latter were popular heroes who were later described as among the most effective figures in the revolt.

Francisco Inca moved just in time, for as soon as the viceroy learned of his whereabouts he sent orders to the lieutenant of the corregidor of Huarochirí, José Antonio de Salazar y Ugarte, to arrest him. The message reached the lieutenant in the mining district of Yauli, and he and the miners decided to act quickly, for "the natives were already less obedient, and showed very little respect."[16] The Spaniards were given additional warning by the parish priest of Huarochirí, Tomas José de Orrantia, member of a wealthy colonial family, who wrote telling them of the organization of the rebellion and urging rapid action.

On July 19, Salazar and a small company of men left for the village of Huarochirí in search of Francisco Inca, leaving other men behind to follow if needed. But the habit of careless contempt for the Indians died slowly, and the small company, divided by rivalries between Spaniards and American-born members of European society, or criollos, was hobbled by its attitudes. Plans for action were completely at variance with the fact of an aroused and angry population. The Europeans refused to believe that the Indians would not cower and disperse at the sight of a whip in the hands of a member of European society, and provided for their safety by spending the night braiding cat-o'-nine-tails by their campfires. These whips were vicious implements when they were wielded by a man against an unarmed person, and the Europeans hung them on their saddles, confidently expecting that "seeing them, the Indians will tremble with fear."[17]

The reality turned out to be very different. The Europeans had some initial success, capturing Francisco Inca's wife in his pastures and driving his cattle down to Huarochirí, where they organized a bullfight in the town square. They were further lulled by Don Andrés, the kuraka, who promised that he would deliver them Francisco Inca and then left for Lahuaytambo to help prepare the Indian assault on Huarochirí, assured that the Europeans would remain in the town. They did. By Saturday, July 25, a large group of Europeans was in the town of Huarochirí, including most of the local representatives of the colonial state. The past corregidor, Don Francisco de Araujo y Rio, ignored warnings of revolt to go to Huarochirí to meet with the judge assigned to carry out his *residencia*, or evaluation of his conduct in office. He brought with him his son-in-law, Juan José de Orrantia, knight of the Order of Santiago and brother of the parish priest of Huarochirí, as well as two other parish priests of the province, a friar, and additional clients and traveling companions. Araujo and his party lodged with his son-in-law the priest, while lieutenant Salazar and his company of sixteen men put up in the town council building a half-block away.

Lulled by Don Andrés's promise to deliver Francisco Inca, the Europeans kept no watch that night, and after dark some 300 people from the various villages that joined the rising came down into the town from the steep slopes of the ayllu Suni above the valley. They met in the house of one of the leaders, the kuraka of the waranqa Chaucarima, to make final plans. The two alcaldes of Huarochirí were present at the meeting; one of them was an active participant, but the other slipped out to warn the Europeans—though with little success. His offer to guide Salazar and his party to safety brought him only a beating from the Spaniard, who ordered him as alcalde to go out and arrest the rebels. The Indians attacked at about 10 P.M., and the Europeans finally realized the seriousness of the situation. The man sent to warn the people lodged in the priest's house was killed. Those at the cabildo barricaded themselves in, but the Indians set fire to the building, forcing the Europeans to retreat into the inner courtyard with the records of the province. Some of the Europeans argued for leaving the building and trying to shoot their way through the Indians. When Salazar opposed this tactic, the group split and seven of the men attempted it anyway, wounding a few Indians and trying to flee down one of the streets leading off the plaza; but they were followed and stoned to death at the edge of town.

At dawn on Sunday, Salazar, still safe with the rest of his men inside the adobe walls of the cabildo, which could not burn, sent a mulatto servant out to find out the fate of the other Europeans. He too was killed, leaving only eight men of the original sixteen alive in the cabildo. Salazar called the rest of his men together, most of them wounded from the stones hurled by the Indian rebels, and proposed that each man take what he could of the 4,000 pesos in the community treasury, stuff as much of the provincial records as he could into his shirt, and make a run for the priest's house. They agreed. As soon as they left the building, the rebels killed one man and took three prisoners. Three more, with dozens of bleeding wounds from the barrage of stones, collapsed and died in the plaza. Salazar, badly wounded in the jaw, made it to the priest's house, but the frightened people inside refused to open the door and when the lieutenant tried to climb over the wall into the patio he was brought down by a stone hurled by a woman and then killed. The Indians killed two of their prisoners but freed the third, who used his darker skin to pose as a member of the Indian elite from another province and convinced the rebels to let him go.[18]

Thus only one of the members of Salazar's small company escaped death. The ex-corregidor Araujo and his son-in-law also fell victim to the rebels, who met following their victory and decided that all of the Spaniards other than the priest would be killed. Araujo was warned of the decision by a village cantor of the church, and the two men attempted to flee the village down back streets. Both were caught and killed.[19] The Indians moved quickly to consolidate their first major victory and protect themselves against reprisals. Their tactics elicited the admiration of the diarist Sebastián Francisco de Melo, a trained soldier. A group of about 80 men was sent to burn the bridges on the road into the mountains from Lima, and to block the narrow roadway with stones. Another group of 200 was stationed in the hills above the settlement of Cocachacra, on the road that followed the Rímac River into the mountains, where they waited to bombard with stones any troops coming from Lima. Still other groups were stationed in the plaza of Huarochirí to guard the village and sent to the other villages of the repartimiento to warn the people and organize them for resistance. Francisco Inca and his father-in-law, Don Juan Pedro de Puipuilibia, withdrew to their home village of Lahuaytambo to direct the operation.

A little over a week after the Indians determined to rebel, they had eliminated most of the Spaniards in the province outside the mining region and were in virtually complete control. Only the parish priests remained, to say masses for the rebels as they demanded. The rebels followed the model of the Spanish militia in their organization of the province. Each group of rebels had its leader, assigned a military title from Captain-General to Sergeant-Major and Field Master. The local groups were coordinated with the leadership, consisting of Francisco Inca, Don

Juan Pedro, and a third man apparently unrelated to the provincial power group but described by the Spaniards as the bravest and most capable of all the rebels. With access to the province from Lima barred by determined Indians and the established rebel community led by Juan Santos at their backs, the rebels seemed invulnerable. The news of the rising that reached Lima, carried by a few soldiers who were not in Huarochirí at the time of the attack and a priest who fled the town, terrified the population of the capital. Rumor armed 3,000 Indians with European weapons rather than the rocks and slings they had used so effectively against the Spaniards.[20] The viceroy also regarded Huarochirí as strategic for the safety of Lima, for he noted that the province was the neck that joined Lima to the highlands, adding that "if [the province] were to continue in rebellion, its proximity to this City [Lima] would make it a refuge for delinquents who would disturb its tranquility and cause a great deal of harm."[21]

Yet less than twenty days after the Indians' first victory, the revolt was virtually over. The leaders, Francisco Inca and Don Juan Pedro, were in Lima, captured and handed over to the Spaniards by members of their own society. The Spaniards in the mining region of Yauli, with Indian troops made up of their own workmen, attacked Huarochirí and dispersed its defenders. Demoralization set in as the people began to fear the reprisals of the state, and one village after another, stimulated by rumors of defection and betrayal by their leaders, turned on those leaders and handed them over to the Spaniards in the hope of clemency for themselves. The united front of the waranqas Colcaruna, Chaucarima, and Checa—at least three of the five waranqas of the repartimiento of Huarochirí—dissolved by the time a force of 600 armed and mounted men from the cream of Lima's aristocracy arrived in Huarochirí.

How did it happen? What were the reasons for the failure of the rebellion after its initial success? The answers are not as obvious as they might appear from the summaries of the affair prepared in Lima. Peasant revolts have not generally been successful in historical or modern times. The isolation of the peasantry from the wider society, the lack of a tradition of coordination and organization among isolated household farmers, the mutual suspicion of neighbors born of the isolation and competition that is an omnipresent part of existence for the peasant farmer—all of these factors, and more, have been offered in explanation of the common failure of peasant movements. But the Andean communities were not based upon the isolated household unit; there was a tradition of social interaction on a far wider scale than is characteristic of either a European peasantry or the Andean highland communities today. And provincial society, despite the local self-sufficiency of the rural community, was not isolated and cut off from the European society that dominated it and absorbed its production.

The structure of colonial administration, with its local political organization imposed by the Spaniards together with the kuraka hierarchy whose roots reached back to the Inca Empire, kept alive both a sense of historical continuity and links to the ruling European society in the highland communities.

The factors that played a large role in both the organization of the rebellion of 1750 and its defeat derive primarily from the colonial experience. That experience distorted traditional social groups and gave them new orientations. It created other groups, and it gave all of the members of native Andean society an enemy and a focus for their frustration and their anger. And yet the colonial system also introduced division and suspicions that, in the end, could not be overcome, at least in the short time available to the leaders of the rebellion. Well-founded suspicion bred hesitation and disunity, which in turn hobbled the cooperation and dedication needed to broaden a rebellion that had to expand or die. Even then it is difficult to imagine how the Indian rebels could have succeeded. The jungle territory in which the rebels led by Juan Santos barricaded themselves from the Spanish authorities for over two decades was not on the main route into the highlands. Santos's territory did not lie close to Lima and therefore represent an omnipresent threat to the colonial state. The events in Huarochirí were sufficient to mobilize a generally sloppy and poorly organized citizen militia, for the members of that militia were aroused by the direct challenge not only to their authority but also to their lives and their property. And yet, without falling into the trap of thinking that we can offer a blueprint of how the rebellion should have been run—the armchair rebel's easy solace—we can still learn a great deal about the impact of two centuries of colonial rule upon the people of Huarochirí by examining closely the organization and conduct of the rebellion and the social divisions that contributed to its defeat. The story of the rebellion of 1750 offers a valuable opportunity to see the product of the developments discussed in the preceding chapters, as the members of Andean society in Huarochirí challenged the exploitation upon which the colonial system was founded and maintained.

One of the principal elements of the rebellion of 1750 that bears examination is the character and the sources of its leadership. Viceroy Superunda regarded the Indian population of Lima as the source of sedition. He complained that young boys were brought to the religious houses of the city as servants of the friars, and that once there they learned trades, became part of the city population, and refused to return to their villages. And, he added, it would be unwise to have these people in the provinces, since they were so "accustomed to Spanish ways, intelligent, and with ideas above their station due to their easy and continual dealings with the

Spaniards."[22] Popular opinion attributed the plots against the government to these skilled craftsmen who filled "all of the mechanical professions for lack of Spaniards, who disdain to occupy themselves at such tasks."[23] The skilled Indian population of Lima was considerable. From quite early, Indians appear not only as skilled workmen but as masters of trades in the cities.[24] One authority calculated that by 1612, the Indian artisans in Lima included 323 tailors, 129 shoemakers, and 80 silk weavers—to mention only the professions with the most Indian practitioners.[25] Indians did join the trade guilds, and obtained the rank of master, although by the eighteenth century, at least, many of the trades had separate guilds for Spaniards and Indians, each with its own chief master.[26] The separation was probably a reaction by the Indians to discrimination within their guilds, for the case of the Indian tailors' guild, approved as a separate guild in 1731, shows that the Indians sought the separation.[27]

These people were in their appearance and habits very like the members of European society among whom they lived and worked. They, and even their women, wore European-style rather than Indian-style clothing. They participated fully in the European money economy, tending to invest their earnings in urban property—stores or houses that were rented out for income—rather than in land for cultivation. They spent their money on luxury clothing or jewelry, and saved, like their European counterparts, by buying objects of gold and silver such as *tembladera*, a vase of hammered gold or silver whose paper-thin sides could be sliced or clipped to get a bit of metal to buy goods or pay debts. They drank tea from silver- and gold-inlaid *mates*, and a number owned Negro slaves.[28] In the eighteenth century, even their choice of trade within the skilled professions reflected the same preferences shown by members of Spanish society. An eighteenth-century observer complained that the urban Indians avoided the crafts involving hard labor such as those of the blacksmith, stonecutter, or mason, preferring instead to be painters, weavers, tailors, shoemakers, musicians, or jewelers—all further removed from the manual labor despised by the members of Spanish society.[29] Contracts of apprenticeship among the Indians in Lima in the eighteenth century do show a clear preference for such trades as tailor, shoemaker, or painter.[30] Superunda, again, felt strongly that the contradiction between the economic status and life styles of these people and the barriers to their full access to the honors and careers open to members of European society was the origin of their opposition to the colonial system.

The lack of distinction in clothing and the fine cloth they wear (in the matter of which we should institute no changes) spoils them, and puts them in such a state that it becomes insufferable to them not to be permitted access to offices and dignities that, if such were entrusted to them, would mean handing command over to them, or raising them to such a status that, with more enterprise and opportunity, they would attempt to seize it.[31]

The only member of the group arrested in the Lima conspiracy of 1750 whose occupation we know was Francisco Inca, who was a ranking member of the Indian potters' guild of the city. But other members of the group were undoubtedly skilled. The person who prepared a map of the central part of the city with the points of attack marked on it was a painter. Another of the plotters was a trader, who used his profession to make contact with Juan Santos by accompanying the soldiers that guarded the people sent to harvest coca on the edge of the jungle. A third was a surgeon from the province of Santa who fled home and was later apprehended there.[32]

Though the skilled artisans may well have been, as Superunda argued, the major people responsible for the plots against Spanish authority in Lima, the provincial revolt drew its leaders from the local power elite, in particular the kurakas. The two interim kurakas of the repartimiento of Huarochirí and one of the waranqa kurakas were crucial to the rebellion, convinced to join by Francisco Inca, the skilled artisan intermediary between the Lima plotters and his home province. The kurakas could meet with the organizers of the rebellion in Lima when they accompanied the Indians sent down to do mita service on the haciendas outside Lima down along the coast. They had grievances of their own against the colonial system: the 1729 census of Huarochirí still provided the basis for mita and tribute assessments in 1750, and the kurakas were responsible for those assessments and held liable for any shortages. Angered by these pressures, both Don Andrés and his brother Don Juan Pedro agreed to join the rebellion. Their role in the original plan was to obtain the participation of the adjoining provinces, and when the plot was discovered and an order sent to arrest Francisco Inca, they played important roles in the subsequent rising of their province on its own.[33] The ex-kuraka of the repartimiento of Chaclla, Juan del Espíritu Santo Macas Sacllapoma, who had retired from office owing to "age and incapacity," sent his son to offer the support of Chaclla despite the silence of his nephew, Pedro Julcarilpo, who was serving as interim kuraka in his stead. Macas's support apparently weighed in the decision of fifteen villages of Chaclla to join the rebellion following a message from Don Andrés and the rebels in Lahuaytambo.[34]

But the fabled authority of the kuraka was not without limits. There is considerable evidence in this case that the Indians were quite capable of acting on their own, as they had done in the province in the 1730's, in order to maintain and preserve their traditional ceremonies and rituals.

The autonomy shown by the local community—to the point of ignoring or even attacking the kuraka—was in evidence here as well. The people clearly preferred their established leaders to play a part in the movement, and were willing to place them at its head, but the kuraka who went against his people's wishes was likely to find himself wishing for Spanish protection. And since the kurakas did move far more easily between European and Indian societies than their village kinsmen, they were subject to suspicion of alliance with the authorities. The familiarity of the kurakas with the representatives of the European bureaucracy could be used in support of the rebellion, as Andrés de Borja did by going directly to Huarochirí before the Indian attack on the town to reassure the Spanish authorities of his loyalty and his aid in the search for Francisco Inca. The Europeans, used to the kurakas' compliance, did not question his protestations and were surprised by the nighttime attack in which the kuraka himself was a major leader.

Pedro Julcarilpo, the reluctant kuraka of Chaclla, found his relationship with the Spaniards his undoing in the rebellion. He clearly did not sympathize with the rising, but he kept silent, particularly after a kuraka of one of the waranqas of Chaclla argued against joining the people of Huarochirí and was nearly killed by the angry villagers and his mestizo son-in-law. The Spanish diarist Francisco de Melo was able to turn the kuraka's vacillation to the benefit of the Europeans. He wrote a false letter purporting to be an answer to one of his *compadres*, or ritual co-parents, in the village of Huanza where he was known to have stood as a godparent for many people. The letter read:

Beloved *compadre*:
   I received your letter, in which you asked permission to kill my *compadre* Don Pedro Julcarilpo and bring me his head. Do not do it, because I know that he is a loyal vassal of His Majesty, and once he knows that I am on my way to Huarochirí with more than 400 soldiers armed with good shotguns, he will quickly come personally to give me the obedience that he owes to the King my Lord. If he does not, you may execute him as you offered, cutting off his head, and I will reward you in the name of His Majesty.[35]

After closing the letter and mutilating it a little, Melo sent a *compadre*, bound to him by ties of ritual kinship, to drop the note in Julcarilpo's patio where he would discover it. The kuraka, terrified that his people would kill him for betraying them, fled to Yauli in search of Spanish protection.

The close ties that the provincial elite maintained with the members of European society cut both ways. Behind the façade of loyalty, a kuraka who had the trust of his people could do a great deal to further a rebellion. But without the unqualified loyalty and support of the people under his authority, the kuraka was exposed to the effect of all the rumors that circulated freely in a period of fear and high tension. Astute members of European society obviously realized the value of having ties among the Indians. Those ties accounted for much of the effectiveness of Melo's rumors fomenting suspicion between people—particularly between local communities and their kurakas, whose day-to-day contacts with Europeans and whose exploitation of their people were well known. The same factors affected the nontraditional members of the provincial political elite—the alcaldes and officials of the Church—whose loyalties in the rebellion were divided. Unfortunately, there is no information in the data available on the rebellion of 1750 to explain why one alcalde became a leader of the rebellion and another warned the Spaniards of the plans developed in the meetings he attended.[36]

A closer look at the stimuli to rebellion in 1750 will help us understand the impact of the colonial regime and the opportunities that were available to—and used by—people to formulate an ideology differentiating themselves from their European masters. It cannot, however, explain why some people subscribed to that ideology to such a degree that they would risk exposure and a painful death, whereas others chose to ally with the Europeans and betray their fellows. The rebellion of 1750 constituted a break from the traditional passive resistance of the Andean community described in Chapter Eight. It was thoroughly secular, despite strains of mysticism in the justification and appeals of plotters in Lima. Viceroy Superunda argued that the major stimulus for rebellion among the urban Indians was their failure to gain access to the offices and status open to members of European society, and certainly the highly urbanized character of the participants in Lima shows clearly through a letter found on one of the organizers. Evidently intended as an organizing tool, this letter reveals a considerable degree of familiarity with the history of the empire of which Peru was a part. At least one of the organizers of the Lima rising learned to read and write as a servant in the palace of the Marqués of Villagarcia, and one of the leaders of the provincial rebellion was described as "familiar with all the worldly histories."[37] Throughout one finds a thoroughly Catholic sense of indignation and an appeal to divine law and morality. The letter calls upon the Indians, both gentlemen and the "common estates," in the name of the Holy Trinity to oppose their persecution. "Even the mestizos among us, sons of noble women [*cacicas*] endure the same persecution, for God has his limit and for 200 and more years we have been cut off from our ancestors and we will be consumed and not even faint signs will remain of the natives of these kingdoms."[38] One hears overtones of the traditional structure of Andean society and the role played by the ancestors and deities of the local communities, but the Andean elite had to have a detailed knowledge of their lines of

descent if they were to have any claim to elite rank, which as we have
seen depended upon descent from the preconquest kuraka elite. The importance of linear descent, of limited value in traditional Andean society,
was considerable in Spanish culture. Indeed, purity of blood and linear
descent, made legal requirements for office-holding in the sixteenth century, were still among the criteria for preferment in the eighteenth. The
author of this letter echoed Superunda's assertion that the Indian elite
deeply resented the contempt shown toward them by the Europeans and
the barriers, de facto though not legal, to their social and political advancement. As the writer complained, "for two centuries, now going on
three, there has been no place for us nor for our sons; though we send
them to study in monasteries, they languish in hard labor in the service
of the Spaniards and in obrajes and mines."[39] The ending is an impas-
sioned appeal:

We as Christian Catholics appeal to God and our honor. How long must we live
in the lethargy of ignorance? We must restore our kingdom as other nations have
done; like Portugal and the two Sicilies did. . . . Those impulses stimulate us to
elect a Captain General as the Israelites chose Moses to lead them from the cap-
tivity of Pharoah . . . [and] as the other kingdoms have done. The removal of this
heavy yoke will bring us eternal fame in the immortal annals and confront many
nations with the strength of our valor.[40]

The writer of this appeal wrote for people who opposed the Spaniards
in terms of European values. He found in the professed tenants of the
Catholic religion and the history of the European states the terms and the
framework with which to confront the class that ruled and benefited from
the colonial system. He had some knowledge of both European and bib-
lical history, and he knew that his society had been defeated; he needed
no detailed history of the regime under which he lived or of other movements of resistance to compose his letter. No forbidden books needed to
be read in order to conceive the ideas expressed in his letter. Study of the
Bible and of the basic materials available to any member of European society—and undoubtedly to an acculturated Indian in the capital—provided sufficient raw material to define the Indians' condition and justify their
resistance.

The concerns of the provincial leaders of the rebellion of 1750 were not
those of the urban Indians, although it is more than likely that the kurakas
of Huarochirí were at least aware of the arguments of the urban plotters,
since they met in the house of Francisco Inca when they came down to
Lima with a contingent of mita laborers. But the kurakas had other concerns, as pressing as those of their urban kin and perhaps more immediate: their personal wealth was threatened by the continuing decline of
the population of their province and by the difficulties they were experi-

encing in trying to get a recount in order to bring tribute and labor levies back into line with population. Both Don Andrés and Don Juan Pedro spent time in jail for tribute debts prior to 1750, and both lost their riding mules to the corregidor for their failure to obtain the moneys charged to the people under their authority.[41] The officials of the Indian cabildo and of the Church also had reason for resentment, since they were increasingly forced into the role of collector for corregidor and priest.

Even given the difficulties of building any coherent picture of the objectives and attitudes of the provincial kurakas, we can certainly see the immediate reasons for their discontent and their willingness to subscribe to the rebellion. It is harder to get a glimpse of the attitudes of the mass of the Indian population in Huarochirí, although in some cases their actions in the course of the rebellion provide a graphic picture of their feelings toward the representatives of Spanish colonial authority. In his description of the ambitions of the urban Indians, Viceroy Superunda expressed his confidence in the basic docility of the people in the rural areas, whose "humble treatment and affairs, in proportion to their condition, maintain them more subject and controlled."[42] But how "controlled" did the people remain during the rebellion of 1750? How did they respond to their oppression?

The treatment of the ex-corregidor of Huarochirí, Don Francisco de Araujo y Rio, who stood high in the colonial aristocracy, is a vivid example of the Indians' feelings about the colonial system. Attempting to escape from Huarochirí following the Indians' first successful attack, Araujo was discovered by a rebel who offered to help him, saying "you are my corregidor; I have always loved you, and you me. Come with me and I will defend you. But you know that the Indians hate you because you made them carry stones, and in order to appease their anger put this stone on your back and carry it."[43] Despite the ex-corregidor's desperate promise to donate 2,000 pesos to the village church, the man made Araujo carry a heavy rock on his back for several blocks until he reached the edge of the village. There, still carrying his burden, Araujo was stoned to death by the Indians who were waiting for him.

The ritual debasement that the Indians forced on their ex-corregidor was brutally apt. In the sixteenth century the mita was more familiar and acceptable to members of Andean society than tribute levies that could not be phrased in Andean terms, but by the seventeenth and particularly the eighteenth centuries, the mita had become the symbol of the colonial system, dreaded and hated by the people forced to leave their lands and homes to work for the members of European society in the mines, on the haciendas, on the roads, or elsewhere according to the demands of the colonial authorities. And the rebel's greeting to his ex-corregidor—"I have always loved you, and you me"—reproduces virtually word for word the salutation that commonly accompanied the corregidor's orders to village or provincial officials who had to execute his orders and collect his debts among their fellows.[44]

The hypocrisy of Spanish colonial officialdom, which protested at every level that the exploitation of the Indians was for their own good, is made particularly clear and vivid by its reversal in Araujo's case. The treatment of the ex-corregidor was brutal, but its impact on us depends less on the brutality itself than on the fact that the parties in the exchange have reversed roles, that the Spaniard is on the receiving end. This reversal of roles points up the brutality of the "normal" day-to-day interactions between Indians and Europeans, for the Europeans maintained their authority by treating the people they administered with obvious contempt as more animal than human. Their behavior was an important part of the mechanisms of local control, for the fact of such behavior was a constant reminder to the Indians of the force that stood behind the Europeans. Only on extraordinary occasions when the people could stand no more did they turn upon their oppressors.

The mechanisms of social control in colonial society depended far more upon constant contact between European and Indian than upon any show of force. The front-line troops of the colonial system were not soldiers, but the people who spoke the language of the Indian people, who were willing to stand as godparents to their children or sponsors at their marriage, and who would do small favors for their ritual kinsmen—favors that generally proved to be to their own benefit. These people were often sympathetic to the Indians who worked for them and among whom they lived, as long as the Indians showed them the respect and submission due a superior from an inferior. The basic class division in the rural provinces was here, in the line drawn between Indian and Spaniard. The line was maintained by the entire apparatus of Spanish colonial society, and as Francisco de Toledo had perceived more than 200 years earlier, the presence of the members of European society among the Indians not only did not threaten the system, but preserved it.

Not everyone fell neatly into one society or the other in the colony. There were many people who participated to some degree in both groups and who could not be clearly defined by their external appearance as belonging to one or the other. This fact could be effectively used by a person to his own advantage, as it was in the rebellion of 1750. One of the men who made up part of the Spanish company sent down from Yauli in search of Francisco Inca at the beginning of the rebellion was a mestizo. He was captured by the rebels, but when they were about to kill him he demanded to see Francisco Inca, whom he told that he was himself the son of a kuraka and had met the Spaniards in Yauli on his way to offer the support of the Indians of Tarma for the rebellion. He said that he had accompanied the Spaniards to Huarochirí only to cover the real purpose of his mission, and he promised that if the rebels freed him he would return within four days with at least 4,000 men from Tarma. The man's dark skin and his willingness to present himself as an Indian convinced the rebels, who were eager to believe that they were going to receive aid from other provinces. He was freed, fed, and provided with money for his return to Tarma, and he immediately fled to Lima to inform the Spanish authorities in the capital of the events. [45]

At the intersection of Spaniard and Indian, only someone who was personally known to the people on either side could be clearly identified, for by the eighteenth century there were few physical differences that distinguished a member of Indian society from a member of the dominant European group. This is not to say that a Spaniard from the peninsula, separated from the people born and raised in Peru by speech, habits, and bearing as well as by physical appearance, could be mistaken for anything else than he was; but a member of colonial society, particularly one raised outside the capital, could "pass" with far greater ease. The leadership of the rebellion was itself drawn from people who stood in this boundary zone between Spaniard and Indian, people whose identification, by themselves and by the authorities, was as members of the subject Indian class despite the culture traits, habits, and even attitudes that they shared with people defined as part of the dominant class.

The members of European society in the rural areas proved in the end to be the bulwark of the colonial regime. Many of these people were respected by the Indians, for whatever reason, and used the respect that the Indians had for them in the service of the colonial authorities. The parish priests of Huarochirí were spared by the Indian rebels in 1750, for the Indians felt that they needed Catholic services even if they were free of their European masters. The Church had not succeeded in inculcating the Indians with its message of submission to the colonial regime, but it had made itself indispensable in the Indian provinces. To the degree that the members of Andean society accepted the Catholic faith, even if they added it to traditional beliefs and ceremonies rather than replacing them, they had to protect the priests who administered the Catholic ceremonies. The refusal of the Spanish authorities to permit the growth of an Indian priesthood was an essential part of the structure of colonial rule, for in refusing to permit a native priesthood, the colonial Church assured the presence of people who identified with the colonial regime among the Indians. And people who did not participate directly in the colonial bureaucracy could also perform a function similar to that of the parish priests, able to undermine and defeat a rebellion by virtue of the knowledge they had about the structure of the native Andean communities and the tensions that existed within them.

Sebastián Francisco de Melo is an example of the importance to the state of Spaniards or members of European society among the Indians. Melo had ties of ritual kinship, or *compadrazgo*, throughout Huarochirí that functioned in normal times to assure him of a labor supply to work his mineral claims in Yauli. These ties proved particularly important in 1750, when the people rose against the Spanish authorities. The rebels killed the ex-corregidor, as we have seen, and the lieutenant of the corregidor and others known to them as directly associated with the structure of provincial rule, but they did not move against Melo, who in turn used his ties in the Andean communities to destroy the rebellion. His knowledge of the structure of local society enabled him to set the villages of the province against one another and destroy the unity of the revolt. He wrote 22 letters, one to each village in the repartimiento of Huarochirí, with the following message, always addressed to a village other than the one to which he sent it:

Sons, Alcaldes, and principales of the village of . . . :
     I received your letter in which you tell me that you are loyal vassals of His Majesty, and that only fear of the rebels of . . . brought you into the rising. But I pardon you in the name of His Majesty if you will hand over to me, dead or captive, Francisco Ximenez Inca, Juan Pedro, the governor Francisco [sic] de Borja, Felix Puipuilibia, Bartolomé de la Cruz, and Phelipe Ripsi, all of which I thank you for in the name of the King our Lord, and you will be rewarded with lands.[46]

Melo used the services of a forastero woman who bore no love for the Indians of Huarochirí because they charged her rent for the pastures she used in seeing to it that the letters reached villages other than those to which they were addressed. To add verisimilitude, each letter contained the names of some people he knew in the town to which the letter was addressed whose loyalty to the rebellion, like that of the interim kuraka of Chaclla, was likely to be questionable. In his diary, Melo noted that he chose always to drop the letters in towns opposite one another.[47]

Melo was well aware of the competition between villages and the battles over land between neighbors that were increasingly common in the eighteenth century, and his tactic was surely sufficient to introduce discord among those that had been united, as he put it. One specific example that Melo noted, the exchange of letters between Langa and Lahuaytambo, suggests that he knew the villages very well indeed. Lahuaytambo and Langa were directly across the river from each other but in different waranqas. Further, each village was the capital of its waranqa and the principal residence of the elite lineage of that unit—the Puipuilibias of

Chaucarima, the waranqa of which Lahuaytambo was the principal village, and the Cajahuaringas of Langasica. Whether by accident or by design, Melo here chose two villages that were very likely to be at odds, with the further complicating factor that the interim kuraka of the repartimiento of Huarochirí in 1750 was the hereditary kuraka of Lahuaytambo, a Puipuilibia. Melo need not have been aware of any more than the rivalries between waranqas and kuraka lineages, but he managed to hit upon one of the many social "fault lines" of Huarochirí in the eighteenth century.

The tactic was brilliantly successful. On August 2, Don Juan Pedro de Puipuilibia went to Langa to recruit support for the rebellion. The villagers, their suspicion aroused by Melo's letter, attempted to seize him, and he was obliged to flee to a compadre in the village of Chorrillos, part of the waranqa Langa, where the suspicions aroused by the letter proved greater than the ties of ritual kinship. Afraid of betrayal by the other villages, the people of Chorrillos and Langa moved first, seizing Don Juan Pedro and his brother Don Andrés and sending them down to Lima, thus earning for Langa the title of "loyal village."[48] So before the soldiers from Lima ever left the capital for Huarochirí, the rebellion lost part of its leadership, leaving the people disorganized and fragmented. The rest of the leaders fell within a few days to the Spanish forces coming from Lima and from Yauli under Francisco de Melo. Thus ended the rebellion of 1750.

The punishment of the rebels was intended as a warning to the rest of the population that they would not soon forget. All of the people were ordered to present themselves at the plaza of Huarochirí on August 17. More than a thousand men, as many women, and many children were there. They entered the plaza through a line of soldiers, dressed colorfully and armed. These were not the soldiers who actually fought in the rebellion, most of whom were Indians or at least Spaniards and Spanish-Americans familiar to the Indians. They were the cream of the Spanish and Spanish-American aristocracy from Lima, dressed in the most imposing uniforms, as well as the mulatto regiments, also imposing. The people were seated in the plaza and tightly packed, and Melo spoke to them in Quechua, warning them that anyone who cried out during the executions would be executed himself. Then the executions began: each of the seven men condemned to death was brought into the plaza, tied to the gallows, shot dead, and then hanged. Then those sentenced to beatings were brought out, also tied to the gallows, beaten, and their hair cut short. After this spectacle, the general pardon signed by the viceroy for the province as a whole was read, and the people were dismissed. The bodies of the dead men were cut into pieces, and the dismembered heads, legs, and arms exhibited in the villages of the provinces. The rebellion was over. Melo was named lieutenant of the province for his services to the Crown, and one of his first tasks was to collect from the Indians more than 150,000 pesos that the corregidor had distributed in the repartimiento de mercancías.[49]

By 1751, the province was back to normal. The only change was that the Contaduría de Tributos finally ordered the census that the kurakas had petitioned for without success for two decades. Save for references to the rebelliousness and ill temper of the people of Huarochirí in petitions submitted by members of Spanish society fighting protests by the Indians, there was no evidence of any change in the province. But evidently neither side forgot the experience, for 30 years later, in 1783, there was another rising in Huarochirí when a man named Felipe Velasco, who took the name of Túpac Inca Yupanqui, presented himself as the successor to Túpac Amaru II and attempted to lead a rebellion. Little more is known about the rebellion of 1783, which is generally presented as a last sputter of the great fire that swept the southern part of the Andes in 1780–82. After 1783, the viceroy decided that Huarochirí was a danger to the security of the kingdom and converted the provincial official to a military officer with full military authority over the region. Huarochirí became in effect an occupied region under military rule.[50]

But despite the political maneuvers and adjustments that followed the rebellions of 1750 and 1783, there was no alteration in the basic condition of the population except to make the force that underwrote the colonial relationship more open and visible. One of the first acts of the Spaniards after the defeat of the rebellion of 1750 in Huarochirí was to replace the principales and alcaldes whose loyalty to the Spanish regime they considered questionable with others whom they defined as "less seditious and more loyal."[51] The response of the members of European society to any demands from the Indians was to attempt to reinforce the mechanisms of local control by eliminating Indians from positions of responsibility. A proposal for the reorganization of local Indian administration submitted to the colonial authorities by a parish priest in the 1770's suggested that the mestizos living among the Indians and renting community lands be given land by the state, thus binding them more closely to the state than to the native communities, and added that a mestizo might be named to the Indian cabildo as a minor official but with some jurisdiction to serve as an informer for the colonial authorities, "since as he would no longer be obligated to them [the Indians], he would be sure to reveal their secrets."[52] There is no evidence that this advice was followed, but in 1778 the Spanish inspector-general of Peru, Antonio de Areche, decreed that the position of teacher in the Indian parishes could not be entrusted to

Indians but had to be given to Spaniards or, if they were not available, to persons of mixed descent.[53]

All of these measures worked toward the same ends: the destruction of community autonomy and the construction of more ties binding people within the Indian communities to the colonial state. This mechanism, in a multitude of different forms, was perhaps the most important of all the factors that maintained the colonial system. In the course of the long centuries of colonial rule, the efforts of the authorities to reorganize Indian society in order to make such ties to the state a part of the pattern of local social relationships were met with determined resistance by the Indians. The local political elite erected by colonial legislation to direct the political and ceremonial life of the villages established and populated by the state did not turn out to be as compliant as the architects of the colonial system originally planned. The Indians could not reject the institutions imposed by the state; they incorporated them and used them to protect their own. Many of the people who held office in the colonial power elite instituted by the Europeans also held positions of respect and prestige in terms of their own culture. The principal example of this is the overlap between this group and the group of people who were responsible for preserving and maintaining the traditional ceremonies linked to the prosperity and preservation of the local kin groups or ayllus. The presence of alcaldes and of cantores and sacristans of the Church in this latter group is ample evidence of the success of the community in adapting colonial institutions to its own needs and objectives.

And yet there were real limits to how far the Andean community could maintain its traditions and its cohesion while absorbing and using the structures imposed by the Spaniards. The acculturation of the traditional elite, in particular the kurakas and their lineages, not only established links between the dominant European society and the Indians, links that the kurakas could use both for their own enrichment and to protect their communities, but also gave the kurakas experience with the Europeans and insight into the culture of their masters that led them to see the Spaniards as not so different from themselves except for their privileged position in the colonial system. But acculturation was also a bait that some—and not only kurakas—could not resist: a chance to share in the profits of the colonial system, to buy acceptance from the members of European society by becoming their loyal supporters and servants. And some did take the bait, accepting the hatred of their fellows in exchange for economic benefits and control over others in their communities. But though the loyal Indian might gain some profit thereby, he could never become a member of European society. Even the kurakas found that they were barred from full membership in the ruling class by the contempt of the members of European society and the barriers they raised to block their participation.

One other aspect of the system of "divide and rule" that was the defining characteristic of the colonial system also stands out as basic to the defeat of the Indian rebellions. By the eighteenth century, the traditional cooperation that bound large groups of people together in common labor and celebration was undermined and fragmented. Groups that had once gathered regularly to celebrate one another's feast days no longer did so. The major feast days and celebrations of provincewide deities faded and died. Local groups struggling to survive took what they could of one another's land, as they had for centuries, but without the limitations imposed by common membership in larger social groups. The Spanish court system rather than the kuraka became the arbiter in the quarrels that arose from such encroachment, and in the long run the decision of the courts in any particular case mattered little, for the Spanish legal tradition refused to conceive that both parties in a dispute could be right and undermined cooperation by awarding full control to one side at the expense of the other.

All of these processes, discussed in far more detail in the preceding chapters, contributed to the steady fragmentation of the larger social units of Andean society and the isolation of the local community. With nothing to maintain the interaction that held together traditional Andean society and restrained its inherent competitiveness, the local communities fragmented into isolated, mutually suspicious units. And these smaller units, already suspicious of one another's motives and ready to believe the worst of their neighbors, were easy prey to the kind of tactics used by Melo. Unity and cooperation under such circumstances became almost impossible, and suspicion was common and close to the surface—perhaps because it was so often merited. The class line that divided colonial society was very real but not easily distinguished except for those occasions of crisis when everyone had to declare his allegiance. Even then the fearful and the suspicious could be swayed by both threats and offers of personal advantage, and there were also many people who found it difficult to put their trust in the members of their own society who took advantage of them in normal times.

The basic division between conqueror and conquered, between Spaniard and Indian, was the foundation of the colonial system, for it enlisted all of the members of European society—the society of the conquerors—in the preservation of the system that benefited them. And for the Europeans who administered the system, this dichotomy—before which the graded hierarchy of rank and status that according to the political theory of the eighteenth century was the foundation and bulwark of all monarchical systems faded into insignificance—was at the same time something to be deplored and the basis of the colonial state. And as long as it existed, the hatred of Indian for Spaniard and the periodic rebellions of the Indians against the system that absorbed their labor and their goods would continue. The Spaniards saw this clearly. Viceroy Superunda, in summarizing the causes of the rebellion of 1750 in Huarochirí, described vividly the basic structure of the colonial system. For the two could not be separated. The exploitation of the members of one society by the members of another was the basis of the colonial state, and as long as that was true, any attempt by the Indians to alter the terms and the conditions of exploitation would be perceived—correctly—as a challenge to the system itself. Superunda, who well understood the dynamic he did his best to preserve, deserves the last word on the origin of the rebellion of 1750 and its larger meaning.

The real and permanent cause of the restlessness of the Indians is that in all conquered nations to which the rulers are joined by marriage, in the course of generations the two groups can no longer be distinguished from one another except for the matter of their origins, and they merge, becoming a single people, both recognizing their sovereign. But when the diversity of customs, the accident of color, or the baseness attributed to the dominated impedes those links and the nations remain separated from one another, there is never a lack of discontented vassals or malignant spirits, and the dominated are easily infected by the wish to evade what they view as the repression of their freedom, and to change a government that, although just and moderate, they view with inherited hatred and constant envy. [54]

As the viceroy clearly saw, the structure of colonialism made rebellion inevitable, for as long as an entire society, with its own traditions and culture, was exploited by and for the benefit of people defined as another society, the antagonism between ruler and ruled was part of the dynamic. The changing structure of the economy of Europe in the eighteenth century could not help but affect the overseas territories, as the graded ranks and statuses of colonial society were increasingly compressed to fit the overall dichotomy of the colonial equation. The people who were regarded and regarded themselves as Indians became more and more a class, defined by its opposition to another class that lived from their labor and their poverty. The process was by no means complete in 1750, and lasted well into the republican period, but the outlines of the social attitudes and the structures of the independent state of Peru can be perceived by the middle of the eighteenth century.

Conclusion

IN THE Introduction to this study, I stated that my aim was the delineation of the colonial relationship that took form in the course of the centuries of Spanish colonial rule. What do I mean by the term "colonial relationship"? I mean essentially a system founded upon violence, upon the conquest of one society and culture by another, and the organization of a political system in which the people defined as belonging to one society—the descendants of the conquered—provide the goods and the labor that support another group of people, defined as belonging to the society of the conquerors. Now this relationship of dominance and exploitation was not at the forefront of every interaction between people in the colonial world. There were poor, indigent Europeans and wealthy, powerful Indians. But the superstructure of colonial society, the state and the laws that gave it form and maintained it, had as its purpose the maintenance of the division between the two societies and the organization of the flow of surplus from the conquered Indian society to the dominant European population and from there to the metropolis in Spain.

The Spanish colonial system in America took form at the beginning of the European expansion that culminated in the triumph of capitalism in Europe and the creation of a European world system dominated by the capitalist mode of production. Latin America was incorporated into the European system at a time when the socioeconomic structures of the European states were still essentially feudal. But the political integration of feudalism was fragile at best, and could hardly be expanded to become the basis of a political system that stretched beyond an ocean. The traditional feudal solution to the integration of new conquests into the European states had been to grant the new territories to lords linked by feudal ties to the monarch of the ruling state. But this solution no longer functioned even in Europe in the sixteenth century, where the chain of parcelized sovereignties that linked peasant to lord and lord to overlord had already begun to weaken and break.

The political system that emerged in the Andes in the sixteenth century was not imported whole by the conquerors; there were no existing models of colonialism upon which to build. The system that emerged was laboriously constructed over the decades from the capture of the last Inca ruler in 1533 to the definitive organization of the colonial state in the 1570's and 1580's, and it drew upon both medieval tradition and precedent and local conditions. The conquerors did not seek to introduce new relations of production in the Andes, or even, in the early years, new kinds of property relations. The basic assumption of the conquest period—an assumption that continued with only limited changes into the mature colonial state system—was that the native Andean population would continue to live and produce as it had in the past, only adding to its traditional activities the tasks and goods demanded of it by the new European masters. The Spaniards attempted to superimpose upon the traditional Andean forms of production a feudal superstructure by means of which they could appropriate the labor and the goods of the local economy. But the grafting of a series of servile demands upon the productive capacities of a primitive, essentially tribal economy undermined the productive power of Andean society, already severely weakened by disease, and threw the entire structure of the conquest period into crisis.

During the conquest period, the new kingdom of Peru was organized by and for the conquerors, who functioned as quasi-feudal lords without ever obtaining any formal juridical authority from the Spanish Crown. But as the number of Spaniards in the new colony grew and the native Andean population fell sharply, the conquerors found themselves in competition for Indian labor with other, newer arrivals. Their response was to attempt to convert their de facto control over native labor into a juridical right, thereby using the power of the state to exclude other members of Spanish colonial society in Peru from access to that labor. The Crown was called upon to protect the new ruling class of Peru from its own excesses and to ensure its control over the surplus extracted from the conquered Andean population. But as was clear to all contemporaries, the devolution of authority over the Indians to the conquerors would have made them into a full-fledged feudal aristocracy—at a time when the "new monarchies" in Europe were locked in struggle with their own native nobilities. The 1560's were years of struggle in Europe between the centralizing monarchs and their recalcitrant nobilities, who sought to regain the political authority they had gradually lost in the course of the fifteenth and sixteenth centuries.

The resolution of the struggle in the Americas was the product not of decision but of inertia. The Crown continued to temporize through the 1580's, attracted by the generous offers with which the encomenderos sweetened their pleas for feudal jurisdiction, but at the same time unwilling to surrender the authority too recently wrested from its own nobility at home to a new one overseas. The crisis was surmounted by the organization of the colonial state system—an apparatus that guaranteed the wealth and social power of the aristocracy of the new overseas colony while reserving to the colonial bureaucracy the exercise of juridical authority. The Spanish state did not attempt to transform the relations of production that governed the production and distribution of goods within native Andean society. Rather, under the rule of Francisco de Toledo, Viceroy of Peru from 1569 to 1582, a structure of colonial government emerged that was built largely upon the neofeudal principles of European absolutism. Toledo gave coherent form to the ideological premises of Spanish rule in Peru and left the colony with a political structure that remained virtually unchanged throughout the Spanish colonial period.

The colonial state and its representatives—the royal bureaucracy and the Catholic Church—became the intermediaries between the native Andean population and the members of Spanish colonial society. Legally, members of Spanish and Indian societies in the Andes were defined as distinct "republics," each subject to the King of Spain and assigned distinct and theoretically complementary roles in the economic and social system of colonial Peru. The Indians labored and the Spaniards ruled.

The legal and political bureaucracy elaborated in the colony was a stopgap solution to the glaring problem of political integration; it was obvious that the Crown was hardly in a position to enforce its claim to the loyalty of its overseas population if that population chose to deny it. The ties that bound the colonies to Spain were primarily political. Peru, like Spain, was predominantly an agrarian society in which a peasant population, in this case Indian, was expected to produce the foodstuffs and basic goods consumed by the European colonists. The ties between Spain and Peru depended ultimately upon the state's monopoly of access to the Indian population and its ability to reward or punish by the provision or withdrawal of access to Indian goods and labor. There was no real economic interdependence between Spain and Peru; dependence went the other way, for the Crown depended heavily upon the remission of silver from Potosí. Hence the heavy emphasis placed by Spanish authorities upon the importance of the aristocracy, regarded as the bulwark of royal power. As long as social position and political power emanated from Castile, the Crown could expect to retain control over its oveseas population. Titles of nobility, sumptuary legislation, and the whole unwieldly apparatus of pomp and circumstance that bounded the lives of the Spanish colonial population were part of the cumbersome but effective mechanisms of political control. Those mechanisms were intended to gain and retain the loyalty of the powerful members of Spanish colonial society, the elite that monopolized political and economic position in the colony.

The apparatus of control over the native Andean population was both simpler and more direct. It rested upon the presence of the civil and religious bureaucracy of the Spanish colonial state—the corregidor de indios and parish priest. In addition to having specific duties, such as implanting Catholic doctrine for the priest and collecting tribute and judging local grievances for the corregidor, these officials were responsible for the surveillance of a potentially hostile population and for its control in case of the failure of the more tacit day-to-day mechanisms of control.

But many additional factors made of the colonial system a complicated, often contradictory web of social relations mixing the medieval world that was passing and the modern world that was coming into being. The rise and expansion of the Atlantic trading economy was the basis of the very existence of Spain's overseas colonies, whose own internal economies developed in direct response to the demands of international commerce. The colonial economy of the Andes was structured around the overseas demand for precious metals, and the economic structures of colonial society—haciendas, manufactories, etc.—were by-products of the export-oriented dynamism generated by the mines.

The direct links between the colonial world and the distant overseas metropolis were the merchant houses that dominated international trade, profiting in the exchange of silver for the goods demanded by the Spanish society that grew up in the Andes. The effects of the commercial revolution that began in the sixteenth century have been studied in the case of Europe, and clearly contributed to the growth of capitalism there. But in the Americas, and particularly in the Andes, the long-term impact of the predominant role of commerce in the history of colonial society has as yet been inadequately studied. In Mesoamerica, where a commercial system was imposed upon societies already integrated and interrelated through trade and exchange, the result seems by the eighteenth century to have been a rapidly developing society on the model of Western Europe, with a wealthy elite actively involved in both commerce and the modernization of the techniques of production, particularly in the export sector.

But in the Andes, the long-term process of change initiated by the incorporation of the area into the European world brought different consequences. There, the societies that became the productive foundation of the new colony were organized on different principles from those of Mesoamerica. In the Andes, local communities gained access to goods or resources not immediately available through other means than exchange or trade. By seeking and maintaining access to distant resource areas, cultivated either by seasonal migrants or by resident colonists—mitmaq— these communities achieved a degree of self-sufficiency that assured their members of desired goods without recourse to exchange outside the group. Through both conquest and incorporation, large polities could be established over vast territories, and complicated state structures could be maintained by the extraction of a portion of the surplus product of the component groups. This pattern was similar enough to the tribute pattern of other state systems, in the Americas and elsewhere, to permit the invading Europeans to equate the state structures of both Mesoamerica and the Andes, and to apply to both certain preconceptions drawn from their experience of European state systems.

The imposition of the structures and the requirements of a commercial market-oriented system upon the Andean productive system in the long run undermined local productive patterns and relations in favor of a growing orientation toward market production in the rural communities, and also gradually destroyed the productive structures evolved to deal with this alpine environment, leaving a local peasantry impoverished and at a real disadvantage in relation to the world economy into which it was forcibly drawn. The Andes today have been widely classified as a "problem environment" barely capable of sustaining the people who live there. In terms of modern Western technologies, alpine landscapes are largely unproductive. Their soils are poor, and the volume of labor that must be invested in making them productive yields little profit in terms of modern capitalist calculations. A contemporary agricultural economist has aptly summarized the problem facing the rural communities in the Andes today:

With the growth of commercial agriculture and in general of capitalism, what had once been an advantage became a liability. The great variety of soil types and climate within a small area produced sharp diseconomies of scale in production and constituted an obstacle to the organization of medium-sized and large modern agricultural enterprises. Mechanization decidedly favors the flat areas that are so scarce in the Andes. The improvement of transport and the extraordinary growth of commerce permit a complementarity of diet without the need of microregional geographic specialization, which is replaced by the social specialization of the producers. [1]

Those of us interested in the history of societies can never forget that societies exist in given geographical spaces that are themselves the product of long-term interaction with the people who inhabit them. There is no such thing as a "natural" landscape; "good" and "bad" environments are defined as such in terms of a given productive system. The Andes were once a rich land, perceived as such by the invading Europeans. It was a land that produced in abundance, and that supported the pomp and circumstance of a considerable ruling class while at the same time providing a modest existence for the majority of the population.

In the Andes, the main thrust of both the measures of the colonial state and the expansion of a commercial system (countered and contradicted by the measures of the state itself) was the fragmentation and dissolution of the rural community into smaller and smaller units. The aim of the state was, in brief, the creation of local self-sufficient peasant communities whose surplus could be appropriated by the colonial bureaucracy to pay the costs of its own administration and control as well as to subsidize the Spanish colonial elite. The needs of state control and administration fostered suspicion toward traditional elites and ceremonies and contributed to the persecution and destruction of the traditional ceremonial practices and beliefs that were part of the integrative mechanisms of large communities that, although they functioned on a day-to-day level as separate units, came together to extend, repair, and maintain the productive resources upon which the prosperity of the larger group depended. The economic demands of the state forced the local communities to participate, at least to a limited degree, in the European economic system that was introduced into the new colony, appropriating lands and resources best suited for the productive system introduced from Europe.

The expansion of commerce and the growing participation of the members of the Andean communities in the European market system, both through compulsion and through choice, further pushed the fragmentation and eventual dissolution of the Andean rural community. The culmination of this process was the penetration of the concepts and the values of private property inside the community itself, the internal differentiation of the community into rich and poor, and the eventual creation of a wealthy peasant sector and a dispossessed, landless group forced to seek their means of survival outside the community in the labor market provided—or in this case, largely not provided—by a growing capitalist system of production. In other words, the end product of the long-term process of change initiated in the colonial period was the creation of the preconditions for the development of capitalism.

Throughout the Andes, however, this long-term process was impeded, even halted, by the determined resistance of the local community, the policies of the state, and the contradictions of the world economy. The society erected on the foundation of the surplus extracted from the Andean population depended ultimately upon the survival of the productive power of that population—and the particular relationship that evolved in the Andes between the land and the people who inhabited and used it was the basis of that survival. To the degree that the productive structures of traditional Andean society—buttressed and reinforced by the ceremonies, beliefs, and sociopolitical relationships discussed throughout this volume—were undermined, the long-term productive capacity of the Andean community was itself weakened and eaten away. The contrast between the descriptions of rural prosperity in the sixteenth century and the despairing or contemptuous comments about rural poverty in the eighteenth were obvious even to contemporaries. The only solution, within the context of a precapitalist structure with a minimum of local capital accumulation, was to protect the local Andean community to the degree that such protection was both possible and conceivable within the political and ideological context of eighteenth-century Europe. Such protection was only partially possible, and the result was the gradual but irreversible fragmentation of the Andean community as the integrative mechanisms that once bound local groups into large entities—even ethnic units—were weakened and eroded. The smaller and more limited the social unit, the more exposed and the weaker it was, and the more likely to be absorbed into the commercial, mercantile organization of European colonial society. As the threads that bound the Andean web of production together weakened and broke, the web itself shrank, and a structure that had once been resilient and strong became rachitic and shaky, providing those within it only the solace of shared poverty.

But despite this bleak picture, the local Andean community survived throughout the colonial period, especially in areas that were particularly inimical to European methods of exploitation and land use, such as Huarochirí. Large areas of the Andes remained primarily the province of local communities, and in others, despite the penetration of European forms such as the great estate or hacienda, the members of European society were themselves forced to adopt many of the traditions and patterns of cultivation developed by Andean cultures over millennia in order to survive, becoming in the process less "capitalist," or market-oriented. The gradual fragmentation of Andean rural society produced not isolated household farms but small, isolated, and semiclosed peasant communities that were on the defensive not only against the representatives of the state or of the dominant ruling society, but also against their neighbors and competitors for the rapidly shrinking resource base available to a society that no longer had the labor power to extend its resources or bring lost resources back into production. This peasantry did not entirely lose its traditions, and the more educated and able members of Andean society not only preserved those traditions—often the basis of their own social position—but also sought in the course of the latter part of the colonial period to reconstruct their past, often drawing upon the history of their conquerors to fill in the pieces of the story that had been forgotten or eliminated by the construction of colonial culture and society. For the most part, these efforts at revivification were undertaken by an Andean elite, rather than being joined to the resentment against the overseas metropolis growing among the members of European society born and raised in the colony. The policies of the Spanish colonial state were successful to the extent that the elite of the colony never made common cause with the conquered majority against the Crown, as some had feared would happen in the sixteenth century, before differences of culture and tradition became the basis of a quasi-racial division that was stronger and more lasting than any laws or rules could have ever been. In the colonial world, status and position depended heavily upon access to the state and the state bureaucracy, and that in turn was financed by the surplus extracted from the people defined as Indian. The taxes of the Crown and the feudal rent of the nobility were merged in the tribute levied upon the Indians and distributed to members of European society in the form of grants, perquisites, and offices. The Peruvian aristocracy, unlike its European counterparts, based its social and economic position upon its access to the state and had little reason to lead its exploited peasantry in rebellions against the exactions of the Crown, as many who were eager to obtain a larger portion of the surplus extracted from the peasant population did in Europe. The role of champion of an exploited peasantry in the colony fell to the Indian elite.

The strength of the colonial structure, organized through the patronage powers of the colonial state, is testified to by its durability. Even after the colonial elite finally severed the political ties that had bound it to Spain until 1821, it sought to maintain the internal relations inherited from the colonial world, relations upon which its social and economic predominance had been built. The new states attempted to open themselves to the European world market of the nineteenth century while preserving internally the colonial relations that assured their appropriation of the surplus generated by the people defined as Indian. But the colonial state, itself the product of a world that had passed away, could not just be transformed into the skeleton of an autonomous polity by an elite eager to maintain the colonial dichotomy of the world it had destroyed. The long wars of independence, followed by the tensions and turbulence of the first half of the nineteenth century, themselves the product of the ambiguous nature of the transition to independence, left the state structure weak and disorganized, and the social relations articulated in terms of that state themselves in flux.

The neocolonial state that took form in the second half of the nineteenth century was built not upon a strong state, but upon a relatively weak one, in which much of the structure of domination devolved upon local political elites. The weakness of the central state had important consequences, for the colonial state—through its direct interference in the productive process, forcing people to perform labor and to provide surplus by virtue of their assignment to a particular social group rather than in response to a market—had slowed down the process of "modernization" that consisted essentially in the expropriation of the rural population and the rise of a market-oriented elite. For a regime that lacked capital, this immobilization was functional, but it could work only as long as the central state, or the bureaucratic network that supported it, remained relatively strong.

But political independence brought different conditions. The state was weak, not strong, and could not extend its influence much beyond the coast. The former colonial elite, the criollos and their hangers-on, were too few to run the political system. The sharp dichotomies between Indian and European, as well as the marginal position of mestizos and poor ex-Europeans, could not be tolerated any longer, for the elite needed lesser elites to maintain local control independent of a central government. With political decentralization, much of the highlands became an area of relatively small landholding, with the ex-Europeans competing for land and power with the former Indian elite. In that process the two groups seem to have merged—a process that is indicated by the changing meaning of the term "Indian." The idea of a rich, acculturated, Europeanized Indian elite became a contradiction in terms in a way that it never was in the colonial period, even as late as the last years of the eighteenth century.

In some parts of the country, in particular the coast and some areas of the highlands, the door was opened to a process of rapid consolidation of large estates by an elite eager to participate in the international market. The story of the growth of the great estate and its varied forms, on the coast and in the sierra, has in recent decades become a topic of great interest, particularly since the Agrarian Reform of 1969 focused attention on this historical formation. But where there was little level land available, or where rich mineral resources did not attract national and, later, international capital, the peasant community, direct heir of the Andean tradition, remained predominant. In Huarochirí, where small landholding was the norm in the colonial period, the productive structure does not seem to have changed to any great degree. The province still sent foodstuffs to Lima and workers to the mines, but as in other areas the population became a mixed peasant one, a typical neocolonial structure that was split not by major divisions but by a thousand petty quarrels. Its villages fragmented until even ayllus split, and within villages the elites that had appropriated lands and power could not expand their operations by much, and remained bound by the structures of their villages, since their sphere of action was limited to an area that extended little beyond the village itself. It makes little sense today to worry about who is Indian and who is not in Huarochirí, for that would tell us little about the patterns of exploitation, the reasons for the distribution of wealth and poverty in the region.

Given the poverty that is the long-term product of the subordination of the Andean population to a mode of production in direct conflict with the productive structures evolved over millennia in the Andes, is it possible to say anything about the meaning of political independence for the people that have been the subject of this study? Is there any real difference between the situation of the Andean population in the colonial period and today? In terms of the immediate present, of conditions today, it can be argued that there is not, that the century and a half since political independence has only intensified the patterns and the structures evolved in the course of the colonial period. But in terms of potential, of the creation of the conditions for change in the future, political independence, though it brought few or no direct benefits to the members of rural society, introduced new elements that must be taken into account in order to understand the political struggles of this century.

Political independence did not mean independence for the people regarded as Indian in Peru. Even their legal status remained unchanged for decades after Spain formally recognized the loss of its Andean colony. But though formal political independence from Spain had little direct relation to the struggles undertaken by the members of Andean society and described in the case of Huarochirí in Chapter Nine, it was still an important—in fact an essential—step in the long struggle for freedom. The ideology of the revolt described in Chapter Nine, and of other revolts like it, was nationalistic, but in terms of a nationalism built on a cultural identification with an Indian past. The political independence of Peru was not built on that identification, and was not fought for in those terms or by people who subscribed to them.

The independence of Peru ended the colonial equation of colonials and natives. It ended the identification on the part of the elite of the colony with an outside polity. The ex-colonizers, or a segment of them, did inherit the new state, and the racism characteristic of the colonial equation remained, and in some cases even increased. The contradiction of the Peruvian case is that the anticolonial dream of the colonized was in fact realized by a segment of those who regarded themselves as part of the society of the colonizers—much as if the Algerian wars of independence had left in Algeria, as the elite, the ex-French colonists born in the colony. The distorted interactions of the colonial relationship continued to define the members of the society.

But after political independence, it became conceivable that a member of the elite could defend, honestly and totally, a group defined as Indian, for both could share an identity as Peruvians. Independence did not realize that dream, but it made it conceivable. The elimination of the sharp dichotomy between Indian and European, with the consequent disappearance of an Indian elite, also eliminated the group within Indian society that had begun in the latter part of the colonial period to formulate a separate ideology of its own. With a single country in which all must exist together, the development of a unity of purpose and ideology built upon common class interests rather than cultural identifications or preconceptions has become possible. But that common purpose will demand more than formal political ideology and protestations of faith. It will require a revolution in attitudes and preconceptions that will make it possible to find human value in the struggle for dignity and worth wherever it is found, in the countryside or in the city, on the factory line or behind a *taqlla*, in the wisdom of the academy or the wisdom of the farmer who creates his home and his work from the mud and dirt of his land.

Reference Matter

Notes

Complete authors' names, titles, and publishing data for sources cited in the Notes are given in the Bibliography. The following abbreviations are used in the Notes:

AA   Archivo Arzobispal, Lima
AGI   Archivo General de Indias, Seville
ANP   Archivo Nacional de Perú, Lima
BNP   Biblioteca Nacional de Perú, Lima

Introduction

1. On this point see Sánchez-Albornoz, *Indios y tributos en el Alto Perú*, and Larson, "Economic Decline."

2. There is a large ethnographic literature from the Andes. For a particularly fine recent example dealing with Central Peru, see Mayer; for Huarochirí in particular, see Matos Mar et al.

3. Much of our knowledge of the pre-Inca origins of Andean institutions stems from the work of John V. Murra; see, for example, his articles "On Inca Political Structure," "New Data on Retainer and Servile Populations," and "Social Structural and Economic Themes."

4. See for example Foster-Carter.

Chapter One: The Human Landscape

1. Avila, *Dioses y hombres de Huarochirí*, p. 137.

2. Virtually any standard geography of Peru presents this image of the country; the sources I have used in the preparation of the following pages are principally Koepcke; Raimondi; Dollfus, *Les Andes centrales*; von Tschudi; and Schweigger.

3. All Andean farmers are well aware of the distinct zones of the sierra slopes; I received a clear, concise description of them from Sr. Hector Chuquimuni of the Comunidad of Yambilla, Huarochirí, in 1968. For more academic or scholarly descriptions, see Dollfus, *Les Andes centrales*, pp. 223–30; and von Tschudi, pp. 213–25.

4. For estimates of population statistics in 1535, see Dobyns, "Estimating Aboriginal American Population," and Chapter Four below. For population statistics in 1940, see República del Perú . . . , *Censo Nacional*.

5. See, for instance, Murra, "El 'Control Vertical.' "
6. Thomas C. Patterson, personal communication.
7. A description of the struggle of various ethnic groups over the coca lands of Quives can be found in Rostworowski de Diaz Canseco, "Etnohistoria de un valle costeño."
8. Avila, "Relación," p. 255.
9. Dillehay, p. 27.
10. Avila, *Dioses y hombres de Huarochirí*, p. 243: "Los Jesuítas en Huarochirí—1571," document no. 1.
11. Testimony of Don Francisco Conapariaguana, kuraka of Guarapa, in Ortíz de Zúñiga, vol. 2, p. 29.
12. Huaman Poma de Ayala, p. 64.
13. Avila, *Dioses y hombres de Huarochirí*, p. 63.
14. See in particular Mayer.
15. See Morris and Thompson.
16. John Thatcher, field notes, 1968 field season (survey designation PV50), Huarochirí–Upper Mala Valley.
17. See Rowe, "The Age Grades"; for colonial testimony on the Inca census categories, see Huaman Poma de Ayala, pp. 195–232.
18. Huaman Poma de Ayala, pp. 195–232.
19. *Ibid.*, p. 848.   20. Isbell, pp. 99–108; Lounsbury.
21. Huaman Poma de Ayala, p. 848.   22. González Holguín, p. 77.
23. Polo de Ondegardo, "Relación," p. 117.
24. González Holguín, p. 167.
25. Avila, *Dioses y hombres de Huarochirí*, pp. 39, 175.
26. Bastien, p. 42; for material on Huarochirí, see ANP, Seccion Histórica, "Derecho Indígena," cuaderno 149, ff. 7–7v, 19v–25.
27. Santo Tomás, *Gramática*, p. 129.
28. Rowe, "Inca Culture," pp. 253–56.
29. Bastien, p. xxiv.
30. Avila, *Dioses y hombres de Huarochirí*, p. 65.
31. González Holguín, pp. 39–40.
32. Avila, *Dioses y hombres de Huarochirí*, pp. 169–83.
33. "Declaración de Don Martín Cari, cacique principal de la parcialidad de Anansaya," in Diez de San Miguel, p. 35.
34. Avila, *Dioses y hombres de Huarochirí*, pp. 169, 173, 181.
35. *Ibid.*, pp. 171, 173.   36. Solá and Urioste.
37. Diez de San Miguel, p. 35.   38. González Holguín, p. 40.
39. Sr. Hector Chuquimuni, personal communication, Huarochirí, 1968.
40. Testament of Margarita Macuy Sacsa, ayllu Sangallalla, Huarochirí, 1 de Mayo de 1631, in ANP, Seccion Histórica, "Testamentos de Indios." Although the document title refers to a woman, who apparently carried on litigation about lands based upon the wills of male ancestors, it was a man who left the testament in 1631.
41. "Autos que siguío Doña Juana Salazar . . . sobre propriedad de unas tierras," ANP, Seccion Histórica, "Derecho Indígena," cuaderno 149 [1684].
42. AA, Visitas de Huarochirí, legajo 1, ff. 2–2v.
43. See for example Bastien, pp. 93–94.
44. "Declaración de Don Martín Cari," in Diez de San Miguel, p. 35.

45. Testimony of Don Francisco Conapariaguana, in Ortíz de Zúñiga, vol. 2, p. 45.
46. Huaman Poma de Ayala, pp. 97–99, 188–220.
47. Loaysa, p. 586.
48. See Chamberlain.
49. Testimony of Gaspar Cayua, *principal* of the village of Quillcay and of Querocalla, in Ortíz de Zúñiga, vol. 2, p. 46.
50. *Ibid.*, p. 47.
51. Avila, *Dioses y hombres de Huarochirí*, p. 161.
52. Matienzo, p. 21.
53. Testimony of Don Francisco Conapariaguana, in Ortíz de Zúñiga, vol. 2, p. 28.
54. Matienzo, p. 21.
55. Testimony of Don Francisco Conapariaguana, in Ortíz de Zúñiga, vol. 2, p. 28.
56. Matienzo, p. 21.
57. Huaman Poma de Ayala, pp. 194–234.
58. Murra, "La Guerre," p. 928; for the specific case of Huarochirí, see AGI, Justicia 413, ff. 163–163v. John V. Murra kindly let me consult a microfilm of this case.
59. Testimony of Don Francisco Conapariaguana, in Ortíz de Zúñiga, vol. 2, p. 29.
60. Rostworowski de Diaz Canseco, *Etnía y sociedad*.
61. Morris, "L'Etude archéologique," p. 944.
62. See Murra, "Social Structural and Economic Themes," p. 51.
63. Testimony of Don Francisco Conapariaguana, in Ortíz de Zúñiga, vol. 2, p. 27.
64. Avila, *Dioses y hombres de Huarochirí*, pp. 169–83.
65. *Ibid.*, p. 181.
66. *Ibid.*, p. 179.
67. *Ibid.*
68. For the basic concept of "verticality," see Murra, "El 'Control Vertical,' " pp. 429–75.
69. González Holguín, p. 243.
70. *Ibid.*
71. Murra, "El 'Control Vertical,' " pp. 466–68.
72. Murra's discussions of Chucuito, of Huánuco, and of the Chillón-Rímac area can be found conveniently collected in a single volume, *Formaciones económicas y políticas del mundo andino*. The major piece is "El 'Control Vertical' " (pp. 59–116), but see also "Un reino aymara en 1567" (pp. 193–224) and "Las autoridades étnicas tradicionales en el alto Huallaga" (pp. 171–92).
73. "Numeración y padrón de los ayllus y pueblos del repartimiento de San Francisco de Chaclla . . . 1726," ANP, Sección Histórica, "Derecho Indígena," cuaderno 232.
74. Registro 1° del Escribano Público Lic. Carlos Rosas Morales, 1884–85, ANP, Sección Notarial [1884], f. 38v; ANP, Sección Histórica, "Derecho Indígena," cuaderno 267 [1741], cuaderno 189 [1705].
75. Rostworowski de Diaz Canseco, "Etnohistoria," p. 19.
76. Dávila Brizeño, p. 78.
77. Cook, ed., *Tasa de la visita general*, pp. 282–84.

78. "Numeración . . . de Chaclla, 1726 [cited in n. 73 above]; Registro 1° . . .
Morales [cited in n. 74 above].
79. Murra, "El 'Control Vertical,' " p. 436.
80. Avila, *Dioses y hombres de Huarochirí*, p. 141.
81. For a summary of the case, see Rostworowski de Diaz Canseco, "Etnohistoria."
82. *Ibid.*, p. 32.
83. "Carta del Padre Juan Gómez a Francisco de Borgia [1571], in Avila, *Dioses y hombres de Huarochirí*, p. 243.
84. Huaman Poma de Ayala, p. 768.
85. Avila, *Dioses y hombres de Huarochirí*, p. 173.
86. *Ibid.*, p. 181.
87. Morris, "The Technology," p. 43–46.
88. González Holguín, p. 324.
89. Huaman Poma de Ayala, p. 245.
90. Morris and Thompson, pp. 350–51.
91. John Thatcher, field notes, Huarochirí, 1968, site PV47-31.
92. Dollfus, "Les Andes intertropicales," pp. 895–903.

Chapter Two: The Sons of Pariacaca

1. Dávila Brizeño, pp. 61–78.
2. *Ibid.*, p. 62.
3. *Ibid.*, p. 78.
4. Avila, *Dioses y hombres de Huarochirí*, p. 173.
5. Murra, "El 'Control Vertical.' "
6. " 'Real cédula que se guarden a los indios sus usos y costumbres no siendo claramente injustos (Peru),' Badajoz, 23 de Septiembre de 1580," in Konetzke, vol. 1, doc. no. 394, pp. 529–30.
7. The lands of the cofradías were often created from the lands assigned to the support of the Inca deities, but despite that geographical overlap, it is difficult to find any continuity between Andean institutions and the Catholic Church; see Polo de Ondegardo, "Informe," pp. 182–87.
8. ANP, Sección Histórica, "Derecho Indígena," cuaderno 284, ff. 68v–70v, 192.
9. *Ibid.*, cuaderno 189 [1705], f. 3; ANP, Sección Histórica, "Titulos de Comunidades," legajo 5, cuaderno 44.
10. For example, see Dávila Brizeño, p. 70: ". . . fue el primer encomendero deste dicho repartimiento de Guadocheri."
11. Avila, *Dioses y hombres de Huarochirí*, p. 111.
12. See the breakdown of administrative divisions in the *visita* of Francisco de Toledo, summarized in Vásquez de Espinosa, p. 648; the repartimientos of Mamaq, Chaclla, and Huarochirí were divided into the same number of waranqas throughout the colonial period; see the description in Melo, ff. 2v–3v.
13. Avila, "Relación," p. 257.
14. Dávila Brizeño, p. 78; "Provisión de retasa del tributo que deben pagar los Indios del Repartimiento de San Francisco de Chaclla . . . 1705," ANP, Sección Histórica, "Derecho Indígena," cuaderno 189, ff. 3–3v.
15. Rostworowski de Diaz Canseco, *Etnía y sociedad*, p. 81; AGI, Justicia 413, ff. 163–63v (microfilm consulted through the courtesy of John V. Murra).

16. Registro 1° del Escribano Público Lic. Carlos Rosas Morales, 1884–85, ANP, Sección Notarial [1884], f. 38v; "Provisión de retasa . . ." (cited in n. 14 above), ff. 3–3v.

17. ANP, Sección Histórica, "Títulos de Comunidades," mandados protocolizar [1711–1832]; *ibid.*, legajo 11, cuaderno 94 [1717–85].

18. Moore, p. 99; see also Rowe, "Inca Culture," p. 263.

19. There has been considerable scholarly disagreement about the time span to be assigned to the Inca Empire, but archaeologists, on the basis of their own data, are increasingly in agreement with the estimates first proposed in 1945 by Rowe in "Absolute Chronology in the Andean Area."

20. ANP, Sección Histórica, "Títulos de Comunidades," legajo 8, cuaderno 63.

21. *Ibid.*, f. 12.

22. Zambrano, p. 1.

23. Santo Tomás, *Gramática*, p. 128.

24. Avila, *Dioses y hombres de Huarochirí*, p. 153.

25. *Ibid.*, pp. 23–25.

26. *Ibid.*, p. 77. On the basis of internal evidence, it is clear that the narrator of the tales was a Checa.

27. *Ibid.*, p. 53.

28. Testimony of Don Cristóbal Xulca Condor, in Ortíz de Zúñiga, vol. 1, p. 35.

29. Avila, *Dioses y hombres de Huarochirí*, p. 137.

30. Matienzo, pp. 20–21.

31. Rostworowski de Diaz Canseco, "Etnohistoria," p. 47.

32. Polo de Ondegardo, "Relación," p. 147.

33. *Ibid.*, p. 144.

34. *Ibid.*, p. 147.

35. Polo de Ondegardo, "Informe," p. 181.

36. Avila, *Dioses y hombres de Huarochirí*, p. 144.

37. Palomino Flores, p. 78.

38. Avila, *Dioses y hombres de Huarochirí*, pp. 35–45. The version of the myth that follows is my translation from the Spanish of José María Arguedas, corrected against the manuscript translation from Quechua to English by Solá and Urioste, consulted through the courtesy of Donald Solá.

39. Avila, *Dioses y hombres de Huarochirí*, p. 37.

40. Huaman Poma de Ayala, p. 848.

41. Avila, *Dioses y hombres de Huarochirí*, p. 67.

42. *Ibid.*, pp. 65–67.

43. Arriaga, p. 71.

44. See Murra, "Cloth and Its Functions."

45. Arriaga, p. 50; Berthelot, pp. 957–58.

46. In local village societies today, for example, the people who are most suspect as the source of witchcraft and ill will are often one's kin. See Bastien, pp. 93–94.

47. Arriaga, p. 118.

48. González Holguín, p. 40.

49. *Ibid.*, p. 37.

50. Arriaga, p. 49.

51. Avila, *Dioses y hombres de Huarochirí*, p. 111.

52. *Ibid.*, p. 39.

53. *Ibid.*, p. 111.

54. *Ibid.*, p. 159.

55. Arriaga, p. 47.

56. Avila, *Dioses y hombres de Huarochirí*, p. 89.

57. *Ibid.*, p. 113.
58. Arriaga, pp. 28–30.
59. "Causa criminal de hechicería contra María Huánico mestizà del pueblo de Quinti y Cicilia Canchasuyo del ayllu Curitupia, San Lorenzo de Quinti" [Jan. 25–May 26, 1660], AA, Visitas de Idolatría, legajo 2, cuaderno 21.
60. Arriaga, p. 68.
61. "Letter from Father Luís de Teruel, 1621," quoted in Arriaga, p. 155: "Causa criminal contra Isabel Choqui del ayllu Cullana del pueblo de San Juan de Tantaranche, anexo de Quinti," AA, Visitas de Idolatría, legajo 3, cuaderno 1.
62. "Causa criminal contra Lucía Suyu Cargua, Juan Baptista y Juana Sacsahuaria, todos del pueblo Quinti, ayllu Hualcaraya" [Apr. 22–May 14, 1660], AA, Visitas de Idolatría, legajo 2, cuaderno 14.
63. "Carta del padre Fabían de Ayala al arzobispo" [Dec. 4, 1611], in Avila, *Dioses y hombres de Huarochirí*, p. 252.
64. *Ibid.*, pp. 105, 127; Arriaga, p. 15.
65. Avila, *Dioses y hombres de Huarochirí*, p. 87.
66. Avila, "Relación," p. 255.
67. Avila, *Dioses y hombres de Huarochirí*, pp. 65, 79, 103; the name yañca was clearly specific to Huarochirí, whose population did not speak Quechua as a first language; the function of the priests of the wak'as, equivalent to the yañca, is also described by Arriaga, pp. 32–33.

In addition to the ritual specialists, there were a large number of diviner/spell-casters in Andean local society, who cast the futures of people about to set out on a trip or undertake an important activity. They also set or countered spells, located lost objects, and treated illness. They were less important people than priests, and their services to individuals were paid for with gifts of food or drink that supplemented household production. After the Spanish conquest, with the persecution of the ritual specialists, the distinctions between specialist and diviner/spell-caster began to blur and the two kinds of activity sometimes fused. See Arriaga, p. 36.

68. Avila, *Dioses y hombres de Huarochirí*, pp. 101, 103.
69. Arriaga, p. 28.
70. Avila, *Dioses y hombres de Huarochirí*, p. 181.
71. *Ibid.*, p. 65 (translation corrected against that of Solá and Urioste).
72. Thomas C. Patterson, personal communication. The agricultural cycle is complicated in the central Andes, which are only 12° from the equator, and there is considerable variation in harvest and planting times from valley to valley, and even within valleys. In general, land is prepared for cultivation about July or August, and the rains wet the earth and signal the beginning of planting. Crops are harvested about June, technically the winter solstice, for so close to the equator, the growing season depends more upon rains than upon the small seasonal variations in temperature.
73. Avila, *Dioses y hombres de Huarochirí*, p. 79. It is not easy to reconstruct the calendar for the celebration of the major festivals, since after the Spanish invasion, people disguised the feasts of the wak'as by setting them to coincide with the holy days of Catholic saints, frequently the saints after whom the villages were named, thus preserving the festivals of the wak'as in the face of the local village priest, with, of course, slight necessary adjustments in the times of the celebrations.
74. *Ibid.*, pp. 65, 79.

75. *Ibid.*, pp. 67, 79, 85.
76. *Ibid.*, p. 69.
77. John V. Thatcher, field notes, Huarochirí, 1968, site PV50-90.

Chapter Three: Tribes Become Peasants

1. Quoted in Morris, "Peru's Golden Treasures," p. 8.
2. Marx, p. 36.
3. Miguel de Estete, "Noticia del Peru" [1535], quoted in Murra, "Cloth and Its Functions," p. 717.
4. Zuidema, "Reflexiones."
5. Rowe, "Absolute Chronology," p. 267.
6. *Ibid.*, pp. 269–71; see also Rowe, "Inca Culture."
7. Rowe, "Inca Culture," p. 281.
8. *Ibid.*, p. 208; Rowe, "Absolute Chronology," pp. 271–72.
9. Rowe, "Absolute Chronology," pp. 277–79, and map facing p. 273.
10. *Ibid.*, pp. 276–77.
11. Zuidema, "Reflexiones," esp. pp. 57–60.
12. Cabello Balboa, p. 320.
13. Zuidema, "Reflexiones," pp. 59–60.
14. Murra, "On Inca Political Structure," pp. 30–41.
15. Murra, "La Guerre," pp. 929–32; see also Rowe, "Inca Culture," pp. 206–8.
16. Murra, *La organización económica*; and Murra, "La Guerre," pp. 933–34.
17. For an extremely suggestive example of the kind of work that can be done, see Wachtel, "Hommes d'eau."
18. Much of this work has been done by John Murra since 1956. See the collection of his writings entitled *Formaciones económicas y políticas del mundo andino*; for an evaluation of research on Andean society and his suggestions for further work, see Murra, "Current Research and Prospects in Andean Ethnohistory."
19. Cobo, pp. 77–82, 204, 206–7, 262.
20. Huaman Poma de Ayala, p. 64.
21. Rostworowski de Diaz Canseco, "Etnohistoria," p. 39.
22. Levillier, *Don Francisco de Toledo*, vol. 2, p. 19.
23. Polo de Ondegardo, "Informe," pp. 133–34.
24. For a detailed study of the long document that relates the story of the dispute between the Canta and the Chaclla peoples over the coca fields of Quives, see Rostworowski de Diaz Canseco, "Etnohistoria," pp. 7–61.
25. Dávila Brizeño, p. 78. The peoples of Huarochirí also had access to *lomas* pastures on the coast, probably also granted by the Incas, since their conquests did not reach to the coast prior to their absorption into the Inca state.
26. Polo de Ondegardo, "Informe," p. 135.
27. Dávila Brizeño, p. 62.
28. Rostworowski de Diaz Canseco, "Etnohistoria," p. 21.
29. Avila, *Dioses y hombres de Huarochirí*, pp. 109–11, 114–19, 131–35.
30. Murra, "Una apreciación," pp. 433–34.
31. See Murra, "Social Structural and Economic Themes," p. 54, for a discussion of the responsibilities of the kuraka to the Inca state.
32. Cabello Balboa, p. 274.
33. Polo de Ondegardo, "Informe," p. 165.

34. Murra, "On Inca Political Structure," p. 34.
35. Polo de Ondegardo, "Informe," p. 185.
36. *Ibid.*, p. 149.
37. John Murra has provided much of the stimulus that made the publication of these invaluable sources possible. We now have three volumes available: Ortíz de Zúñiga (2 vols.); and Díez de San Miguel.
38. "Testimonio de Gaspar Cayua," in Ortíz de Zúñiga, vol. 2, p. 47.
39. See Garcilaso de la Vega, p. 289.
40. Díez de San Miguel, p. 92.
41. Avila, *Dioses y hombres de Huarochirí*, p. 129.
42. Cobo, p. 122.
43. Avila, *Dioses y hombres de Huarochirí*, p. 129; see also pp. 114–19, 131–35.
44. See, for examples of such myths, Avila, *Dioses y hombres de Huarochirí*, pp. 109–11, 131–35.
45. See Murra, "Social Structural and Economic Themes," pp. 52–53, and "New Data."
46. Polo de Ondegardo, "Informe," p. 139.
47. See Chapter One.
48. See Rostworowski de Diaz Canseco, "Etnohistoria," pp. 19, 47.
49. The project is still in process; for preliminary reports and tentative conclusions, see Morris, "State Settlements," "Master Design," "The Identification of Function," and "L'Etude archéologique."
50. See Avila, *Dioses y hombres de Huarochirí*, pp. 109–11, 131–35.
51. *Ibid.*, pp. 131–35.
52. Julien; see also Chapter Two above.
53. Huaman Poma de Ayala, p. 359.
54. Menzel, pp. 220–21, 232–33.
55. Dávila Brizeño, p. 74.
56. Thatcher, p. 5; also John Thatcher, field notebook, June 27, July 5, Aug. 20, 1968, site PV50-200.
57. Cieza de León, p. 46.
58. *Ibid.*, p. 70.
59. *Ibid.*, p. 65.
60. Menzel, p. 232.
61. Matienzo, p. 24.
62. Huaman Poma de Ayala, p. 347.
63. Murra, "Social Structural and Economic Themes," pp. 53–54.
64. Morua, vol. 1, p. 62.
65. Morris, "The Technology and Organization," pp. 43–44.
66. Rostworowski de Diaz Canseco, "Etnohistoria," p. 24.
67. Morris, "The Technology and Organization," p. 44, and "Master Design," pp. 62–64. Unless otherwise noted, the material on Huánuco Pampa is based upon these sources, and upon Morris's other articles listed in n. 49 above.
68. Cieza de León, p. 109.
69. Huaman Poma de Ayala, p. 299.
70. Morris, "The Infrastructure of Inka Control," pp. 14–17.
71. Huaman Poma de Ayala, p. 251.
72. Polo de Ondegardo, "Relación," p. 57.
73. Murra, "The Mit'a Obligations," pp. 5–8.
74. Cobo, p. 110.
75. Pedro Pizarro, quoted in Morris, "The Technology and Organization," p. 45; see also Rowe, "What Kind of a Settlement Was Inca Cuzco?," p. 60.

76. Huaman Poma de Ayala, p. 243.
77. Polo de Ondegardo, pp. 109–10.
78. *Ibid.*, p. 58.
79. For the sometimes tense relationship between the wak'as and the Inca state, see Rowe, "Inca Culture," p. 293; see also Hemming, pp. 56–57.
80. Rowe, "Inca Culture," p. 302.
81. Avila, *Dioses y hombres de Huarochirí*, p. 129.
82. Unless otherwise noted, the discussion of the site is based upon my field notes from the 1968 field season, NSF project on the culture history of the western slopes of the Andes, directed by Thomas C. Patterson, Temple University. Field notebook no. 2 (site PV47-25), pp. 1–24; field notebook no. 4 (sites PV47-28 and PV47-32), pp. 17–40, 77–86.
83. In Avila, *Dioses y hombres de Huarochirí*, pp. 73, 85, 89, Chaupiñamca appears as the sister of Pariacaca; her marriage to Pachacamac is told of by Dávila Brizeño, p. 75, who as a Spaniard was probably more likely to learn of the official state tradition than of local stories.
84. Huaman Poma de Ayala, p. 234.
85. Avila, *Dioses y hombres de Huarochirí*, p. 75.
86. Field notebook no. 4, 1968, p. 39, Aug. 5, 1968. The Fábrica Patama, scheduled for construction in 1968, was built and the site destroyed by 1970.
87. Site PV47-25, field notebook no. 2, 1968, pp. 1–24; see also Max Uhle's report on the site in Uhle, pp. 51–52.
88. Identification provided by Thomas C. Patterson.
89. Avila, *Dioses y hombres de Huarochirí*, p. 127.
90. *Ibid.*, p. 113.
91. Murra, "La Guerre," p. 930.
92. Levillier, *Don Francisco de Toledo*, vol. 2, p. 108.
93. Avila, *Dioses y hombres de Huarochirí*, p. 131.
94. *Ibid.*, p. 133. 95. *Ibid.*, p. 135.
96. Wachtel, "The Mitimas." 97. *Ibid.*, p. 3.
98. Morua, vol. 1, pp. 90–93.
99. Rostworowski de Diaz Canseco, "Succession," p. 425.

Chapter Four: The Age of the Conquerors

1. "El Lic. Espinosa al Emperador, Panamá, 10 de Octubre de 1533," in Porras Barrenechea, *Cartas del Perú*, p. 67.
2. Porras Barrenechea, *Las relaciones primitivas*, pp. 65–66.
3. For a useful general summary of the conquest of Peru, see Hemming, *The Conquest of the Incas*, esp. pp. 23–316.
4. Lockhart, *The Men of Cajamarca*, p. 23.
5. The discussion of Spanish society that follows relies heavily upon the work of John H. Elliott; see especially his *Imperial Spain, 1469–1716*.
6. *Ibid.*, p. 109.
7. *Ibid.*, p. 111–12.
8. *Ibid.*, p. 113.
9. My memory of the proverb dates to graduate lectures by Robert Padden; a poem of similar import is found in Bagú, p. 125.
10. Lockhart, *Men of Cajamarca*, p. 32.
11. Pike, pp. 22–34.

12. *Ibid.*, pp. 25–26.

13. Lockhart, *Men of Cajamarca*, pp. 667–70, 142–43.

14. Hemming, pp. 74, 556; Lockhart, *Men of Cajamarca*, p. 13. Some 13,420 pounds of gold and 26,000 pounds of silver were melted down at Cajamarca. Calculations of their worth in contemporary terms do not take into account changing currency values or prices, whose fluctuations make estimates of limited value. Still, the figure of over half a billion dollars provides an approximate yardstick against which a reader can estimate the plunder of the conquest.

15. Lockhart, *Men of Cajamarca*, p. 96.

16. See Espinosa Soriano, *Destrucción*, pp. 50, 63–68.

17. For a detailed account of the rapid changes of Inca rulers during this period, see Hemming, pp. 87–96, 119–26.

18. Espinosa Soriano, *Destrucción*, pp. 50, 158–63.

19. Hemming, pp. 130–36.

20. *Ibid.*, pp. 169–88, gives a full description of the looting that accompanied the conquest.

21. Espinosa Soriano, *Destrucción*, pp. 70–76, 93–96.

22. "El Lic. Espinosa al Emperador, Panamá, 10 de Octubre de 1533," in Porras Barrenechea, *Cartas del Perú*, p. 68.

23. "Francisco de Barrionuevo al Emperador, Panamá, 19 de Enero de 1534," in *ibid.*, p. 96.

24. "La Audiencia de la Isla Española al Emperador, Santo Domingo, 30 de Enero de 1534," in *ibid.*, p. 99.

25. "Los Oficiales de Puerto Rico al Emperador, San Juan, 26 de Febrero de 1534," in *ibid.*, p. 100.

26. "Pascual de Andagoya y el Lic. Espinosa a la Audiencia de Santo Domingo, Panamá, 27 de Julio de 1536," in *ibid.*, pp. 218–19.

27. Kubler, "The Neo-Inca State," pp. 189–203; also Hemming, pp. 238–55, 274–76.

28. Espinosa Soriano, *Destrucción*, p. 112.

29. Avila, *Dioses y hombres de Huarochirí*, p. 105.

30. *Ibid.*, pp. 105–7.

31. *Ibid.*, p. 107.

32. Espinosa Soriano, *Destrucción*, p. 122.

33. The account, the "información de Jatunsausa," was prepared by Don Francisco Cusichaca, kuraka principal of the Saya of Jatunsausa, whose father had allied with Pizarro in 1533. The quipu records and native declarations were translated by a bilingual noble, Don Martín, and submitted to the Crown in support of Don Francisco's petition for office and recognition for his services. The petition provided the documentary basis for Espinosa Soriano's *Destrucción del Imperio de los Incas* and was also used by John V. Murra in a study of Andean classificatory systems, "Las etno-categorías de un *khipu* estatal," in *Formaciones económicas y políticas del mundo andino*, pp. 243–54.

34. Vega, p. 81.

35. Espinosa Soriano, *Destrucción*, pp. 68, 97, 129, 154, 182.

36. Murra, "Las etno-categorías," cuadro IV, facing p. 252.

37. Browman. A llama gives birth only about every two years, so the loss of such a large number of animals would also have depressed the birth rate significantly, reducing the size of the llama herds in subsequent years; the herds were largely females, which were kept for breeding and not sacrificed.

38. Hemming, p. 35.

39. For a summary of the benefits and responsibilities of the encomendero, see Lockhart, *Spanish Peru*, p. 21.

40. Lockhart and Otte, eds., p. 150.

41. See Anderson, pp. 19–20, 408–10.

42. See Díez de San Miguel and Ortíz de Zúñiga; the records of the inspection and census carried out under the authority of Pedro de la Gasca in the 1540's—our earliest such source to date—are now being prepared for publication by María Rostworowski de Diaz Canseco.

43. Espinosa Soriano, "El alcalde mayor indígena," p. 202.

44. BNP, doc. A-36, Libros Notariales de Diego Gutiérrez, 1545–55, Lima, Aug. 7, 1550, f. 279 (information provided by James Lockhart).

45. Santillán, p. 57.

46. Huaman Poma de Ayala, p. 554.

47. See the example of the encomendero Lucas Martínez Vergazo in the brilliant thesis of the young Peruvian historian Efraín Trelles Aréstegui, "Lucas Martínez Vergazo: Funcionamiento de una encomienda peruana inicial" (Pontifícia Universidad Católica del Perú, Lima, 1980).

48. Hemming, p. 148.

49. Espinosa Soriano, *Destrucción*, p. 154.

50. Helmer, p. 42.   51. Berthelot, pp. 948–58.

52. Dávila Brizeño, p. 69.   53. *Ibid.*, pp. 75–76.

54. See Sempat Assadourian, pp. 12–28.

55. For a description of the techniques of mining during the conquest period, see Sempat Assadourian, pp. 24–26.

56. Murra, "Aymara Lords," pp. 231–43.

57. Matienzo, p. 132.

58. Spalding, "Kurakas and Commerce," pp. 591–92.

59. Loredo, *Alardes y derramas*, pp. 126–31.

60. *Harkness Collection . . . Documents from Early Peru*, pp. 128, 110.

61. *Ibid.*, p. 101.

62. Trelles Aréstegui, pp. 32–41 (cited in n. 47 above).

63. Libro notarial de Hernando de Caçalla, Archive of Guillermo Gayoso G., Huánuco, Perú, Book IV (1567), ff. 1, 44.

64. Only 64 percent of the llamas were actually sent to market by the encomendero or his mayordomo, but another 35 percent of the llamas demanded in tribute were paid for by the Indians at a price above the market price in Potosí, so for the purpose of this calculation it has been assumed that they were sold—to the Indians from whom they were demanded in the first place! Trelles Aréstegui, esp. pp. 219–52 (cited in n. 47 above).

65. *Ibid.*

Chapter Five: The Colonial System

1. Dobyns, "Estimating Aboriginal American Population."

2. María Rostworowski de Diaz Canseco, personal communication, 1980.

3. Dobyns, "An Outline of Andean Epidemic History to 1720."

4. *Ibid.*; see also Smith, "Despoblación de los Andes centrales en el siglo XVI." Population data from 1542 should be available when Rostworowski de Diaz Canseco completes her study of the tribute reassessments based on population counts of the native Andean population in that year.

5. Lockhart, *Spanish Peru*, p. 12.

6. *Ibid.*, p. 16.

7. "Carta a S.M. del Virrey Marqués de Cañete, Panamá, 11 de Marzo de 1556," in Levillier, ed., *Gobernantes del Perú*, vol. 1, p. 259.

8. Jara, p. 52.

9. On the close link between the Crown's finances, its American territories, and the Spanish enterprise in Europe, see Elliott, *Imperial Spain*, pp. 161–204, 287–89; and Elliot, *Europe Divided*, pp. 56–60.

10. "Los oficiales de Sevilla al Emperador, Sevilla, 1535," in Porras Barrenechea, *Cartas del Perú*, pp. 184–85.

11. "Fray Tomás de Berlanga al Rey," Nombre de Dios, 3 February 1536, in Porras Barrenechea, *Cartas del Perú*, p. 196.

12. "Pedro de la Gasca a S.M.," Lima, 25 September 1548, in Levillier, ed., *Gobernantes del Perú*, vol. 1, p. 212.

13. Quoted in Lockhart, *The Men of Cajamarca*, p. 141.

14. "Robles al Cardenal Sigüenza, Panamá, 20 de Setiembre de 1539," in Porras Barrenechea, *Cartas del Perú*, p. 374.

15. "El Lic. Vaca de Castro a María de Quiñones, su mujer, Cuzco, 28 de Noviembre de 1542," in Porras Barrenechea, *Cartas del Perú*, p. 511; the English quotation is in Lockhart and Otte, eds., p. 177.

16. On the stormy history of the New Laws, see Simpson, pp. 123–44.

17. Polo de Ondegardo, "Relación," p. 130.

18. "Pedro de la Gasca a S.M.," Lima, 25 September 1548, in Levillier, ed., *Gobernantes del Perú*, vol. 1, pp. 211–12.

19. *Ibid.*, pp. 143, 199–200.

20. Sánchez Bello, pp. 420–75.

21. Levillier, ed., *Gobernantes del Perú*, vol. 2, p. 494.

22. *Ibid.*, p. 572.

23. Sánchez Bello, p. 479.

24. *Ibid.*

25. Lohmann Villena, "Etude préliminaire," p. ix.

26. Wachtel, "Rebeliones y milenarismo," pp. 110–12, 117–123.

27. *Ibid.*, pp. 113–14; Lohmann Villena, "Etude préliminaire," p. ix.

28. Juan de Salinas Loyola, "Las encomiendas del Perú, 1569," in Jiménez de la Espada, vol. 1, p. 56.

29. See, for example, the letter of the parish priest Francisco de la Calzada of Potosí to his sister in Spain in 1577, in Lockhart and Otte, eds., pp. 252–55.

30. Zabálburu and Sancho Rayon, eds., vol. 6, p. 274.

31. "Instrucciones a los comisarios reales," in Zabálburu and Sancho Rayon, eds., vol. 6, p. 7.

32. Rowe, "The Incas Under Spanish Colonial Institutions," p. 156.

33. "Carta de los Comisarios a S.M. sobre la perpetuidad y otras cosas," in Zabálburu and Sancho Rayon, eds., vol. 6, pp. 52–55.

34. Matienzo, p. 98.

35. "Carta de los Comisarios a S.M. . . . ," in Zabálburu and Sancho Rayon, eds., vol. 6, p. 52.

36. This argument was frequent in the early years after the conquest; for a discussion of these issues, see Lohmann Villena's "Etude préliminaire," pp. vii–ix, and also his "La restitución por conquistadores y encomenderos."

37. "Carta de Fray Domingo de Santo Tomás a Su Majestad sobre la perpetuidad, 16 de marzo de 1562," in Lissón Chávez, ed., vol. 2, p. 198.

38. *Ibid.*, p. 199.
39. "Copia de una carta escrita a Su Majestad sobre los negocios de las Indias," *Nueva coleccion*, vol. 6, pp. 218–59.
40. *Ibid.*, p. 254.
41. *Ibid.*, p. 255.
42. *Ibid.*
43. "Carta de los Comisarios a S.M. . . .," in Zabálburu and Sanchez Rayon, eds., vol. 6, p. 48.
44. *Ibid.*
45. Elliott, *Europe Divided*, p. 107.
46. "Carta de los Comisarios a S.M. . . .," in Zabálburu and Sanchez Rayon, eds., vol. 6, p. 62; on the separatist sentiments of distant nobilities, see also Lynch, vol. 1, pp. 337–45.
47. "Carta de los Comisarios a S.M. . . .," in Zabálburu and Sanchez Rayon, eds., vol. 6, pp. 62–63.
48. *Ibid.*, pp. 58–59.
49. *Ibid.*, p. 63.
50. Sánchez Bello, p. 497.
51. Bronner, "Peruvian Encomenderos in 1630."
52. Matienzo, p. 98.
53. The major biography of Toledo remains that of Levillier, *Don Francisco de Toledo*, which dates from the 1930's. A new study of the life and times of this major figure sorely needs to be written.
54. See Anderson, pp. 40–56.
55. The variety of taxes and forms of access to labor that replaced feudal relationships in Europe has been described by B. F. Porshnev as "centralized feudal rent," a definition that also fits the colonial system elaborated in Peru between 1550 and 1580. See Anderson, p. 35.
56. "Real cédula que se guarden a los indios sus usos y costumbres no siendo claramente injustos (Perú), Badajoz, 23 de setiembre de 1580," in Konetzke, ed., vol. 1, p. 529.
57. These "reductions" are discussed in Chapter 7 in detail.
58. Polo de Ondegardo, "Relación," p. 172.
59. Levillier, ed., *Gobernantes del Perú*, vol. 1, pp. 20–23.
60. Helmer, "La visitación de los Indios Chupachos."
61. Santillán, p. 81.
62. "Carta de D. Francisco de Toledo a S. M., Cuzco, 1 de marzo de 1572," in Levillier, ed., *Gobernantes del Perú*, vol. 4, pp. 113–15; also "Memorial que D. Francisco de Toledo dió al Rey del estado en que dejó las cosas del Perú [1581]," in Beltrán y.Rózpide, pp. 67–85.
63. See Cook, ed., *Tasa de la visita general*, for the population figures and tribute assessments of the Audiencias of Cuzco and Charcas (the Audiencia of Lima is not included).
64. ANP, Sección Histórica, "Derecho Indígena," cuaderno 189 [1705], and cuaderno 287 [1726–52].
65. *Recopilación de leyes*, Libro VI, Tít. V, ley xviii; on the legal position and rights of the kuraka, see Solórzano, vol. 1, chap. 27, pp. 405–15; on other exemptions, see ANP, Sección Histórica, "Derecho Indígena," cuaderno 189 [1705], f. 27v.
66. *Recopilación de leyes*, Lib. VI, Tít. V, ley lix.

67. On the organization and the subsequent history of the encomienda in Peru, see Belaunde Guinassí, *La encomienda en el Perú*.

68. Cook, ed., *Tasa de la visita general*, p. 283.

69. "Cuadro de remates de las especies que en los corregimientos de su distrito pertenecieron a esta Real Caja del Cuzco este año de 1647," Archivo Histórica del Cuzco, document no. 7.

70. For a fuller explanation of this process, see Sempat Assadourian.

71. On the mita, see Ballesteros, Lib. II, tít. XVIII, ord. iii: "cédula del servicio personal [1609]"; *Recopilación de leyes*, Lib. VI, tít. XII, ley xxii.

72. *Aranzel de los jornales que se han de pagar a los indios así voluntarios, mingados, alquilas, y agregados a las haciendas de españoles, como mitayos, y de obligación, en todo género de trabajo* . . . (Los Reyes, 1687). Copies of this rare publication can be found in the Biblioteca Nacional, Madrid, and in the Biblioteca de la Escuela del Derecho, University of Buenos Aires, Argentina. A microfilm is available in the Biblioteca Nacional, Lima.

73. "Carta de D. Francisco de Toledo a S. M., Cuzco, 1 de marzo de 1572," in Levillier, ed., *Gobernantes del Perú*, vol. 4, p. 109.

74. Memorandum of Francisco de Melo, ANP, Sección Histórica, "Derecho Indígena," cuaderno 287 [1726–52], 2 unnumbered pages, and cuaderno 189 [1705], ff. 2–7; also the "Relación que el Príncipe de Esquilache hace al Señor Marqués de Gualdacazar sobre el estado en que deja las provincias del Perú [1621]," in Beltrán y Rózpide, p. 241.

75. Cornblit, pp. 24–27; see also Sánchez-Albornoz, *Indios y tributos en el Alto Perú*, esp. chap. 3: "Una dicotomía indígena: originarios y forasteros," pp. 35–64.

76. "Razón del contador de Retasas, José de Orellana, al virrey Conde de Superunda," in Fuentes, ed. and comp., vol. 4, appendix, pp. 7–15. The last population counts in the archbishopric of Lima prior to the 1780's were taken around 1754, the date of Orellana's summary, so for that area—and that area only—the figures he presents can be assigned with some certainty to sometime in the first half of the eighteenth century.

77. TePaske, "The Fiscal Structure of Upper Peru and the Financing of Empire."

78. Moreno Cebrián, *El corregidor de indios*.

Chapter Six: The Shrinking Web

1. "Estado geográfico del virreinato del Perú, sus intendentes, partidas, doctrinas, pueblos, anexos y sus pobladores con distinción de clases y sexos como se manifiesta [1790]," AGI, Estado, 75. James F. King kindly provided me with a photocopy of this document.

2. For a general discussion of the early gold-hunting period in the Americas, see Chaunu and Chaunu, vol. 8; on the treasure hunt in Huarochirí itself, see Avila, *Dioses y hombres de Huarochirí*, pp. 105, 107.

3. Dávila Brizeño, pp. 75–76.

4. *Ibid.*, p. 67.

5. *Ibid.*, p. 77.

6. *Ibid.*, p. 62.

7. Santillán, p. 94.

8. Dávila Brizeño, p. 77.

9. See Sempat Assadourian, pp. 23, 34–36.

10. Vásquez de Espinosa, pp. 442.

11. Cobo, p. 319.

12. Sempat Assadourian, pp. 28–34.

13. "Relación de oficios que se proveen en al gobernación de los reinos y provincias del Perú [1583]," in Levillier, ed., *Gobernantes del Perú*, vol. 9, p. 191. Population figures for the Audiencia of Lima are unfortunately not contained in the otherwise indispensable edition of the Toledo *Visita* by Noble David Cook.

14. Vásquez de Espinosa, p. 438.

15. "Razón de los tributarios de la provincia de Huarochirí [1779–80]," "Libro primero de los cargos y distribución del Ramo de Tributos de las provincias de la jurisdicción de este virreinato de Lima según las últimas matrículas de cada uno de ellas [1781]," ANP, Sección Histórica, unclassified.

16. Kubler, "The Quechua in the Colonial World," pp. 334–40.

17. Dávila Brizeño, p. 62.

18. ANP, Sección Histórica, "Derecho Indígena," cuadernos 284 [1751] and 286 [1752].

19. *Ibid.*

20. *Ibid.*, cuaderno 699 [1711].

21. See, for example, *ibid.*, cuaderno 284 [1751], especially ff. 75–78v.

22. See *ibid.*, cuaderno 699 [1711].

23. "Testamento de José de la Cruz, 11 de abril de 1713," ANP, Sección Histórica, "Testamentos de Indios," legajo 2.

24. See, for example, the case of the coca lands of Quives in Rostworowski de Diaz Canseco, "Etnohistoria."

25. As the kuraka of Chaclla noted regarding the lands of Quives, "they knew nothing about selling or buying chacaras, nor was there any such custom." Rostworowski de Diaz Canseco, "Etnohistoria," p. 9.

26. "Indice del repartimiento de tasas, de las provincias contenidas en este libro hechas en tiempo del Exmo. Sr. D. Francisco de Toledo [copy of 1785]," Archivo General de la Nación Argentina, Sala 9:17-2-5, f. 42; see also Romero, "Libro," p. 165.

27. *Recopilación de leyes*, Lib. VI, Tít. III, ley xix [1560].

28. "Autos promovidos por el Bachiller Melchor de Segura, 1661," AA, Visitas de Huarochirí, legajo 1, ff. 1–2v, 9; ANP, Sección Histórica, "Tierras de Comunidad," legajo 11, cuaderno 94 [1717–85].

29. "Testamento de José de la Cruz" [cited in n. 23 above]. The definition of a *tabla*, a plot of land that can be cultivated by a single person in one day, was provided to me by Delfin Zúñiga, of Huánuco and New York.

30. "Autos promovidos por el Bachiller Melchor de Segura, 1661," AA, Visitas de Huarochirí, legajo 1, ff. 2–2v.

31. *Ibid.*, ff. 1–2v, 9. Contemporary villages in the province can be located on the map entitled "Perú, Departamento de Lima, Mapa del Perú," issued by the Oficina Cartográfico Nacional in 1956. The scale is 1:500,000. Library of Congress, map division, 927-B.

32. Field notes, 1968.

33. Solórzano Pereira, chap. 12, book 6, punto 2.

34. *Recopilación de leyes*, Lib. IV, Tít. XII, ley xviii [1642, 1646].

35. See Burga, pp. 97–103.

36. "Cédulas y provisiones," 21, no. 2, pp. 441–42.

37. *Ibid.*, p. 440.

38. *Recopilación de leyes*, Lib. IV, Tít. XII, ley xix.

39. Burga, pp. 99–100.

40. "Indice temático de la compilación (ordenanzas sobre tierras)," p. 468.

41. ANP, "Titulos de Comunidades," mandados protocolizar, Chaclla; ANP, Sección Histórica, "Derecho Indígena," cuaderno 825; ANP, "Tierras de Comunidades," legajo 11, cuaderno 94.

42. Cook, ed., *Padron de los indios*.

43. ANP, Sección Histórica, "Derecho Indígena," cuaderno 189 [1705], ff. 14v–18; cuaderno 287 [1726–53], ff. 2v–6 (inconsistent pagination).

44. *Ibid*., cuaderno 287 [1726–53], ff. 1v–3v (inconsistent pagination).

45. "El común del pueblo de San Miguel de Visu . . . 1781," BNP, Sala de Manuscritos (C-2869), ff. 1–3v.

46. ANP, Sección Histórica, "Derecho Indígena," cuaderno 189 [1705], ff. 4–4v; cuaderno 188 [1706], especially ff. 1–1v, 6v–7, 10v–11.

47. Melo, "Diario histórico," f. 37; and Francisco de Melo, memorandum on mita arrangements in ANP, Sección Histórica, "Derecho Indígena," cuaderno 287 [1726–53] (2 unnumbered pages).

48. For a description of the mita de tambos, see Dávila Brizeño, p. 73; Vaca de Castro; "Relación de los pueblos"; and Concolorcorvo, pp. 389–90.

49. ANP, Sección Histórica, "Derecho Indígena," cuaderno 287 [1726–53] (2 unnumbered pages); cuaderno 189 [1706]; and cuaderno 272 [1745].

50. Melo, "Diario histórico," f. 6.

51. Porlier, Bancroft Library microfilm, reel 2, ff. 3, 32v–33, 35.

52. ANP, Sección Histórica, "Derecho Indígena," cuaderno 353 [1773–75], ff. 22–27, 77–78, 84–84v. In certain *doctrinas*, the rate was six pesos, two reales per 100 sheep, and three pesos, six reales per 100 goats.

53. The tariff of Liñan y Cisneros is summarized in the "Visita de San Pedro de Casta, 1721," AA, Visitas de Huarochirí, legajo 1, f. 7. I have failed to locate either the tariff of Mogrovejo, or any summary of its contents.

54. *Ibid*., f. 4.

55. "Arancel de derechos parroquiales . . . de la ciudad y obispado de Nuestra Señora de la Paz [1768]," in *Perú: Papeles varios*, document no. 8, Museo Mitre, Buenos Aires (microfilm copy in *Documents microfilmed by C. G. Crampton: Peru and Bolivia*, Bancroft Library, reel 1). "Arancel de derechos eclesiásticos parroquiales . . . formado por el Ilustrísimo Sr. D. D. Juan Manuel de Moscoso y Perales [1780]," in *Perú: Papeles varios*, document no. 9, Museo Mitre, Buenos Aires.

56. For examples of the additional levies added to the tribute for the Church, see the tribute assignments in ANP, Sección Histórica, "Derecho Indígena," cuaderno 189 [1705], ff. 21–21v; and cuaderno 287 [1726–53], ff. 4–4v (pagination inconsistent).

57. See Spalding, "El corregidor," p. 129.

58. See the comments of the Viceroy Conde de Superunda on this point cited in Moreno Cebrián, p. 274; see also the estimates of expected profits from the repartimiento, in lists that circulated in the viceroyalty, summarized in Moreno Cebrián, pp. 78–79.

59. Cited in Moreno Cebrián, p. 274.

60. *Ibid*., p. 338.

61. Calculations are based upon the population figures found in the sources listed in Table 1, using the number of tributaries as a rough guide to the number of households.

62. Melo, "Diario histórico," f. 48. Population figures are based on the "Razón que da D. José de Orellana . . . de los indios de todas clases que se consideran existentes en los arzobispados y obispados que abajo se expresan . . . [1754]," in Fuentes, vol. 4, anexos o documentos, p. 7.

63. Per capita figures are calculated on the basis of the tariff lists in Moreno Cebrián, pp. 317–55, and the population statistics in appendix 4 of Fisher, *Government and Society in Colonial Peru*.

64. See, for example, the documents "Causa fecha contra el B.r José de Vargas, 1648," and "Causa contra el L.do Perez de Vivero, 1606," both in AA, Visitas de Huarochirí, legajo 1.

65. Such personal services were expressly forbidden, but the source materials testify to their existence. The material in AA, Visitas de Huarochirí, contains an abundance of testimony regarding the exactions of the priest; on the corregidor, see the material in ANP, Sección Histórica, "Derecho Indígena,"—for example, cuaderno 187 [1703], ff. 21, 43.

66. Palata, chaps. 8, 20.

67. ANP, Sección Histórica, "Derecho Indígena," cuaderno 188 [1705], ff. 9–9v.

68. *Ibid.*, cuaderno 665 [1807]; "Carta escrita por D. José Gabriel Túpac Amaru al visitador Don José Antonio Areche, antes de ser tomado prisionero [1781]," in Miller, vol. 1, Appendix A, p. 420.

69. Juan de Manrique, "Informe en consequencia de órden de Gálvez, 29 de julio de 1782 . . . Potosí, 16 de febrero de 1783," BNP, "Papeles varios" (microfilm copy in *Documents microfilmed by C. G. Crampton: Peru and Bolivia*, Bancroft Library, reel 3).

70. Melo, f. 1v.

71. "Informe del fiscal," ANP, Sección Histórica, "Derecho Indígena," cuaderno 283 [1750], ff. 3–3v.

72. *Ibid.*, cuaderno 283 [1750], f. 3v.

73. See Varese, pp. 82–85.

74. ANP, Sección Histórica, "Derecho Indígena," cuaderno 825, esp. ff. 86–89; also Melo, "Diario histórico," f. 4.

75. *Descripción del virreinato del Perú*, p. 78.

76. Salinas y Córdoba, pp. 247, 252–53.

77. Bueno, p. 33.

78. ANP, Sección Histórica, "Derecho Indígena," cuaderno 825, f. 89.

79. *Ibid.*, f. 123v.

80. *Ibid.*, ff. 86–87.

81. *Ibid.*, cuaderno 267, f. 36.

82. See, for example, the dispute in ANP, "Tierras de Comunidad," legajo 2, cuaderno 16.

83. "Títulos de la comunidad de Chaclla," ANP, "Títulos de comunidades," mandados protocolizar, f. 25.

84. ANP, "Tierras de Comunidad," legajo 5, cuaderno 44.

85. Melo, "Diario histórico," f. 19v.

86. ANP, Sección Histórica, "Derecho Indígena," cuaderno 288, f. 1v.

87. Salinas y Córdoba, p. 245.

88. Bravo de Lagunas y Castilla, pp. 184–88.

89. Salinas y Córdoba, p. 253.

90. *Ibid.*, p. 254.

91. ANP, Sección Histórica, "Derecho Indígena," cuaderno 287 [1726–53], ff. 2–2v, 4–5 (pagination inconsistent).

92. Moro Chimo Capac, reel 3.

93. ANP, Sección Histórica, "Derecho Indígena," cuaderno 149, ff. 19–25.

94. "Testamento de José de la Cruz, 11 de abril de 1713," ANP, Sección Histórica, "Testamentos de Indios," legajo 2, unclassified.

95. ANP, Sección Histórica, "Derecho Indígena," cuaderno 699 [1711], f. 36v.

96. "Causa criminal de hechicería contra D. Francisco Julcarilpo y su cuñada Da. Francisca de Oría, 1730," AA, Visitas de Idolatría, legajo 3, cuaderno 15. Much of my work with these materials, which are now being edited and prepared for publication by Guillermo Cox, was originally made possible by John H. Rowe, who graciously gave me access to the transcripts he had made of these documents in 1952.

97. Surnames from the 1750's were drawn from the census of Huarochirí in 1751: ANP, Sección Histórica, "Derecho Indígena," cuaderno 284, 286; contemporary surnames were obtained from conversations in Huarochirí and from a visit to the local cemetery for a survey of tombstones (field notes, 1968).

98. A *tembladera* is a vase made of hammered gold or silver that got its name because its sides were so thin that they vibrated under the impact of a breath of wind. These vases were used as a form of savings in colonial society, since bits of metal could be clipped or cut from their sides to use as payment. A *mate* is a cup, usually made of a carved gourd, that is used for drinking tea made of the *mate* leaves imported from Paraguay.

99. "Causa criminal de hechicería contra Don Francisco Julcarilpo y su cuñada Da. Francisca de Oría, 1730," AA, Visitas de Idolatría, legajo 3, cuaderno 15.

100. "Causa criminal contra Gerónimo Pumayauri, 1700," AA, Visitas de Idolatría, legajo 4, cuaderno 49.

101. Lynch, vol. 1, pp. 198–99.

102. Conde de Superunda, "Relación de gobierno," in Fuentes, vol. 4, p. 137.

103. For the most capable and persuasive statement of this argument, see Céspedes del Castillo.

104. Sánchez-Albornoz, "La saca de mulas."

105. *Ibid.*, p. 262, n. 3.

106. "Parecer del M.R.P. Diego Josef Merlo . . . sobre la consulta que hace el Gral. D. Manuel de Elcorrobarrutia . . . si le será lícito hacer su repartimiento . . . ," in Paz, vol. 2, pp. 308–12.

107. The tariff lists of the legalized repartimiento de mercancías are reproduced in Moreno Cebrián, pp. 317–55.

108. *Ibid.*, p. 88. 109. *Ibid.*, p. 338.

110. Macera, "Introducción," p. 11. 111. *Ibid.*, p. 24.

112. Moreno Cebrián, pp. 317–54.

113. ANP, "Tierras de Comunidades," legajo 8, cuaderno 63.

114. *Ibid.*, legajo 2, cuaderno 16.

115. Quoted in *ibid.*, f. 64v.

116. *Ibid.*, legajo 5, cuaderno 44.

117. Inventory of the properties of Pedro Julcarilpo contained in the "Causa criminal de hechecería contra D. Francisco Julcarilpo y su cuñada Da. Francisca de Oría, 1730," AA, Visitas de Idolatría, legajo 3, cuaderno 15.

Chapter Seven: The Cutting Edge

1. Chamberlain, "The Concept of the 'Señor Natural'."
2. On Huaman Poma, see his *Nueva corónica y buen gobierno*, and Wachtel, "Pensamiento salvaje y aculturación."
3. Stern, "Algunas consideraciones," p. 227.
4. "Libro del notario público Diego Gutiérrez, 1550," BNP, Sala de Manuscritos (A-36), ff. 279v, 449v; "Libro del notario público Diego Gutiérrez, 1545–1555," ANP, Sección Notarial, ff. 501–2. Documents brought to my attention by James Lockhart.
5. Espinosa Soriano, *Destrucción del Imperio de los Incas*.
6. Polo de Ondegardo, "Copia de unos capitulos," p. 276.
7. Matienzo, pp. 50–53.
8. The first royal cédula ordering the foundation of Indian towns in Peru was promulgated in 1549, during the administration of Pedro de la Gasca. See Espinosa Soriano, "El alcalde mayor indigena," pp. 200–201; see also Matienzo, *Gobierno del Perú*, p. 48.
9. See Spalding, "El kuraka," pp. 42–45.
10. On the activities of the Indian elite in the civil wars among the Spaniards, see Huaman Poma de Ayala, pp. 410–13; on the role of the elite in the rebellion of Manco Inca, see *ibid.*, p. 407.
11. "Memorial para el buen asiento," p. 173.
12. *Ibid.*, p. 167.
13. *Ibid.*
14. Toledo, "Carta a la corona, 20 de marzo de 1573," in Levillier, ed., *Gobernantes del Perú*, vol. 5, pp. 27–31.
15. "Memorial que D. Francisco de Toledo dió al Rey . . . del estado en que dejó las cosas del Perú," in Beltrán y Rózpide, p. 86.
16. Toledo's proposals for the organization of Peruvian colonial society are outlined in his "carta de D. Francisco de Toledo a Su Majestad, Cuzco, 1 de marzo de 1572," in Levillier, ed., *Gobernantes del Perú*, vol. 4, pp. 48–208.
17. *Ibid.*, pp. 130–32.
18. *Ibid.*, p. 118.
19. Romero, "Libro de la visita general," pp. 163–72.
20. *Ibid.*, pp. 163–64.
21. *Recopilación de leyes*, Lib. VI, Tít. III, ley xviii [1618].
22. Romero, "Libro de la visita general," p. 191.
23. Dávila Brizeño, p. 70.
24. *Ibid.*, pp. 70–71, 74, 76.
25. The number of towns in the province is derived from *ibid.* The population of the province as recorded in the general census ordered by Francisco de Toledo is contained in the "Relación de oficios que se proveen en la gobernación de los reinos y provincias del Perú [1583]," in Levillier, ed., *Gobernantes del Perú*, vol. 9, p. 191.
26. Matienzo, p. 48.
27. The ordinances of Toledo dealing with the structure of Indian village government form the first nine títulos of Book 2 of Ballesteros, *Tomo primero de las ordenanzas del Perú*. The structure of the Indian cabildo is outlined in Tít. I, órdenes i–xiii.

28. *Ibid.*, órden i; *Recopilación de leyes*, Lib. VI, Tít. III, ley xv [1618].

29. This assertion is based upon a survey of cases presented to the Audiencia by the Indians contained in ANP, Sección Histórica, "Derecho Indígena." See also the lists of alcaldes there in cuadernos 354, 283 [1751], and 284 [1752]. The latter two are based on the censuses of Huarochirí and Chaclla in 1751–52.

30. For the laws regulating the duties and conduct of the alcalde, see Ballesteros, Lib. II, Tít. II, órdenes i–XXXVI.

31. *Ibid.*, Tít. I, órden viii.

32. *Ibid.*, órden iv.

33. "De una carta," p. 234.

34. "Carta a S. M. del Lic. Castro, Los Reyes, 12 de enero de 1566," in Levillier, ed., *Gobernantes del Perú*, vol. 3, p. 137.

35. *Recopilación de leyes*, Lib. VI, Tít. III, leyes vi, vii.

36. Ballesteros, Lib. II, Tít. VIII, órden iii.

37. Toledo was ordered to institute schools in repartimientos; see the "Despacho a Toledo, 28 de diciembre de 1568," in Lissón Chavez, ed., vol. 2, doc. 8, p. 452. Toledo ordered that a school be established in each repartimiento, staffed by a hispanized or *ladino* Indian; Ballesteros, Lib. II, Tít. VIII, órden iii. The first cédula that I have found specifying schools in each village with a resident priest is dated 1685: "Real cédula que se enseñe a los indios la lengua española y se pongan escuelas, Madrid, 7 de julio de 1685," in Konetzke, ed., vol. 2, doc. 520, pp. 766–67. The inspectors who visited the priests of the Archbishopric of Lima, however, required the village priests to maintain a school in their doctrinas as early as the mid-seventeenth century. See "Visita de Chaclla, 1642," in AA, Visitas de Huarochirí, legajo 1.

38. See, for example, "Visita de Chaclla, 1642," and "Visita de San Pedro de Casta, 1721," in AA, Visitas de Huarochirí, legajo 1.

39. Toledo specified a salary in kind: Ballesteros, Lib. II, Tít. VIII, órden iii. In the eighteenth century, however, the schoolmasters were paid 30 pesos per year out of the tribute moneys since, according to the Contaduría de Tributos, community funds were lacking. See the "Retasa del repartimiento de Huarochirí, 1753," ANP, Sección Histórica, "Derecho Indígena," cuaderno 287, ff. 7v–8 (pagination inconsistent).

40. Ballesteros, Lib. II, Tít. VIII, órden iii.

41. *Recopilación de leyes*, Lib. VI, Tít. III, leyes vi, vii.

42. "Cédula real por la que se ordene a las autoridades de Quito prohiban el abuso de los que por ociosidad se dedican a la música, setiembre de 1565," in *Colección de Reales Cédulas dirigidas a la Real Audiencia de Quito*, vol. 1, p. 130.

43. Huaman Poma de Ayala, p. 448.

44. Matienzo, p. 51.

45. "Carta de D. Francisco de Toledo a S. M., Cuzco, 1 de marzo de 1572," in Levillier, ed., *Gobernantes del Perú*, vol. 4, pp. 116–17.

46. Loayza, "Memorial de las cosas del Perú tocantes a los indios [1586]," p. 586.

47. See, for example, the salaries specified in ANP, Sección Histórica, "Derecho Indígena," cuaderno 189 [1705], f. 19, and cuaderno 287 [1726–53], ff. 3v–4, f. 4 (inconsistent pagination).

48. *Recopilación de leyes*, Lib. VI, Tít. VII, leyes i, ii.

49. Espinosa Soriano, "El alcalde mayor indígena," pp. 222–24.

50. Dávila Brizeño, p. 70; "Los jesuitas en Huarochirí—1577," in Avila, *Dioses y hombres de Huarochirí*, p. 245.

51. Espinosa Soriano, "El alcalde mayor indígena," pp. 221–24; Don Sebastian Quispe Ninavilca's title of office can be found on pp. 262–66.

52. "Prevenciones hechas por el Lic. Castro para el buen gobierno del reino del Perú . . . Los Reyes, 1565," in Levillier, ed., *Gobernantes del Perú*, vol. 3, pp. 117–18.

53. Ballesteros, Lib. II, Tít. I, órden vii.

54. Matienzo, p. 51.

55. Huaman Poma de Ayala, pp. 687, 809.

56. Diez de San Miguel, p. 434.

57. Huaman Poma de Ayala, p. 768 (quote), and pp. 492, 791.

58. "Consulta del consejo de las Indias sobre las proposiciones que hizo el Capitán Andrés de Deza pidiendo que los españoles pueden vivir libremente en pueblos de indios [1628]," in Konetzke, ed., vol. 2, doc. 201, p. 310.

59. Huaman Poma de Ayala, p. 539.

60. "Carta de D. Francisco de Toledo a S. M., Cuzco, 1 de marzo de 1572," in Levillier, ed., *Gobernantes del Perú*, vol. 4, p. 128.

61. *Ibid.*, pp. 127–29.

62. See the Council of the Indies' decision regarding Andrés de Deza's petition of 1628, in Konetzke, ed., vol. 2, doc. 201, p. 310.

63. See Ayans, "Breve relación de los agravios que reciben los indios que ay desde cerca del Cuzco hasta Potosí [1596]." See also "Representación de la ciudad del Cuzco, en el año de 1768, sobre excesos de corregidores y curas," in *Relaciones de los vireyes y audiencias que han governado el Perú*, vol. 3, pp. 207–306; ANP, Sección Histórica, "Derecho Indígena," cuaderno 187 [1702], ff. 21, 43ff.

64. "Real cédula sobre que los indios vivan en sus tierras y casas, Tordesillas, 12 de julio de 1600," in Konetzke, ed., vol. 3, doc. 41, p. 63.

65. "Carta del Arzobispo de Lima, D. Pedro Villagomez, sobre la memoria de D. Pedro de Loma y D. Francisco de Ugarte, en razón de la reducción de los indios a sus pueblos [1663]," in Lissón Chávez, ed., vol. 5, doc. 2,094, p. 364.

66. ANP, Sección Histórica, "Derecho Indígena," cuaderno 284 [1751], ff. 81, 154–64; "Razón de los tributarios de la provincia de Huarochirí [1779–80]," in "Libro primero de los cargos y distribución del Ramo de Tributos de las provincias de la jurisdicción de este virreinato de Lima según las últimas matrículas de cada uno de ellas [1781]," ANP, Sección Histórica, unclassified; and ANP, Sección Histórica, "Derecho Indígena," cuaderno 189 [1705], f. 3.

67. "Causa criminal contra Don Sebastían Quispe Ninavilca, mestizo al revés, May 17, 1660," AA, Visitas de Idolatría, legajo 2, cuaderno 13; "Causa contra el Lic. Juan Bernabé de la Madris, Melchor de Lumbria y Doña Francisca Melchora, mestiza de Huarochirí," AA, Visitas de Idolatría, legajo 4, cuaderno 33.

68. The lowest-ranking kurakas paid tribute unless they were specifically noted as nobles; see ANP, Sección Histórica, "Derecho Indígena," cuaderno 284 [1751], ff. 115–17, 132–32v; cuaderno 286 [1752], ff. 80v–84.

69. The Indian *colegios*, originally provided for by Toledo, did not actually begin functioning until a half-century later. See Rowe, "Movimiento nacional Inca," p. 5.

70. "Causa criminal de hechicería contra Isabel Huanay, 1642," AA, Visitas de Idolatría, legajo 2, cuaderno 8.

71. "Causa criminal de hechicería contra María Pomaticlla, 1660," AA, Visitas de Idolatría, legajo 4, cuaderno 32, f. 6.

72. Rivera, "El Malku," p. 17.

73. "Causa criminal de hechicería contra Gerónimo Pumayauri, Langa, 1700," AA, Visitas de Idolatría, legajo 4, cuaderno 49.

74. Complaints about the appropriation of land by kurakas are common; references can be found throughout the ANP, Sección Histórica, "Derecho Indígena."

75. "Títulos de la comunidad de Chaclla," ANP, Títulos de comunidad, mandados protocolizar.

76. Rivera, "El Malku," pp. 10, 14–16; "Causa criminal de hechicero de oficio seguido contra Don Francisco Julcarilpo y su cuñada Doña Francisca de Oría, 1730," AA, Visitas de Idolatría, legajo 3, cuaderno 15. For further material on the mercantile and financial activities of the Andean elite, see Larson, "Caciques," p. 89.

77. "Consulta del Consejo de las Indias sobre los memoriales de Don Jerónimo de Limaylla, indio de la provincia de Jauja, Madrid, 26 de marzo de 1678," in Konetzke, ed., vol. 2, doc. 451, pp. 653–56.

78. "Real cédula . . . mandando a los Virreyes, Audiencias, Gobernadores, Arzobispos y Obispos de las Indias cuiden con particular atención de que los indios sean admitidos en las religiones, educados en los Colegios, y promovidos según su méjor capacidad, 11 de setiembre de 1766," in Paz, vol. 2, pp. 282–88.

79. Campbell, p. 34.

80. "Relación que escribe el Conde de Superunda . . . de los principales sucesos de su gobierno . . . 1756," in Fuentes, ed. and comp., vol. 4, p. 284.

81. Juan and Ulloa, p. 321.

82. Rowe, "Colonial Portraits."

83. "Relación que escribe el Conde de Superunda," in Fuentes, ed. and comp., vol. 4, p. 98; see also Rowe, "Movimiento nacional inca," pp. 8–10.

84. See Macera, "Informaciones geográficas del Perú colonial."

85. ANP, Sección Histórica, "Derecho Indígena," cuaderno 187 [1703], f. 4.

86. *Ibid.*, f. 11.

87. Hoyo, p. 168.

88. "Carta del Arzobispo de Lima, D. Pedro Villagómez, sobre la memoria de D. Pedro de Loma y D. Francisco de Ugarte en razón de la reducción de los indios a sus pueblos [1663]," in Lissón Chávez, ed., vol. 5, doc. 2,094, p. 400.

89. ANP, Sección Histórica, "Derecho Indígena," cuaderno 699 [1711], f. 12v.

90. *Ibid.*, cuaderno 286 [1752], f. 133v.

91. "Real cédula para que se atienda al remedio de los agravios que los caciques hacen a los indios, Madrid, 2 de marzo de 1690," in Konetzke, ed., vol. 2, doc. 563, pp. 124–25.

92. ANP, Sección Histórica, "Derecho Indígena," cuadernos 284 [1751] and 286 [1752]. Estimates of the composition and size of the Indian nobility are based upon the repartimientos of Huarochirí and Chaclla only, since no people recognized as noble appear in the census of the repartimiento of Yauli, newly organized and incorporated into the province of Huarochirí in the mid-eighteenth century.

93. Melo, f. 6; ANP, Sección Histórica, "Derecho Indígena," cuaderno 284.

94. Field notes, 1968 season, Huarochirí, Book 3, pp. 45–46. Note, however, that the Cajahuaringas in 1750 were kurakas not of Huarochirí, but of the neighboring waranqa of Chaucarima. Such relocation of elite lineages happened in the colonial period, and may well have taken place after political independence also.

95. Rowe, "Movimiento nacional inca," p. 25.
96. Rivera Serna, p. 144.

Chapter Eight: Belief and Resistance

1. Lohmann Villena, "La restitución."
2. Elliott, *Imperial Spain*, p. 97.
3. *Ibid.*, pp. 210–11.
4. See the description by Cristóbal de Molina, quoted in Hemming, pp. 172–73.
5. Duviols, *La Lutte*, pp. 82–83.
6. For the decrees of the first Conciliar Council of Lima regarding the Indians, see Vargas Ugarte, vol. 1, pp. 3–35.
7. Duviols, *La Lutte*, p. 39; Vargas Ugarte, vol. 1, constituciones nos. 38, 39, pp. 29–32.
8. Vargas Ugarte, vol. 1, constitución 38, p. 29.
9. *Ibid.*
10. Quoted in Duviols, *La Lutte*, p. 41.
11. On the Taki Onqoy, see Ossio, ed., especially the articles by Millones and Wachtel, pp. 83–142.
12. Cristóbal de Molina, cited in Wachtel, "Rebeliones y milenarismo," pp. 121–22.
13. See Chapter Two above.
14. Testimony from the investigation by Cristóbal de Albornoz into the Taki Onqoy, quoted by Wachtel in "Rebeliones y milenarismo," p. 137, n. 75.
15. Testimony quoted by Wachtel in "Rebeliones y milenarismo," p. 137, n. 77.
16. See the descriptions of the worship of the wak'as Chaupiñamca and Pariacaca of Huarochirí in Avila, *Dioses y hombres de Huarochirí*, pp. 67, 75, 85–89. Craig Morris has also reported the presence of what appears to be the remains of an oracle in Huánuco Viejo, located during his excavations there. Verbal communication, 1975, Columbia University.
17. Millones, "Un movimiento nativista," p. 88.
18. Testimony quoted by Wachtel in "Rebeliones y milenarismo," p. 137, n. 71.
19. *Ibid.*, p. 144.   20. *Ibid.*, p. 123.
21. Matienzo, pp. 6–11, quote on p. 11.   22. *Ibid.*, p. 11.
23. Toledo's "Libro de la Visita," quoted in Duviols, *La Lutte*, p. 124.
24. See Elliott, *Imperial Spain*, pp. 99–100.
25. Population figures from 1572 are drawn from the summaries in Vásquez de Espinosa, pp. 644–65; those for 1792 are taken from Fisher, p. 6, and from the "Estado geográfico del virreinato del Perú, sus intendentes, partidas, doctrinas, pueblos, anexos y sus pobladores con distinción de clases y sexos como se manifiesta [1791]," AGI, Estado, 75, photocopy courtesy of James F. King.
26. For an example of the priests' zealousness for state over faith, see the letter of the Viceroy Conde de Superunda to the Crown, Lima, Sept. 24, 1750, in F. Loayza, ed., pp. 161–62.
27. See Bocanegra, *Ritual formulario*, copy consulted through the courtesy of John H. Rowe.
28. Duviols, *La Lutte*; the records of the investigations can be found in AA, Visitas de Idolatría, spanning the period from the 1640's to the 1730's.
29. See the biography of Avila by Pierre Duviols in Avila, *Dioses y hombres de Huarochirí*, pp. 218–29.

30. *Recopilación de leyes*, Lib. V, Tít. VII, ley xxi; Lib. III, Tít. X, ley xxii; Lib. VI, Tít. VI, ley vii. Solórzano Pereira, Book 2, cap. 30, punto 27.

31. Quoted by Duviols in Avila, *Dioses y hombres de Huarochirí*, p. 218.

32. Duviols, "Bio-bibliografía de Francisco de Avila," *Dioses y hombres de Huarochirí*, p. 218.

33. "Estado geográfico del virreinato del Perú [1791]" (cited in n. 25 above).

34. Avila, "Relación."

35. Arriaga (page references in subsequent notes are to the English translation).

36. The edict opening the investigation was read in the church of Huarochirí on Jan. 11, 1660; final sentencing of the accused and the carrying out of the sentences took place on May 28, 1660. AA, Visitas de Idolatría, 2 legajos.

37. *Ibid.*, legajo 2, cuaderno 16.

38. See, for example, the "Causa criminal de hechicería contra Lorenzo Llacsayauri y su muger, Juana Tantamallao, ayllu Llaguas, San Lorenzo de Quinti," *ibid.*, legajo 2, cuaderno 23.

39. "Causa contra Inez Chumbiticlla, ayllu Huancaya, San Lorenzo de Quinti," *ibid.*, legajo 2, cuaderno 25.

40. For the recommendations to the inspectors of idolatry, see Arriaga, pp. 115–16, 126.

41. "Causa criminal contra María Pomaticlla, ayllu Queripa, San Lorenzo de Quinti," AA, Visitas de Idolatría, legajo 4, cuaderno 32, f. 12.

42. Arriaga, p. 114.

43. The data that follow have been extracted from the eleven distinct idolatry investigations in AA, Visitas de Idolatría.

44. "Causa criminal de hechicería contra María Huanico, mestiza, ayllu Llaguas, San Lorenzo de Quinti," AA, Visitas de Idolatría, legajo 2, cuaderno 21.

45. "Causa criminal de hechicería contra Lorenzo Llacsayauri . . . " (cited in n. 38 above).

46. *Ibid.*, ff. 12–13, 16v.

47. *Ibid.*, ff. 14v–16.

48. "Causa criminal . . . contra María Huanico" (cited in n. 44 above), f. 7.

49. "Causa criminal contra el Lic. Juan Bernabé de la Madris, Melchor de Lumbria, y Doña Francisca Melchora, mestiza, San Lorenzo de Quinti, 1660," AA, Visitas de Idolatría, legajo 4, cuaderno 33.

50. *Ibid.*

51. "Causa criminal contra D. Sebastián Quispe Ninavilca," AA, Visitas de Idolatría, legajo 2, cuaderno 13.

52. "Causa criminal contra María Pomaticlla . . . " (cited in n. 41 above), ff. 5v–6.

53. "Causa criminal contra Lucía Suyu Cargua, Juan Baptista, y Juana Sacsahuaria, ayllu Hualcaraya, San Lorenzo de Quinti, 1660," AA, Visitas de Idolatría, legajo 2, cuaderno 14, f. 4v.

54. *Ibid.*, ff. 1v–2.

55. "Causa criminal contra Isabel Choqui, ayllu Collana, San Juan de Tantaranche, 1660," AA, Visitas de Idolatría, legajo 3, cuaderno 1.

56. "Causa criminal de hechicería contra Lorenzo Llacsayauri . . . " (cited in n. 38 above), ff. 9–11.

57. "Causa criminal contra Lucía Suyu Cargua . . . " (cited in n. 53 above), ff. 2–2v.

58. *Ibid.*; and "Causa criminal contra Isabel Choque . . ." (cited in n. 55 above).
59. Avila, *Dioses y hombres de Huarochirí*, pp. 69–71.
60. "Causa criminal contra Juan de Rojas, 1723," and "Causa criminal contra Francisco Julcarilpo, 1730," AA, Visitas de Idolatría, legajo 3, cuadernos 9, 15.
61. "Causa criminal contra Francisco Julcarilpo . . ." (cited in n. 60 above), cuaderno 15, f. 12.
62. "Causa criminal contra Juan de Rojas . . ." (cited in n. 60 above), cuaderno 9.
63. González Holguín, p. 232.
64. "Causa criminal contra Francisco Julcarilpo . . ." (cited in n. 60 above), f. 11.
65. Duviols, *La Lutte*, p. 179.
66. Francisco de Avila, quoted in Duviols, *La Lutte*, p. 179.
67. Clayton, "Local Initiative and Finance in Defense of the Viceroyalty of Peru."

Chapter Nine: The Challenge to Colonialism

1. "Copia de una carta escrita en Lima sobre el levantamiento de los indios en el año de 1750," Biblioteca Colombina, Seville, Mss. 63-6-29, tomo de varios. Copy obtained through the courtesy of John H. Rowe.
2. See Campbell, pp. 34–35.
3. Rowe, "The Incas Under Spanish Colonial Institutions," p. 157.
4. José de Mugaburu, *Diario de Lima*, pp. 131–32.
5. See F. Loayza, ed.; see also Varese, pp. 60–85. More work on the rebellions of the seventeenth and eighteenth centuries is currently being done by John Rowe and Scarlet O'Phelan. See, for example, O'Phelan's recent "El Sur Andino" and "Túpac Amaru y las sublevaciones del siglo XVIII." Their work should do much to fill out our sketchy outline of Indian resistance to Spanish colonial rule.
6. Sotelo, pp. 38–41.
7. For classic examples of the two extremes mentioned, see the Conde de Superunda's letter to the Crown, Sept. 24, 1750, in F. Loayza, ed., pp. 161–78, and "Relación y verdadero romance que declara la inconsiderada y atrevida sublevación, que intentaron hazer los indios mal acordados, y algunos mestizos, en la ciudad de Lima," in Sotelo, pp. 21–24.
8. Melo, "Diario histórico del levantamiento de la provincia de Huarochirí."
9. Conde de Superunda, in F. Loayza, ed., pp. 161–62.
10. *Ibid.*, pp. 162–63.
11. "Copia de una carta . . ." (cited in n. 1 above), f. 1; José Antonio Manso de Velasco, Conde de Superunda, "Relación que escribe . . . [1756]," in Fuentes, ed. and comp., vol. 4, p. 22.
12. "Copia de una carta . . ." (cited in n. 1 above), ff. 1–2.
13. *Ibid.*, f. 2; and Conde de Superunda, in F. Loayza, ed., p. 166.
14. Conde de Superunda, in F. Loayza, ed., p. 166.
15. "Copia de una carta . . ." (cited in n. 1 above), f. 3.
16. Melo, "Diario histórico," f. 7.   17. *Ibid.*, f. 8.
18. *Ibid.*, ff. 12–12v.   19. *Ibid.*, ff. 13–13v.
20. *Ibid.*, f. 4.
21. Conde de Superunda, in F. Loayza, ed., p. 169.

22. *Ibid.*, p. 177.
23. *Ibid.*, p. 175.
24. Harth-Terré and Márquez Abanto, pp. 409, 433–34; Lee and Bromley, eds., *Libros de cabildo de Lima*, vol. 14 (1602–5), pp. 435–36.
25. Romero, *Historia económica*, p. 141.
26. For example, see ANP, Sección Histórica, "Cabildo (Gremios)," legajo 20, documents without order or title from 1781–82 and 1767–77. See also the article "Ordenanzas del Gremio de Zapateros," pp. 10–11.
27. ANP, Sección Histórica, "Cabildo (Gremios)," legajo 20, documents without order or title from 1767–77, case from 1777.
28. See, for example, the testaments in ANP, Sección Histórica, "Testamentos de Indios," legajo 1; and in ANP, Sección Notarial, the "Registros de escrituras públicas" of Francisco Cayetano de Arredondo (1710–18 and 1727–31), Francisco Roldán (1734–42), and Francisco Huamán Minayulli (1778–79 and 1780–81). See also Harth-Terre, "On the Discovery of Documents."
29. Concolorcorvo, "El lazarillo," p. 378.
30. See the contracts of apprenticeship scattered through the "Registros de escrituras públicas" in ANP, Sección Notarial—for example, of Francisco Huaman Minayulli [1780–81], ff. 27v–28, 670–72; and of Francisco Cayetano de Arredondo [1727–31], ff. 588, 771–72.
31. Conde de Superunda, in F. Loayza, ed., p. 175.

32. *Ibid.*, pp. 171–72.   33. Melo, f. 6v.
34. *Ibid.*, ff. 27–27v.   35. *Ibid.*, f. 18v.
36. *Ibid.*, f. 9v.   37. *Ibid.*

38. "Copia de una carta . . . " (cited in n. 1 above), f. 6. I have modified the text somewhat, since the grammar and form of the original—although not the style—are extremely rough.
39. *Ibid.*, f. 6v.
40. *Ibid.*
41. Melo, f. 6v.
42. Conde de Superunda, in F. Loayza, ed., p. 175.
43. Melo, f. 13v.
44. See, for example, the letter of a corregidor to the Indian alcaldes quoted in Chapter Seven.
45. Melo, ff. 12–12v; the arrival of Robladillo, the mestizo, in Lima is recorded in "Copia de una carta . . . " (cited in n. 1), f. 12, postscript.

46. Melo, ff. 20–20v.   47. *Ibid.*, f. 20v.
48. *Ibid.*, f. 30v–31.   49. *Ibid.*, ff. 46v–48v.
50. Sotelo, pp. 38–47.   51. Melo, f. 51.
52. Hoyo, p. 183.

53. "Instrucción que los corregidores y comisionados nombrados por la visita general de tribunales de justicia, y real hacienda de estos reynos, deben observar provisionalmente para la formación de nuevos padrones de tributarios . . .," included in the "Instrucción de revisitas o matrículas formada por el Señor Don Jorge Escobedo y Alarcón . . . [1784]," Museo Mitre (Buenos Aires), Papeles diversos, Lima, 1768–84, doc. 1, cap. 29.
54. Conde de Superunda, in F. Loayza, ed., p. 176.

Conclusion

1. Caballero, pp. 113–14.

Bibliography

I. Introduction

The Bibliography that follows provides a partial introduction to some of the topics and preoccupations of those scholars who have attempted to reconstruct the history of a people and a society that left no autonomous records of their own. Moreover, the culture discussed in the preceding pages was not that of the people who left the only record we have of it—of its beliefs, its practices, and its behavior. The Europeans who conquered the people inhabiting the Andes in the sixteenth century used those people to labor for them. They exploited them, reorganized them for their own benefit, and even had children by them. But their attempts to comprehend the culture and the attitudes of the people they subjugated were distorted by their own culture, through which they had to filter the information they obtained on the Andean peoples, and in terms of which they interpreted that information.

Today, almost a half millennium later, how do we go about reconstructing a culture that has been in large measure lost to us? The descendants of the people conquered in the sixteenth century still live in the Andes, but their culture—like their physical and genetic characteristics—has been thoroughly transformed by centuries of subjugation to and contact with a culture imposed from outside. The behavior and attitudes of the predominantly peasant groups descended from the people who once ruled the Andes are today the subject matter of anthropologists interested in the analysis and interpretation of what are called "non-Western" cultures—those different from our (and their) own. Until recently, the history of the peoples of the Andes prior to the arrival of the Europeans has been the province of the archaeologists, whereas the history of those peoples under European rule has been the province of the historians, who were trained to study the evolution of European bureaucracy or the structures of colonialism. This division of labor has truncated the history of the societies that inhabited the Andes at the moment of their conquest. It has left the impression, not always intentional, that the conquered majority offered little or no resistance to its subjugation, and that the new rulers reproduced the European cultures from which they had come with little or no modification stimulated by the culturally distinct majority among whom they lived.

This image, simple and attractive to those who belonged or felt they belonged to the European elite, was always challenged by the facts. The Andes were the site of massive and desperate rebellions both during the period of European rule and after it—rebellions that make a mockery of the notion of "the passive Indian." Historians and other scholars found themselves faced with the necessity of explaining these events within the historical framework they had built for themselves, an enterprise that was not always successful and that left many questions for later generations to ponder. The most honest and dedicated among these scholars—and there were many such—did not hesitate to present these events in ways that stimulated questions about the nature of the colonial system and the alleged passivity and submissiveness of the conquered peoples. With the accumulation of more materials and the construction of the foundations for a solid history of the Andean area, new generations chose to make these questions the center of their attention.

Interest in the history of Andean society under European rule, and the impact of the Europeans upon the people they conquered, focused initially, as might be expected, upon the mechanisms of colonial rule. The reports of early eyewitnesses; the debates over the proper way to administer the new possessions, which filled the years after the European invasion both in the new colony and in Spain; the administrative structures that were developed and the protests against both their excesses and, not infrequently, their very existence by concerned members of the dominant society—all formed the basis of scholarly research. Until the second half of this century, the source materials available for the study of native Andean society consisted largely of the documents generated by the colonial bureaucracy, carefully collected, edited, and published by scholars whose work laid the foundation for later interpretation.

A rapid survey of Part III of this Bibliography, which for reasons of space has been principally confined to materials to which some direct reference is made in the text, will make it immediately clear how much of the work done today continues to rely heavily upon administrative and bureaucratic records. In a reaction against the often schematic and formalized vision of the past projected through those records, many of us have tended to denigrate the importance of the work done by the first generations of scholars who devoted themselves to the publication and analysis of memorials and reports, law codes, and the vast body of material produced by a bureaucracy whose slowness and attention to detail have been condemned by the very historians who are now profiting from those qualities. Without the foundations laid by these scholars, we would lack the essential framework upon which to raise our own "revisions" of their interpretations. Nor can we now dispense with administrative history or reconstruction. The more we learn about the mechanisms of taxation, about the operation and the customs of justice, about the details of local administration, the better able we will be to make creative use of the data ground out by the colonial bureaucracy.

Part III of the Bibliography also contains a sample of the kind of work that I have found useful in seeking to apply the data contained in administrative sources. Anthropologists and ethnologists have contributed a great deal to Andean history, both in volume and in value. Although the specific interpretative models offered by some—though by no means all—anthropologists ignore the elements of time and process that are the focus of history, concentrating instead upon the organization of static "structures" or "systems," the disciplines of anthropology and of history have been drawing closer to each other in recent years, and continued interchange of both concepts and methodologies promises to enrich the work of scholars in both disciplines. In particular, those of us involved in historical research, and especially those of us who must depend heavily upon administrative records, could learn a great deal from the research methodology of the anthropologists. Good fieldwork depends heavily upon asking open-ended, procedural questions of informants, and avoiding as much as possible the kind of question that implicitly or explicitly structures and limits the response. Thus, rather than asking an informant "Why do you do these things in this way?" or "What is the meaning of . . . ?"—questions that are largely incomprehensible to anyone but an academic of Western culture trained to seek, and to produce, abstract explanations of events and behavior—a good field anthropologist is much more likely to ask a question like "What happens if . . . ?" or "What do you do when . . . ?"

Perhaps surprisingly, the administrative records yield far more when interrogated from this perspective than when questioned for abstractions. They are the products of practical minds asking practical questions for specific purposes, and though the purposes need not have any direct relation to the aims and objectives of the historian, we can learn a great deal by attempting to reconstruct or to comprehend what questions the material we read tried to answer. An example of this kind of record is provided by the summaries of disputes over land between communities of Huarochirí brought before the viceregal court. Court records of all kinds are, in effect, raw field data, the record of social interactions in which norms and values are tested and redefined (if under somewhat atypical and strained conditions), much as relationships are tested and redefined in the course of day-to-day existence. The conclusion of the conflict—the decision of the judge—is often of relatively little value. But the process itself—the arguments presented, the alliances revealed, the changing size and composition of the social groups in conflict as the dispute progresses—reflects the social mechanisms, the patterns of alliance and schism, and the networks that bind the society together.

The trial records themselves are also a useful corrective to interpretations based upon law codes and court decisions alone, for specific laws were often ignored by colonial tribunals in favor of local traditions. The Spanish Crown did stipulate that local tradition should be respected except when specifically contradicted by Spanish legislation or religious principles, but the Audiencias carried this general rule even further, ignoring the general regulations regarding land distribution laid down in the sixteenth century in favor of local tradition until the latter part of the eighteenth century. This may be regarded as one more example of the laxity of the colonial bureaucracy, or it may provide a useful counterpoint to the strict interpretation of colonial reality in terms of its legislation. However we choose to view it, it is worth remembering that the law is made by its application rather than by its promulgation, and local circumstances always exercise a considerable influence upon how rules are applied.

The judicial records of the colonial Church, in particular its investigations into native religious practice (or idolatry, as it was called), are also invaluable for documenting social organization, for they consist essentially of the day-to-day records of the ecclesiastical court and permit us to follow the actions and reactions of the people involved in these investigations in great detail. The value of such materials lies in the wealth of specific detail they contain; though daunting and often repetitious, they bring us that much closer to the daily lives and the cultural assumptions of the people we seek to understand. This observation may explain in part the extremely small proportion of material from the Archive of the Indies in Seville, the traditional repository of information for historians of the colonial period, cited in this study. I do not wish to argue that the Archive of the Indies is of little or no worth for studies of this kind; the substantial contributions of María Rost-worowski de Diaz Canseco, the bulk of whose work rests upon material preserved in that great repository, are sufficient in themselves to contradict any such assertion. I remain convinced that much valuable information can be found in the seat of colonial government, but I would also like to emphasize the importance for the social historian of the records that remained in the ex-colonies. What these records lack in volume and completeness they make up in detail. There are often great gaps in them, and they may also be poorly preserved, but these were the working documents of colonial administration. The detail of daily life is often abstracted and summarized in the general reports prepared for the upper levels of any bureaucracy. The minister sees less of the detail, by necessity, than the local police chief, and the latter sees less than the "cop on the beat." The working copies of censuses and tribute lists, marked over with corrections and additions, when they can be found, are a great deal more informative about local conditions than the clean copies prepared for the central administration.

Another discipline upon which I have drawn heavily in the preparation of this work is archaeology, again not only for specific data in interpretations but also for the perspective contained in the work of at least some of its practitioners who have made creative and productive use of documents as well as of the more traditional sources. The work of scholars like Craig Morris and Tom Patterson is stimulating in itself, and it is useful for the historian to learn something of the working methods of archaeology if possible, in order to be able to use the work done by people in this field without being forced to accept the conclusions and the theories that the fieldwork is presented to support.

We could also profit immensely from a dose of the patience of the archaeologist, who is forced to postpone conclusions until after sifting through a significant sample of the mountainous remains of refuse left by people in the course of their daily lives. For in social history as well, much of our most significant data consists of bits and pieces of seemingly disparate information that yield up their meaning only when combined with other bits and pieces. The data we use must be worked and reworked, broken down and recombined—often with information not contained in written records. And at least some of the basic assumptions upon which people built their culture and the practices through which they ensured their survival and even their prosperity emerge only from direct experience of the environment in which they lived. In the case of the Andes, where geography and environment have been major conditioning factors in the evolution of human societies, this is particularly true. Even today, planners and "development" experts—both Peruvian and from outside Peru—trained in the best traditions of Western technology find that their efforts to restructure the local landscape to their specifications often have side effects that accelerate the destruction and impoverishment of that landscape. In this situation, any contribution that can be made to understanding the interaction of human societies and their environment is a potential contribution to the future as well. In that enterprise, the historian and scholar can profit from a good pair of boots, a fascination with the landscape, and a healthy respect for the possible wisdom of traditions that appear, from both historical records and field experience, to have survived the test of time and the efforts of experts on behalf of more recent fashions.

Though I would insist that our understanding of our past and of the origins of the present increases through the constant, considered confrontation of theory and the mass of detail that is the historian's source material, I want finally to emphasize once more the importance of both sides of this equation. In a reaction against the dry, dull summaries of the positivist school, which forswore interpretation on the grounds that the facts would "speak for themselves," at least some contemporary studies have attempted to renovate those summaries by superimposing upon them a theoretical outline that is at best confusing, and at worst even duller than the originals. In generating theory as well as in testing that theory, we cannot dispense with basic research and rely upon the materials of others who have "done their time" in the archives and libraries. For theory, if it is not to become a mere suitcase into which we stuff information, must be continually revitalized by confrontation with data that bring up the difficult and often embarrassing questions of how well that theory really "fits" the reality we seek to comprehend. And finally, the historian's subject matter is ultimately not structures, not abstractions, but people: human groups and societies in the process of constructing, changing, and living their lives. And it is when these people communicate the flavor and tone of their lives and their attitudes in a document—an infrequent but immensely valuable occurence—that we find the reward, and the delight, of the practice of history.

II. Archival and Library Collections

Virtually all of the unpublished data upon which this study is based have been gathered in archives and document collections in the Americas, north and south. As I have noted earlier, I do not want to imply that I regard the massive body of data in the great repositories of the Spanish Empire as unimportant. I have used material from Spain that was brought to my attention by friends and colleagues, and that material lived up to all the traditional expectations about the value of the great Archive of the Indies. Two particularly useful such documents, cited in the text, were the dispute over the coca lands of Quives between the kurakas of Canta and Chaclla, located and used by Waldemar Espinosa Soriano and María Rostworowski de Diaz Canseco, and the charts summarizing the first general census of Peru in 1791, collected by Professor James F. King, who graciously permitted me to consult his copy of the material. Nonetheless, I have found that for local and regional history, the sources to be found in the Americas are generally more than adequate; and frequently, since they are not summaries prepared for superior officials in the seat of government, they contain more detail than similar materials in Madrid or Seville.

The great majority of the sources used in this study may be found in the National Archive of Peru (Archivo Nacional del Perú) and in the National Library (Biblioteca Nacional del Perú), both located in Lima. The colonial sources dealing with Indian society in the National Archive's extensive holdings are to be found primarily in the collections entitled "Derecho Indígena, " "Tierras y Haciendas," and "Títulos de Comunidades," all of which are ordered in an easily consulted, well organized card catalog for the convenience of researchers. A decade ago, there was a considerable body of uncataloged material in the archive, and I worked with and prepared a list of contents of a collection of wills and testaments from the Indian barrio attached to Lima, Santiago del Cercado, and from outlying villages in the valley of Lima. The collection, entitled "Testamentos de Indios," provides valuable insight into the daily lives of Indian people of only moderate income living in and around Lima during the colonial period. The sections entitled "Tierras y Haciendas" and "Títulos de Comunidades" deal with land disputes between Indians and Spaniards, and among the Indians themselves. The "Derecho Indígena" collection consists primarily of cases concerning Indians brought before the Audiencia of Lima and of the records of Indian administration, such as population counts and tribute and mita assessments. Substantial parts of the collection, as well as documents from other parts of the National Archive, have been published in the invaluable *Revista del Archivo Nacional del Perú*, which has been appearing intermittently since the early years of the century.

The notarial section of the Archive has become better known to historians in recent years owing to the extensive use made of its materials by James Lockhart and others who have demonstrated in their work the importance of these records for social history. The notarial section contains a virtually complete series of the notarial records of Lima since the Spanish conquest of Peru. There have been losses, some of which have subsequently appeared in other libraries abroad (as, for example, the collection of notarial records from the conquest period known as the Harkness Collection, which now resides in the Library of Congress). But despite this, the notarial collection has suffered less loss and mutilation than other, more immediately "flashy" sections of the archive. In my own work, I found the three "escribanos de Indios"—notaries who provided services for the members of Indian society in Lima and its environs during the eighteenth century—particularly valuable.

The documentary materials in the Sala de Investigaciones of the Biblioteca Nacional del Perú are both valuable and accessible. Since the great fire that destroyed a large part of the library several decades ago, the surviving documentary materials, many of them burned around the edges, have been carefully preserved and ordered. The Sala also boasts a card catalog that presents all of its documentary holdings in chronological order.

Another extremely valuable archive for the study of the history of the native Andean peasantry (as well as for social history in general) is the Archivo Arzobispal del Perú, the repository of the administrative and other records of the Archbishopric of Lima. I made extensive use of the inspection records of the Indian parishes, as well as of the census data drawn up for the purposes of ecclesiastical administration. But for my purposes, the most valuable holdings of the Archivo Arzobispal were the records of the idolatry investigations carried out in the archbishopric from the 1630's to the early years of the eighteenth century. These day-to-day transcripts of interrogations, punishments, and all the other aspects of this colonial witch-hunt are among the few sources in which the members of Andean society speak directly in their own voices; and although the sources are essentially records of coercion and violence, a considerable amount of local practice and a sense of the personalities of the people involved come through. The complete records of the idolatry investigations contained in the Archivo Arzobispal are now being prepared for publication by Guillermo Cook of Lima.

Outside Lima, the notarial records kept in many provincial cities and towns constitute a largely untapped source of information on provincial social and economic life. Notarial records are private property, and documents dating back to at least the seventeenth century (and in a number of cases the sixteenth) have been handed down from notary to notary. The current owners of these records are, in my experience, generally people who have a full understanding of the historical value of the materials in their care, and who are eager to contribute to the reconstruction of the history of their provinces and their country. I have visited notarial archives in a number of provincial cities in Peru and have uniformly been received warmly and generously. In this study, I have drawn upon material from the notarial archives of Huánuco and of Huaraz. Sr. Guillermo Gayoso G., notary of Huánuco, has records in his collection that date to the 1560's and include not only the kind of material one would expect to find in a notarial office but also local censuses, judicial records, and other sources on the early history of Huánuco. He graciously permitted me to invade his office for a full month, during which time I was barely able to skim the surface of this rich collection. In Huaraz, Sr. Victor Alvarado also permitted me to work in his archive, thus giving me the chance to see material that later disappeared under tons of mud and rock in the great earthquake and landslide that devastated the Callejón de Huaylas, destroying half of Huaraz itself, in 1970.

In Peru, in addition to the archives, an essential source for understanding Andean history is the land itself, both for the actual information it contains and for the lessons it teaches to those willing to study. A walk in the Andes is an experience in history, in which the walker can see at firsthand the record left by past Andean cultures. The foundations of houses built and lived in long before the Europeans invaded the Andes are now occupied by the contemporary descendants of those people, who have raised their straw-mat or stone and mud walls upon those same foundations. Abandoned fortress walls and low pyramids bear witness to the conflicts and the ceremonies of the past, and it is possible to see the techniques of pre-European agriculture still practiced in areas far from urban centers. Preconquest traditions are still maintained, with admixtures from the centuries following the entry of the Europeans; and the old tales once told to explain the origins and the customs of the people who inhabited and cherished the land are still repeated by older members of the highland communities. And the time spent walking the land and talking to people often brings insights that illuminate previously unclear or confusing data.

There is also a great deal of material on colonial Peru outside the Andes. The Archivo General de la Nación Argentina in Buenos Aires, an area that was part of the viceroyalty of Peru until 1776, contains copies of Peruvian records that were sent to Buenos Aires when that city became the capital of the new viceroyalty of La Plata, whose territory included the area of Upper Peru, now Bolivia. For example, copies of the great *visita* of Viceroy Francisco de Toledo in the 1570's were made in the eighteenth century for the southern part of the Andean area and can be consulted in Buenos Aires today, whereas the Lima originals have long since disappeared. And the Argentine National Archive contains a wealth of invaluable material on eighteenth-century Bolivia that is making it possible for scholars to reconstruct a good deal of the social and demographic history of rural society in that part of the *altiplano*.

The Peruvian materials in the Museo Mitre in Buenos Aires are also rich, surely in part because General Mitre was a historian of considerable skill and ability as well as president of his country. The documents in the Peruvian collection include material on the *visita* of Peru by Antonio de Areche in the 1780's as well as considerable data on the Indian revolts that periodically shook the viceroyalty from the middle of the seventeenth century. Among the latter material is a diary of the revolt that took place in Huarochirí in 1750, written by a Spaniard who was at that time a miner in the province and later became the lieutenant to the corregidor, an apparently active and able official whose actions were remembered and referred to by the Indians well into the nineteenth century. The diary, prepared as part of the author's plea for some reward from the viceroy for his efforts and presented to Viceroy Amat y Junient in 1761, is an invaluable source that illuminates not only the Indian revolt but also the attitudes and assumptions of the social sector of which the author was a part.

Finally, the United States has also become the repository of valuable materials from and about the Andes, as a result in part of the collecting fever of its citizens, who later donated their treasures to U.S. libraries and repositories, and in part of the wonders of modern microfilm techniques. The Yale University Library has a wonderful collection of Peruvian colonial manuscripts, unfortunately stored away in boxes and unordered or classified. I was able to use materials from this collection because of the efforts of scholars who have microfilmed these data as well as other materials on colonial administration and Indian revolt in the Andes and left them in the Bancroft Library of the University of California at Berkeley. The Bancroft, though principally concentrating its holdings on western Americana, also contains on film a considerable body of material from the Spanish colonial archives in Seville dealing with colonial South America. Microfilm in the Bancroft Library as well as other microfilmed sources consulted for this study are referred to in the notes in terms of both the location of the available microfilm and the repository of the original document.

III. Individual Works Cited in the Notes

Anderson, Perry. *Lineages of the Absolutist State*. London, 1974.

Arriaga, Father Pablo José de. *Extirpacion de la idolatría en el Perú*. Trans. by L. Clark Keating as *The Extirpation of Idolatry in Peru*. Lexington, Ky., 1968.

Avila, Francisco de. *Dioses y hombres de Huarochirí: Narración quechua recogida por Francisco de Avila* (1598?). Trans. by José María Arguedas. Lima, 1966.

————. "Relación que yo el Dr. Francisco de Avila, cura y beneficiado de la cuidad de Guánuco, hize por mandado del Sr. Arçobispo de Los Reyes acerca de los pueblos de indios de este Arçobispado . . . [1611]," in Avila, *Dioses y hombres de Huarochirí*, pp. 255–59.

Ayans, Antonio del. "Breve relación de los agravios que reciben los indios que ay desde cerca del Cuzco hasta Potosí [1596]," in Rubén Vargas Ugarte, ed., *Pareceres jurídicos en asuntos de indios* (Lima, 1951), pp. 35–88.

Bagú, Sergio. *Estructura social de la colonia*. Buenos Aires, 1952.

Ballesteros, Tomás de. *Tomo primero de las ordenanzas del Perú* [1685]. Lima, 1752.

Bastien, Joseph W. *Mountain of the Condor*. New York, 1978.

Basto Girón, Luís J. "Las mitas de Huamanga y Huancavelica," *Perú Indígena*, no. 13 (1954), pp. 2–28.

Belaunde Guinassí, Manuel. *La encomienda en el Perú*. Lima, 1945.

Beltrán y Rózpide, Ricardo. *Colección de las memorias o relaciones que escribieron los virreyes del Perú acerca del estado en que dejaban las cosas generales del reino*. Madrid, 1921.

Berthelot, Jean. "L'Exploitation des métaux précieux au temps des Incas," *Annales: Economies, Sociétés, Civilisations*, 33, nos. 5–6 (Sept.-Dec. 1978), pp. 948–66.

Bocanegra, Juan Pérez. *Ritual formulario, e institucion de curas, para administrar a los naturales de este Reyno, los santos sacramentos del Baptismo, Confirmacion, Eucarista y Viatico, Penitencia, Extremauncion y Matrimonio, con advertencias muy necesarias.* Lima, 1631. A text for use in the Cuzco area written in Spanish and Aymara-Quechua.

Braudel, Fernand. "Histoire et sciences sociales: la longue durée," *Annales: Economies, Sociétés, Civilisations,* 13, no. 4 (Oct.-Dec. 1958), pp. 725–53.

Bravo de Lagunas y Castilla, Pedro José. *Voto consultivo, que ofrece al excelentíssimo señor don José Antonio Manso de Velasco, Conde de Superunda . . . .* Lima, 1761.

Bronner, Fred. "Peruvian Encomenderos in 1630: Elite Circulation and Consolidation," *Hispanic American Historical Review,* 57, no. 4 (1977), pp. 633–59.

Browman, David. "Demographic Correlations of the Wari Conquest of Junin," *American Antiquity,* 41, no. 4 (Oct. 1976), pp. 465–77.

Bueno, Cosme. *Geografía del Perú virreinal.* Lima, 1951.

Burga, Manuel. *De la encomienda a la hacienda capitalista: el valle de Jequetepeque.* Lima, 1976.

Caballero, José Maria. *Agricultura, Reforma Agraria y pobreza campesina.* Lima, 1980.

Cabello Balboa, Miguel. *Miscelanea Antartica: una historia del Perú antiguo* [1586]. Lima; 1951.

Campbell, Leon. "The Army of Peru and the Tupac Amaru Revolt," *Hispanic American Historical Review,* 56, no. 1 (Feb. 1976), pp. 31–57.

Carrió de la Bandera, Alonso (pseud. Concolorcorvo). "El lazarillo de ciegos caminantes (1777)," in Juan Pérez de Tudela, ed., *Biblioteca de autores españoles,* vol. 122 (Madrid, 1959), pp. 245–407.

————. *Reforma del Perú.* Introduction by Pablo Macera. Lima, 1951.

"Cédulas y provisiones sobre repartimientos de tierras," *Revista del Archivo Nacional del Perú,* 20, no. 1 (1956), pp. 151–70; 20, no. 2 (1956), pp. 417–46; 21, no. 1 (1957), pp. 192–235; 21, no. 2 (1957), pp. 396–472; 22, no.1 (1958), pp. 218–20; 22, no. 2 (1958), pp. 455–71.

Céspedes del Castillo, Guillermo. *Lima y Buenos Aires: Repercusiones económicas y políticas de la creación del virreinato del Rio de la Plata.* Seville, 1947.

Chamberlain, Robert S. "The Concept of the 'Señor Natural' as revealed by Castilian Law and Administrative Documents," *Hispanic American Historical Review,* 19, no. 2 (1930), pp. 130–37.

Chaunu, Pierre, and Huguette Chaunu. *Seville et l'Atlantique.* Paris, 1955–56. 8 vols.

Cieza de León, Pedro de. *El Señorío de los Incas.* Lima, 1967.

Clayton, Lawrence A. "Local Initiative and Finance in Defense of the Viceroyalty of Peru: The Development of Self-Reliance," *Hispanic American Historical Review,* 54, no. 2 (May 1974), pp. 284–304.

Cobo, Bernabé. *Historia del Nuevo Mundo. Obras del padre . . .,* ed. Francisco Mateos. In *Biblioteca de autores españoles,* vols. 91, 92 (Madrid, 1956).

Colección de documentos inéditos para la historia de España. Madrid, 1842–95 (Kraus Reprint, 1964–66). 112 vols.

Colección de Reales Cédulas dirigidas a la Audiencia de Quito, 1538–1600. Quito, Archivo Municipal, vol. 1, 1935.

Collier, George A., Renato Rosaldo, and John D. Wirth, eds. *The Inca and Aztec States, 1400–1800: Anthropology and History.* New York, 1982.

Concolorcorvo. See Carrió de la Bandera, Alonso.

Cook, Noble David, ed. *Padrón de los indios de Lima en 1613.* Lima, 1968.

————. *Tasa de la visita general de don Francisco de Toledo.* Lima, 1975.

Cornblit, Oscar. "Society and Mass Rebellion in Eighteenth-Century Peru and Bolivia," *Latin American Affairs (St. Antony's Papers)*, no. 22 (Oxford, 1970), pp. 9–44.

Dávila Brizeño, Diego. "Descripción y relación de la provincia de los Yauyos toda, Anan Yauyos y Lorin Yauyos," in Marcos Jiménez de la Espada, ed., *Relaciones geográficas de Indias*, vol. 1 (Madrid, 1881), pp. 61–78.

Descripción del virreinato del Perú. Rosario, Argentina, 1968.

Díez de San Miguel, Garci. *Visita hecha a la provincia de Chucuito por Garci Díez de San Miguel en el año 1567*. Paleographic version by Waldemar Espinosa Soriano. Lima, 1964.

Dillehay, Tom. "Pre-Hispanic Resource Sharing in the Central Andes," *Science*, 204, no. 4388 (Apr. 1979), pp. 24–31.

Dobyns, Henry. "Estimating Aboriginal American Population: An Appraisal of Techniques with a New Hemispheric Estimate," *Current Anthropology*, 7, no. 4 (1966), pp. 395–449.

_____. "An Outline of Andean Epidemic History to 1720," *Bulletin of the History of Medicine*, 37, no. 6 (Nov.-Dec. 1963), pp. 493–515.

Dollfus, Olivier. *Les Andes centrales du Pérou et leurs piédmonts*. Lima and Paris, 1965.

_____. "Les Andes intertropicales: une mosaique changeante," *Annales: Economies, Sociétés, Civilisations*, 33, nos. 5–6 (Sept.-Dec. 1978), pp. 895-903.

Duviols, Pierre. "Un Inedit de Cristóbal de Albornoz," *Journal de la Société des Americanistes*, 56 (1967), pp. 7–39.

_____. *La Lutte contre les réligions autochtones dans le Pérou colonial*. Lima and Paris, 1971.

Elliott, John H. *Europe Divided, 1559–1598*. London, 1968.

_____. *Imperial Spain, 1469–1716*. New York, 1963.

Espinosa Soriano, Waldemar. "El alcalde mayor indígena en el virreinato del Perú." *Anuario de Estudios Americanos*, vol. 17 (Seville, 1960), pp. 183–300.

_____. *Destrucción del Imperio de los Incas*. Lima, 1973.

Febres Villarroel, Oscar. "La crisis agrícola en el Perú en el último tércio del siglo XVIII," *Revista Histórica*, 27 (1964), pp. 102–99.

Fisher, John. *Government and Society in Colonial Peru: The Intendant System, 1784–1814*. London, 1970.

Flores Galindo, Alberto. *Sublevaciones populares y sociedad colonial: Tupac Amaru, 1780*. Lima, 1976.

_____. "Tupac Amaru y la sublevación de 1780," in *idem*, pp. 271–323.

Foster-Carter, Aiden. "The Modes of Production Debate," *New Left Review*, 107 (Jan.-Feb. 1978), pp. 58–66.

Fuentes, Manuel Atanasio, ed. and comp., *Memorias de los virreyes que han gobernado en el Perú, durante el tiempo del coloniaje español, impresas de orden suprema*. Lima, 1859. 6 vols.

Garcilaso de la Vega, "El Inca." *Primera Parte de los Comentarios Reales de los Incas*, in Fr. Carmelo Saenz de Santa Maria, S.J., ed., *Biblioteca de autores españoles*, vol. 133 (Madrid, 1960).

Geografía del Perú virreinal. See Bueno, Cosmé.

González Holguín, Diego. *Vocabulario de la lengua general de todo el Perú llamado lengua qquichua o del Inca*. Lima, 1952.

The Harkness Collection in the Library of Congress. Documents from Early Peru. The Pizarros and the Almagros (1531–1578). Washington, D.C., 1936.

Harth-Terré, Emilio. "Cauces de españolización en la sociedad indo-peruana de Lima virreinal." Lima, 1964. Pamphlet.

_____. "On the Discovery of Documents Which Reveal the Negro Slave Trade Among the Lower-Class Indians During the Viceregal Government in Peru." Lima, 1961. Pamphlet.

_____, and Alberto Márquez Abanto. "Las bellas artes en el virreynato del Perú: perspectiva social y económica del artesano virreinal en Lima, siglo XVI," *Revista del Archivo Nacional*, 26, no. 2 (July-Dec. 1962), pp. 353–446.

Helmer, Marie. "La visitación de los Indios Chupachos: Inka et encomendero, 1549," *Travaux de l'Institut Français d'Etudes Andines*, vol. 5 (Lima-Paris, 1955–56), pp. 3–50.

Hemming, John. *The Conquest of the Incas*. New York, 1970.

Hoyo, Juan Josef del. "Estado y economías de los naturales del Perú que se dicen indios y medios simplísimos de corregir [1772]," in Carlos A. Romero and Horacio H. Urteaga, eds., *Colección de libros y documentos referentes a la historia del Perú*, series 1, vol. 4 (Lima, 1917), pp. 161–204.

Huaman Poma de Ayala, Felipe. *Nueva corónica y buen gobierno (Codex peruvien illustré)*, in *Travaux et Memoires de l'Institut d'Ethnologie*, vol. 23 (Paris, 1936).

"Indice temático de la compilación (ordenanzas sobre tierras)," *Revista del Archivo Nacional*, 22, no. 2 (July-Dec. 1958), p. 468.

Isbell, Billie Jean. *To Defend Ourselves: Ecology and Ritual in an Andean Village*. Latin American Monographs No. 47. Austin, Texas, 1978.

Jara, Alvaro. *Tres ensayos sobre economía minera hispanoamericana*. Santiago de Chile, 1966.

Jiménez de la Espada, Marcos, ed. and comp., *Relaciones geográficas de Indias*. Madrid, 1881–97. 4 vols.

Juan, Jorge, and Antonio de Ulloa. *Noticias secretas de America*. London, 1826.

Julien, Catherine J. "Inca Decimal Administration in the Lake Titicaca Region," in Collier et al., eds., *The Inca and Aztec States*, pp. 119–51.

Keith, Robert G. *Conquest and Agrarian Change: The Emergence of the Hacienda System on the Peruvian Coast*. Cambridge, Mass., 1976.

Koepcke, María. *Corte ecológico transversal en los Andes del Perú central con especial consideración de las aves. Parte I: Costa, vertientes occidentales y región alto-andina*. Memorias del Museo de Historia Natural "Javier Prado." Lima, 1954.

Konetzke, Richard, ed. *Colección de documentos para la historia de la formación social de Hispanoamérica (1493–1810)*. Madrid, 1953–58. 3 vols.

Kubler, George. *The Indian Caste of Peru, 1795–1940*. Washington, D.C., 1952.

_____. "The Neo-Inca State (1537–1572)," *Hispanic American Historical Review*, 27, no. 2 (May 1947), pp. 189–203.

_____. "The Quechua in the Colonial World," *Handbook of South American Indians*, vol. 2 (Washington, D.C., 1946), pp. 331–410.

Larson, Brooke. "Caciques, Class Structure and the Colonial State in Bolivia," *Nova Americana* (Turin), 3 (1979), pp. 197–235.

_____. "Economic Decline and Social Change in an Agrarian Hinterland: Cochabamba in the Late Colonial Period." Ph.D. diss., Columbia University, 1978.

Lee, Bertram T., and Juan Bromley, eds. *Libros de cabildo de Lima*. Lima, 1935– (14 vols. to date).

344   Bibliography

Le Roy Ladurie, Emmanuel. *The Peasants of Languedoc*. Trans. with an introduction by John Day. Urbana, Ill., 1974.

Levillier, Roberto. *Don Francisco de Toledo, supremo organizador del Perú, su vida, su obra (1515–1582)*. Buenos Aires, 1935–40. 4 vols.

————, ed. *Gobernantes del Perú. Cartas y papeles, siglo XVI. Documentos del Archivo de Indias*. Madrid, 1921–26. 14 vols.

Lewin, Boleslao. *La rebelión de Tupac Amaru y los orígenes de la emancipación americana*. Buenos Aires, 1957.

Lissón Chavez, Emilio, ed. *La Iglesia de España en el Perú. Colección de documentos . . . Sección primera: Archivo General de Indias*. Seville, 1943–56. 5 vols.

Loayza, Francisco A., ed. *Juan Santos, el invencible (manuscritos del año de 1742 al año de 1755)*. *Los pequeños grandes libros de historia americana*, series 1, vol. 2. Lima, 1942.

Loayza, Rodrigo de. "Memorial de las cosas del Perú tocantes a los indios [1586]," *Colección de documentos inéditos para la historia de España*, vol. 94 (Madrid, 1889), pp. 554–605.

Lockhart, James. *The Men of Cajamarca*. Berkeley, Calif., 1972.

————. *Spanish Peru, 1532–1560: A Colonial Society*. Madison, Wisc., 1968.

————, and Enrique Otte, eds. *Letters and People of the Spanish Indies*. London and New York, 1976.

Lohmann Villena, Guillermo. *El corregidor de indios en el Perú bajo los Austrias*. Madrid, 1957.

————. "Etude préliminaire," in Juan de Matienzo, *Gobierno del Perú* (Lima-Paris, 1967).

————. *Las minas de Huancavelica en los siglos XVI y XVII*. Seville, 1949.

————. "La restitución por conquistadores y encomenderos: un aspecto de la incidencia Lascasiana en el Perú," *Anuario de Estudios Americanos* (Seville), 23 (1966), pp. 21–89.

Loredo, Rafael. *Alardes y derramas*. Lima, 1942.

————. *Los repartos*. Lima, 1958.

Lounsbury, Floyd G. "Aspects du système de parenté inca," *Annales: Economies, Sociétés, Civilisations*, 33, nos. 5–6 (Sept.-Dec. 1978), pp. 991–1005.

Lynch, John. *Spain Under the Hapsburgs*. New York and London, 1965. 2 vols.

Macera, Pablo. "Informaciones geográficas del Perú colonial," *Revista del Archivo Nacional del Perú*, 28, nos. 1 and 2 (1964), pp. 133–252.

————. "Introducción" to Alonso Carrió de la Bandera, *Reforma del Perú* (Lima, 1951).

————. *Mapas coloniales de haciendas cuzqueñas*. Lima, 1968.

Marx, Karl. *Grundrisse*. Trans. and ed. David McLellan. New York, 1971.

Matienzo, Juan de. *Gobierno del Perú (1567)*. Ed. and with a prologue by Guillermo Lohmann Villena. Lima-Paris, 1967.

Matos Mar, José, et al. *Las actuales comunidades de indígenas: Huarochirí en 1955*. Lima, 1958.

Mayer, Enrique José. "Reciprocity, Self-Sufficiency, and Market Relations in a Contemporary Community in the Central Andes of Peru." Ph.D. diss., Cornell University, 1974.

Melo, Sebastián Francisco de. "Diario histórico del levantamiento de la provincia de Huarochirí, escrito por Sebastián Francisco de Melo, Sargento Mayor de tropas arregladas, Justicia Mayor y Teniente General en dicha provincia, quien lo presenta al Excmo. Señor D. Manuel de Amat Y Junient, Caballero de la Orden de San José, Mariscal de Campo de los Reales Ejércitos, Virrey gobernador y Capitan General de los reinos del Perú. Pachachaca, 20 de Octubre de 1761." Ms., Museo Mitre, Buenos Aires, Arm. B, C. 19, P. 1, No. de orden 4.

Memorial de las historias del Nuevo Mundo Piru [1630]. Lima, 1957.

Menzel, Dorothy. "The Inca Occupation of the South Coast of Peru," in John H. Rowe and Dorothy Menzel, eds., *Peruvian Archaeology: Selected Readings* (Palo Alto, Calif., 1967), pp. 217–34.

Miller, General William. *Memorias del General Miller al servicio de la república del Perú.* Trans. General Torrijos. Madrid, n.d. 2 vols.

Millones, Luís. "Un movimiento nativista del siglo XVI: el Taki Onqoy," in Juan Ossio, ed., *Ideología mesiánica del mundo andino* (Lima, 1973), pp. 83–94.

_____. "Nuevos aspectos del Taki Onqoy," in Juan Ossio, ed., *Ideología mesiánica del mundo andino* (Lima, 1973), pp. 95–102.

Moore, Sally Falk. *Power and Property in Inca Peru.* New York, 1958.

Moreno Cebrián, Alfredo. *El corregidor de indios y la economía peruana en el siglo XVIII.* Madrid, 1977.

Moro Chimo Capac, Vicente. "Manifiesto de los agravios, vexaciones, y molestias que padecen los indios del reyno del Perú . . . [1722]." Madrid, 1732. Microfilm, Bancroft Library, University of California, Berkeley.

Morris, Craig. "L'Etude archéologique de l'échange dans les Andes," *Annales: Economies, Sociétés, Civilisations,* 33, nos. 5–6 (Sept.-Dec. 1978), pp. 936–47.

_____. "The Identification of Function in Inca Architecture and Ceramics," in *Actas y Memorias del XXXIX Congreso Internacional de Americanistas* (Lima, 1971), vol. 3, pp. 135–44.

_____. "The Infrastructure of Inka Control in the Peruvian Central Highlands," in Collier et al., eds., *The Inca and Aztec States,* pp. 153–71.

_____. "Master Design of the Inca," *Natural History,* 85, no. 10 (1976), pp. 58–67.

_____. "Peru's Golden Treasures." American Museum of Natural History exhibition catalog. New York, 1977.

_____. "State Settlements in Tawantinsuyu: A Strategy of Compulsory Urbanism," in Mark P. Leone, ed., *Contemporary Archaeology: A Guide to Theory and Contributions* (Carbondale, Ill., 1972), pp. 393–401.

_____. "The Technology and Organization of Highland Inca Food Storage." Ph.D. diss., University of Chicago, 1967.

_____, and Donald E. Thompson. "Huánuco Viejo: An Inca Administrative Center," *American Antiquity,* 35, no. 3 (1970), pp. 344–62.

Morua, Fray Martin de. *Historia General del Perú.* Madrid, 1962–64. 2 vols.

Mugaburu, José de. *Diario de Lima (1640–94).* 2 vols. Vols. 7 and 8 of Romero and Urteaga, eds., *Colección de libros y documentos referentes a la historia del Perú* (Lima, 1917–18).

Murra, John V. "Una apreciación etnológica de la visita," postscript article in Díez de San Miguel, *Visita hecha a la provincia de Chucuito* (Lima, 1964).

_____. "Aymara Lords and Their European Agents at Potosí, "*Nova Americana* (Turin), 1, no. 1 (1978), pp. 231–43.

_____. "Cloth and Its Functions in the Inca State," *American Anthropologist,* 64, no. 4 (Aug. 1962), pp. 710–28.

————. "El 'Control Vertical' de un máximo de pisos ecológicos en la economía de las sociedades andinas," in Iñigo Ortíz de Zúñiga, *Visita de la provincia de León de Huánuco en 1562*, vol. 2 (Huanuco, 1972), pp. 429–76.
————. "Current Research and Prospects in Andean Ethnohistory," *Latin American Research Review*, 5, no. 2 (Spring 1970), pp. 3–36.
————. "Las etno-categorías de un *khipu* estatal," in *Formaciones económicas y políticas del mundo andino*. Lima, 1975.
————. *Formaciones económicas y políticas del mundo andino*. Lima, 1975.
————. "La Guerre et les rébellions dans l'expansion de l'état Inka," *Annales: Economies, Sociétés, Civilisations*, 33, nos. 5–6 (Sept.-Dec. 1978), pp. 927–35.
————. "The Mit'a Obligations of Ethnic Groups to the Inka State," in Collier et al., eds., *The Inca and Aztec States*, pp. 237–62.
————. "New Data on Retainer and Servile Populations in Tawantinsuyu," in *Actas y Memorias del XXXVI Congreso Internacional de Americanistas* (Seville, 1966), vol. 2, pp. 35–45.
————. "On Inca Political Structure," in Vern F. Ray, ed., *Systems of Political Control and Bureaucracy in Human Societies. Proceedings of the 1958 Annual Spring Meeting of the American Ethnological Society* (Seattle, Wash., 1958), pp. 30–41.
————. *La organización económica del estado Inca*. Mexico City, 1978.
————. "Social Structural and Economic Themes in Andean Ethnohistory," *Anthropological Quarterly*, 34, no. 2 (Spring 1961), pp. 47–59.
O'Phelan, Scarlet. "El Sur Andino a fines del siglo XVIII: cacique o corregidor," *Allpanchis Phuturinqa*, 11–12, nos. 11–12 (1978), pp. 17–32.
————. "Túpac Amaru y las sublevaciones del siglo XVIII," in Flores Galindo, *Sublevaciones populares y sociedad colonial*.
"Ordenanzas del Gremio de Zapateros, 13 de abril de 1792," *Revista del Archivo Nacional del Perú*, 22, no. 1 (Jan.-June 1958), pp. 7–22.
Ortíz de Zúñiga, Iñigo. *Visita de la provincia de León de Huánuco en 1562*. Huanuco, 1967–72. 2 vols.
Ossio, Juan A., ed. *Ideológica mesiánica del mundo andino*. Lima, 1973.
Palacio Atard, Vicente. *Areche y Guirior. Observaciones sobre el fracaso de una visita al Perú*. Seville, 1946.
Palata, Duque de la. "Aranzel de los jornales que se han de pagar a los indios así voluntarios, mingados, alquilas, y agregados a las haciendas de españoles, como mitayos, y de obligación, en todo genero de trabajo. . . . " Los Reyes, 1687.
Palomino Flores, Salvador. "Duality in the Socio-Cultural Organization of Several Andean Populations," *Folk*, 13 (1971), pp. 65–88.
Patterson, Thomas C. *America's Past: A New World Archaeology*. Englewood Cliffs, N.J., 1973.
————. "Chavin: An Interpretation of Its Spread and Influence," in Elizabeth P. Benton, ed., *Dumbarton Oaks Conference on Chavin* (Washington, D.C., 1971), pp. 29–48.
————. "The Emergence of Food Production in Central Peru," in Stuart Streuver, ed., *Prehistoric Agriculture* (Garden City, N.J., 1971), pp. 181–207.
————. "Population and Economy in Central Peru," *Archaeology*, 24, no. 4 (1971) pp. 316–21.
Paz, Melchor de. *Guerra separatista. Rebeliones de indios en Sud América: la sublevación de Túpac Amaru*. Lima, 1952. 2 vols.

Pike, Ruth. *Aristocrats and Traders: Sevillian Society in the Sixteenth Century.* Ithaca, N.Y., 1972.

Polo de Ondegardo, Juan. "Copia de unos capítulos de una carta . . . para el doctor Francisco Hernández de Liébana," in Zabáburu and Sancho Rayon, eds., *Nueva colección de documentos inéditos para la historia de España,* vol. 6 (Madrid, 1896), pp. 274–81.

————. "Informe del Lic. Polo de Ondegardo al Lic. Briviesca de Muñatones sobre la perpetuidad de las encomiendas en el Perú [1561]," *Revista Histórica* (Lima), 13 (1940), pp. 125–96.

————. "Relación de los fundamentos acerca del notable daño que resulta de no guardar a los indios sus fueros [1571]," in Carlos A. Romero and Horacio H. Urteaga, eds., *Colección de libros y documentos referentes a la historia del Perú,* series 1, vol. 3 (Lima, 1916), pp. 45–188.

Porlier, Antonio. "Libro de cédulas, autos acordados, y otros instrumentos pertenecientes a los indios, año de 1769," book 2. Yale University Library; microfilm in Bancroft Library, University of California, Berkeley, in *Documents Relating to Peru.*

Porras Barrenechea, Raul. *Cartas del Perú (1524–1543).* Lima, 1959.

————. *Las relaciones primitivas de la conquista del Perú.* Paris, 1937.

Raimondi, Antonio. *Notas de viajes para su obra "El Perú."* Lima, 1943. 2 vols.

Recopilación de leyes de los reynos de las Indias, mandados imprimir y publicar por la Ma. Católica del Rey D. Carlos II. Facsimile ed., Madrid, 1943. 3 vols.

"Relación de los pueblos que midan en el tránsito de la ciudad de Lima a la de Chuquisaca . . . ," in *Juicio de límites entre el Perú y Bolivia: Prueba Peruana* (Barcelona, 1907), vol. 3, pp. 232–50.

"Relación de oficios que se proveen en la gobernación de los reinos y provincias del Perú (1583)," in Roberto Levillier, ed., *Gobernantes del Perú* (Madrid, 1925), vol. 9, pp. 128–226.

Relaciones de los vireyes y audiencias que han gobernado el Perú. Madrid, 1872.

República del Perú, Ministerio de Hacienda y Comercio. *Censo Nacional de Población y Ocupación, 1940. Vol. I: Resúmenes generales.* Lima, 1944.

Rivera, Silvia. "El Malku y la sociedad colonial en el siglo XVII: el caso de Jesús de Machaca," *Avances* (La Paz), 1 (1978), pp. 7–27.

Rivera Serna, Raul. *Los guerrilleros del centro en la emancipación peruana.* Lima, 1958.

Rodríguez Casado, Vicente, and Florentino Perez Embid, eds. *Manuel de Amat y Junient, virrey del Perú, 1761–1776. Memoria de Gobierno.* Seville, 1947.

Romero, Carlos Alberto. "Idolatrías de los indios Huachos y Yauyos," *Revista Histórica* (Lima), 6, no. 2 (1918), pp. 180–97.

————. "Libro de la visita general del virrey D. Francisco de Toledo, 1570–1575," *Revista Histórica* (Lima), 7, no. 2 (1924), pp. 113–216.

————. "Rebeliones indígenas en Lima durante la colonia," *Revista Histórica* (Lima), 9 (1928), pp. 317–37.

————, and Horacio H. Urteaga, eds. *Colección de libros y documentos referentes a la historia del Perú.* Lima, 1916–41. 24 vols.

Romero, Emilio. *Historia económica del Perú.* Buenos Aires, 1949.

Rosenblat, Angel. *La población indígena y el mestizaje en América.* Buenos Aires, 1945. 2 vols.

Rostworowski de Diaz Canseco, María. *Etnía y sociedad: costa peruana prehispánica.* Lima, 1977.

_____. "Etnohistoria de un valle costeño durante el Tahuantinsuyu," *Revista del Museo Nacional del Perú,* 35 (1967–68), pp. 7–61.

_____. "Nuevos aportes para el estudio de la medición de tierras en el Virreinato o Incario," *Revista del Archivo Nacional del Perú,* 28, nos. 1 and 2 (1964), pp. 31–58.

_____. *Señoríos indígenas de Lima y Canta.* Lima, 1978.

_____. "Succession, Co-option to Kingship, and Royal Incest Among the Inca," *Southwestern Journal of Anthropology,* 16, no. 4 (1960), pp. 417–27.

Rowe, John H. "Absolute Chronology in the Andean Area," *American Antiquity,* 10, no. 3 (Jan. 1945), pp. 265–84.

_____. "The Age Grades of the Inca Census," *Miscellanea Paul Rivet. Octogenario Dicata,* vol. 2 (Mexico City, 1958), pp. 499–522.

_____. "The Chronology of Inca Wooden Cups," *Essays in Pre-Columbian Art and Archaeology* (Cambridge, Mass., 1961), pp. 317–41.

_____. "Colonial Portraits of Inca Nobles," in Sol Tax, ed., *The Civilizations of Ancient America: Proceedings of the XXIX International Congress of Americanists,* vol. 1 (Chicago, 1951), pp. 258–68.

_____. "Inca Culture at the Time of the Spanish Conquest," *Handbook of South American Indians,* vol. 2 (Washington, D.C., 1946), pp. 183–330.

_____. "The Incas Under Spanish Colonial Institutions," *Hispanic American Historical Review,* 37, no. 2 (May 1957), pp. 155–99.

_____. "Movimiento nacional inca del siglo XVIII," *Revista Universitaria del Cuzco,* 107 (1955), pp. 3–33.

_____. "What Kind of a Settlement was Inca Cuzco?," *Ñawpa Pacha* (Berkeley, Calif.), 5 (1967), pp. 59–67.

Salinas y Córdoba, Fray Buenaventura de. *Memorial de las historias del Nuevo Mundo Piru* [1630]. Lima, 1957.

Salinas Loyola, Juan de. "Las encomiendas del Perú, 1569," in Marcos Jiménez de la Espada, ed., *Relaciones geográficas de Indias,* vol. 1 (Madrid, 1881), p. 56.

Sánchez-Albornoz, Nicolas. *Indios y tributos en el Alto Perú.* Lima, 1978.

_____. "La saca de mulas de Salta al Perú, 1778–1808," *Anuario de Instituto de Investigaciones Históricas,* no. 8 (Rosario, Argentina, 1965), pp. 261–312.

Sanchez Bello, Ismael. "El gobierno del Perú, 1550–1564," *Anuario de Estudios Americanos,* vol. 17 (Seville, 1960), pp. 407–524.

Santillán, Fernando de. "Relación del orígen, descendencia, política y gobierno de los Incas," in *Tres relaciones de antiguedades peruanas* (Asunción del Paraguay, 1950), pp. 33–134.

Santo Tomás, Fray Domingo de. *Gramática o arte de la lengua general de los indios de los reynos del Perú.* Facsimile ed. prepared by Raul Porras Barrenechea. Lima, 1951.

_____. *Lexicon, o vocabulario de la lengua general del Perú.* Facsimile ed. prepared by Raul Porras Barrenechea. Lima, 1951.

Schweigger, Erwin. *El litoral peruano.* Lima, 1947.

Sempat Assadourian, Carlos. "La producción de la mercancía dinero en la formación del mercado interno colonial," *Economía* (Lima), 1, no. 2 (Aug. 1978), pp. 9–55.

Silva Santisteban, Fernando. *Los obrajes en el virreinato del Perú.* Lima, 1964.

Simpson, Lesley Byrd. *The Encomienda in New Spain.* Berkeley, Calif., 1950.

Smith, C. T. "Despoblación de los Andes centrales en el siglo XVI," *Revista del Museo Nacional del Perú*, 35 (1969), pp. 77–91.

Sola, Donald, and Jorge Urioste. "The Sons of Pariacaca." Unpublished English translation of the Quechua text of the first chapters of Avila, *Dioses y hombres de Huarochirí*. A comparison of the original text, José María Arguedas's translation, and this English version is instructive.

Solórzano Pereira, Juan de. *Política Indiana* [1647]. Madrid and Buenos Aires, 1930.

Sotelo, Hildebrando. *Las insurrecciones y levantamientos en Huarochirí y sus factores determinantes*. Lima, 1942.

Spalding, Karen. *De Indio a campesino: cambios en la estructura del Perú colonial*. Lima, 1974.

_____. "El corregidor de indios y las origenes de la hacienda serrana peruana," in Spalding, *De Indio a campesino*, pp. 127–46.

_____. "El kuraka y el comercio colonial," in Spalding, *De Indio a campesino*, pp. 31–60.

_____. "Kurakas and Commerce: A Chapter in the Evolution of Andean Society," *Hispanic American Historical Review*, 54, no. 4 (Nov. 1973), pp. 581–99.

_____. "Social Climbers: Changing Patterns of Mobility Among the Indians of Colonial Peru," *Hispanic American Historical Review*, 50, no. 4 (Nov. 1970), pp. 645–64.

Stern, Steve J. "Algunas consideraciones sobre la personalidad histórica de don Felipe Guaman Poma de Ayala," *Histórica*, 2, no. 2 (Dec. 1978), pp. 225–28.

_____. "The Challenge of Conquest: The Indian Peoples of Huamanga, Peru, and the Foundation of a Colonial Society, 1532–1640." Ph.D. diss., Yale University, 1979.

TePaske, John J. "The Fiscal Structure of Upper Peru and the Financing of Empire," in Karen Spalding, ed., *Essays in the Political, Economic, and Social History of Colonial Latin America* (Newark, Del., 1982), pp. 69–94.

Thatcher, John. "A Seriation of the Ceramics from Huarochirí," unpublished paper, 1969.

Torres de Mendoza, Luís, ed. *Colección de documentos inéditos, relativos al descubrimiento, conquista y organización de las antiguas posesiones españolas de América y Oceania*. Madrid, 1864–84. 42 vols.

Uhle, Max. *Pachacamac: Report of the William Pepper Peruvian Expedition of 1896*. Pittsburgh, Pa., 1903.

Vaca de Castro, Cristóbal. "Ordenanzas de tambos (1543)," *Revista Histórica* (Lima), 3, no. 4 (1908), pp. 427–92.

Varese, Stefano. *La sal de los cerros*. Lima, 1968.

Vargas Ugarte, Rubén. *Concilios Limenses*. Lima, 1951–54. 3 vols.

Vásquez de Espinosa, Antonio. *Compendio y descripción de las Indias occidentales*. Washington, D.C., 1948.

Vega, Andrés de. "La descripción que se hizo en la provincia de Xauxa por la instrucción de Su Majestad," in Marcos Jiménez de la Espada, ed., *Relaciones geográficas de Indias*, vol. 1 (Madrid, 1881), pp. 79–95.

Villagomez, Pedro de. *Exhortaciones e instrucciones acerca de los indios del Arzobispado de Lima* [1649]. Vol. 12 of Carlos A. Romero and Horacio H. Urteaga, eds., *Colección de libros y documentos referentes a la historia del Perú* (Lima, 1919).

Von Tschudi, Juan Jacobo. *Testimonio del Perú, 1837–1842*. Lima, 1966.

Wachtel, Nathan. "Hommes d'eau: le problème Uru (XVIᵉ–XVIIᵉ siècle)," *Annales: Economies, Sociétés, Civilisations*, 33, nos. 5–6 (Sept.-Dec. 1978), pp. 1127–59.

_____. "The Mitimas of the Cochabamba Valley: The Colonization Policy of Huayna Capac," in Collier et al., eds., *The Inca and Aztec States*, pp. 199–235.

_____. "Pensamiento salvaje y aculturación: el espacio y el tiempo en Felipe Guaman Poma de Ayala y el Inca Garcilasco de la Vega," in *Sociedad e ideología*, pp. 163–228.

_____. "Rebeliones y milenarismo," in Juan A. Ossio, ed., *Ideología mesiánica del mundo andino* (Lima, 1973), pp. 103–42.

_____. *Sociedad e ideología*. Lima, 1973.

_____. *La Vision des vaincus. Les Indiens du Pérou devant la conquête espagnole: 1530–1570*. Paris, 1971.

Zabálburu, Francisco de, and José Sancho Rayon, eds. *Nueva colección de documentos inéditos para la historia de España y de sus Indias*. Madrid, 1894–96. 6 vols.

Zambrano, Fray Juan. "Relación de la filiación de sangre y nobleza de don Bartholo García y Espilco, por el padre fray Juan Zambrano [1732]," with an introduction and notes by John H. Rowe. Berkeley, Calif., 1970. Pamphlet series of *Ñawpa Pacha*.

Zuidema, R. T. *The Ceque System of Cuzco: The Social Organization of the Capital of the Incas*. Leiden, 1964.

_____. "Reflexiones sobre la concepción histórica de los Incas," *Runa: temas de ciencias sociales* (Ayacucho), 1, no. 1 (Nov. 1967), pp. 55–62.

Index